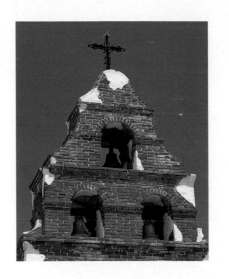

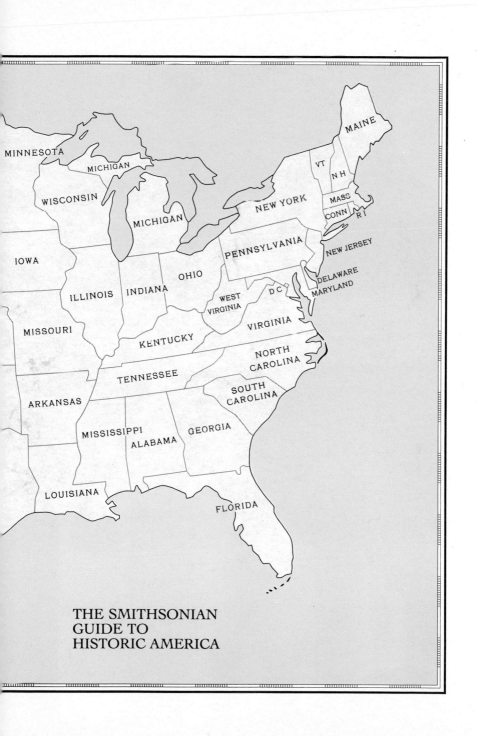

THE SMITHSONIAN
GUIDE TO
HISTORIC AMERICA

THE
SMITHSONIAN
——— GUIDE TO———
HISTORIC AMERICA
THE PACIFIC STATES

TEXT BY
WILLIAM BRYANT LOGAN
SUSAN OCHSHORN

SPECIAL PHOTOGRAPHY BY
CHUCK PLACE

EDITORIAL DIRECTOR
ROGER G. KENNEDY
DIRECTOR OF THE NATIONAL MUSEUM
OF AMERICAN HISTORY
OF THE SMITHSONIAN INSTITUTION

Stewart, Tabori & Chang
NEW YORK

Smithsonian Books
WASHINGTON, D.C.

Published in 1989 by Stewart, Tabori & Chang, Inc., 740 Broadway,
New York, NY 10003.

FRONT COVER: Mission San Carlos Borromeo, CA
HALF-TITLE PAGE: Mission San Miguel, CA
FRONTISPIECE: Old San Luis Lighthouse, CA
BACK COVER: San Simeon, CA

SERIES EDITOR: HENRY WIENCEK
EDITOR: MARY LUDERS
PHOTO EDITOR: MARY JENKINS
ART DIRECTOR: DIANA M. JONES
ASSOCIATE EDITOR: BRIGID A. MAST
ASSISTANT PHOTO EDITORS: BARBARA J. SEYDA, FERRIS COOK
EDITORIAL ASSISTANT: MONINA MEDY
DESIGN ASSISTANT: KATHI R. PORTER
CARTOGRAPHIC DESIGN AND PRODUCTION: GUENTER VOLLATH
CARTOGRAPHIC COMPILATION: GEORGE COLBERT
DATA ENTRY: SUSAN KIRBY

LIBRARY OF CONGRESS CATALOGING-IN-PUBLICATION DATA

Logan, William Bryant.
    The Pacific States.

    (The Smithsonian guide to historic America)
    Includes index.
    1. Pacific States—Description and travel—1981-   —Guide-books.
2. Alaska—Description and travel—1981-   —Guide-books. 3. Hawaii—Description and
travel—1981-   —Guide-books. 4. Historic sites—Pacific States—Guide-books. 5. Historic
sites—Alaska—Guide-books. 6. Historic sites—Hawaii—Guide-books.
I. Ochshorn, Susan. II. Place, Chuck. III. Kennedy, Roger G. IV. Title. V. Series.
F852.3.L63 1989   917.904'33   89-4591
ISBN 1-55670-102-0
ISBN 1-55670-106-3 (pbk.)

Distributed by Workman Publishing, 708 Broadway, New York, NY 10003

Printed in Japan

10 9 8 7 6 5 4 3 2 1
First Edition

C O N T E N T S

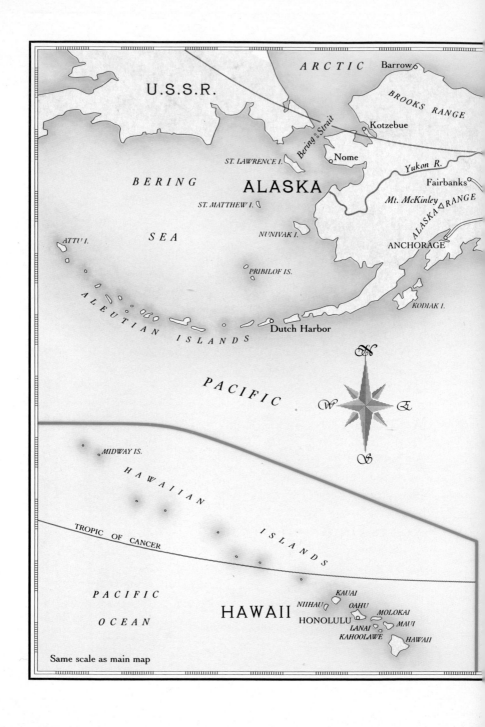

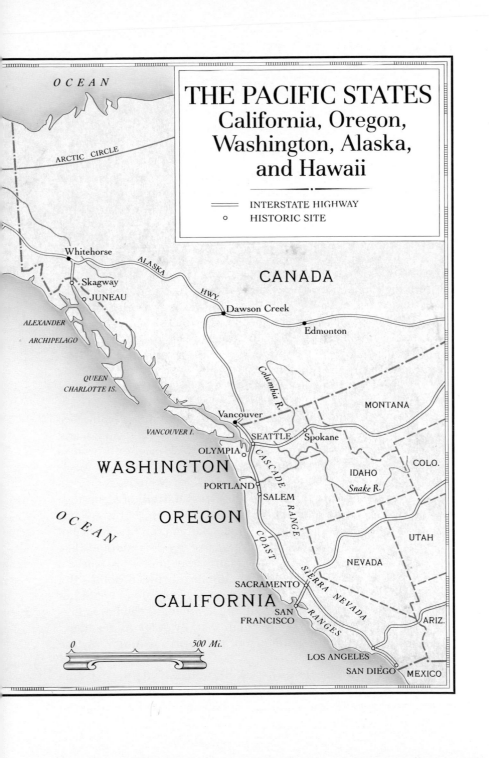

THE PACIFIC STATES
California, Oregon, Washington, Alaska, and Hawaii

═══ INTERSTATE HIGHWAY
○ HISTORIC SITE

OCEAN

ARCTIC CIRCLE

Whitehorse

ALASKA

Skagway

HWY.

JUNEAU

Dawson Creek

CANADA

ALEXANDER
ARCHIPELAGO

Edmonton

QUEEN
CHARLOTTE IS.

Columbia R.

MONTANA

Vancouver

VANCOUVER I.

SEATTLE Spokane

OLYMPIA

CASCADE

IDAHO

COLO.

WASHINGTON

PORTLAND

Snake R.

SALEM

RANGE

OCEAN

OREGON

COAST

UTAH

NEVADA

SACRAMENTO

SIERRA NEVADA

CALIFORNIA

SAN
FRANCISCO

RANGES

ARIZ.

0   500 Mi.

LOS ANGELES

SAN DIEGO MEXICO

INTRODUCTION

ROGER G. KENNEDY

The Pacific states are so called not because their inhabitants are more noticeably benign than others; they are unified by a region of water in a way that has more to do with their history than a traditional, landbound view of things would suggest. They are deployed about the northeastern quadrant of the Pacific Ocean—a modest description that might lead one to think they are closer together than they are. The Pacific, taken as a whole, is the largest single element in the geography of the globe; one of its quadrants is an immense expanse by comparison with the relatively modest ranges of wave and trough shared by the five Gulf states, the two Long Island Sound states, or the four Lake Michigan states. The members of each of these minor maritime congeries could float messages to each other in bottles, but only the Pacific states came into the present century with a history in which water was more important than land.

Americans do not customarily center a story upon a featureless watery terrain, at the edges of which are shorelines; most Americans, like the Russians (about whom more in a moment), are a continental people. To most of us, emigration does not imply traveling over water—though to a Polynesian, a Nantucketer, or an Aleut it might. Instead we think of the Oregon Trail, of Conestoga wagons, of Mormon handcarts, of pack trains, railways, and highways—it requires some effort of imagination even to conceive of dog teams and the Yukon. Furthermore, most of our land travel (like that of the Russians) has been across fairly level grasslands, where a straight line on a map is the shortest distance between points. But Polynesian navigators knew a thousand years ago that they could not set sail directly for any ultimate goal; the invisible tugs and pressures of wind and current required of them that, in order to get there, they warp the theoretical geometry of the earth's maritime surface with elaborate calculations.

In the age of paddle and sail, Hawaii was at the extreme northeastern reach of a triangular pattern of canoe-borne emigration that had been important in human affairs for a thousand years before Russians or Americans arrived on the scene. Along this ancient pathway moved thousands of migrants, sometimes as a few people in a single craft, sometimes in fleets under the command of chiefs. They went island by island, eastward first from the southeastern edges of Asia, to create a new culture on the islands of the central Pacific. Then, after a long pause, they moved again, northward to Hawaii.

The medieval Polynesian achievement staggers the imagination: By A.D. 300 the Samoans had colonized Tahiti and the Marquesas, and during the next 500 years the islanders spread not only across the open ocean to Hawaii but also in the opposite direction, to New Zealand. By the fifteenth century there were 200,000 of them living on the Hawaiian archipelago, a number that remained fairly stable until the onset of Europeans and European diseases in 1778. The population was reduced to fewer than 35,000 by 1900.

In the Far North, human settlement was much older. The earliest linking of Siberian and Alaskan cultures—presaging ours with the Russian—dates to between 11,000 and 8,000 years ago and is seen in the similarity of ancient artifacts found in Siberia and America. There is substantial archaeological evidence in the region to support the hypothesis that the ancestors of the American Indians passed through it on their way to populate North America. Once in place on this side of what became the Bering Strait, some of these people showed a remarkable predilection for staying put: The settlement of Anangula in the Aleutian Islands lasted longer than the Roman Empire.

There are rumors aplenty of Japanese and Chinese voyages to the western coast and of Russian castaways there in the seventeenth century, but the original inhabitants of our five-state region discovered Europeans digging in upon their shores with clear intention to remain only in the eighteenth century. Juan Rodriguez Cabrillo had touched the California coast in 1542, and Sir Francis Drake made a landfall there fifty years later. These first probes were events chiefly interesting to map- and myth-makers—they were not serious intrusions. Though the Manila galleons made landfalls at Cape Mendocino as early as 1600, and Sebastian Vizcaino established a base at Monterey to protect their passage southward, California was only pricked along its western skin until Father Junipero Serra commenced the laying down of missions after 1769.

OVERLEAF: *Forsyth Glacier on Mount Saint Helens before the eruption in 1980.*

Very shortly thereafter, the Russians put down their first permanent settlement in North America at Unalaska in the eastern Aleutians; after a precarious winter or two, it was firmly established by the time the American Revolution began. Our history—the stories of common men and women living their daily lives without the presence of any court chroniclers or commissioned biographers—bears remarkable similarities to the history of these Russian pioneers. While we tend to regard the log cabin as a western European contribution to this continent, the Russians had perfected the form by the fifteenth century, and as one of them proudly said in the 1840s, "a Russian is everywhere the same. No matter where he chooses to live, whether it be in the Arctic Circle or in the glorious valleys of California, he everywhere puts up his national log cabin." And we have a common history of fur hunting and fur trading. The famous Captain James Cook did not arrive in the North Pacific until 1778, almost 200 years after Drake, but the fur traders had probably preceded him. Russians had reconnoitered the North American coast as far south as what is now British Columbia.

Cook was not commissioned to make a survey of natural resources, however. His assignment was to test the possibilities of taking a Northwest Passage from the Pacific to the Atlantic, and that test he performed. Pressing through the Bering Strait into the fogs and ice floes of the Arctic Ocean, Cook put a final quietus upon the dream of an alternative to the long voyage around Spanish South America. He returned to the Hawaiian Islands, where he was the first European to intervene in the civil wars among the residents (who needed no discovering by him) and paid for that intervention with his life.

Visitors appeared in Hawaii from another direction as well. The continental inconvenience around which Cook had sought a Northwest Passage had a Southwest Passage, but a very distant one, around the Horn. Mariners who followed that passage on their way to San Francisco or the Northwest Coast found that the imperatives of Pacific winds and currents created a navigational triangle, with its western and most pleasant vertex at Honolulu. Before the narrow waist of America was cut by order of Theodore Roosevelt to allow for a canal across Panama, Boston traders had to sail a jump-rope course around and under the feet of that landmass. Then they were impelled to move not northward along the South American coast but northwestward to Hawaii before pressing back eastward to

California or the Oregon Country. This would have been true even if
the South American coast had been friendly, which in the hands of
the Spanish Empire it was not.

Yankee traders went around the Horn and then to the mouth of
the Columbia River well before Lewis and Clark reached it overland.
By 1807, New Englanders knew more about Oahu and Nootka than
they knew about Saint Louis. They saw Mauna Loa before they saw
Pikes Peak. Every important early English or American explorer
came to Alaska and Oregon by way of Hawaii. This was true of Cook
in the 1770s, of Robert Gray at the end of the 1780s, and of George
Vancouver in the early 1790s. They established the route to the fur
ports and, fifty years later, for the suppliers to the mining frontier of
California.

This was the sequence: furs first, then gold, and much later, the
harvesting of the forests. Some people farmed where and when they
could, but it was not until the twentieth century that agricultural
products from this region became very important in world markets.
Instead, Americans and Russians were engaged in a converging
campaign of destruction of fur-bearing animals. Insatiable, brutal,
relentless, heedless, and improvident, the pursuit of fur on the part

*In the 1840s Paul Kane painted this scene of Indians near Fort Colville in eastern
Washington drying salmon in lodges made from mats hung on poles.*

of European hunters had led to the near-extermination of wild fur-bearing animals first in Europe itself and then in many parts of eastern America and western Siberia. A historian of modern Russia has depicted its eastward expansion as being essentially a sequence of conquests "of successive river basins . . . the speed of expansion being determined by the exhaustion of fur-bearing animals in each successive basin." At about the time Puritan merchants in England first introduced the conical beaver hat, the Stroganof family of merchants was turning a displaced army of Cossacks away from their own salt-mining domain, near the Urals, toward the neighboring khanate of Sibir. Within a single lifetime these Cossacks and their sons exhausted several river basins. They reached the Pacific shore in 1638. In the North Pacific, the fur hunt and fur trade also induced the indiscriminate degradation and, in some instances, slaughter of the native peoples who had since ancient times lived in a balanced, self-renewing relationship with the animals of the North.

From the outset of English invasion of North America, the native peoples were perceived chiefly in utilitarian terms—as agents to hunt for fur or later, after the fur-bearing animals had been exterminated, as no longer usable and therefore as impediments to other uses of the land. It has been wisely observed that the indelible image of Indians as hunters was fixed in the European mind not because that was their essential character or occupation when Europeans first came among them, but because that was how the Europeans used them: as units of production, as hide-seekers.

It may seem strange to stress the fur trade so heavily in an essay dealing with California and Hawaii as well as with the north-coast Pacific states, but even if we revert to overland history, it was American fur traders who came that way first to California, and it was other fur traders who intervened at the pivot of modern Hawaiian history. Their cannon enabled the king of Hawaii to complete his conquest of the islands and later the traders brought Hawaii into the imperial contests of Great Britain, Russia, and the United States.

The convergence of European fur hunters from east and west upon the North Pacific came after the long scouring of two continents for fur. From the lower Volga and Dnieper valleys, Russians pressed eastward toward the Pacific as, out of the Appalachian highlands, American pioneers pressed westward toward the same destination. By the end of the eighteenth century, Russians and Americans were selling beaver hair to the same customers.

During the 1780s and 1790s the commanders of Russian forts sumptuously entertained British and American sea captains; a Spanish administrator in California was even willing to consider a Russian administrator as a son-in-law. There was a bloodless "Nootka Sound Crisis" among the imperial powers in 1790, after which Spain courteously relinquished the exclusive claim to Vancouver Island, marking the first stage in its withdrawal from the North Pacific.

These were the decades in which the native populations were being decimated by war and disease—especially in the North, where the Russians did not trade furs in exchange for commodities as did the English, Dutch, and French, relying instead upon extracting furs as tribute from native populations. The rigor of their means of extraction, together with the diseases the newcomers carried, produced even worse losses than those resulting from European disease and warfare in North America. The Russians' systematic program of elimination reduced the native population in the region under Russian control by 90 percent, but only after the most effective resistance to European imperialism offered anywhere in North America. Russian efforts to apply the same methods in Hawaii were successfully resisted by a relatively densely settled, centrally governed, and technologically sophisticated people.

European diseases wrought their usual consequences from Kauai and Vancouver to Santa Barbara. War and radical changes in social structure ravaged the densely settled region we now call the Pacific Northwest. Villages of great architectural sophistication were depopulated and some left uninhabited. Buildings of heavy planks laid upon frameworks of post-and-beam (more European in appearance than any others on the continent) were left eerily empty, presided over by immense wooden sculptures. These "totem poles," removed to serve purely ornamental purposes in New York and Washington, continue to justify gasps of wonder—urban Americans seldom expect such grandeur from people they have been taught to think of as "savages" or "nomads" or "hunter-gatherers."

The decline of Spanish power in the Northwest after Spain abandoned Nootka in 1790 was followed by the revolt of California from Mexico and its ultimate acquisition by—some would say merger with—the United States. California settled into statehood in 1850, without passing through territorial status. The Russians had eight years earlier simplified matters by selling their California base, Fort Ross, to John Sutter, a private citizen. (Fort Ross was named not for some Anglo-American named Ross but by the Russians for "Rossia.") Alaska was sold later, but only after a Hawaiian adventure. Since Alaska was not hospitable to the traditional food crops grown by Russians, Hawaii, fertile and fecund, assumed a fresh importance to them. Russian ships arrived off Hawaiian ports in 1804, and there is evidence they intended to establish a base there in 1808. To the end of the 1850s, many of the needs of Alaska's fur-gatherers were answered on the shores of Kauai and Oahu, where beachheads were established.

The Russian presence in Hawaii was most welcome to American skippers during the War of 1812. There was a powerful British fleet in the Pacific, so American ships were "sold" to the Russians and operated by the Russian American Company. The company proposed to reciprocate this stratagem in the 1850s, offering to "sell" Alaska to a San Francisco ice company (with a right of repurchase three years later). This was, again, to keep an asset out of the hands of the British, with whom the tensions were gathering that would lead to the Crimean War.

One of the American vessels conveniently transferred to the Russians, the *Atahualpa*, renamed the *Bering*, was cast ashore on Kauai during a gale, and the local prince availed himself of the conventions of the law of salvage to make off with its cargo. Under the pretext of liberating that cargo, the Russian American Company sent a German surgeon, Georg Anton Schaeffer, to Kauai on an American ship to secure a base and then see what might be done on Oahu.

Schaeffer complied; from 1815 to 1818, he filibustered about the islands, building Fort Elizabeth of lava blocks on the south shore of Kauai, Forts Alexander and Barclay on the north coast, and the beginnings of another at Waikiki on Oahu. The Russian flag flew briefly over the Kauai forts until Schaeffer was sent packing by the

Hawaiians. The Russian emperor declined to support Schaeffer's endeavors. Though two years later the czar created a flurry of diplomatic activity by claiming the North American coast nearly as far south as Nootka, he made no mention of Hawaii.

The Crimean War of 1854–1856 led to the abandonment of Alaska by the Russians in 1867. The weakness of the Russian armed forces in the Pacific was demonstrated by the pummelling of Siberia's ports by a British squadron. Fearing that the British would take this opportunity to add Alaska to Canada, the Russians made their offer to sell Alaska to the ice company. The expansionary Americans were thereby alerted. Though its economic value had declined steeply as the fur seals were exterminated, Alaska was a possession worth keeping out of the hands of the British. The price required—two cents an acre—was reasonable, so Alaska was purchased in 1867, though it was not effectively governed by the United States for decades thereafter.

The Hawaiian Islands remained independent, though their central government was "advised" by Americans and their arable land engrossed by American corporations. In the 1890s a series of nationalistic revolts threatened those arrangements. After members of the Hawaiian royal family joined in these last efforts to resist the Americanization of the islands, the kingdom was replaced by a republic in 1894, and four years later Hawaii became a territory of the United States. It is noteworthy that a new power in the North Pacific, Japan, vigorously protested that step. As the Russians backed away, the Japanese took their place, and a contention commenced with the United States from the Philippines to the Aleutians. However, the ruins of Fort Elizabeth, now moldering in the underbrush on the bank of the Waimea River, remind us that the United States might have had to purchase not only the forty-ninth but also the fiftieth state from the Russian emperor.

LOS ANGELES
AND
SOUTHERN
CALIFORNIA

OPPOSITE: *Mission San Diego de Alcalá, the first of the twenty-one missions established by the Spanish in what is now the state of California.*

For many years Los Angeles was viewed as an oddity and an exception, but when the time comes to decide on the prototypical city of the twentieth century, the City of the Angels may be chosen. It is not just a city in the nineteenth-century sense, but a vast combination—part city, part county, part patchwork of towns—embracing an entire coastal plain and even jumping mountain ranges to find more land for development. The official city alone occupies almost 465 square miles, although when the sprawl into the Los Angeles lowlands is taken into account, the total urban area approaches five times that figure. Los Angeles has grown not by gradual accretion but by booms, as many as five, each abetted by the city's entrance into a typical twentieth-century enterprise. The first was real estate itself, and the lure was the climate and leisure. Then came a kind of imported agriculture headed by the citrus industry; next, the oil industry and the automobile; then the movies; and finally the aircraft industry and the military/industrial complex.

Los Angeles is situated on a linked set of broad, primarily flat plains, isolated from the rest of California by mountain ranges. The Los Angeles lowlands stretch from the San Fernando Valley in the north to the San Jacinto Basin in the south, ringed by ranges of hills and mountains, from the Santa Monicas in the northwest, through the Santa Susanas, San Gabriels, San Bernardinos, San Jacintos, Santa Anas, and San Joaquins. Only the ocean offers an easy outlet.

The landscape is comparatively recent, having appeared in its present form only a few million years ago. Faulting and folding made the mountains, and the gradual uplift of the sea floor created the broad alluvial coastal plain. The Palos Verdes Hills at the southern end of the arc of Santa Monica Bay were, in fact, once an island, and it is possible to see the strata marking different sea levels on the hills' seaward face. The region is still in the process of formation, partly by what one geographer describes as "fundamental earth disturbances," which most people know as earthquakes.

Chumash Indians had lived here for many centuries before the first white man's sail appeared off the coast. In 1542 Juan Rodríguez Cabrillo sailed past San Pedro Bay, naming it Bahía de los Humos (Bay of the Smokes), presumably for the pall of smoke that Indian campfires left hanging over the lowlands. The word smog was coined only in the mid-twentieth century—to describe conditions in Los Angeles—but it seems that the very first white to see the Los Angeles Basin saw the aboriginal version of the same phenomenon: human waste-smoke trapped by marine air in the mountain-ringed plain.

Ferdinand Deppe's 1832 painting of Mission San Gabriel Arcángel, just north of Los Angeles, is the earliest known painting of a California mission.

In 1769 José de Gálvez, Inspector General of New Spain (Spain's highest official in Mexico), dispatched Gaspar de Portolá and Father Junípero Serra on the Sacred Expedition to plant mission colonies in Alta (upper) California—so-called to differentiate it from Baja (lower) California, the peninsula below the 30th parallel. The Spanish wanted to secure their claims to upper California lest the Russians or English establish footholds there. The Sacred Expedition proceeded by land and sea to San Diego, from where Portolá's band marched north to the future sites of Los Angeles, Monterey, and San Francisco (along the way they discovered the La Brea tar pits and experienced an earthquake strong enough to throw them to the ground). They blazed the famous El Camino Real, or Royal Road, which today survives as Route 101, marked with signs bearing a mission symbol. Father Serra established nine missions; his successor, Father Fermín Lasuén, founded another nine; and three missions were started later, from San Diego to Sonoma. In the six and a half decades of the missions' work, some 88,000 Indians were baptized into the Catholic faith.

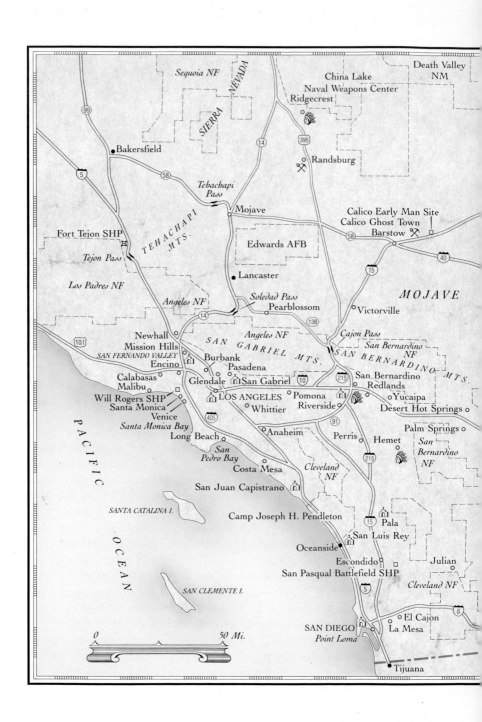

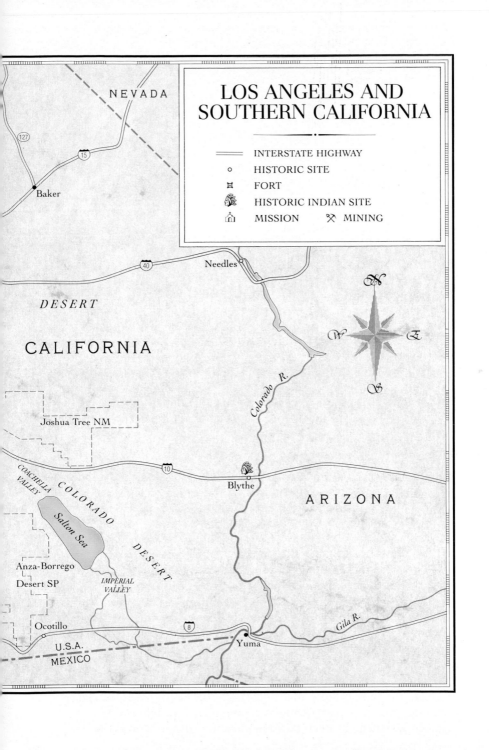

NEVADA

LOS ANGELES AND SOUTHERN CALIFORNIA

- ═══ INTERSTATE HIGHWAY
- ○ HISTORIC SITE
- ⊟ FORT
- 🪶 HISTORIC INDIAN SITE
- ⛪ MISSION   ⚒ MINING

127

15

Baker

DESERT

40   Needles

CALIFORNIA

Joshua Tree NM

Colorado R.

10   Blythe

A R I Z O N A

COACHELLA VALLEY

COLORADO

Salton Sea

DESERT

Anza-Borrego
Desert SP   *IMPERIAL VALLEY*

Ocotillo   8   Yuma   *Gila R.*

U.S.A.
MEXICO

Gauchos in a Horse Corral, *an 1877 painting by James Walker, shows the Mexican*

Conversion was only one goal. The missionaries also set out to train the Indians—hunters and gatherers by custom—to till fields and raise livestock in the settled manner of Europe. To this end the missions were granted huge tracts of land, hundreds of thousands of acres, by the Spanish government (the Spanish saw no irony in this taking of Indian land for the purpose of training Indians to a way of life in which they had little interest). The government intended ultimately to turn the land over to the Indians when they had demonstrated their abilities as farmers—a goal that was perpetually elusive.

The year after Mexico achieved its independence from Spain in 1821, the inhabitants of California, the Californios, declared themselves to be a part of the new Mexican republic. In 1833 the Mexican government decided to begin the transfer of mission lands

origins of the California cowboy (detail).

to the Indians, a process known as secularization. Only half of the land was to be given to the Indians directly; the other half was to be parcelled out to Californios who would manage these lands and share the proceeds with the Indians. As it turned out, the secularization of the missions was the occasion for ill-disguised larceny on a grand scale. The Indians were by and large cheated out of their holdings as the missions were converted into vast, private *ranchos.*

The Californios made several attempts at self-governance, partly to ensure for themselves the largest possible parcels of secularized land. In 1831 the Californios revolted against the Mexican governor: The opposing forces traded artillery shells in a "battle" at Cahuenga Pass. Although no one was hurt, the governor was recalled to Mexico. In 1836 the Californios declared themselves a free state within the republic of Mexico with Juan Bautista Alvarado as governor and Mariano G. Vallejo as military commander. The secularization of mission lands went on apace. In 1845 another governor from Mexico clashed with the Californios at Cahuenga Pass—again the Mexicans gave up, and Pío Pico became governor.

At this time the U.S. government, nervous about potential British ambitions in the West, was considering ways of acquiring California. In 1842 President Tyler's administration unsuccessfully attempted to buy the territory from Mexico, an offer that was repeated by President Polk, at a price of $25 million. As it turned out, events along the Texas-Mexican border determined California's future. The Mexican War, devoutly hoped-for by American expansionists, broke out along the Rio Grande in early 1846. On July 7, at Monterey Bay, Commodore John D. Sloat declared California part of the United States. In the account of one sailor who was present at the "conquest" of San Francisco on the next day, "in less than 48 hours from the first hoisting . . . the Yankee Colors were flying at every important post in Upper California and the U. States in bloodless possession of that beautiful Country."

Prior to the official U.S. declarations, a group of American irregulars, eager to lay their hands on as much acreage as possible, and abetted in their scheme by the adventurous Lieutenant Colonel John Charles Frémont, had captured the weak Californio garrison at Sonoma and declared the existence of the independent Bear Flag Republic, which lasted but one month, June 10 to July 9, 1846. The designated U.S. military and civil governor of the new land, Stephen Kearny, was already on his way to California from Santa Fe at the head of one hundred dragoons. At San Pasqual a troop of Californio cavalry tried and failed to expel Kearny. In January 1847 Kearny took part in the successful attack on Los Angeles. Commodore Richard F. Stockton and Frémont, disregarding Kearny's authority, briefly governed California themselves.

The following entries radiate from the city's early-nineteenth-century center, El Pueblo de los Angeles, then describe sites to the northeast, in downtown Los Angeles, Hollywood, and northern and western Los Angeles. Sites along the urban area's coastline are covered next, followed by descriptions of Pasadena and the regions to the north, east, and south of Los Angeles. Then the chapter covers San Diego, Palm Springs and the southern desert, the California portion of the Mojave Desert, and Death Valley.

The first Los Angeles aqueduct, shown here at its dedication on November 5, 1913, inaugurated the city's second boom by supplying water for the increasing population.

L O S   A N G E L E S

Though Gaspar de Portolá's expedition camped in the vicinity of Los Angeles's future center in 1769—at the time, it was an Indian village called Yang-na—it was not here but in the nearby San Gabriel Valley that the Spaniards directed their first colonization efforts in the area. Mission San Gabriel Arcángel, founded in 1771, preceded the town by a decade.

The settlement of El Pueblo de Nuestra Señora la Reina de los Angeles del Río de Porciuncula—the Town of Our Lady the Queen of the Angels by the Porciuncula River—was founded at the order of Spanish governor Felipe de Neve on September 4, 1781. In agrarian Spanish, rather than mercantile English, style the town was situated not at a convenient port but near a river, high enough to be above the floodplain but low enough to be easily irrigated by the river. The town was laid out on a rectangular grid encompassing about twenty-eight square miles, centered on a plaza, with home and farm sites for twenty-four families. In fact, only twelve families were persuaded to take the risk. These forty-four settlers from Sinaloa were the seed of the West's great metropolis.

Despite its favorable climate, Los Angeles had problems: The mountains isolated it, it had poor harbors, and fresh water was comparatively scarce. Cattle brought the first real wealth to the town. When the missions were secularized in 1834 and their land divided among the Mexican Californians, the *pueblo* (town) of Los Angeles was rechristened a *ciudad* (city).

The people of Los Angeles were a spirited group. It took the U.S. forces several battles before they were finally able to secure the city for the United States in 1847, just in time to see the value of the cattle ranches skyrocket with the new demand for beef created by the gold rush to the north. Although times should have been good, most Californios were already in the process of losing their land to the novel and, to them, unintelligible legal system the Yankees brought with them from the East. What cunning lawyers could not extract, the supposedly equable climate did: A drought in 1856, followed by floods in 1861 and an even worse drought from 1862 to 1865, put the ranchers in a position from which few could recover.

The stage was set for the city's first boom. In 1870, Los Angeles boasted only 5,000 residents; plans were afoot for a real cathedral (Saint Vibiana) and a real theater. Then came the Southern Pacific Railroad. The city had to give away land, money, and its own local railroad to convince the "Octopus" of the SP to make Los Angeles a stop, but the results seemed promising when the population reached 11,000 by 1880, four years after the railroad's arrival. The real boom came after 1886, however, when the competing Santa Fe Railroad reached Los Angeles. In the ensuing fare wars and promotional campaigns—the city's own Chamber of Commerce was active in the Midwest, and the railroads fought so hard that the fare from Kansas City declined to one dollar—land values rose over 500 percent. By 1890 Los Angeles had quintupled in size. Through the following decade, the railroads helped make the area's citrus and other produce known far afield, and the first oil strikes added to the city's wealth. By the turn of the century, the population had doubled again, to around 100,000.

Water, the movies, and a seaport quadrupled Los Angeles's extent and tripled its population in the years of the second boom, from 1900 until the First World War. The construction of a deepwater port at San Pedro—after a long fight against the forces of the Southern Pacific, which preferred a site that the company owned at Santa Monica—supplied one of the city's needs; the completion of the Los Angeles Aqueduct in 1913, running almost 250 miles from the Owens River east of the Sierras to the San Fernando Valley, supplied the water needed to fuel growth. Furthermore, it gave the city reason to annex more territory, and outlying towns a potent reason for agreeing to be seized. In between, the movie business turned Hollywood from a sleepy community into a bustling part of the city.

In the third boom, beginning in 1920, settlers poured in, giving the city a population of nearly 1,250,000 by decade's end. Major oil strikes at Signal Hill, Huntington Beach, and Santa Fe Springs almost tripled L.A.'s already respectable output of oil. After a tremendous building boom in the 1920s and the rapid expansion of the motion picture industry, which had just entered the era of the talkies, the Depression hit Los Angeles hard. Real recovery—the fourth boom—was led by the city's importance as a military manufacturing center during World War II. The aircraft designers were crucial to the military effort, and their companies were the backbone of postwar military and civilian flight. Engineers such as Glenn Martin, Donald Douglas, and John Northrop founded companies whose names are almost synonymous with flying.

EL PUEBLO DE LOS ANGELES HISTORIC MONUMENT

The city's downtown has generally migrated south and west over the years, but the center of the old Spanish settlement has been preserved, together with those structures that were a part of its nineteenth-century evolution. This park preserves the third site occupied by the Spaniards—heavy rains had forced them to move higher above the floodplain in 1815 and again in the late 1820s. The original quadrangular plaza is now circular; the once unpaved Wine Street is now the Mexican marketplace called Olvera Street; but a good deal of historical interest remains.

The **Avila Adobe** is a reconstruction of a one-story adobe house built in about 1818 by a prominent rancher and later mayor. The original was damaged in the 1971 earthquake and torn down. It has been refurnished to show the sort of furniture and decorative items

The kitchen of the Avila Adobe, restored to its 1840s appearance, was used for bathing as well as cooking. The bed in the master bedroom, opposite, is spread with a Chinese shawl.

that would have graced the home of a Mexican cattleman during the 1840s. At that time the hide-and-tallow trade was booming, so the interiors reflected goods brought by traders from around the world, as well as Spanish colonial pieces. Next door is the **Plaza Substation,** built in 1904 as one of the network of power stations that ran Los Angeles's once-fine streetcar system. Across Olvera Street is the **Pelanconi House.** Built between 1855 and 1857, it is the oldest brick house still standing in the city; the craft of brick firing had been brought to the city by Jesse Hunter only a few years before. The 1887 Eastlake-style **Sepulveda House** next door, also of brick, is being restored to reflect middle-class Mexican-American taste of the late nineteenth century; it houses the park's visitors center.

The cluster of buildings on the south side of the plaza shows nineteenth-century developments. The oldest is the 1858 **Masonic Hall,** which still serves as the group's meeting hall and as a small museum of Freemasonry. The **Merced Theatre** (1870) and the grand Italianate **Pico House** hotel (1870) represent the area's last efforts to remain at the center of a city that was expanding westward. The latter was built by Pío Pico, the last Mexican governor of California.

Tucked into the southeast corner of the plaza itself is the Old Plaza Firehouse No. 1, the city's first official firehouse, built in 1884. Now restored, it contains nineteenth-century firefighting equipment, plus the turntable that made it possible to keep the engine facing front without having to back the horses in. West of the plaza, across Main Street, is the **Old Plaza Catholic Church**, completed in 1822 and still in use today. Although its simple architecture is reminiscent of the mission churches, it was never a mission itself.

LOCATION: *Visitor Center:* 620 North Main Street. HOURS: *Sepulveda House:* 10–3 Monday–Friday; 10–4:30 Saturday; *Avila Adobe, Old Plaza Firehouse, and Masonic Hall:* 10–3 Tuesday–Friday, 10–4:30 Saturday–Sunday. FEE: None. TELEPHONE: 213–628–1274.

The Spanish-style **Union Passenger Terminal** (800 North Alameda Street), a Depression-era project completed in 1939, was the last of the great train stations built in the United States. It was originally

Zuni kachina dolls, representations of spirits, are part of the large collection of Indian artifacts at the Southwest Museum in Los Angeles.

designed as a series of thirty connected structures, the spaces
between which were supposed to make it more stable during
earthquakes. North of Union Passenger Terminal at **Heritage Square**
(3800 Homer Street), is a collection of Victorian residences moved
from other areas of the city. The **Hale House** (Heritage Square,
818–449–0193) is a particularly fine redwood Queen Anne-style
home of the 1880s, furnished with period items.

   El Alisal (200 East Avenue 43, 818–222–0546) is the house
Charles Lummis built with the help of Indian craftspeople between
1857 and 1910. A Harvard-educated journalist, author, librarian, and
archaeologist, Lummis was devoted to the region's Spanish heritage
and built his house as a personal expression of the Hispanic-inspired
style that fascinated him. Constructed of boulders, concrete, hand-
hewn beams, and telephone poles, El Alisal was the scene of many
literary and artistic gatherings. It displays objects collected by
Lummis on his travels in the southwest. It is also the headquarters of
the Historical Society of Southern California.

SOUTHWEST MUSEUM

One of the great museums in the country for the artifacts of
America's native peoples, the Southwest Museum consists of a
warren of halls and exhibits set in a 1914 Mission Revival building
designed by Sumner Hunt. The comprehensive collections cover a
territory larger than the museum's name suggests, ranging from the
Navajo Southwest to the Eskimo North, and as far east as the Indians
of the Great Plains. Among the many collections on display, the
basketry is particularly remarkable. The museum was founded by
Charles Fletcher Lummis, one of the first modern Californians to
appreciate the state's Spanish heritage. In 1897, Lummis founded
the Landmark Society, one of the first organizations to preserve
California's missions. In 1903, he began the Southwest Society as the
Los Angeles chapter of the American Institute of Archaeology. The
society sponsored anthropological and ethnographic research and
collecting, and by 1907 had amassed a noteworthy collection. The
museum also maintains the **Casa de Adobe** (4605 North Figueroa
Street), a re-created mid-nineteenth-century Spanish Colonial
hacienda, built in 1918 by the Hispanic Society of California.

   LOCATION: 234 Museum Drive, off the Pasadena Freeway. HOURS:
   11–5 Tuesday–Sunday. FEE: Yes. TELEPHONE: 213–221–2163.

The eclectic Los Angeles City Hall, opposite, designed by John C. Austin, John and Donald Parkinson, and Albert C. Martin, Sr., contains elements of many different architectural styles. The elaborate Byzantine decoration in the interior rotunda, above, was designed by Austin Whittlesey.

DOWNTOWN LOS ANGELES

Downtown Los Angeles—a vaguely defined locale southeast of the multi-layered junction of the Santa Ana, Harbor, Pasadena, and Hollywood freeways—preserves few traces of the nineteenth century. In its frenzies of growth Los Angeles sacrificed many of its landmarks. Still, the surviving monuments, civic, commercial, and religious, possess vestiges of a traditional character that some do not expect to find in Los Angeles. The twenty-seven-story Los Angeles **City Hall** (200 North Spring Street) is no longer the tallest building in the city, although when the construction began in 1926, a special ordinance had to be passed to allow it to surpass the statutory thirteen-story limit. A solid tower set above a broad colonnaded base, it is striking inside and out, due to the opulent use of marble, wood, and Malibu tile. There is a fine view of the city from the twenty-seventh-floor terrace.

Nearby **Saint Vibiana Cathedral** (114 East Second Street) is a good copy, built in 1876, of the Baroque Church of San Miguel del

Puerto in Barcelona. The **Wells Fargo History Museum** (333 South Grand Avenue, 213–253–7166) features a complete facsimile of a gold rush-era Wells Fargo office, a collection of stagecoaches, and the Dorsey gold collection, consisting of gold samples and mining tools. Henry Wells and William G. Fargo, the two Eastern financiers who established the American Express Company, founded Wells, Fargo & Co. in New York in 1852 to provide postal, banking, and transportation services to California's Gold Rush territory. The company quickly became one of the region's most important financial institutions—by 1855 there were fifty-five Wells Fargo agencies in California.

In the southern end of the downtown area are two architectural landmarks: the ship-shaped **Coca-Cola Building** (1334 South Central Avenue), complete with portholes and two huge, inset bottles of Coke, built between 1935 and 1937, and the equally exuberant **Herald Examiner Building** (1111 South Broadway), completed by Julia Morgan for William Randolph Hearst in 1913, in a flamboyant Mission Revival style. Southwest of the downtown area is **Exposition Park** (Figueroa Street and Exposition Boulevard), the site of the 1932 and 1984 Olympics and now a center for museums and sports facilities. The University of Southern California is nearby.

The **California State Museum of Science and Industry** (Figueroa Street and Exposition Boulevard, 213–744–7400) is a vast complex of exhibits, including a mathematics exhibit designed by Charles Eames, satellites, rockets, models of the human body, and a history of the state's industrial development. This is the largest U.S. science museum outside of the Smithsonian Institution. Adjacent is the **California Afro-American Museum** (600 State Drive, 213–744–4700), dedicated to Afro-American achievements in the arts, politics, education, and sports. The museum offers changing exhibitions and maintains a sculpture garden, theater, and research library.

NATURAL HISTORY MUSEUM
OF LOS ANGELES COUNTY

This museum contains fine dioramas and exhibits relating to modern animals, as well as significant collections of vertebrate and invertebrate fossils. The displays on pre-Columbian Meso-American culture are justly famous. An entire hall is devoted to the history of California and the Southwest from 1540 to 1940; exhibits include a cutaway model of Juan Rodríguez Cabrillo's ship, the *San Salvador,* dioramas depicting early Indian life; re-creations of an early Spanish adobe and an Indian straw hut; and displays on the gold rush and the movie industry. Real California gold can be seen in the Gem and Mineral Hall, along with an array of gems and descriptions of how they are created.

LOCATION: 900 Exposition Boulevard. HOURS: 10–5 Tuesday–Sunday. FEE: Yes. TELEPHONE: 213–744–3414.

The **Hancock Memorial Museum** (213–743–5213) occupies a wing of the marine sciences building on the south side of the central quadrangle of the University of Southern California campus. It consists of a foyer and four original rooms from the mansion of Ida Haraszthy Hancock, the daughter of Agoston Haraszthy and wife of Los Angeles pioneer Henry Hancock. The rooms—a reception hall, English library and dining room, and a music salon in the Louis XV style—date from 1907 and contain some of her fine collection of furnishings, including items from the Mexico City Chapultepec Palace of Emperor Maximilian and Empress Carlota. The reception hall features Carrara marble stairways, murals depicting the ruins of Pompeii and Herculaneum, and a large stained-glass window.

Los Angeles's most universally recognized landmark is the Hollywood sign, which cost the developers of "Hollywoodland" $21,000 in 1923. A group of concerned celebrities restored it in 1974 at the cost of $27,500 per letter.

Amid smoke and spray William Beaudine directs a silent comedy. Beaudine was one of Hollywood's most prolific directors, with hundreds of low-budget films to his credit.

HOLLYWOOD

This wedge of Los Angeles set against the Santa Monica Mountains (here called the Hollywood Hills), about eight miles west of downtown, was part of the ranch of Don Tomás Urquídez in the 1850s. A man named Horace Wilcox christened the area Hollywood and set about selling house lots in 1887. In 1910, when the town agreed to be annexed to Los Angeles in order to take advantage of Owens Valley water, it had only about 4,000 residents.

The fledgling movie industry had begun its emigration from the East to Los Angeles in 1906, the year in which the city's first studio was started. The movie industry was slow to expand in its early years because a monopoly called the Motion Pictures Patent Company controlled critical camera and film-processing patents. Filmmakers who lacked patent licenses sought remote spots, such as Southern California, to escape the monopoly's lawyers. They also came to Los Angeles for the relentlessly sunny climate—a boon to moviemakers on a tight schedule. The Los Angeles chamber of commerce described the region's allure in an advertisement: "Environment certainly affects creative workers. You realize surely the importance in such essentially sensitive production as the making of Motion Pictures the vital importance of having every member of an organization awake in the morning and start to work in a flood of happy sunshine. Cold rain and slushy snow do not tend to the proper mental condition for the best creative work."

The first moviemakers to establish themselves in Hollywood were William and David Horsley, who had been shooting Westerns in New Jersey and wanted more accurate scenery. In 1911 the brothers set up shop in a tavern at Sunset Boulevard and Gower Street, shooting Hollywood's first moving picture, *The Law of the Range. The Squaw Man,* directed in 1913 by Cecil B. De Mille and produced by Samuel Goldwyn, was the first feature-length film shot entirely in Hollywood. A decade later, Hollywood had 50,000 residents and a billion-dollar industry. The **Hollywood Studio Museum** (2100 North Highland Avenue, 213–874–2276) is located in the former horse barn De Mille used for shooting *The Squaw Man.* Originally situated at Selma and Vine streets, it was moved to the Paramount lot and transferred to its present location in 1985. The museum has changing exhibits about the history of motion pictures.

Perched on the slopes of Mount Lee is the **Hollywood Sign,** with letters fifty feet high by thirty feet wide, put up in 1923 to advertise a housing development called Hollywoodland. When the city took ownership of the hillside and the sign in 1949, officials chopped the "land" off the end, leaving the sign as we know it today.

A neon dragon guards the marquee of Mann's—originally Grauman's—Chinese Theatre, where honored Hollywood stars still leave their foot- and handprints in the sidewalk.

Mann's Chinese Theatre (6925 Hollywood Boulevard) and the Egyptian Theatre (6712 Hollywood Boulevard), two symbols of Hollywood, were constructed for Sid Grauman, an entrepreneur who conceived the notion of grand movie premieres, with the stars arriving like royalty and the fans straining to touch them. The Egyptian Theatre opened in 1922 with a showing of Douglas Fairbanks, Jr., in *Robin Hood.* The Chinese, finished in 1927, contains the famous forecourt full of the signatures, handprints, and footprints of scores of stars. (The tradition is said to have begun when one of them stepped in wet cement by accident.)

The **Chateau Marmont Hotel** (8221 Sunset Boulevard, 213–656–1010), where the likes of Howard Hughes and Greta Garbo once lived, is a Hollywood version of a Norman chateau. Many early stars are buried at the **Hollywood Memorial Park Cemetery** (6000 Santa Monica Boulevard)—Tyrone Power, Douglas Fairbanks, Jr., and Rudolph Valentino among them.

Aline Barnsdall, an oil heiress, bought the land now called Barnsdall Park (4800 Hollywood Boulevard) early in the century and

Frank Lloyd Wright placed bands of stylized cast-stone hollyhocks, Aline Barnsdall's favorite flower, on her East Hollywood house, known as Hollyhock House.

A Hollyhock House mantelpiece decorated with a geometric design.

commissioned Frank Lloyd Wright to design a house and cultural center. The result is the 1921 **Hollyhock House** (4808 Hollywood Boulevard, 213–662–7272), now restored and furnished much as Wright prescribed. The hollyhock flower is used as an abstract decoration on the house and its furnishings. The **Rudolph M. Schindler House** (833 North Kings Road, 213–651–1510) was built by Schindler in 1921 and 1922. The young Viennese architect had come to the United States to work with Frank Lloyd Wright and to Los Angeles to supervise construction of Wright's Hollyhock House. Schindler's own house was his laboratory for testing ideas about materials and modernist forms, and adapting simple construction techniques to the southern California climate. Designed around a series of interlocking garden courts, the house is constructed of concrete and canvas, creating a simple camp-like structure.

   Cahuenga Pass, near the junction of the Hollywood and Ventura freeways, was the site of two battles in 1831 and 1845—virtually bloodless artillery exchanges—between Californios and forces of the Mexican governors. In both battles the governors were defeated. Near here, too, the Mexican forces led by Andrés Pico, the brother of Pío Pico, came to terms with the American Lieutenant Colonel John Charles Frémont on January 13, 1847, ending Mexican-American hostilities in the state. A marker at 3919 Lankershim Boulevard in North Hollywood commemorates the site.

Wilshire Boulevard stretches sixteen miles from the downtown area to the sea, passing various socioeconomic and ethnic enclaves and such landmarks as the 1929 Art Deco **Bullocks Wilshire** department store (3050 Wilshire Boulevard) and the La Brea tar pits. Oil wells dotted the landscape several blocks north of Wilshire.

GEORGE C. PAGE MUSEUM OF LA BREA DISCOVERIES

Here is the richest single deposit of Pleistocene life yet discovered; the remains of over 200 different species, some of them extinct, have been recovered from the sticky morass in which they were snared and then entombed. (Rain puts a deceptive cover of water over the thick tar that lies beneath, so that the deadly pools resemble water holes.) The remains of sloths and mammoths, camels and birds, even of a 9,000-year-old woman have been recovered from the pits, since the 1906 discovery that the tar contained fossils. The pits had been known to human inhabitants for centuries before. When the Spaniards arrived, the Indians were already using the sticky pitch to

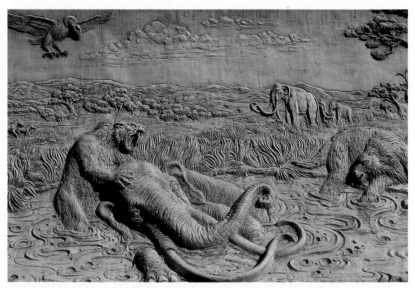

A section of the diorama in the George C. Page Museum of La Brea Discoveries shows an artist's re-creation of some of the now-extinct denizens of prehistoric Los Angeles.

caulk boats and waterproof baskets; the Europeans used the pitch on the roofs of their houses. Some of the early Spanish settlers thought the black tar was the cause of earthquakes and speculated that it might flow from a volcano. The museum houses the remarkable paleontological collection that has been dug from the tar pits over the years, including a section showing work in progress. The fossil collection numbers over 1 million pieces, one-tenth of which are on display. Bones, dioramas, and holographic images are used to give a vivid picture of what the area was like 40,000 years ago.

LOCATION: 5801 Wilshire Boulevard, Hancock Park. HOURS: 10–5 Tuesday–Sunday. FEE: Yes. TELEPHONE: 213–936–2230.

Also in Hancock Park is the **Los Angeles County Museum of Art** (5905 Wilshire Boulevard, 213–857–6111), which has some of the world's finest collections of Tibetan, Nepalese, and Indian materials, Islamic paintings, and Assyrian and other Near Eastern artifacts. Founded in 1910, the museum also has a fine collection of American art from the post–World War II period.

BEVERLY HILLS

Although entirely surrounded by the city of Los Angeles, Beverly Hills is an independent city. This enclave of palatial homes started out in 1906 as a speculative residential tract named for Beverly Farms, Massachusetts. It began to take on the character it retains today when the **Beverly Hills Hotel** (9641 Sunset Boulevard) was built in 1912. **Pickfair** (1143 Summit Drive, private), the first and still among the most famous of the area's mansions, was the home of Mary Pickford and Douglas Fairbanks, Sr., who bought an existing hunting lodge in 1919 and renovated it in a fancy Colonial Revival style. At 905 Loma Vista Drive is an equally opulent, slate-roofed, Tudor-style house called **Greystone Mansion** (213–550–4654), built in 1928 by oilman Edward L. Doheny, Sr., who had made the first big Los Angeles oil discovery in 1892. Its landscaped grounds are now a city park. Doheny first struck oil at First Street and Glendale Boulevard very near downtown Los Angeles. He made his real oil fortune in Mexico and the federally owned Elk Hills Reserve in Kern County. In 1923 Doheny was implicated in the Teapot Dome scandal: He was accused but acquitted of having bribed Secretary of the Interior Albert B. Fall to obtain the lease to drill for oil at Elk Hills.

The Santa Monica Pier, most famous for its large carousel, complete with a turn-of-the-century Wurlitzer organ.

C O A S T   S I D E

Along the gentle curve of Santa Monica Bay are the towns of Malibu, Santa Monica, and Venice. **Malibu** was first a Spanish ranch, then a vast property belonging to Frederick Hastings Rindge and later to his widow. Development, chiefly of luxury beach cottages, began in the mid-1920s. **Santa Monica** was first intended to be Los Angeles's seaport, but lost out to San Pedro at the turn of the century. Thereafter, it developed slowly as a beach resort. In the 1940s, an airport and aircraft manufacturing plants contributed to a rapid urbanization. The **Santa Monica Pier** (Ocean and Colorado avenues), built between 1904 and 1921, is a charming, well-preserved playland, a reminder of Santa Monica's resort days. The **Santa Monica Heritage Museum** (2612 Main Street, 213–392–8537), an 1890s house, displays turn-of-the-century furnished rooms on its first floor.

The area called **Venice,** south along the coast, was founded in 1904 by tobacco heir Abbott Kinney. He ordered canals dug, brought in gondolas from Venice, Italy, and invited Sarah Bernhardt to perform on the Venice pier at the area's opening. He hoped for a center for wholesome entertainment and living. Within two decades, however, all but three of the canals had been filled in as health hazards, and water shortages had forced the area's annexation to Los Angeles. An oil boom in the 1930s caused derricks to rise where Kinney had envisioned monuments.

WILL ROGERS STATE HISTORIC PARK

The rambling but palatial ranch house of the humorist, philosopher, movie star, and trick roper has been preserved in Pacific Palisades as a state historic park. The 186-acre park features views that look eastward over Los Angeles and westward to the Pacific Ocean. Originally a small cottage, the house was enlarged to thirty-one rooms in 1928, when the Rogers family began occupying it full time. The furnishings are much as Rogers left them: rustic, comfortable, with

The double-height living room of Will Rogers's California ranch house, where he lived from 1928 until his death in 1935, was used for indoor rope-trick practice.

collections of Indian rugs and basketry. Rogers, who actually did start his career as a cowboy, had among his prized possessions a mounted calf, said to have been given to him by friends who were tired of being roped themselves.

LOCATION: 14253 Sunset Boulevard, Pacific Palisades. HOURS: *Park:* 8–6 Daily; *House:* 10–5 Daily. FEE: Yes. TELEPHONE: 213–454–8212.

J. PAUL GETTY MUSEUM

The Getty museum is housed in a faithful reconstruction of the Villa dei Papyri, a Roman country house built around a peristyled courtyard. The original stood in Herculaneum, Italy, where it was buried by Mount Vesuvius's eruption in A.D. 79. The museum's courtyard features gardens, mosaics, multicolored marble, and fountains.

Oil magnate J. Paul Getty was responsible for both the building and the original collection, and the bequest he left the museum on his death has made it the most richly endowed museum in the world. Its collection of Greek and Roman statuary is superb. One of the most famous pieces, a fourth-century B.C. bronze, possibly by Lysippus, was acquired in 1977, but a good part of the collection was obtained by Getty himself beginning in the 1930s. The second floor contains pre-twentieth-century Western European paintings, drawings, and sculpture; decorative arts; and nineteenth- and twentieth-century photographs.

LOCATION: 17985 Pacific Coast Highway, Malibu. HOURS: 10–5 Tuesday–Sunday. Parking reservations are required. FEE: None. TELEPHONE: 213–458–2003

WAYFARERS CHAPEL

Devotees of Emanuel Swedenborg have a great Swedenborgian Church in San Francisco and the magnificent Wayfarers Chapel in Rancho Palos Verdes, designed by Lloyd Wright, son of Frank Lloyd Wright. Made almost entirely of glass set in a wood frame and surrounded by a grove of redwoods and gardens, the chapel commands the heights looking out over the Pacific. In fulfillment of

OPPOSITE: *The J. Paul Getty Museum in Malibu, which opened in 1974, re-creates the Villa dei Papyri, a Roman villa from the first century B.C. that was buried in the A.D. 79 eruption of Mount Vesuvius.*

the plans of Elizabeth Schellenberg, it was completed in 1951. Exhibits on Swedenborgianism and Helen Keller (a noted Swedenborgian) are on display.

LOCATION: 5755 Palos Verdes Drive South, Rancho Palos Verdes. HOURS: 9–5 Daily. FEE: None. TELEPHONE: 213–377–1650.

The small but interesting **Lomita Railroad Museum** (250th Street and Woodward Avenue, Lomita, 213–326–6255) is housed in a replica of a nineteenth-century Massachusetts railroad station. The engine and other rolling stock on display date from about 1900.

SAN PEDRO

One of the most important harbors on the West Coast, San Pedro was once so shallow that oceangoing ships had to be unloaded offshore and the goods brought to land by skiff. The harbor was improved somewhat during the 1850s, but the area did not experience dramatic growth until about 1900, when federal funds were finally approved to enlarge the port. The **Cabrillo Marine Museum** (3720 Stephen White Drive, 213–548–7562) features southern California marine life and a seashell collection. A plaque on the grounds of Fort MacArthur Military Reservation marks the site of the 1823 Casa de San Pedro, the first commercial structure on the bay.

Housed in what was once a ferry building, the **Los Angeles Maritime Museum** (Berth 84, Sixth Street, 213–548–7618) features several walk-in naval exhibits, including the bow and bridge of the cruiser Los Angeles. A good collection of ship models is also part of the museum, as is a graphic history of San Pedro harbor. The careful renovation of the building has preserved a good deal of memorabilia from ferry days. The Point Fermin Lighthouse (south end of Gaffey Street at Paseo del Mar) was built in 1874 on a promontory overlooking the Pacific. It went out of use in 1942.

WILMINGTON

A white frame house, **Drum Barracks** (1052 Banning Road, 213–548–7509), is all that remains of Camp Drum, a Union Army camp established here in 1861 and abandoned in 1871. The camp was Federal headquarters for the entire Southwest during the Civil War, and from 1861 to 1863 was the terminus for a camel-borne trade

The largest airplane ever built, Howard Hughes's Spruce Goose, *is now on display in Long Beach. Surrounding the wooden plane is an exhibit detailing Hughes's contributions to aviation history.*

route. It is now operated as a Civil War museum. A strong Union supporter and the man most responsible for the development of Los Angeles harbor, Phineas Banning built a striking twenty-three-room Greek Revival house in 1864, now preserved as the **General Phineas Banning Residence Museum** (401 East M Street, 213–548–7777). It is the finest example of its style in southern California, and the interior has been carefully restored and furnished with many original Banning pieces, along with other appropriate Victorian furnishings.

LONG BEACH

Long Beach was incorporated just before the turn of the century, as a beach community. In 1921 oil was discovered on **Signal Hill,** and the field was at one time the largest in the United States, delivering over 250,000 barrels per day. Long Beach harbor is the final resting place of the huge British ocean liner, *Queen Mary* (Pier J, 213–435–3511), now completely refurbished in all its Art Deco glory. The 81,000-ton ship was built in 1934 and retired in 1964 after more than 1,000 Atlantic crossings. The ship is now home to a 364-room hotel, and it also contains exhibits including a sound-and-light reenactment of a collision at sea and a display depicting the ship's role in World War II. A mammoth of airborne transport, the *Spruce Goose*, is preserved inside a geodesic dome next to the *Queen Mary*, as part of the same complex. This wooden airplane, 80 feet tall, with a wingspan of over 320 feet, was built by Howard Hughes to ferry troops and tanks during World War II, but it was not finished until 1947, and it flew only once, for about one minute. Models of the plane's eight huge engines, plus memorabilia of Howard Hughes's career as an aviator and builder of airplanes, are also on display.

A cedar-shingled 1912 Craftsman-style house contains the **Long Beach Museum of Art** (2300 East Ocean Boulevard, 213–439–2119). The first-rate collection of modern and southern California art is complemented by an interesting sculpture garden and substantial holdings in video art and modern German art.

Rancho Los Cerritos Historic Site

A Maine family sent three cousins west to California during the 1850s; the Flints and Bixbys became large-scale ranchers, and the Bixbys, who managed the southern California holdings, became one of the area's most prominent families. Later this 1844 Monterey-style adobe house and the neighboring Rancho Los Alamitos were owned by the Bixby clan. From this house—first built by Jonathan Temple—the Bixbys ran a 27,000-head sheep ranch from 1866 until 1881. The house has been somewhat modified, but it is furnished with Bixby-era pieces, and its fine Italianate garden has been partially preserved.

LOCATION: 4600 Virginia Road. HOURS: 1–5 Wednesday–Sunday. FEE: None. TELEPHONE: 213–424–9423.

Rancho Los Alamitos (6400 Bixby Hill Road, 213–431–3541), an adobe structure, was built by the Spanish in about 1806, but it has been much modified over time. Members of the Bixby family lived here from 1878 until 1968, and the furnishings reflect their long occupancy; some of the cabinets and wardrobes were carved by John Bixby himself. While the house is interesting in itself, the important California native-and-exotic-plants garden, dating from the 1920s, is also impressive. Also on the grounds are barns, stables, and other period farm buildings.

Catalina Island's Casino, in Avalon, its only town, contains a museum, a movie theater, and a ballroom that once drew crowds of more than 6,000 to its dances.

CATALINA ISLAND

About thirty miles southwest of Los Angeles harbor is Catalina Island, with its main town of Avalon. Named by the explorer Sebastián Vizcaíno in 1602, the island later served as a temporary base for otter hunters, who killed or drove away the native population. After the United States seized California, it passed from hand to hand, as a private fiefdom, until chewing-gum magnate William Wrigley bought the whole island in 1919 from the Bannings and developed Avalon as a resort center. The **Catalina Island Museum** (1 Casino Way, 213–510–2414), housed in the Wrigleys' 1929 Casino Building, contains exhibits on the Indian peoples and the history, prehistory, and natural history of the island, as well as photos and artifacts from the early resort days.

SAN GABRIEL VALLEY

The San Gabriel Valley stretches out east of Los Angeles in a bowl formed by the San Gabriel Mountains to the north, the San Jose Hills to the east, and a scattering of other ranges to the south. Pasadena lies at its near end, Pomona just beyond its far end. The Spaniards established their first settlement in the Los Angeles area here, and founded the Mission San Gabriel Arcángel in 1771. Under the padres of San Gabriel, the first grapes and oranges were cultivated in California, where they were grown until the 1930s.

PASADENA

In 1872 Thomas B. Elliott of Indianapolis and a group of friends bought part of an old ranch in the San Gabriel Valley, originally naming it the California Colony of Indiana, and later, Pasadena, the latter being an Ojibwa word for "crown of the valley." The city boomed, busted, and boomed again along with the real estate speculation during the last quarter of the nineteenth century; in 1890 it initiated the New Year's Day Tournament of Roses to promote southern California's climate. In the early 1900s it was one of the wealthiest cities in the country, a prosperity reflected in the **Tournament House** (391 South Orange Grove Boulevard, 818–449–4100), a Mission Style mansion built for the chewing-gum king, William Wrigley, Jr., between 1908 and 1914.

Gamble House

With its Japanese-inspired lines and impeccable craftsmanship, the Gamble House is one of the most important houses in the United States—a definitive example of the Arts and Crafts movement in this country. Built as a vacation home for David H. Gamble in 1908, it is the work of the brothers Charles and Henry Greene. The hand-wrought interior is as remarkable as the Craftsman-style exterior, and the house is furnished as conceived by the Greenes, including furniture, rugs, and Tiffany glass.

LOCATION: 4 Westmoreland Place. HOURS: 12–3 Thursday–Sunday. FEE: Yes. TELEPHONE: 818–793–3334.

OPPOSITE: *The 1908 Gamble House, designed by Charles and Henry Greene, who had been greatly influenced by the Japanese pavilion at the 1893 Chicago World's Columbian Exposition.* OVERLEAF: *The teak-panelled Gamble House entrance hall contains furnishings designed by Charles Greene.*

Pasadena Historical Society

Housed in a turn-of-the-century mansion of Beaux-Arts design, the historical society's museum is a combination of house museum, cultural museum, and Finnish folk-arts museum. The furnishings on display were gathered by the original owners, the Fenyes family, once leaders of Pasadena society and literary culture. The basement holds a collection of artifacts and photographs relating to the city's history. A member of the family married the Finnish consul during the 1940s, and the couple began to assemble the finest collection of Finnish crafts outside of Finland, housed in a separate building.

LOCATION: 470 West Walnut Street. HOURS: 1–4 Tuesday, Thursday, and Sunday (except third Sunday of each month). FEE: Yes. TELEPHONE: 818–577–1660.

Norton Simon Museum of Art

On view at this museum are seven centuries of European paintings, sculpture, and tapestries, dating from the Renaissance to the twentieth century, including works by Raphael, Rubens,

Still Life: Lemons, Oranges, and a Rose *by the Spanish painter Francisco de Zurbarán is one of the masterpieces in the collection of the Norton Simon Museum in Pasadena.*

Impressionist and Post-Impressionist paintings are a specialty of the Norton Simon Museum, whose collection includes Henri Matisse's The Black Shawl, *or* Lorette VII.

Rembrandt, Watteau, Goya, Manet, van Gogh, Renoir, Degas, Cezanne, and Picasso. Complementing the western art is a collection of Asian sculpture from India and Southeast Asia spanning a period of 2,000 years. The museum was founded in 1924 as the Pasadena Art Institute. The present building, designed by Thornton Ladd, opened to the public in 1969 as a museum specializing in contemporary art, which failed. It was reorganized and remodeled in 1974 under the direction of businessman Norton Simon. Nearly all of the works on display were collected by Simon and his wife, the actress Jennifer Jones, whose interest in India led to the collection of Asian sculpture.

LOCATION: Colorado and Orange Grove boulevards. HOURS: 12–6 Thursday–Sunday. FEE: Yes. TELEPHONE: 818–449–3730.

El Molino Viejo (1120 Old Mill Road, San Marino, 818–449–5450) was the first water-powered gristmill to be built in southern California, constructed in 1816 by Indians from the Mission San Gabriel. The simple adobe structure was used as a home after 1833, and today is maintained by the California Historical Society, which has its southern California headquarters here and uses the space for rotating exhibits on the region's history.

The Huntington Gallery, built in 1910 as Henry E. Huntington's residence, was designed by Myron Hunt and Elmer Grey. OPPOSITE: *Allegorical figures representing the seasons decorate the mausoleum of Huntington and his wife, Arabella. Built in 1933 on the grounds of the Huntington estate, the mausoleum was designed by John Russell Pope, the architect of the Jefferson Memorial in Washington, DC.*

THE HUNTINGTON LIBRARY, ART GALLERY, AND BOTANICAL GARDENS

Henry E. Huntington, the nephew of Big-Four railroad tycoon Collis P. Huntington, inherited his uncle's stake in the Southern Pacific, sold it, and helped to create Los Angeles's once-successful mass transit system. He owned vast tracts of land in southern California. On a choice 207-acre site in San Marino, he had built a palatial Neoclassical residence in 1910, a library in 1925, and remarkable gardens of twelve specific styles, including a cactus and succulents garden that is perhaps the finest of its kind in the world.

In 1919 he endowed a museum, library, and gardens. The collection of eighteenth- and nineteenth-century British and French painting and decorative arts is among the finest in the world. (It includes Gainsborough's *Blue Boy.*) The library, likewise, boasts a world-class collection of rare manuscripts and books. Among the bibliographic treasures on display are a Gutenberg Bible, a collection of

OPPOSITE AND ABOVE: *The Mission San Gabriel, which had the oldest and, at one time, the largest vineyards in California.*

Shakespeare's works, the manuscript of Benjamin Franklin's *Autobiography,* and a set of Audubon's *Birds of America.* Outside, there are Shakespeare gardens, herb gardens, Zen gardens, the succulents garden, and one of the world's largest collections of camellias.

LOCATION: 1151 Oxford Road, San Marino. HOURS: 1–4:30 Tuesday–Sunday. FEE: Yes. TELEPHONE: 818–405–2100.

MISSION SAN GABRIEL ARCANGEL

Founded in 1771, San Gabriel was the fourth mission established by Father Junípero Serra, and it was to become one of the most prosperous. The church, built in 1806, has narrow windows and Moorish features, perhaps suggested by the great cathedral/mosque of Córdoba in Spain. The main facade is on the side wall to the north—an unusual design for a mission church. The large bell tower on the south side was built to replace an earlier one destroyed by an earthquake. Almost 2,000 Indians worked the mission lands and helped tend more than 40,000 head of cattle. At its height, Mission San Gabriel controlled 1.5 million acres, including the San Gabriel Valley, south to the ocean and east to the San Bernardino Mountains.

The mission is closed indefinitely due to earthquake damage, but the cactus gardens and a reconstructed eighteenth-century kitchen are open to the public.

LOCATION: 537 West Mission Drive, San Gabriel. HOURS: 9:30–4:15 Daily. FEE: None. TELEPHONE: 818–282–5191.

LOS ANGELES STATE AND COUNTY ARBORETUM

This 127-acre garden of exotic flora and fauna lies on part of what once was the flamboyant E. J. "Lucky" Baldwin's great estate, in the town called Arcadia that he founded. The plantings show clearly the exotic species—Australian, South African, and Mediterranean—that can adapt to the California climate. (Hollywood has been delighted with the gardens as a setting, having used them in everything from *The African Queen* to *Roots*.) The **Queen Anne Cottage and Coach Barn** on the grounds were built in the middle 1880s, when the elderly silver tycoon married a 16-year-old bride. The **Hugo Reid Adobe** house next door was built in 1839 by the Scotsman Hugo Reid, owner of the Rancho Santa Anita from 1841 to 1847. There is also a restored 1890s Santa Fe Railroad station on the grounds.

LOCATION: 301 North Baldwin Avenue, Arcadia. HOURS: 9–4:30 Daily. FEE: Yes. TELEPHONE: 818–446–8251.

WORKMAN AND TEMPLE HOMESTEAD MUSEUM

In 1841 William Workman and John Rowland led the first overland settlement expedition to California from Taos, New Mexico, where both men had been trappers and traders. Already married to Mexican women and accustomed to Hispanic ways, they had no trouble securing a 48,790-acre land grant from the Mexican governor—particularly when Rowland offered to pay $1,000 in gold in back taxes on the spot and promised to care for the Indians who lived on the land. The Workman home was built in 1841 of plain adobe and Victorianized in 1872; the exterior has been restored to its 1872 appearance. A fine 1923 Spanish Colonial Revival home built for Workman's grandson, Walter P. Temple, has been restored inside and out and furnished with period and original furnishings. The pedimented mausoleum in the cemetery can also be visited. Pío Pico, the last Mexican governor of California, is also buried here. This site, one of the state's true historical treasures, features excellent interpretive tours.

LOCATION: 15415 East Don Julian Road, City of Industry. HOURS: 1–4 Tuesday–Friday, 10–4 Saturday–Sunday; closed the fourth weekend of every month. FEE: None. TELEPHONE: 818–968–8492.

John Rowland, the partner of William Workman, originally lived just across the creek from his friend in the **John Rowland Home** (16021 East Gale Street, 818–336–7644), one of the oldest brick houses still standing in southern California. Like Workman, he had married a Mexican woman, and they shared the ranch life, running cattle and raising grapevines and fruit trees. When Rowland's first wife died, however, he met and married a young widow from Kentucky, Mrs. Charlotte Gray. To delight her, he built this brick house in 1855 in a Southern plantation style (it was later slightly remodeled). The descendants of John Rowland lived here, and the interior preserves many of their furnishings.

The **El Monte Historical Museum** (3150 North Tyler Avenue, El Monte, 818–444–3813) commemorates the nineteenth-century history of El Monte, once a separate town and now contiguous with East Los Angeles. The museum features a re-created general store, barber shop, police station, and school from the 1850s, and the interior of a late-nineteenth-century house.

WHITTIER

This town was founded by Quakers late in the last century and named for Quaker poet John Greenleaf Whittier. It contains **Casa de Pío Pico** (6003 Pioneer Boulevard, 213–695–1217), the home of

California's last Mexican governor. He bought the 9,000-acre ranch on which the home is situated after the close of hostilities between U.S. troops and the Californios in 1847, but the first house he built here was swept away by a flood in 1883. The thirteen-room adobe structure, the second home on the site, has suffered earthquake damage, but the park surrounding the house is open to the public.

POMONA

Named for the Roman goddess of fruits, Pomona was long an orchard center, though today its economy centers on high-tech light industry. Its past, as with so many other towns in the region, is the story of a ranch and of partners. **La Casa Primera de San José** (1569 North Park Avenue, 714–623–2198) is the oldest surviving house in town, built by Don Ignacio Palomares in 1837, to be the headquarters of his part of the Rancho San José, a 15,000-acre spread that he shared with Don Ricardo Vejar. Some of the orange trees planted by his son in the 1860s here are still alive. The one-story adobe building is restored and furnished in late nineteenth-century fashion. In 1854 Don Ignacio built himself a second and larger home, with thirteen rooms, which is today known as **Adobe de Palomares** (491 East Arrow Highway, 714–620–2300). Though it was abandoned by the mid-twentieth century, the city has since restored it, furnishing it with mid-nineteenth-century antiques, including some originally owned by Don Ignacio's family. The **Phillips Mansion** (2640 Pomona Boulevard, 714–623–2198), a three-story, mansard-roofed Second Empire structure, was built in 1875 by Louis Phillips, who took over the management of the Palomares-Vejar ranch after it went bankrupt in the 1860s. It is now restored and furnished according to the taste of the period.

SAN FERNANDO VALLEY

There are about 177 square miles to the San Fernando Valley, set among mountain ranges northwest of downtown Los Angeles. The area is both hotter and drier than the nearby coastal plain. Originally called Encino Valley—*encino* being Spanish for live oak—it was a place where early Chumash and Shoshonean peoples came to gather acorns. The Spanish colonized it comparatively late, when Father Serra's successor, Father Lasuén, established Mission San Fernando Rey de España in 1797. The mission was the seventeenth to be founded along El Camino Real and was intended as a halfway link between the missions San Gabriel Arcángel and San Buenaventura. After secularization of the mission lands, which comprised much of the valley, Mexican ranchers took vast tracts but lost them piece by piece to drought, to invading Yankees, and to Yankee lawyers. Two events put the Valley, as it is colloquially known, on the modern map: the arrival of the Southern Pacific Railroad in 1874 and of Owens Valley water in 1913. The first eliminated isolation; the second, drought, though to get the water, in 1915, the Valley had to agree to be annexed to Los Angeles. A suburban quilt of pastel stucco houses replaced what was once farmland.

GLENDALE

The city of Glendale was created during the 1880s land boom that followed the extension of the Southern Pacific into the Valley. Also known as the "Original Mud Block Adobe," the **Catalina Adobe** (2211 Bonita Drive, private), was built for Catalina Verdugo in the 1830s. She was the blind daughter of the grantee of the surrounding ranch in 1784, Don José María Verdugo.

Forest Lawn Memorial Park

The most famous cemetery in California, Forest Lawn is as much a symbol of southern California's culture as is any abode of its living residents. The names of those buried here are inscribed on plaques set flush to the lawn. What distinguishes the memorial park are its "public" buildings. There are full-scale reproductions of several old European churches, as well as facsimiles of Michelangelo's sculptures; a huge stained-glass version of Leonardo's *The Last Supper*; a Roman temple (containing the remains of oilman Edward L. Doheny); and two of the largest paintings in the world, one of the Crucifixion and the other of the Resurrection.

LOCATION: 1712 South Glendale Avenue. HOURS: 8:30–5 Daily. TELEPHONE: 213–254–3131.

BURBANK

Burbank is named for one of the men who first developed it during the 1880s. It began to grow in the 1920s, when the Lockheed Aircraft Corporation was founded here. Its motion picture and television studios have placed Burbank among the entertainment capitals of the world. The **Gordon R. Howard Museum** (1015 West Olive Avenue, 818–841–6333) includes a well-restored 1887 Eastlake-style house with late nineteenth-century furnishings; an interesting collection of antique automobiles; an exhibit depicting the history of Lockheed Aircraft; and life-size vignettes depicting the early days of Burbank—Dr. David Burbank's dental office, Al Jolson making the first talkie, a country store—furnished with many original items.

ENCINO

Encino and most of the towns nearby were small farming communities until after the Second World War. During the eighteenth century, the Franciscans had camped in the area while scouting a site for Mission San Fernando Rey. The **Los Encinos State Historic Park** (16756 Moorepark Street, 818–784–4849) shows two stages in the slow early development of Encino. It preserves the 1849 **De la Osa Adobe,** a nine-room ranch house, and the 1872 **Garnier Building,** of solid limestone with stucco exterior covering and a gabled roof. The houses belonged to successive owners of the Rancho de los Encinos, and both have been restored.

In nearby **Calabasas** is another notable adobe house, the **Leonis Adobe** (23537 Calabasas Road, 818–712–0734). The once simple 1844 mud-block structure, remodeled into a Monterey-style two-story house during the 1870s, is restored and well furnished in the style of its later period. On the same site is the 1875 **Plummer House,** moved here from Hollywood and restored with period wallpaper, carpeting, and furniture. It also contains a museum with interpretive exhibits. The one-and-a-quarter-acre property is set up like a ranch, with livestock and a 1912 barn.

MISSION HILLS

The San Fernando Valley Historical Society is headquartered in the **Andrés Pico Adobe** (10940 Sepulveda Boulevard, 818–365–7810), built in 1834 and altered in the 1870s, when a second story and wooden floors were added. Andrés Pico was the brother of Pío Pico, the last Mexican governor of California, and the house remained in the family until 1899. It later fell into ruins and was restored in 1930.

Mission San Fernando Rey de España

The nineteen semicircular arches of the surviving *convento* of the mission are strong reminders of its original status and prosperity. The building, the largest free-standing adobe structure in California, served as quarters for visitors to the great cattle-ranching and farming mission, founded in 1797. (The mission church itself had fallen into ruins even before it was finally destabilized by a 1971 earthquake, but it has now been well restored.) An extensive collection of artifacts and reconstructed period rooms show what life was like in the days before the influence of the missions weakened.

LOCATION: San Fernando Mission and Sepulveda boulevards, Mission Hills. HOURS: 9–5 Daily. FEE: Yes. TELEPHONE: 818–361–0186

The Mission San Fernando Rey de España, established by Father Junípero Serra's successor Father Fermin Lasuén in 1797, was the fourth mission he founded in a four-month period.

NORTHERN ENVIRONS

North of the city of Los Angeles, but still within Los Angeles County, the land turns to mountains and then to desert in a rapid transition from urban setting to wild landscape. East of the high San Gabriels begins the Mojave Desert, with old mines, new military bases, and the remains of experimental fringe communities.

NEWHALL

One of the pioneer oil-well sites in California lies in nearby Pico Canyon, named for Andrés Pico, who ran a coal-oil business here. Still on the spot is the well called **Pico No. 4,** the first successful commercial well in California, drilled in 1876. It was this strike and the subsequent ones in the surrounding Newhall Field that led to the formation of the Standard Oil Company of California. The

The dining room of William S. Hart's ranch house contains a large portrait of Hollywood's first cowboy star.

hamlet of **Mentryville,** named for Charles A. Mentry, who drilled that first successful well, is situated on Route 5 near Pico Canyon Road. His home there (27201 West Pico Canyon Road, 805–254–1275) has been restored.

Vásquez Rocks County Park (10700 West Escondido Canyon Road, Agua Dulce, 818–268–0840) preserves massive sandstone rock formations as well as incised petroglyphs. In the 1850s the area served as a hideout for the bandit Tiburcio Vásquez, who is said to have left a treasure hereabouts.

The **William S. Hart County Park and Museum** (24151 San Fernando Road, 805–254–4584) was the estate of Hollywood's first star of cowboy movies, William S. Hart. About half of the estate, including his Spanish-style ranch house, has been preserved for public use at Hart's request, and the home is much as he left it, including his remarkable collections of Navajo rugs and antique firearms, as well as works by his friend Charles M. Russell, the Western artist. The less elaborate ranch house has also been preserved.

California's first gold strike was made in 1842 in **Placerita Canyon Park** (19152 West Placerita Canyon Road, 805–259–7721), now a 350-acre preserve of oak woodlands and chaparral. Francisco López was digging wild onions when he turned up some gold on his knife. A small local rush ensued, but nothing like what was to happen farther north seven years later. A state marker commemorates the spot, known as "The Oak of the Golden Dream," since the strike was made near an oak tree.

EDWARDS AIR FORCE BASE

Located in the semi-arid Antelope Valley, Edwards Air Force Base is the largest aerospace research and flight-test facility in the country and is the location of the Air Force Flight Test Center, the NASA Ames Dryden Flight Research Facility, and the Air Force Astronautics Laboratory. The tradition of high-speed aircraft research at Edwards goes back to the dawn of the jet age; it was here that then-Captain Charles Yeager first broke the sound barrier. The base is the landing site for the space shuttle.

LOCATION: Off Route 14 or Route 58, 100 miles north of Los Angeles. HOURS: *Air Force Flight Test Center:* Group tours by appointment. *NASA:* Tours at 10 and 1 Monday–Friday. FEE: None. TELEPHONE: *USAF:* 805–277–3517; *NASA:* 805–258–3446.

A marker four-and-a-half miles east of Pearblossom on Route 138 commemorates the **Llano del Rio Colony,** one of California's most important experiments in socialist, communal living. The colony was founded in 1914 by Job Harriman, the defense lawyer for the McNamaras, leftists who dynamited the *Los Angeles Times* building. At its height the colony had more than 1,000 residents, but it disbanded in 1918, with some members moving to Louisiana.

EASTERN   ENVIRONS

The residential and farming region east and south of Los Angeles is an assemblage of inland valleys, forming a rough triangle hemmed in by mountains. The Spanish found the area too desolate for a mission. The first explorers passed through in 1772, but it was not until Father Dumetz appeared in 1810 that the area became known by a Spanish place name: San Bernardino.

SAN BERNARDINO

The town was founded in March 1851 by remnants of the Mormon Battalion, an army unit that had been recruited in Iowa to fight in the Mexican War, arrived in California in early 1847, and disbanded without seeing action. San Bernardino's neat grid of streets and dedication to productive agriculture provided a model for the valley for the next century. Friction between Mormons and non-Mormons in San Bernardino caused the Mormons to depart for Salt Lake City in 1857, leaving the fledgling town to serve as a considerably more raucous supply center for the mines of the Mojave. The city retains few monuments to its first settlers; at Arrowhead Avenue and Court Street is a **marker** for the the Mormon Stockade, raised in 1851.

Near the city are several Indian reservations and one gigantic phenomenon of unusual interest, the **Arrowhead** (three miles north of the intersection of Fortieth Street and Route 18), a huge and perfectly shaped arrowhead incised on the side of a mountain. It covers more than seven acres and seems to point straight to a hot spring.

RIVERSIDE

Founded in 1870, the city of Riverside quickly became an important citrus center. At the corner of Magnolia and Arlington avenues is the

Parent Washington Navel Orange Tree, the foundation of the entire California navel orange industry. It is one of two trees propagated from slips from Bahía, Brazil, obtained in 1873 by the U.S. Department of Agriculture. The **Riverside Municipal Museum** (3720 Orange Street, 714–782–5273), housed in the 1912 post office, contains exhibits and artifacts of local history from the Indian period, Spanish exploration, and the twentieth century. The museum also operates **Heritage House** (8193 Magnolia Avenue, 714–689–1333), an 1891 Queen Anne house that has been restored to reflect the taste of the 1890s. The **Jensen-Alvarado Ranch** (4307 Briggs Street, Rubidoux, 714–369–4302) is being restored as a living history farm, with brick ranch buildings dating to the 1870s and orchards and vineyards. The **March Field Museum** at March Air Force Base (Route 215, 714–655–3725), the oldest military air base in the West, dates from 1918. The museum contains a collection of thirty-nine vintage aircraft, as well as memorabilia, photos, and uniforms.

REDLANDS

This city, once prosperously agricultural, was named for the color of its soil. It has preserved a number of Victorian homes, including the onion-domed **Morey Mansion** (190 Terracina Boulevard, 714–793–7970), built in 1890 and now an inn. The 1897 **Kimberly Crest House** (1325 Prospect Drive, 714–792–2111) is a chateauesque mansion with Italian gardens and citrus groves. Decorated in a French Revival style, the home is furnished with a collection of antique pieces, some as old as the Renaissance, others including Tiffany lamps. Another Victorian house contains the **Historical Glass Museum** (1157 North Orange Street, 714–797–1528), whose exhibits trace the history of American glassware.

The **San Bernardino County Museum** (2024 Orange Tree Lane, 714–792–1334) is known for its outstanding mammal and bird collections, as well as dioramas and artifacts spanning the area's history. The **Lincoln Memorial Shrine** (125 West Vine Street, 714–798–7632) was not created until 1932, but it contains one of the most important collections of Lincoln memorabilia in the West, largely composed of books, pamphlets, and other paper items, with some fine portraits and busts of Lincoln. The **San Bernardino Asistencia** (26930 Barton Road, 714–793–5402) was an outpost of Mission San Gabriel, established in 1819 as a center for the local Indian converts. It has been restored, with dioramas, artifacts, and exhibits on the life of converts and priests during the 1830s and 1840s. A portion of the *zanja,* or irrigation ditch system, the first irrigation project in the valley, can also be seen.

The town of **Yucaipa,** whose name comes from the Shoshonean word for "marshy place," contains the **Sepulveda Adobe** (32183 Kentucky Street, 714–795–3485), dating from 1842, said to be the oldest surviving residential structure in the county. It has been restored with antiques and reproductions of the period.

Toward the southern end of the inland valley system is the town of **Perris,** with its **Orange Empire Railway Museum** (2201 South A Street, 714–657–2605). The museum has a collection of 150 pieces of railway equipment, mainly from southern California and offers rides on some of the old cars. Indian petroglyph sites are to be seen near the town of **Hemet,** east of Perris. Among them is **Maze Stone County Park** (California Avenue, 714–787–2551), which is named for a mysterious labyrinthine pattern to be found on one of its stones.

O R A N G E   C O U N T Y

South of the city, Orange County was split off from Los Angeles County in 1889. Its first center of European settlement had been in the south at San Juan Capistrano, the mission established by Father Serra in 1776. After secularization of the missions, the coastal plain on which the county is located was broken into several large land grants. Two of these, totaling 93,000 acres, were combined during the 1870s by James Irvine. Large parts of his ranch were still intact until the middle of the twentieth century, but elsewhere in the county, particularly in the north, orange growing boomed, followed by urban development. The first Valencia orange groves were planted near present-day Fullerton in the early 1870s.

ANAHEIM

Anaheim, founded in 1857 by German settlers as an experimental agricultural colony, was named for the nearby river, the Santa Ana, and the German word for home, *heim.* The **Mother Colony House** (414 Northwest Street, 714–999–1850), an unadorned redwood frame house, was the first in the colony, built for its founder, George Hansen. The house is now a museum devoted to the history of

Anaheim. The Polish actress Helena Modjeska and the novelist Henryk Sienkiewicz founded a short-lived Polish communal experiment also located at Anaheim. After it failed, Modjeska took up her acting career again, and built a house in the coast-range canyon now named for her, naming the retreat Arden after the forest in Shakespeare's *As You Like It,* but it is today known simply as the **Modjeska Home** (Modjeska Canyon Road, private). Designed by Stanford White, the 1888 frame house is undergoing restoration.

COSTA MESA

This town, whose name was chosen by the real estate promoters who founded it in 1915, is the location of **Diego Sepulveda Adobe**, probably built early in the nineteenth century as a shelter for Indians herding cattle for the Mission San Juan Capistrano. Later it became the home of Diego Sepulveda, who won this part of the mission's land in the great land-grant boom after secularization. The one-story adobe is restored and furnished with artifacts suggesting how it looked during different periods of its nineteenth-century occupancy.

MISSION SAN JUAN CAPISTRANO

This was the seventh of the Franciscan missions founded in upper California. Its first church was dedicated by Father Junípero Serra in 1776. The great church whose ruins now stand on the site was completed after almost a decade's work in 1806, and was the most ambitious structure the padres attempted in California. The stone church had interior vaulting surmounted by four domes. Scarcely six years after it was finished, the domes crashed down in an earthquake, killing forty Indian neophytes. The church was not rebuilt and the ruins are now surrounded by gardens. A new church, modeled precisely on the ruined stone church, has been constructed on the grounds. Period rooms and exhibits are also on display. Also on the grounds is the **Serra Chapel,** an unpretentious adobe structure thought to have been constructed in 1778. If that date is correct, it is the oldest Spanish church surviving in California. It has been restored and fitted with a Baroque Spanish reredos.

LOCATION: Ortega Highway and Camino Capistrano, San Juan Capistrano. HOURS: 7:30–5 Daily. FEE: Yes. TELEPHONE: 714–493–1424.

*Arcades like this one at San Juan Capistrano shaded the mission's priests and other work-
ers from the insistent California sun.*

S A N   D I E G O

San Diego Bay, protected from the Pacific by the narrow Silver
Strand, was visited by Juan Rodríguez Cabrillo in 1542 and by
Sebastián Vizcaíno in 1602, who named it after San Diego de Alcalá,
a Franciscan saint. The settlement was founded in 1769 by the
Sacred Expedition, led by Gaspar de Portolá and Father Junípero
Serra, who had come from Baja California to bring upper California
under Spanish control and to establish a system of missions. Father
Serra founded Mission San Diego de Alcalá, the first of the Spanish
missions in upper California.

As a mission San Diego has pride of primacy, but it was never
very successful. For example, in 1800 scarcely more than 150 Indian
converts lived there, while other missions counted their converts in
the thousands. Nor did the presidio that Portolá founded
concurrently with the mission show great promise of expansion;
early on, it was outstripped by Monterey, which became capital of
upper California, and the nearby San Carlos de Borromeo Mission,
where Father Serra resided.

Not until the Santa Fe Railroad broke San Diego's isolation in 1885, joining the then-small city to the rest of the continent, did the population begin to increase. During the ensuing boom, the famous Hotel del Coronado was built in 1888 on the narrow-necked Coronado peninsula. The author Henry James, who stayed at the hotel in 1905, said he would stay awake intentionally to listen to the ocean. James was favorably impressed with southern California: "The days have been mostly here of heavenly beauty, and the flowers, the wild flowers just now in particular, which fairly rage, with radiance, over the land, are worthy of some purer planet than this."

World War I was the real turning point for San Diego. The city and its surrounding area were chosen as the location for important military bases, and the great Panama–California International Exposition of 1915–16 celebrated the city's new muscle and important position due to the newly opened Panama Canal. Balboa Park, created for that exposition, is still an important cultural center of the city. The Second World War made San Diego even more important as a military base for operations in the Pacific theater. The postwar era brought the aerospace and electronics industries to the area. Between the beginning of World War II and 1960, San Diego's population nearly quadrupled.

On Point Loma, a finger of land jutting out from San Diego, is the **Cabrillo National Monument,** commemorating the first European landing on the west coast of the United States. Juan Rodríguez Cabrillo's flotilla of three Spanish vessels entered what is now San Diego Bay on September 28, 1542, more than two centuries before the Spaniards colonized the area. Near the spot is the restored **Old Point Loma Lighthouse** (Point Loma, 619–557–5450), built in 1855. Rising more than 400 feet above sea level, the light worked nonstop for almost forty years. Today it is open for tours, and the view from the top is excellent.

On San Diego Bay near Lindbergh Field is **Spanish Landing Park** (Harbor Drive), containing a monument marking the place where the sea and land contingents of the Sacred Expedition met in 1769. The *San Antonio* and the *San Carlos* put into port on May 4 and 5. A week later, the footsore overland party appeared.

MARITIME MUSEUM

This museum is in reality three vintage ships, each refitted and restored to near-original condition. The most spectacular is the *Star of India,* an iron three-masted bark built as a full-rigged ship on the

Isle of Man in 1863, which carried cargo and migrating humanity more than twenty times around the world and is today the oldest merchantman still afloat. An elegant steam yacht, the *Medea,* built in 1904, and the *Berkeley,* a San Francisco–Oakland ferryboat of 1898, are also part of the museum.

LOCATION: 1306 North Harbor Drive. HOURS: 9–8 Daily. FEE: Yes. TELEPHONE: 619–234–9153.

OLD TOWN

San Diego city life centered in this area from 1821 until the coming of the Santa Fe Railroad in the 1880s. Bounded by Wallace, Congress, Twiggs, and Juan streets, this plaza is now a state historic park, where many structures of the middle nineteenth century are preserved. It contains both adobe and frame structures, some of the latter shipped around the Horn and set up on the plaza. The 1867 **Seeley Stable** (Calhoun Street) now houses a fine museum of horse-drawn vehicles, branding irons, saddles, and other equestrian items. **La Casa de Bandini** (Calhoun and Mason streets), now a restaurant, dates from 1829. Juan Bandini, who had arrived as a skipper, stayed to marry the daughter of a prominent citizen; his home was the social focal point of the old town. The second story was added later when the premises were converted into a hotel. (It also served some time as a pickle factory.) **La Casa de Estudillo** (Mason Street) was built in 1827 by José María de Estudillo, captain of the San Diego presidio. It has been refurnished in the late-Spanish-period style and is open to visitors.

LOCATION: Off Routes 5 and 8. HOURS: 10–5 Daily. FEE: For Seeley Stable. TELEPHONE: 619–237–6770.

JUNIPERO SERRA MUSEUM

The mission-style museum building (built in 1929) stands in Presidio Park. It was built near the site of California's first Spanish mission and presidio, established by Father Junípero Serra and Gaspar de Portolá in 1769. Five years later, the mission was moved inland, to where fresh water was more available, and to keep the Indians

OPPOSITE: *San Diego's Old Point Loma Lighthouse, one of eight Pacific coast lighthouses built in the 1850s after the gold rush had dramatically increased the number of settlers arriving by ship at California ports.*

San Diego boomed after the Santa Fe Railroad reached it in 1885. This ca. 1887

separate from the sometimes turbulent soldiery. The museum contains fine exhibits relating to early European explorations of the California region and to life in the presidio. There is also an outstanding collection of Spanish Renaissance furniture.

LOCATION: 2727 Presidio Drive. HOURS: 10–4:30 Tuesday–Saturday, 12–4:30 Sunday. FEE: Yes. TELEPHONE: 619–297–3258.

The **Gaslamp Quarter,** San Diego's downtown-renewal project, is a sixteen-block area that contains a number of fine nineteenth-century houses, some restored. The district runs between Fourth and Sixth avenues and from Broadway to Harbor Drive. Among the more interesting houses is the 1850 **William Heath Davis House and Museum** (410 Island Avenue, 619–233–5227), headquarters of the

photograph shows the sale of some 2,500 lots at Ocean Beach.

council devoted to restoring the area. Tours of the quarter leave from this house.

The **Villa Montezuma Museum** (1925 K Street, 619–239–2211), an outstanding Queen Anne–style house, was built in 1887 for Jesse Shepard, a noted musician, author, and mystic who lived in San Diego for two years. The home, decorated to his exacting specifications, is particularly rich in wood detailing and art-glass windows.

MISSION BASILICA SAN DIEGO DE ALCALA

The original mission—the first Franciscan mission in upper California—was a thatch-roofed hut on Presidio Hill. After the Spaniards had spent five years trying to convert them to the Spanish faith and way of life, the Indians remained hostile to Father Serra

and burned the first church on the new site. In this attack the
Indians killed Father Luis Jaime, California's first martyr. The next
church was destroyed by an earthquake in 1803. The present simple
white church with its lovely *espadana* is a reconstruction of the
building completed in 1813. Secularization of this mission in 1834
led to the abandonment of the church. During the Mexican–
American War, the U.S. Army occupied the mission grounds and
used the church as a barracks. In 1862 the government returned the
mission to the Catholic church. Original portions of the church's
buttresses and walls were incorporated in the 1931 reconstruction.
The **Father Luis Jaime Museum** on the grounds features a collection
of Native American arts, mission documents, relics, and ecclesiastical
artwork. Nearby are the remains of a **dam and flume,** built in 1813,
among the first irrigation systems in upper California.

> LOCATION: 10818 San Diego Mission Road. HOURS: 9–5 Daily. FEE:
> Yes. TELEPHONE: 619–281–8449.

BALBOA PARK

Center for the city's museums and location of the famous **San Diego
Zoo** (2920 Zoo Drive, 619–234–3153), the park covers 1,400 acres in
the heart of San Diego. It was set aside as a cultural center in 1868,
though most of the Spanish Revival buildings, including some of
those housing the museums, were constructed for the 1915-16
Panama–California International Exposition. Much of the design
and the plantings in the vast park were also created at that time by
Kate Sessions, a noted landscape architect who had her nursery on
the grounds. The zoo itself owes its existence to the exposition, since
it was begun with animals that had been imported for the event.
Other buildings in the park were constructed for the 1935-36
California Pacific International Exposition.

   The **Museum of Man** (1350 El Prado, 619–239–2001), housed
in the handsome Mexican-Baroque California Building designed by
Bertram Grosvenor Goodhue for the 1915-16 exposition, contains
fine exhibits of artifacts concerning the history of man in the New
World, especially of Meso-American, Southwestern, and California
cultures. The **San Diego Museum of Art** (1450 El Prado,

OPPOSITE: *The restored padres' bedroom at San Diego de Alcalá shows the primitive
conditions of the missionaries' lives. The bed is a loose web of leather strips.*

The richly ornamented facade of the San Diego Museum of Art includes statues of three important Spanish painters—Velázquez, Murillo, and Zurbarán. OPPOSITE: *Balboa Park's baroque Casa del Prado is used as a meeting place for a number of local groups.*

619–232–7931) is located in a Spanish Revival building that postdates the exposition, modeled after the University of Salamanca in Spain. Inside is a fine general collection of art, with particular emphasis on European Renaissance and Baroque, Asian, and American art. The **Timken Art Gallery** (1500 El Prado, 619–239–5548), adjacent to the San Diego museum, opened in 1965. It displays European Old Masters, American eighteenth- and nineteenth-century works, and a good collection of Russian icons.

Also in the park are the **San Diego Natural History Museum** (1788 El Prado, 619–232–3821); the **Reuben H. Fleet Space Theater and Science Center** (1875 El Prado, 619–238–1233), featuring films on large screens that surround the audience, as well as over sixty hands-on exhibits; and the **San Diego Aero-Space Museum** (2001 Pan American Plaza, 619–234–8291), with original and reproduction planes and spacecraft.

SAN DIEGO COUNTY

San Diego County, which stretches far to the north and east of the city proper, has a varied character. The Hispanic remains are richest near the coast; inland, in the semi-arid and desert lands, mining settlements and transportation routes are all that mark the past. The following entries extend from north to south in a halo around the city of San Diego.

MISSION SAN LUIS REY DE FRANCIA

San Luis Rey, dedicated in 1798, was the eighteenth of the missions to be established. The large and architecturally refined church and cloister are among the finest in the chain, and the mission was the richest of all in both goods and Indian converts. When counts were made just prior to secularization, San Luis Rey was found to have almost 3,000 neophytes and almost 60,000 head of livestock.

The present cruciform church was built between 1812 and 1815, though it was much restored some time later. A Hispano-Moorish structure with arcades and a dramatic bell tower, the church was so elaborate as to be referred to as a "palace" by some visitors. The interior has restored decorations, some probably originally executed by Indian neophytes. The oldest peppertree in California is still growing on the grounds.

LOCATION: 4070 Mission Avenue, San Luis Rey. HOURS: 10–4 Monday–Friday. FEE: Yes. TELEPHONE: 619–757–3651, ext. 346.

Camp Joseph H. Pendleton (Route 5, north of Oceanside, 619–725–5566), a Marine base established in 1942 on the site of the old Rancho Santa Margarita y Las Flores, preserves several adobe structures. The much remodeled but gracious 1841 **Ranch House,** which now houses the commanding general of the base, is open to visitors. The **Chapel and Bunkhouse Museum** consists of two adobe buildings, the first from 1810 and the second from 1864, now restored with period rooms that show the religious and secular life of the ranch.

Mission San Antonio de Pala (Pala Mission Road, Pala, 619–742–3317) is a very simple church built in 1816 as an outpost of Mission San Luis Rey de Francia. Located on the Pala Indian

The facade of the church at Mission San Luis Rey, named for Saint Louis IX, king of France, includes a niche holding a statue of Saint Francis of Assisi, founder of the Franciscan Order.

Reservation, it has the distinction of being the only mission structure still used primarily by a Native American congregation. The interior decorative painting is particularly fine.

SAN PASQUAL BATTLEFIELD STATE HISTORIC PARK

At this spot on December 6, 1846, was fought one of the few battles of the war for California that actually resulted in significant bloodshed. General Stephen Kearny was marching from Santa Fe at the head of 100 men, including the scout Kit Carson, with orders to assume command of California as military governor. A Californio cavalry group under Andrés Pico intercepted Kearny's column, which was tired after its long overland march. Twenty-two Americans were killed and another sixteen wounded by the lance-wielding Californio cavalry. Kearny retreated, and Carson slipped away to San Diego to summon reinforcements, who arrived on December 11.

The next month Kearny took part in the successful attack on Los Angeles. The fifty-acre park has a visitor center where a short film about the battle is shown.

LOCATION: Off Route 78, 8 miles east of Escondido. HOURS: 10–5 Thursday–Monday. FEE: Yes. TELEPHONE: 619–238–3380.

JULIAN

Northeast of San Diego, amid scattered Indian reservations and ranges of hills, is Julian, the center of an 1870s gold rush to the foothills of the Laguna Mountains. The area is now known more for apples than for nuggets, but the **Julian Pioneer Museum** (2811 Washington Street, 619–765–0227) contains artifacts and photographs of mining days, and the **Eagle Mining Company** (C Street, 619–765–0036) offers a tour of two old mines, with a demonstration of hard-rock mining equipment. The little town itself still has the feel of a turn-of-the-century place; among the prettiest of the old structures is the **Julian Hotel** (Main and B streets), still operating, which is said to have been built by a former slave in 1887.

El Cajon and **La Mesa** are two small communities just outside of San Diego. In El Cajon the **Knox Hotel Museum** (290 North Magnolia Avenue, 619–444–3800), built in 1876 as a way station for drivers hauling gold from Julian to San Diego, has been restored as a museum of turn-of-the-century life. The **San Diego Railway Museum** (4695 Nebo Drive, La Mesa, 619–697–7762) is a reconstructed Victorian depot with a collection of rolling stock from the 1920s.

THE   SOUTHERN   DESERT

The Colorado Desert of California is like a hand seen in profile, cut off at the wrist and with a finger pointing northwest. At its base—near the "wrist" and the Mexican border—is the Imperial Valley, so named by turn-of-the-century promoters who brought the first Colorado River water here and attracted the first homesteaders. Today, the valley is an important center for irrigated agriculture. The northwesterly finger of the desert is the Coachella Valley, a fruit-growing center. Its proximity to Los Angeles via San Gorgonio Pass has made it into an important resort area, centered on Palm Springs. Beyond the two valleys, the Colorado Desert is pure desert, with cacti, creosote, greasewood, and other Sonoran flora. Summer temperatures average 100° F, and an average of only three inches of rain fall each year. The Colorado River, which flows along the desert's eastern boundary, was diverted in 1901 by engineer George Chaffee through a system of canals to irrigate the Imperial Valley. In March 1905 the river flooded into a new canal Chaffee was building, and it rushed into the Imperial Valley, creating a vast lake and forcing the Southern Pacific Railroad to move its tracks out of the way. The lake, called the Salton Sea, was more than eighty feet deep and forty-five miles long; since then, it has shrunk somewhat, but because valley farmers use it as an irrigation outflow it may eventually recover its original size. Originally fresh water, it is now quite salty, becoming more so all the time. The Imperial and Coachella valleys are today major producers of lettuce, tomatoes, beets, cotton, grapefruits, melons, and dates.

PALM SPRINGS

Palm Springs—the "palm" refers to the native Washington palm and the "springs" to the mineral springs known since Indian times—is one of the Southwest's greatest resort areas. Hollywood people were relaxing here as early as the 1920s, having discovered the springs in the shadow of the San Jacinto Mountains while on location, though the town had been founded as a Southern Pacific stop in the 1870s. Palm Springs has gathered its historic remnants at the **Village Green Heritage Center** (221 South Palm Canyon Drive, 619–323–8297). The restored **Cornelia White House,** on the same property, was built in 1893 from railroad ties and served as a guest house for the town's first hotel. Also on the site is the **McCallum Adobe,** an 1884 structure that reflects life before Palm Springs became a resort. The **Palm Springs Desert Museum** (101 Museum Drive, 619–325–7186) has fine collections of Western art and Indian artifacts as well as excellent displays on local natural history and the Cahuilla Indians.

The town of **Desert Hot Springs,** sometimes described as the "poor man's Palm Springs," started out as a hot-springs resort. **Cabot's Old Indian Pueblo Museum** (67616 East Desert View, 619–329–7610) is a

sprawling, four-story, thirty-five-room cement imitation of a pueblo dwelling. Cabot Yerxa built it between 1939 and 1965 (he planned to have 200 more rooms), filling it with Indian artifacts.

The town of **Blythe** is named for Thomas Blythe, an irrigation promoter who founded it in the 1870s and made it the head of the agriculturally prosperous little Palo Verde valley (physiographically a part of the Mojave). About fifteen miles north, off Route 95, is one of the most mysterious monuments in California, the **Indian Lore Monument,** giant intaglios created 5,000 to 7,000 years ago by an unknown people. Carved into the rock are both men and animals, the largest man measuring 167 feet tall and 164 feet from outstretched hand to outstretched hand. The huge figures were discovered in an aerial survey in 1932. Although their purpose is not known, some suspect they were associated with a creation myth.

ANZA–BORREGO DESERT STATE PARK

The park bears a mellifluous double name referring to Spanish explorer Juan Bautista de Anza, who passed through in 1774, and to the bighorn sheep, *borrego,* frequently depicted by aboriginal rock artists in the region. The park is immense, its gorgeous terrain ranging from sea level to around 6,000 feet in elevation. Its passes and canyons were important routes for entering California from the Southwest. The six-foot-high **Peg Leg Smith Monument** (Route S-2, five miles east of Borrego Springs) relates the history of the Borrego Valley's most notable transient, Thomas Long Smith, who after a long career as a trapper came here as a prospector during the 1860s. He turned up in San Diego, ill and babbling about a great Borrego gold mine. The fact that he had more than $1,500 worth of gold dust on his person gave some weight to his story. Unfortunately, he died before he could return to it, and people have been seeking the mine ever since.

LOCATION: Route 8 or Route S-2, 90 miles east of San Diego. HOURS: *Park:* Always open; *Visitor Center:* June through September: 10–3 Saturday–Sunday; October through May: 9–5 Daily. FEE: None. TELEPHONE: 619–767–5311.

OPPOSITE: *Palm Canyon in Palm Springs, where 3,000 native Washington palm trees, which gave the town its name, line the bed of a stream.*

The **Vallecitos Stage Depot** (Route S-2, thirty-one miles north of Ocotillo, 619–694–3049) is an authentic reconstruction of an 1852 stage stop that stood on the spot. It served mail lines, the Butterfield Overland Stage Line, and countless immigrant parties. A nearby state marker commemorates the **Butterfield Overland Stage Route,** near which the rutted tracks of stagecoaches can still be seen. A marker for **Box Canyon** (Vallecitos–Sweeney Pass Road, eight miles south of Route 78) shows the route opened in 1847 by the Mormon Battalion, a group of some five hundred Mormons that had been recruited into the army to fight in the Mexican War. They pried it open, hacking at the rock of the canyon until they had forged a pass for their wagons.

THE MOJAVE DESERT AND DEATH VALLEY

The Mojave and Death Valley—the latter is not really a part of the Mojave but of the Great Basin Desert—provide a hot and concentrated dose of some of the most interesting geology on this planet. Color here comes mainly from the earth: from the dried lakes and the strata of worn mountain ranges with such names as Old Woman, Big Maria, Turtle, Panamint, and Amargosa. Vegetation consists of creosote, saltbush, the Joshua tree, and sagebrush. The animal population is largely nocturnal, though there is considerable diversity of species, particularly among the reptiles and insects. When it is hot, it is very hot, especially in Death Valley, where the average July temperature is 102° F. The Mojave is comparatively gentle, but still forbidding enough that automobile travelers prefer not to cross it in the heat of a summer's day.

Human habitation has always been sparse in this region, except along the Colorado River at California's eastern edge. Hunter-gatherers of Uto-Aztecan stock—the Chemehuevi, the Serrano, and the Koso—eked out a living eating pine nuts, lizards, and whatever else they could extract from the desert. The Mojave, from whom the desert gets its name, were a Hokan people who really lived only on the eastern border of the desert. Unusual among California Indians, they grew crops in the manner of their neighbors from the interior

OPPOSITE: *Ridged sand dunes in Death Valley, named in 1849 by a party of gold hunters who, while searching for a shortcut, were stranded in the extreme heat for several weeks.*

Southwest. Both the Mojave and Death Valley have been explored and settled primarily for their mineral wealth: first gold and silver, then (and more profitably) borax, tungsten, and cement. More recently, the military has cordoned off large areas for air force bases and gunnery ranges.

The entries in this section begin at Needles on the Arizona border, then proceed west to Calico and Victorville, northwest to the town of Mojave, and finally northeast to Death Valley.

NEEDLES

This crossroads town on the Arizona border was founded as a Santa Fe Railroad stop in 1883. It was first located across the Colorado River on the Arizona side and named for the nearby needlelike

When fully loaded, Death Valley borax wagons weighed more than thirty tons and attached to the rear—were hauled by eighteen teams of mules and one team of horses;

mountains there; a few months later the town moved to the California side, and the name came with it. A state monument in town emphasizes the importance of the place as a junction. The **National Old Trails Monument** (Broadway between A Street and Palm Way) commemorates a Mojave Indian trail that paralleled the Colorado River. This was the route used by the explorer Father Francisco Garcés in 1776, the trapper Jedediah Smith in 1826, and other early travelers.

CALICO EARLY MAN SITE

Down the road from the 1880s ghost town of Calico is the site of a ghostly culture perhaps 200 millennia older. Dr. Louis B. Leakey began digging here in the early 1960s, and his researchers claim

required the legendary twenty-mule teams to pull them. The wagons—with water tanks the latter were hitched up next to the wagon to aid in turning.

that some of the more than 12,000 stone tools found on the site are at least 200,000 years old. Since orthodox theory dates man in this region no earlier than 12,000 years ago, there is considerable controversy over the claims. Nevertheless, other finds (such as some at China Lake) may support the older date, so it is possible that these Mojave remains suggest reassessment of the antiquity of human presence in the New World. Tours of the excavations are available.

> LOCATION: Minneola Road, off Route 15. HOURS: Wednesday –Sunday, call for tour times. FEE: None. TELEPHONE: 619–256–3591.

CALICO GHOST TOWN

The town sprang from the earth of the Calico Mountains—so called because of their variegated color patterns—in 1881, following California's richest silver strike. Upwards of 3,000 people lived here at one time, digging the miles of hard-rock tunnels that eventually yielded $13 million in silver. In the aftermath of the McKinley-Bryan presidential race of 1896—when Bryan, the champion of a silver standard, lost to "Gold Bug" McKinley —silver's price plunged, and so did Calico's fortunes.

  The owners of Knott's Berry Farm bought Calico's ghost in 1950 and began an extensive restoration project that has resulted in a tourist-oriented but well-reconstructed mining town. Stores, saloons, houses, including one made of bottles, and part of the old mine shaft have been refurbished and opened for visitors.

> LOCATION: Off Calico Ghost Town Road, Yerma. HOURS: 9–5 Daily. FEE: Yes. TELEPHONE: 619–254–2122.

BARSTOW

This junction town was important as a trail crossing, then as a supply center for the Calico Mountain mines, then as a railway stop. The **Harvey House** (First Street, private) at the railroad depot is a reminder of the string of such depot hotels, all run by Fred Harvey, that once stretched the length of the Santa Fe line. The present Spanish Revival structure, dating from around 1910, replaced the

1885 original, which burned down. It is among the finest surviving examples of a depot hotel.

Victorville, which began as a railroad town, more recently has served nearby George Air Force Base. The **Roy Rogers and Dale Evans Museum** (15650 Seneca Road, Victorville, 619–243–4547) exhibits an odd and interesting assortment of collections: guns, dolls, Western transportation models, and movie memorabilia. Rogers had both his horse, Trigger, and his dog, Bullet, mounted so that they could appear in the museum.

MOJAVE

Although the town takes its name from the Indian tribe, it is about as far from the ancestral home of the Mojave as one can get while still remaining in the Mojave Desert. While not a particularly attractive place, it does have the distinction of being where, in 1883, J. W. S. Perry built the first of the famous twenty-mule-team wagons that hauled borax out of Death Valley to railroad facilities in town. Northeast of Mojave, beyond the junction for Randsburg, is **Red Rock Canyon,** a beautiful formation of buff-, pink-, and red-toned cliffs, once a popular place to shoot Hollywood westerns.

RANDSBURG

This town, and nearby Johannesburg, were created overnight in 1893, when gold was discovered nearby. Both seem to have been named for already rich African mining districts, in hope that history would repeat itself here in the Mojave. The Yellow Aster mine, richest of the gold mines here, eventually yielded $20 million in gold, though the hard-rock mine was later more important for its tungsten than its gold. Randsburg was once important enough to have its own spur of the Santa Fe Railroad. Today, it is a sleepy town, though not a true ghost. Its original buildings were consumed in a series of turn-of-the-century fires, but the **Randsburg Desert Museum** (Butte Avenue, 619–374–2111) preserves photographs and mining artifacts that give a good idea of what the place was like during its boom.

OVERLEAF: *The eroded rock of Golden Canyon near Death Valley's Zabriskie Point.*

MATURANGO MUSEUM

This small museum is in the town of Ridgecrest, adjacent to the China Lake Naval Weapons Center, a huge tract of land west of Death Valley. Periodic tours take visitors onto the naval weapons center, where astonishing numbers of Indian petroglyphs can be seen. The designs, some of them 10,000 years old, appear in jumbled masses on rock outcrops. They feature bighorn sheep and other desert animals, human figures, and mysterious geometric designs.

LOCATION: 100 East Las Flores Street, Ridgecrest. HOURS: 10–5 Tuesday–Sunday. FEE: Yes. TELEPHONE: 619–375–6900.

DEATH VALLEY NATIONAL MONUMENT .

This strangely beautiful and absolutely forbidding 120-mile-long valley was named when parties of prospectors and immigrants bound for California in 1849 tried to use it as a shortcut and emerged only after tremendous hardship. The **Furnace Creek Visitor Center** offers exhibits on the history and the geology of the valley, as well as brochures to guide the traveler. Nearby is **Badwater,** at 282 feet below sea level the lowest place in the United States. The sand dunes of **Stovepipe Wells** were so named because a freshwater spring located here was marked with a stovepipe to keep it from being buried in the dunes. The state historic marker for **Burned Wagons Point** commemorates the spot where the stranded forty-niners burnt their wagons and struggled forward on foot.

The **Harmony Borax Works,** constructed in 1882, has been restored for visitors, complete with one of the famous twenty-mule-team wagons that once carried borax more than 150 miles west to the rail junction at the town of Mojave.

Incongruous in this setting, the opulent Mediterranean-style **Scotty's Castle** was for many years said to be the palace of Walter Perry Scott, a prospector who lived in this cement, tile, stucco, and redwood dwelling. Originally from Kentucky, Scott began his Death Valley career as a teenager, attending to the needs of Nevada-California boundary surveyors in the mid-1880s. He apparently hired on at the Harmony Borax Works and later signed on with Buffalo Bill's Wild West exposition, around 1890. Scott was a better publicity hound than a prospector, receiving financial backing from entrepreneurs such as Chicagoan Albert M. Johnson, who hoped to share a part in Scott's "secret" gold mine. Although it became clear that Scott had no mine, Johnson visited the desert to escape the exigencies of his business life and, in 1922, began to build a permanent desert hideaway. His castle, where Scott lived until his death in 1954, has been restored and is open for tours.

LOCATION: Route 190, 110 miles northeast of Ridgecrest. HOURS: *Park:* Always open. *Visitor Center:* Mid-April through mid-October: 8–5 Daily; mid-October through mid-April: 8–8 Daily. FEE: Yes. TELEPHONE: 619–786–2331.

The twenty-five room Mediterranean-style Scotty's Castle at the northern end of Death Valley.

CHAPTER TWO

THE
CALIFORNIA
INTERIOR

OPPOSITE: *"Goodbye God, I'm going to Bodie" was a common saying among Forty-niners aware of the town's legendary harsh climate and the prevalence of outlaws there.*

The California interior—the rugged northern reaches, the dramatic Sierra Nevada Range, the fertile San Joaquin Valley, and the gold rush towns of the Mother Lode—was settled after the state's coastal areas. Until 1840 most of the region was still the province of the natives who had lived there for centuries and a few intrepid mountain men, fur trappers from the East who explored the Sierra in search of the elusive beaver and pioneered a number of trails in the process. By the middle of the next decade, immigrants had begun traveling overland in wagon trains rather than making the circuitous ocean voyage around the horn of South America or across the Isthmus of Panama. The overland route was direct but rugged, leading through mountain and desert, but the promise of rich farmland and boundless opportunity were powerful lures to these early pioneers. And then there was gold.

The California gold rush started on the American River near present-day Coloma. On January 24, 1848, James Marshall was inspecting a mill he was building for John Sutter when "my eye was caught by . . . something shining in the bottom of the ditch. . . . I reached my hand down and picked it up; it made my heart thump for I felt certain it was gold. The piece was about half the size and of the shape of a pea. Then I saw another. . . ." Neither Sutter nor Marshall grew rich on the discovery. Indeed, most of the thousands who came to make their fortunes went away with little more than enough gold to pay the exorbitant expenses of working their claims. With a certain sense of pride—and irony—they would say that they had "seen the elephant," miners' slang for great expectations followed by disappointment. Nevertheless, the diggings were fabulously productive for those who made the big strikes. It is estimated that in 1849 more than $10 million in gold was taken from the mines; in 1850, more than $40 million; in 1851, more than $75 million; and in the peak year of 1852, more than $81 million. Meanwhile, the population explosion brought rapid development, as transportation and communication systems were quickly set up to serve the miners.

After the gold rush, farmers and ranchers prospered in the San Joaquin Valley, and in the late nineteenth century irrigation opened up new areas to cultivation. Yosemite, first glimpsed by a white explorer in 1851, quickly became one of the nation's first tourist attractions. And in 1869 the transcontinental railroad, first conceived in 1861, was completed; its tracks followed a pioneer trail through the pass where, twenty-three years before, thirty-four members of the Donner Party perished, trapped by an early snow.

A detail from a painting of Forty-niners around a camp fire, by an unknown artist, shows the rigorous life awaiting miners after enduring the hardships of the transcontinental voyage to California. PAGES 108–109: *High peaks in the aptly named Sierra Nevada, or "snowy range."*

This chapter begins in Sacramento, the state capital, then moves northward through the Sacramento Valley to the mountainous inland north before turning southward to follow Route 49 through the gold-rush towns of the Mother Lode. The Sierra Nevada section begins at Donner Pass, one of the main immigrant crossings, then moves south to Lake Tahoe and follows Route 395 along the eastern slopes of the mountains to the once-fertile Owens Valley. At Tehachapi, the southern extreme of the Sierra Nevada Range, the narrative moves to the San Joaquin Valley and roughly follows Route 99 northward from the oil wells around Bakersfield through fertile agricultural lands to Stockton, at the head of the San Joaquin River.

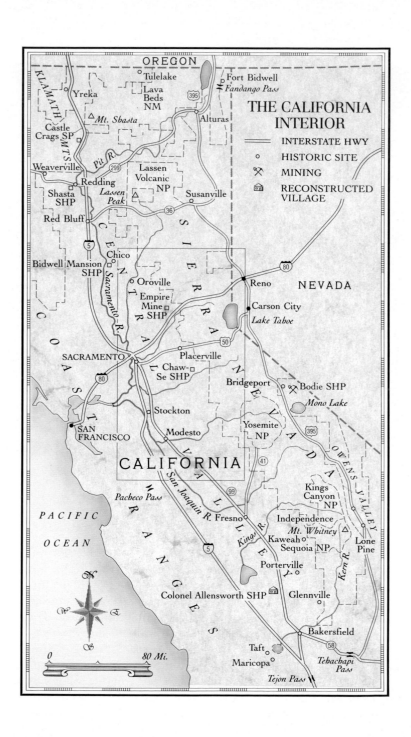

OREGON

Tulelake

Yreka

Lava
Beds
NM

Fort Bidwell
Fandango Pass

△*Mt. Shasta*

Castle
Crags SP

Alturas

THE CALIFORNIA
INTERIOR

	INTERSTATE HWY
○	HISTORIC SITE
✕	MINING
🏠	RECONSTRUCTED VILLAGE

Weaverville

Redding

Lassen
Volcanic
NP

Pit R.

Shasta
SHP

*Lassen
Peak*

Susanville

Red Bluff

Bidwell Mansion
SHP

Chico

Oroville

Empire
Mine
SHP

Reno

NEVADA

Carson City
Lake Tahoe

SACRAMENTO

Placerville

Chaw-
Se SHP

Bridgeport

Bodie SHP

Mono Lake

Stockton

SAN
FRANCISCO

Modesto

Yosemite
NP

CALIFORNIA

PACIFIC

OCEAN

Pacheco Pass

San Joaquin R.

Fresno

Kings
Canyon
NP

Independence

△*Mt. Whitney*

Kaweah
Sequoia NP

Lone
Pine

Porterville

Colonel Allensworth SHP

Glennville

Bakersfield

Taft

Maricopa

*Tehachapi
Pass*

Tejon Pass

0   80 Mi.

N
W · E
S

OWENS VALLEY

Kern R.

Kings R.

Sacramento R.

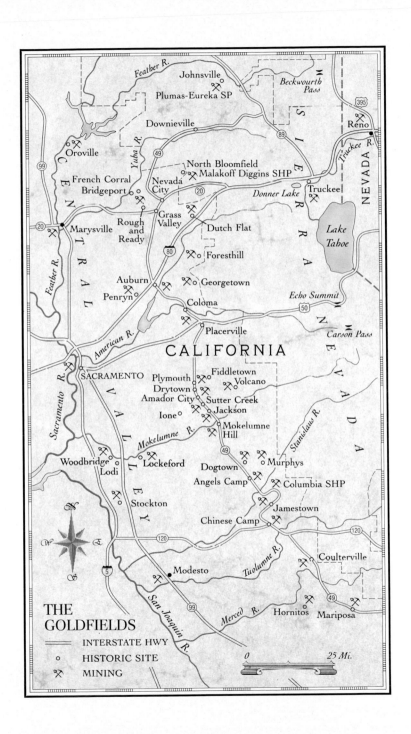

Feather R.

Johnsville

Beckwourth Pass

Plumas-Eureka SP

395

Downieville

89

Reno

S I E R R A

Oroville

99

Yuba R.

49

North Bloomfield
Malakoff Diggins SHP

French Corral
Bridgeport

Nevada
City

20

Donner Lake

Truckee

NEVADA

Truckee R.

Marysville

20

Rough
and
Ready

Grass
Valley

80

Dutch Flat

Lake
Tahoe

Foresthill

Feather R.

Auburn

Penryn

Georgetown

Echo Summit

Coloma

50

American R.

Placerville

N E V A D A

Carson Pass

CALIFORNIA

Sacramento R.

SACRAMENTO

V
A
L
L
E
Y

Fiddletown
Volcano

Plymouth
Drytown
Amador City

Sutter Creek
Jackson

Ione

Mokelumne R.

Mokelumne
Hill

Stanislaus R.

Woodbridge
Lodi

Lockeford

Dogtown

Murphys

49

Angels Camp

Columbia SHP

Stockton

Jamestown

Chinese Camp

120

120

N

W   E

S

5

Modesto

Tuolumne R.

Coulterville

San Joaquin R.

99

Merced R.

Hornitos

Mariposa

49

THE
GOLDFIELDS

——— INTERSTATE HWY

o   HISTORIC SITE

⚒   MINING

0   25 Mi.

THE SACRAMENTO VALLEY

The broad valley of the Sacramento River lies between the Coast
Range to the west and the foothills of the Sierra Nevada to the east,
encompassing the upper third of the larger Central Valley. The traveler Edwin Bryant summed up the joyful emotion he felt when his
party at last crossed the Sierra in 1847 and saw the valley: "A broad
line of timber running through the centre of the valley indicated the
course of the main river, and smaller and fainter lines on either side
of this, winding through the brown and flat plain, marked the channels of its tributaries . . . . I never saw a more beautiful stream."

When Bryant arrived, John Augustus Sutter, a Swiss settler who
had come in 1839, had already created a small empire called New
Helvetia. Partly to thwart the possible expansion of Mexican pioneer
Mariano Vallejo's holdings in the area, the Mexican governor, Juan
Alvarado, had been unusually generous with Sutter, granting him
almost 50,000 acres of valley land and foothills, which Sutter turned
into valuable grazing, farming, and timber property. The discovery
of gold on Sutter's property by his employee James Marshall sparked
a mass migration into the area. Towns leaped into existence at the
beginning of the gold rush. As one miner put it, "In one fortnight's
time $25,000 worth of lots at $250 each were sold. In ten days, seventeen houses and stores were put up, and what was before a ranch—a
collection of Indian huts and a corral for cattle—became a right
smart little city." Sutter's own men deserted him for the mines, and
squatters occupied his territory. He died still fighting to regain it.

Agriculture took a back seat during the gold-rush years, when
the river became the main thoroughfare from San Francisco to the
mines. The region's main towns—Sacramento, Marysville, and others—owed their growth to the wave of travelers and to the necessity
for supply bases.

SACRAMENTO

Sacramento stands on the site of Sutter's Fort, constructed in 1839 as
the center of John Augustus Sutter's New Helvetia land grant. With
the coming of the gold rush, a town grew haphazardly around the
fort, eventually overwhelming it. A traveler in 1850 described it:
"The first view we had of the city was where a line of ships stretches
along the river for nearly a mile, then a few houses loom up mistily

in the fog among the trees . . . . The ships are fast to the shore and seem to be used as storehouses." Everywhere, on ships and on land, there were piles of boxes and supplies. Gambling and drinking went on under tents and in hastily assembled, prefabricated buildings. Gold dust was the currency and was thrown about with abandon: "Everytime it is weighed," wrote a miner, "something is lost, and the business streets of Sacramento will, in a few years, be worth digging up and washing for gold."

Despite several disastrous floods, some semblance of a settlement began to emerge, particularly after the city was chosen to be the state capital in 1854. Sacramento lay on several stagecoach and express routes; during its brief existence from April 1860 to October 1861, the pony express had its terminus there (mail destined for San Francisco continued on by steamboat). The demise of the pony express coincided almost to the day with the completion of the transcontinental telegraph, which also had its terminus in Sacramento. In 1856 Theodore Judah constructed a railroad line, the first in the state, running from Sacramento to Folsom. His ambition was to build a transcontinental railroad. In 1861, with the financial backing of Leland Stanford, Charles Crocker, Mark Hopkins, and Collis P. Huntington, the local businessmen who came to be

A view of Sacramento City drawn on December 20, 1849, nearly two years after gold was discovered fifty miles to the east. The streets are lined with stores selling supplies to miners; one man is selling hotcakes and coffee from a tent.

known as the Big Four, Judah formed the Central Pacific Railroad Company. Eighteen months later, helped along by federal subsidies, the company began laying track eastward. Today, Sacramento is an important processing and shipping center for agriculture, but its biggest business is the state government.

Hugging the waterfront is **Old Sacramento,** a mix of genuine historic sites and modern shops, all preserving the look of the nineteenth-century city. Information is available at the **visitor center** (1104 Front Street, 916–442–7644). The brick **B. F. Hastings Building** (Second and J streets, 916–445–4209), erected in 1852, housed clothing merchants, telegraph offices, the Wells Fargo office, and, from 1855 to 1869, the California Supreme Court. The **courtroom** has been restored to its 1855 appearance, and a recorded dramatization of a contemporary case is played. A **communications museum** pays tribute to printing, the pony express, and the transcontinental telegraph, the last two of which had their terminus in the building.

California State Railroad Museum

This museum occupies four separate structures in Old Sacramento. Exhibits in the **History Building** (125 I Street) include twenty-one

A Great Northern Railway mail car, used between Chicago and Seattle from 1950 to 1970, at the California State Railroad Museum. OPPOSITE: *The museum's collection includes twenty-one restored locomotives and railroad cars.*

locomotives and cars as well as interpretive exhibits tracing the history of rail travel in California and the West. Among the displays are the Central Pacific Locomotive Number 1, the "Governor Stanford," shown emerging from a tunnel in an enormous diorama; an 1888 railroad bridge; and a collection of antique toy trains. The **Big Four Building** (111 I Street), a reconstruction of the Central Pacific Railroad headquarters, houses the library and the Huntington-Hopkins Hardware Store, a re-creation of the 1855 store owned by two members of the Big Four. The **Central Pacific Passenger Station** (Front and J streets) reproduces the original 1870s station, complete with waiting areas, baggage room, and a train shed housing nine locomotives and cars. Next door, the **Central Pacific Freight Depot** has been re-created as it appeared in 1870; it serves as a passenger station for an excursion train that runs down the river.

LOCATION: 125 I Street. HOURS: 10–5 Daily. FEE: Yes. TELE-PHONE: 916–448–4466.

A few blocks from Old Sacramento is the **California State Indian Museum** (2618 K Street, 916–324–0971), displaying craft objects, including a fine basketry collection and dance regalia from the northwest coast, and photographs donated by members of the state's native American population. Photographs show how the artifacts were used in daily and ceremonial life.

Crocker Art Gallery

The original gallery was built by Edwin B. Crocker, brother of Charles Crocker and legal counsel to the Central Pacific Railroad, to house the art collection he and his wife had acquired on a trip to Europe in 1870. A fine example of the Mannerist Italianate villa style, the building was designed by Seth Babson and completed in 1873. The museum has expanded to include the adjacent Crocker residence, an 1853 mansion also designed by Babson in the Italianate style, and a modern wing. The collection focuses on European art from the Renaissance to the present and includes important works by Dürer, Van Dyck, and Rubens; there is also a noteworthy gallery of California art.

LOCATION: 216 O Street. HOURS: 1–9 Tuesday, 10–5 Wednesday–Sunday. FEE: Yes. TELEPHONE: 916–449–5423.

The 1857 **Stanford House** (800 N Street, 916–324–0575) was designed by Seth Babson with a Georgian form and Italianate detail but has been remodeled numerous times. Leland Stanford lived there from 1871 to 1874, and in 1893 it was converted to an orphanage. The house, currently being prepared for restoration, has tours focusing on the techniques used by archaeologists and architects to establish its appearance and structure during various periods.

California State Capitol

The enormous Classic Revival state capitol took fourteen years to build, from 1860 to 1874. The first story is of California granite, the upper floors of brick covered with concrete stucco and painted white. On the walls of the rotunda, late-nineteenth-century paintings of griffins have been re-created to complement the restored interior. State offices have also been restored.

LOCATION: Capitol Mall at Tenth Street. HOURS: June through August: 9–5 Daily; September through May: 9–5 Monday–Friday, 10–5 Saturday–Sunday. FEE: None. TELEPHONE: 916–324–0333.

Larkin Goldsmith Mead's sculpture, Columbus's Last Appeal to Queen Isabella, *has decorated the California State Capitol since 1883, when a prominent Sacramento banker donated it to the state.*

The Governor's Mansion (1526 H Street, 916–323–3047) was built in 1877 for Albert Gallatin, a business associate of Huntington and Hopkins; later occupants included journalist Lincoln Steffens, who grew up here. In 1903 it was sold to the state. The exuberant Victorian mansion was not to the taste of Governor Ronald Reagan, who had a new, ranch-style house constructed in a nearby town. (The next governor, Jerry Brown, refused to occupy the Reagan residence.) The old mansion is now open to the public.

Sutter's Fort

Encompassing the original 1840 adobe fort and the reconstructed compound surrounding it, Sutter's Fort provides one of the most complete visions of frontier California available. John Augustus Sutter, a Swiss immigrant, came to California from Honolulu with a team of eight Hawaiian laborers in 1839. Settling on the land grant of New Helvetia, they first built grass huts in Hawaiian fashion but by 1840 had begun the fort, constructing adobe walls 2.5 feet thick, 18 feet high, and 463 feet long. As a Mexican citizen, Sutter was nominally under the authority of the Mexican governor, but in practice he exercised regal power over his domain, managing his largely Indian labor, interpreting law, and providing lodging and help to the increasing stream of immigrants crossing the Sierra Nevada. It was Sutter who sent help into the Sierra during the winter of 1846–1847 to rescue the Donner Party. With the gold rush—occasioned by James Marshall's discovery at Sutter's Mill in Coloma, about fifty miles east of the fort—Sutter gradually lost almost all that he had built to the prospectors who overran his property, and spent his last years in Washington, fruitlessly seeking compensation.

The monument preserves the original central building, and has reconstructions of the many artisans' shops that were necessary to the self-sufficient management of New Helvetia. There is also a museum, with exhibits on the Donner Party and on John C. Frémont's exploring expeditions.

LOCATION: 2701 L Street. HOURS: 10–5 Daily. FEE: Yes. TELEPHONE: 916–445–4422.

OPPOSITE: *The pediment of the California State Capitol shows the ancient Greek goddess Athena flanked by figures representing Justice, Mining, Industry, and Education. Atop the pediment two statues of Indians, fighting a bear at left and a buffalo at right, complete the ensemble.*

OROVILLE

Oroville started in 1849 as a tent community called Ophir City. At one time, it was the fourth largest town in California, with no fewer than sixty-five saloons. Beginning in the 1860s, Chinese immigrants arrived in force to help work the gold mines in the hills nearby; at its peak the Chinese community numbered 10,000. The 1863 **Chinese Temple** (1500 Broderick Street, 916–538–2496) is now open as a museum. In addition to the main temple room and several smaller traditional rooms, the museum has a tapestry hall, collections of Chinese clothing and shadow puppets, and a modern garden featuring Chinese plants.

The last nonreservation Indian in California was discovered in Oroville in 1911. Ishi, the last of the Yahi tribe, was found in a slaughterhouse (no longer standing) on the Oroville–Quincy Highway at Oak Avenue, where he had wandered in search of food. He spent the rest of his life at the University of California's anthropology museum in Berkeley, relating what was left of Yahi culture.

BIDWELL MANSION STATE HISTORIC PARK

Restored inside and out, this remarkable Italianate villa was built for John Bidwell between 1865 and 1867 by Henry W. Cleaveland, who also designed the first Palace Hotel in San Francisco. Bidwell had been just about everything a pioneer Californian could be. He organized the first overland train of emigrants to California in 1841 and was John Sutter's right-hand man for many years. He discovered gold on the Feather River and mined it for two seasons, then turned to farming on his 26,000-acre ranch. Bidwell was among the first in California to see the value of crop diversity and introduced many new plants, including the casaba melon. As a member of the first California senate, he lobbied for statehood; later, in 1864, he was elected to Congress, where he served a single term. An ardent Prohibitionist and anti-monopolist, he ran for governor three times but was defeated each time; in 1892 he was the National Prohibition Party's candidate for president. The beautifully restored mansion, adjacent to Chico State University, is appropriately furnished.

LOCATION: 525 Esplanade, Chico. HOURS: 10–5 Daily. FEE: Yes. TELEPHONE: 916–895–6144.

The pink stucco Bidwell Mansion in Chico contains twenty-six rooms on its three levels.

RED BLUFF

Named for the reddish cliffs nearby, Red Bluff stands at the head of the navigable portion of the Sacramento River. The town was founded about 1850 and was an important supply center for the Trinity gold mines. A number of handsome Italianate Victorian homes survive. Of particular historical interest is the unpretentious clapboard **John Brown House** (135 Main Street), once the home of abolitionist John Brown's surviving wife and children. Ardent Union supporters in the town took up a collection when the fatherless family arrived in 1864 and installed them in this house; it is currently being restored.

Perched on a bluff above the Sacramento River just northeast of Red Bluff is the **William B. Ide Adobe** (21659 Adobe Road, 916–527–5927), a simple, one-room adobe, built in the early 1850s and furnished with period pieces and reproductions. Ide was one of the party of Bear Flaggers who surprised Mariano Vallejo at Sonoma on June 14, 1846, and he was chosen president of the Bear Flag Republic, which lasted for less than a month. He later became a judge and is reported to have served a short-handed court as judge, court clerk, and both prosecuting and defense attorney of a man accused of horse theft. The defendant was convicted and hanged.

THE   INLAND   NORTH

The inland north may be divided into two sections, both mountainous and sparsely populated. Toward the west is the rugged, forested terrain of the southern Cascades, where mining in the rivers contributed significantly to the gold rush. To the east lie more mountains and the high, dry, volcanic Modoc Plateau. Settlers came early to this region, quickly occupying the scattered fertile valleys with the cattle ranches that persist to this day. A patchwork of Indian tribes occupied the territory before the coming of white settlers, but most is known about the lake-dwelling Modoc. During 1872 and 1873 they fought a bloody war against United States forces for control of their ancestral homeland.

WEAVERVILLE

More than a dozen brick buildings from the 1850s survive on and around Weaverville's Main Street, including the **IOOF Hall** and **Clifford Building,** both with exterior spiral staircases. The ca. 1874 **Weaverville Joss House** (Oregon and Main streets, 916–623–5284) is

An early photograph of Weaverville's Joss House shows its Chinese name—The Temple of the Forest Beneath the Clouds—in characters above the door.

a well-preserved Taoist temple with tapestries and gilded, hand-carved wooden altars brought from a temple in China. A tong war took place in Weaverville in 1854, and some of the weapons used in it are also preserved here. The **J. J. Jackson Memorial Museum** (508 Main Street, 916–623–5211), with exhibits relating to the history of Trinity County, stands nearby. Four miles west of town, on Route 299, are the remains of the **LaGrange Mine.** At peak production, between 1909 and 1915, it was one of the largest hydraulic gold mines in the world.

SHASTA STATE HISTORIC PARK

This state historic park encompasses the ruins of old Shasta, the town that was once the most prominent settlement in the area and the county seat. Most of the town burned down in 1853, but it was soon reconstructed, mainly with iron-shuttered brick buildings whose remains can still be seen. The jail and courthouse have been restored and hold period relics. The graveyard is also notable.

LOCATION: Route 299, 6 miles west of Redding. HOURS: March through October: 10–5 Daily; November through February: 10–5 Thursday–Monday. FEE: Yes. TELEPHONE: 916–243–8194.

Inside the Weaverville Joss House is a table for offerings to the gods of Health, Decision, and Mercy.

Route 5 heading north from Redding leads through the heart of
Shasta-Trinity National Forests, dominated by 14,162-foot-high
Mount Shasta. This volcanic peak is perhaps the most dramatic,
though only the sixth tallest, in California. Joaquin Miller
described it evocatively: "Lonely as God and white as a winter
moon, Mount Shasta starts up sudden and solitary from the heart
of the great black forest." In both Indian and white myths its summit is the seat of occult powers. John Muir and a companion were
trapped on the mountain by a blizzard in 1875; finding providen-
tially located hot springs, they waited out the blizzard—wet and
hot on one side, wet and frozen on the other.

Also on Route 5 lies **Castle Crags State Park** (Castle Creek
Road, off Route 5, 916–235–2684). The odd, dramatic granite
spires here were originally named, by the Spanish, Castillo del
Diablo, the Devil's Castle. One of the crags, Battle Rock, was the
site of a battle between settlers and a party of Modoc Indians in
1855. Miners, lured to the area with tales of gold, consumed or
scattered a good deal of the fish and game on which the Indians
depended. The Modoc retaliated by attacking the settlement and
were driven up to these crags, where a bloody but inconclusive battle ensued. Joaquin Miller claimed that he took part in the battle
and wrote an elaborate description of his exploits. In fact, he was
just a boy at the time and was living in Oregon. A marker near the
park entrance describes the battle.

Yreka, farther north, was founded as a gold-mining camp in
1851. The name probably comes from the Shasta word for "mountain." The area around West Miner and Third streets preserves
some notable early structures. The **Siskiyou County Museum** (910
South Main Street, 916–842–3836) has artifacts from the Indian
period, the gold rush, and later settlement. Adjacent to the museum building is a pioneer village with restored miners' cabins, a
reconstructed church, an original mine shaft, and old mining
equipment. The museum's exhibit of locally mined gold nuggets
can be seen at the **County Courthouse** (322 Fourth Street).

Three and a half miles south of the Oregon border, on the
old Alturas Highway (off Route 139) east of Tulelake, is **Bloody
Point.** Ambushes were frequent here, and in 1850 Modoc Indians
killed more than ninety members of a wagon train party. The little
town of **Newell,** farther south on the highway, was the site of the
Tule Lake Relocation Center, where Americans of Japanese ances-
try were incarcerated during World War II.

LAVA BEDS NATIONAL MONUMENT

In this eerie setting of lava flows, cinder cones, and lava tube caves, a band of about 150 Modoc held off more than 1,000 U.S. soldiers. The trouble began when officials decided to relocate the Modoc to an Oregon reservation in 1869. The tribe's traditional enemies, the Klamath, were located on the same reservation, so a group of Modoc, led by a man named Kientpoos, left to return to their home country. General Edward Canby, the army commander, did not press the issue, but over his objection, federal troops and state militia were sent to bring the Modoc back, precipitating the war that resulted in the death of the Modoc leaders and the relocation of their survivors to the Oklahoma territory.

The park preserves "Captain Jack's Stronghold," the network of caves in which Kientpoos—known as Captain Jack to the whites—and his men took shelter. Also marked are the spot where General Canby was gunned down by the Modoc during a peace parley and the site of Colonel Alvan Gillem's camp, near which he buried many of the 46 soldiers killed in the six-month siege.

LOCATION: Off Route 139, 30 miles south of Tulelake. HOURS: Park is always open. *Visitor Center:* June through August: 9–6 Daily; September through May: 8–5 Daily. FEE: Yes. TELEPHONE: 916–667–2282.

In **Alturas**, the **Modoc County Museum** (600 South Main Street, 916–233–2944) features interesting collections of Indian basketry, firearms, arrowheads, and other artifacts. A walking tour of the town's mainly twentieth-century architecture is also available. About seven miles north on Route 395 is the intriguing **Chimney Rock.** When settler Thomas Denson built a cabin here in 1870, he used this pyramid-shaped rock for his chimney, carving the hearth and flue through the rock.

FANDANGO PASS AND FORT BIDWELL

In California's northeast corner are the remains of Fort Bidwell, now an Indian reservation, established in 1865 to protect settlers and immigrants. Nearby, a poor road climbs to 6,100-foot Fandango Pass, the last great mountain hurdle for immigrants on the Applegate-Lassen overland route to California. The pass is supposedly named for the fandango danced by a wagon train party to celebrate their successful crossing; legend has it that they were massacred by an Indian war party right in the middle of the dance. Nonetheless, this crossing enjoyed great popularity during the gold-rush year of 1849, although the immigrants who used this pass discovered upon crossing it that they were still a long way from Sacramento and the gold fields.

LASSEN VOLCANIC NATIONAL PARK

Located in the northeastern quarter of the state, this park is noted mainly for Lassen Peak, an active plug-dome volcano that rises to almost 10,500 feet. There are many natural wonders here, including hot springs and evidence of the devastation wrought by an early-twentieth-century eruption. Both peak and park are named for Peter Lassen, a pioneer who settled in the area east of here during the 1840s. In 1848 he led a wagon train through this rugged country, supposedly on a shorter route to the Sacramento Valley. The difficulty of the terrain led immigrants to name the route "Lassen's Folly."

LOCATION: Route 89, off Route 36 or Route 44. HOURS: *Park Offices:* 8–4:30 Monday–Friday; *Visitor Center:* June through September: 8–5 Daily. FEE: Yes. TELEPHONE: 916–595–4444.

SUSANVILLE

On the fertile Honey Lake Plain beside the Susan River, Susanville was briefly the capital of the independent territory of Nataqua, founded by Isaac Roop in 1856. Nataqua was never much of a republic, but in 1857 Roop and his associates worked to have it made a part of the projected Nevada Territory, of which he was elected provisional governor. California also laid claim to the area. The dispute simmered until February 1863, when the Plumas County sheriff came to arrest Roop and his party; they barricaded themselves in Roop's cabin, renamed Fort Defiance, and a brief gun battle ensued. Later, when the state line was surveyed, the area became part of California but as its own county, with Susanville as the county seat. The cabin, known as **Roop's Fort,** still stands on North Weatherlow Street; next door is the **William Pratt Memorial Museum,** where artifacts of local history are on display.

GOLD RUSH COUNTRY

At the beginning of 1848 there were perhaps 400 settlers in the Sierra foothills region, which stretches 300 miles from Downieville in the north to Mariposa in the south. It is an attractive, if not fertile, country, cut by many rivers and creeks descending from the Sierra to the valley. In winter the grass rises on the hills, to be followed in spring and early summer by a glorious procession of wildflowers—lupine, Brodiaea, wild mustard, California poppy. In late spring, the grass dries to a golden yellow, framing the dark stands of live oak. At higher elevations spring comes still later, with its alpine wildflowers; the trees are pines; and lichen clings to the rocks.

Thousands of prospectors flocked to these hills beginning in 1848 to pan and sift and dig for gold. They came by boat, crossing the Isthmus of Panama or going around Cape Horn, and they came overland, crossing the Great Basin or following the established Santa Fe trade routes. By the peak gold-rush year of 1852, there were 100,000 miners in the area and 500 towns where previously there had been not one. One popular gold rush institution was the

Hopeful Forty-niners who came to California with visions of finding the ground littered with gold nuggets were quickly disappointed. They labored with pick, shovel, and pan to collect a small amount of gold dust.

International Order of Odd Fellows, a benevolent organization dedicated to offering comfort and assistance to strangers; almost every mining town had an IOOF hall.

The lure of the Mother Lode, as the central section of the mines was known, was not only that gold was abundant, but that it was easily available. The early miners needed little more than a pan and a shovel to ply their trade, working river and creek beds or the "dry diggings," dry riverbeds whose streams had changed their course. Later they resorted to a sort of rocker cradle that sifted the dirt from the gold. As the easily taken placer gold became scarce, some took to diverting whole streams in the hope of working the exposed beds. By the later 1850s, placer mining had given way to expensive, large-scale operations: hydraulic mines that used waterpower to scour hillsides for gold, causing terrible erosion in the process, and the deep hard-rock mines that prospered for many years, some right up to World War II.

Today many of the instant towns of the gold rush are marked by nothing more than a few crumbling shacks, but others have proven more enduring, particularly those that found other livelihoods or have been preserved and restored as parks. The main artery of the gold country is Route 49—named after the Forty-niners, as gold-rush immigrants were known—and almost any route on this highway or beside it will yield the remains of old settlements.

PLUMAS–EUREKA STATE PARK

This lovely state park, whose elevation ranges from 4,000 to 8,000 feet, reveals the true beauty and rugged isolation of the northern mines. A museum houses mining artifacts, a reconstructed assay office, and memorabilia relating to California's first ski area, including the heavy skis on which Snowshoe Thompson once carried the mail over the mountains into Nevada. Also in the park are a stamp mill, used to pulverize ore; a restored Bushman mill; a working blacksmith shop dating from 1900; stables containing mining machinery; the ca. 1900 Moriarty House, a four-room miner's house now furnished with original and period furnishings; and the site of the original ski area, founded about 1860.

LOCATION: Route A-14, 4 miles west of Graeagle. HOURS: 8–4 Daily; call ahead from November through March. FEE: None. TELEPHONE: 916–836–2380.

On Route A-14, surrounded by the park, is the nineteenth-century mining town of **Johnsville.** Many of the original wooden buildings remain, including the two-story **Johnsville Hotel** and the 1906 **Iron Door,** once a general store but now a restaurant, with an iron front door taken from an old powder house.

East of the Plumas-Eureka park, Route 70 follows the 5,221-foot **Beckwourth Pass,** an important immigrant pass during the early 1850s, as it was the easiest crossing of the Sierra Nevada. The famed mountain man James Beckwourth pioneered it in 1851. (His memoirs, *The Life and Adventures of James P. Beckwourth,* published in 1857, are among the most dramatic and entertaining, but least reliable accounts of Western life.) **Downieville** has many Greek and Gothic Revival buildings and a well-preserved Main Street, including storefronts that date from as early as 1852, three years after the town was founded. The **Downieville Museum** (Main Street) houses a small collection of gold-rush photographs and memorabilia, including gold scales and a model of a stamp mill.

A huge pit in **Malakoff Diggins State Historic Park** (23579 North Bloomfield Road, off Route 49, 916–265–2740) testifies to the destructive force of hydraulic mining. Between 1866 and 1884, the year hydraulic mining was banned, the huge operation washed out tons of gravel, using a pressurized water cannon called a monitor, leaving a gash in the mountain 7,000 feet long, 3,000 feet wide, and 600 feet deep. The washed gravel was then processed to remove its gold. The exposed strata of the mountain, with bands of pink and ochre, is in itself a thing of beauty, but farmers whose lands were being ruined by the huge amounts of silt added to the Yuba River brought suit against the miners and eventually achieved a ban. To the east but still within the park is the small mining town of **North Bloomfield,** which contains a number of wooden buildings from the hydraulic mining boom of the 1870s, when the town had a population of almost 2,000. Several buildings, including the general store, have been restored and furnished with period pieces, and the drugstore and saloon have been reconstructed; the latter contains a museum of mining artifacts.

Travelers on Route 80 heading toward Lake Tahoe will pass a state marker and vista point for **Emigrant Gap.** Beginning in 1845, wagon parties following this arduous route—where the Donner Party would later be trapped—faced their final obstacle here, when wagons had to be lowered on ropes down the cliffs into Bear Valley.

DUTCH FLAT

Founded in 1851, Dutch Flat first came to prominence as a hydraulic mining center, then prospered as a supply point for Nevada's Comstock Mines and a stop on the Central Pacific Railroad. As it is one of the few gold-rush towns not to have suffered a devastating fire, it contains an unusual number of pre-1860 structures. Theodore Judah found his first subscriber to the Central Pacific Railroad here, and critics of the railroad contended that the builders secretly planned to terminate the line at Dutch Flat and let the newly built Dutch Flat Wagon Road (which followed the old Donner route) carry on to Virginia City, Nevada, from there. Until it actually crossed the Sierra, the Central Pacific was known to its detractors as the "Dutch Flat Swindle."

NEVADA CITY

Founded in 1849, Nevada City was an important center for placer, hydraulic, and quartz gold mining. Set on a series of tree-covered hills, it contains an unusual number of fine Victorian houses and picturesque commercial buildings, including the 1856 **National Hotel** (211 Broad Street), the 1865 **Nevada Theatre** (401 Broad Street), and the **IOOF Hall** (225 Broad Street). The **American Victorian Museum** (325 Spring Street, 916–265–5804) occupies the 1856 **Miner's Foundry,** the building in which the first Pelton wheel—an invention that facilitated deep quartz mining—was cast in 1878. The museum has a rich collection of Victoriana, including a pipe organ, Staffordshire pottery portrait figures, graphics, and nineteenth-century architectural pieces. The **Nevada County Historical Society Museum** (214 Main Street, 916–265–5468), located in the 1861 Firehouse Number 1, contains a Chinese joss house and exhibits on the Nisinan Indians, the gold rush, and the ill-fated Donner Party.

GRASS VALLEY

The name Grass Valley was originally given informally to the area by immigrants who appreciated the forage to be found here after the

OPPOSITE: *Hydraulic mining at Malakoff Diggins, shown in this photograph from the 1870s, above, yielded some $3,500,000 in gold before the practice was outlawed in 1884. The technique washed out more than 30 million yards of gravel, creating a vast man-made canyon, below.*

difficult Sierra crossing. Some of the most productive quartz gold mines in the state were discovered and worked in this area, and the town preserves many reminders of its history as a mining center and a cradle of California culture. In 1850 a farmer out looking for his cow stumbled on a rock, picked it up, and discovered that it was gold-bearing quartz. The **Gold Hill Marker** (Jenkins Street, between Hawking and French streets) commemorates the spot. Mines, such as Gold Hill, Empire, and North Star, soon sprang up in the area, attracting Cornish hard-rock miners to work them. The powerhouse of the North Star Mine, at the south end of town, now contains the **North Star Mining Museum** (Allison Ranch Road at foot of Mill Street, 916–273–4255), with exhibits on the history of hard-rock gold mining. Among the artifacts on display is a thirty-foot-diameter Pelton wheel, a revolutionary waterwheel that proved efficient enough to run the pumps and machines in the mine's hundreds of miles of tunnels.

Despite a fire in 1855, Grass Valley is comparatively rich in historic buildings. The row of storefronts on Mill Street near East Main Street, with its wooden awnings, is a miniature picture of gold-rush architecture. On Main Street itself is the well-restored **Holbrooke Hotel,** built in 1851. Two surviving homes at 248 and 238 Mill Street were inhabited by Lola Montez and Lotta Crabtree, respectively. Montez was already a legend when she retired briefly to Grass Valley in 1852. She had entertained the crowned heads of Europe with her notorious spider dance and taken a number of lovers—the most prominent, "Mad" King Louis I of Bavaria, made her a countess. She performed both in San Francisco and in the mining towns, taking a year off in Grass Valley, where she kept a trained bear and tutored her neighbor, a child named Lotta Crabtree. Montez retired from the stage in 1856; following a religious conversion, she devoted the rest of her life to helping "wayward women." Crabtree eventually outstripped her mentor, first as a singing and dancing naïf and then as the most highly paid actress of her time, and amassed a fortune of over $4 million, part of which went to build Lotta's Fountain in San Francisco.

Grass Valley was also the birthplace of Josiah Royce, the philosopher and disciple of William James. Born in 1855 to the town's schoolteacher, Royce later attended Harvard and taught there, but his Grass Valley childhood influenced him profoundly. "A child

OPPOSITE: *Nevada City's Firehouse Number 1, built in 1861, is now operated as a museum by the Nevada County Historical Society. Its bell tower and ornate gingerbread decorations are later additions.*

born in one of our far western settlements," he was to write, "grows up amid a community that is a few years older than himself. . . . Yet he shall hear of the settlement of the town as he hears of ancient history, and he shall reverence the oldest, deserted, weather-beaten rotting log cabin of the place . . . quite as much as a modern Athenian child may reverence the ruins of the Parthenon."

Empire Mine State Historical Park

Just southeast of Grass Valley is the site of a mine that operated for more than a century, raising more than 5.8 million ounces of gold from 367 miles of tunnels up to 11,007 feet long and 6,000 feet deep. Guided tours travel down the main shaft and explain the use of headframes and mine machinery still on the site. In 1897 San Francisco magnate William Bourn, then owner of the mine, built the Empire Cottage, a remarkable building of rough-hewn stone trimmed with brick. The house was designed by the great San Francisco architect Willis Polk and has been restored to its 1905 appearance with original and period furnishings.

> LOCATION: 10791 East Empire Street. HOURS: May: 9–5 Daily; June through August: 9–6 Daily; September through April: 10–5 Daily. FEE: Yes. TELEPHONE: 916–273–8522.

The mining town of **Rough and Ready** was founded in 1849 and named for President Zachary Taylor, "Old Rough and Ready," who had served as a general in the Mexican War. Lotta Crabtree, the young protégée of Lola Montez, made her debut as an entertainer here, tap dancing on the anvil in **W. H. Fippen's Blacksmith Shop** (Rough and Ready Highway). The miners signaled their approval by tossing gold nuggets, a practice that would eventually make Crabtree a millionaire. The 1854 **IOOF Hall,** now a Grange hall, is set back on a little hill west of the blacksmith shop.

In the tiny town of **French Corral** a **plaque** (Pleasant Valley Road) marks the location of the first long-distance telephone line in the world, a sixty-mile line built in 1877 to connect the Milton Mining and Water Company headquarters here to French Lake. The system was used to help coordinate the movement of water from the lake for mining purposes. Between Bridgeport and French Corral on Pleasant Valley Road is the **Bridgeport Covered Bridge,** built in 1862 as part of the Virginia Turnpike Company Toll Road.

OPPOSITE: *A somber group of miners prepares to descend by rail into the Empire Mine's 4,600-foot main shaft. The photograph was taken around 1900.*

Looking down the main shaft of the Empire Mine, near Grass Valley, the oldest, richest, and deepest mine in California history.

AUBURN

Auburn was first settled by members of the New York Volunteers, soldiers in the Mexican War who were demobilized in California. It still flourishes in large part because of its strategic position on one of the best routes to the southern mines and over the Sierra, Interstate 80. Deep in a ravine is the oldest part of town, centered mainly on Commercial Street, with a row of false-front stores from the 1850s and 1860s. There are also a number of nineteenth-century buildings on Lincoln Way, including the simple 1892 **fire house,** with a steeply pitched, hipped roof; the domed, Neoclassical **courthouse,** built between 1894 and 1898; the ca. 1894 **IOOF Hall;** and the 1858 **Methodist Church.** The **Gold Country Museum** (1273 High Street, 916–889–4155) contains excellent exhibits on all major mining techniques, from placer mining to hard-rock quartz mining, including a working model of a stamp mill. There are also exhibits on the later history of the area, including its fruit industry. The **Bernhard Museum** (291 Auburn-Folsom Road, 916–889–4156), which will become a living-history farm, now contains three historic buildings: an 1851 farmhouse, furnished with late-Victorian antiques, and winery buildings dating from 1874 and 1881.

In nearby **Penryn,** the **Griffith Quarry Park and Museum** (Taylor and Rock Springs roads, 916–663–1837) tells the story of the important granite quarry established on this site by a Welsh immigrant, Griffith Griffith, in 1864. Stone and ornaments for buildings at Stanford University, Alcatraz federal prison, Fort Point, and the state capitol were quarried and finished here.

The Auburn area was particularly rich in placer gold. Nuggets weighing over twenty-five pounds each were found in the region during 1849 and 1850. Later, hydraulic mining became important. Foresthill Road, proceeding east of town, leads through a number of hamlets that once boasted populations of roistering miners, such as Yankee Jim's and Michigan Bluff. The **Forest Hill Divide Museum** (24601 Harrison Street, Foresthill, 916–367–3988) features displays on the geology, prehistory, and history of the region, including a scale model of the Foresthill Logging Company.

GEORGETOWN

Situated at the northern end of the Mother Lode—the 150-mile vein of gold that accounted for many of the larger strikes—Georgetown has survived while other towns died, owing to the many successful hard-rock mines that flourished around it. Successive fires throughout the nineteenth century destroyed large parts of the old town, although after the first one in 1852 the citizens built Main Street 100 feet wide to slow the spread of any future conflagration. Among the surviving buildings on Main Street are the 1852 brick-and-stone **Wells Fargo Building,** the 1859 **IOOF Hall,** and the 1852 Monterey-style **Shannon Knox House,** said to have been built of lumber shipped around the Horn.

In 1868 John Henry Schnell, a German soldier of fortune who had married into a Japanese family, arrived with a group of Japanese immigrants and attempted to establish a tea and silk plantation near the town of Gold Hill. The Wakamatsu Colony, as it was known, failed after only two years. A **monument** (Cold Springs Road, four miles north of Placerville) commemorates the site; the daughter of one of the settlers is buried nearby.

MARSHALL GOLD DISCOVERY STATE HISTORIC PARK

The gold rush began with James Marshall's discovery of gold here in early 1848, an event now memorialized in this 280-acre park. A working replica of Sutter's Mill, in whose tailrace Marshall first found pea-sized nuggets, is on the site, as are a number of buildings from the town that sprang up near the mill, including Marshall's cabin; two wood frame Greek Revival churches dating from the mid-1850s; an 1852 gunsmith's shop; and as usual, an IOOF Hall. A Chinese store has been restored to its 1859 appearance; its identical neighbor houses a geology museum. A museum contains exhibits about Marshall and Sutter, an authentic Concord stagecoach, and a fine collection of Maidu Indian artifacts. **Marshall's grave,** on a hilltop overlooking the Coloma Valley, is marked by an 1889 statue of the discoverer pointing to where the first flake of gold was found.

LOCATION: Route 49, Coloma. HOURS: *Park:* 8–Dusk Daily; *Museum:* May through September: 10–5 Daily; October through April: 11–4:30 Daily. FEE: Yes. TELEPHONE: 916–622–3470.

PLACERVILLE

Set in a steep ravine near the junction of Routes 49 and 50, Placerville is still an active town with well-preserved historic sites, though most of the original gold-rush buildings were destroyed in an 1856 fire. The town, founded in 1848 as Old Dry Diggins, came to be known as Hangtown after three supposed thieves were hanged here in 1849 and was officially incorporated as Placerville in 1854. The stump of the old hanging tree can still be seen at 305 Main Street.

Although Main Street has suffered modernization some early structures can still be seen, including the 1852 **Fountain-Tallman Building** (524 Main Street) and the 1859 **IOOF Hall** (467 Main Street), both built of native stone. The **Pearson Soda Works** (594 Main Street) is also constructed of native stone, and its first story, which dates from 1859, features a cornerstone and lintels of dressed rhyolite. The second story was added in 1897. The **El Dorado County Historical Museum** (100 Placerville Drive, 916–621–5865) has a collection of gold-rush artifacts and items of nineteenth-century material culture. Several figures of national prominence got their start in

A re-created miner's cabin in the Marshall Gold Discovery State Historic Park, with all the necessities, including a rocker or cradle, an advance on the pan in placer mining technology.

this town. A **marker** commemorates John Studebaker's shop, which once stood at 543 Main Street. Studebaker was a wheelwright here from 1853 to 1858, before returning to his native Indiana, where he founded the buggy factory that later became an important automobile manufacturer. Philip Armour ran a butcher shop in Placerville, and Mark Hopkins, the railroad magnate, had a store in town. Leland Stanford's store was in the little town of Cold Springs, nearby.

Just north of town is **Hangtown's Gold Bug Park** (Bedford Avenue, one mile north of Route 50, 916–662–0832), where two shafts of a hard-rock gold mine are now open for tours. Remains of the stamp mill that once crushed the gold-bearing quartz to facilitate removal of the precious metal may be seen nearby.

The southern mines straddle the heart of Mother Lode country. Route 49, south of its junction with Route 50, passes through small former mining towns like Diamond Springs and El Dorado to arrive at **Plymouth,** which thrived on the quartz mines that operated nearby for more than five decades, extracting over $13 million in gold. The town still boasts an assortment of nineteenth-century structures, including a number of interesting stores built of native stone. The ruins of the headframe of the **Plymouth Consolidated Mines** also survive south of town.

East of Plymouth on Fiddletown Road is **Fiddletown,** a quiet and well-preserved gold-rush hamlet with a number of structures dating from the 1850s. Among the most interesting is the **Chew Kee Store** (Main Street), a rammed-earth house built in 1850 as a Chinese herbalist shop and later used as a general store. The shop and the living quarters in the rear of the building have been restored with original furnishings. Farther east is the town of **Volcano**, named by early settlers who thought the round valley in which it is set was the crater of an extinct volcano. Surrounded by pine-clad mountains, the town has several stone buildings dating to

A pneumatic drill used in the Gold Bug mine, north of Placerville. The mine operated from 1888 until World War II.

The Chew Kee Store served the Chinese population of Fiddletown from 1850 to 1913, when it was given to Fong Chow Yow, the city's last Chinese inhabitant. He kept the store intact until his death in 1965.

the 1850s. Volcano was the first stop for immigrants crossing Carson Pass into California, and during the gold rush it was a thriving town of more than 5,000. The **Saint George Hotel** on Main Street was built in 1864 to serve the influx of miners. The town also preserves a bronze cannon known as "Old Abe" (Consolation Avenue), which was smuggled into Volcano in a hearse during the Civil War by miners sympathetic to the Union, to deter any attempts by Confederate sympathizers to steal gold for the Southern cause.

CHAW-SE STATE HISTORIC PARK

This park preserves an enormous rock with mortar holes in which the Miwok ground acorns, a staple of their diet. Warm water was poured through the acorn meal to leach out toxic tannic acid, and the meal was then boiled into mush or baked into cakes. The Miwok,

A barkhouse is one of several Miwok buildings that can be seen at Chaw-Se State Historic Park, still an important gathering place for the tribe.

who were skilled basket makers, used no pottery but had different baskets, each suited to its particular function, for the various stages of food preparation. The park's cultural center displays these baskets and other crafts, and a Miwok village has been reconstructed nearby.

LOCATION: Pine Grove–Volcano Road, 1.5 miles northeast of Pine Grove. HOURS: *Park:* Dawn–Dusk Daily; *Museum:* April through September: 10–5 Daily; October through March: 11–3 Monday–Friday, 10–4 Saturday–Sunday. FEE: Yes. TELEPHONE: 209–296–7488.

On Route 49 a few miles south of Plymouth stands **Drytown,** one of the gold country's oldest towns. A number of buildings from the 1850s survive, prominent among them the **Old Brick Store** (Main Street and Old Plymouth Road), where George Hearst, father of William Randolph Hearst, ran a mining office and printing press. The elder Hearst failed to make his fortune here but later struck it rich during the Comstock silver rush in Nevada. Farther south, tiny **Amador City** is surrounded by the crumbling headframes of former mines. Most of the town's gold-rush-era buildings have been restored. Nearby **Sutter Creek** is also well preserved, largely owing to the restorations carried out at the end of the nineteenth century, when it was an important center for hard-rock gold mining. The town is a rich mixture of brick, stone, and wood stores, hotels, and homes dating from the 1850s to the 1880s. The Central Eureka Mine, among the most productive and long lived of California's gold mines, was located at the south end of town; it yielded over $34 million in gold before closing down in 1958. **Knight Foundry** (9 Eureka Street), an important source of tools for miners, was founded in 1873 and is still in operation today, the only waterpowered foundry still working in the United States.

West along the Sutter Creek–Ione Back Cutoff is **Ione,** which contains a number of historic buildings, including the red brick **United Methodist Church** (150 West Marlette), dating from the 1860s. The **Preston School of Industry** (Waterman Road), California's first reformatory, was originally located in an 1894 Romanesque Revival complex known locally as "the Castle;" the reform school is now housed in later buildings on the same site.

JACKSON

This is another town that owes its survival to the hard-rock gold mines that surround it. The Argonaut and Kennedy mines, just north of town, were both founded in the 1850s and survived until World War II, yielding at least $70 million in gold between them. The two surviving tailing wheels of the Kennedy Mine were built in 1912, as part of a system that carried mine tailings (discarded rock and gravel) to a central dumping ground. They are preserved in **Kennedy Tailing Wheels Park** (Jackson Gate Road); the ruins of the headframe and stamp mill can also be seen from the park. Nearby, on Argonaut Lane, is the headframe of the Argonaut Mine, where forty-seven miners perished in a mine fire in 1922. The shaft was closed to smother the flames, and by the time rescuers reached the level where the miners had been trapped, all were dead, leaving scrawled on a piece of slate the message "gas too strong."

At the north end of town is **Saint Sava's Serbian Orthodox Church** (724 North Main Street), built in 1894 of wood with a simple tower. The **Amador County Museum** (Church and North streets, 209–223–6386) is located in the A. C. Brown House, an attractive wood frame building raised in the early 1860s. It contains models of the local mines, mining artifacts, Victorian furniture, and a good collection of Miwok basketry.

MOKELUMNE HILL

Named for a subtribe of the Miwok, who once occupied the area, "Mok Hill" was an important placer gold center from 1848 on. The town contains many fine stone buildings, most of them erected after an 1854 fire. The **IOOF Hall** (Center Street) was built by the Adams Express Company shortly after the fire, and the **Hotel Leger** (Main Street) also dates from 1854. During the 1850s, this was perhaps the most turbulent town on the Mother Lode: Mexicans, Chileans, Frenchmen, and Americans, white and black, fought it out for claims so rich that at one time each miner's claim was limited to sixteen square feet. Racism and nationalism were at their ugliest. The town is also supposed to have been frequented by Joaquín Murieta, the bandit who was a sort of Robin Hood to the downtrodden Mexicans of the Mother Lode. So contentious were the citizens of Mok Hill that during one seventeen-week period at least one murder was committed every Saturday night. When it came time to choose a county seat for Calaveras County, a Mok Hill citizen rigged the election so that his town beat out Jackson, leading to a fracas in which Jackson eventually seceded to become the seat of its own county.

MURPHYS

Many fine gold rush–era buildings still stand on this town's tree-lined Main Street, including the restored 1856 **Murphys Hotel** (457 Main Street), whose guests included Mark Twain, highwayman Black Bart, and President Ulysses S. Grant. The **Old Timers Museum,** also on Main Street, contains many artifacts relating to the history of the area, including a gravestone reputed to be that of Joaquín Murieta. Legend has it that Murphys was where the notorious bandit launched his career, after seeing a friend lynched for the alleged theft of a horse. So angry was Murieta that he went on a three-year rampage that began with the murder of all the members of the lynching party.

ANGELS CAMP

Angels Camp was named not for the comportment of its citizens but for two brothers named Angel who opened a store at this site in

OPPOSITE: *The Knight Foundry in Sutter Creek, founded in 1873, produced the tools used by many miners. Still in operation, it recently cast the pilasters used in the restoration of the California State Capitol.*

On the corner of Main and State streets in Columbia, perhaps California's best pre-
served gold rush town, are two brick buildings constructed after a fire in 1854 that con-
sumed most of the town's wooden structures.

1848. The surface gold was quickly exhausted, but the town's deep
quartz mines produced over $19 million worth of gold between 1886
and 1910. Scattered along Main Street are many buildings from the
1850s and 1860s, the most notable of which is the **Hotel Angels**
(1287 South Main Street), where Mark Twain supposedly heard the
story that became "The Celebrated Jumping Frog of Calaveras
County." The town holds a raucous frog jump every year, and a **statue of Mark Twain** stands in Utica Park (Utica Lane and Sams Way).

COLUMBIA STATE HISTORIC PARK

Here, just north of Sonora, the state has restored an entire gold-rush
town. Columbia was founded in 1850 by placer miners, though
greater fortunes came later from hydraulic mining. There is a
restored 1856 brick Wells Fargo office, with original gold scales; the
Fallon Theatre, dating from the 1880s; a reconstructed newspaper

office, stocked with antique printing equipment; and a stagecoach that rides around town.

LOCATION: Off Route 49, 4 miles north of Sonora. HOURS: *Museum:* 8–5 Daily. FEE: None. TELEPHONE: 209–532–4301.

JAMESTOWN

Named for its founder, a placer miner, Jamestown was the first town settled in the southern mines, in 1848. A nugget weighing seventy-five pounds is supposed to have been found in a nearby creek that year, setting off a rush. Later the town was important as a supply center for nearby hard-rock mines. **Railtown 1897** (Fifth Avenue at the reservoir, 209–983–3953), a state historic park, consists of the original shops and offices of the Sierra Railroad, built in 1897 to open the Mother Lode country to the rest of California. The park offers

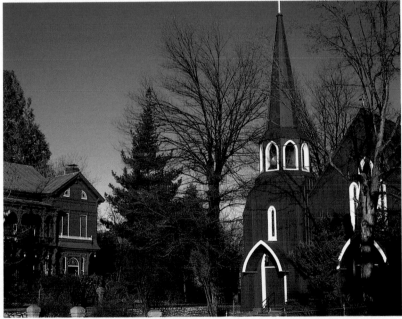

Sonora's 1859 Gothic Revival Saint James Episcopal Church, at right, dates from the town's first wave of prosperity during the gold rush, when it was the second most populous Mother Lode town. The Frank and Ora Morgan Mansion, at left, is a remnant of its second boom from lumber during the 1890s.

steam passenger-train rides and tours of the operating steam round-house. The Sierra Railroad still runs freight over the original tracks.

Just south of Jamestown are the remains of **Chinese Camp,** a gold rush town started by an Englishman who hired Chinese laborers. At one time, there were 5,000 Chinese in residence, and a tong war took place here in 1861. There is little left of the town now, though its Catholic church, brick post office, and Wells Fargo office have survived.

COULTERVILLE

This gold-rush town was founded in 1850 by George Coulter, who set up a tent store to serve the local placer mines. Later there were several important quartz mines in the area. Many early buildings have been preserved, including the adobe **Jeffrey Hotel** (1 Main Street), which opened in 1851 as a Mexican dance hall; and the **Sun Sun Wo Store** (5076 Main Street), a Chinese general store from the early 1850s, still stocked with supplies. The **Northern Mariposa History Center** (Routes 49 and 132, 209–878–3015), a small museum of local history, is located in the 1856 Wells Fargo building and the remains of the Coulter Hotel, which burned in 1899. "Whistling Billy," the railroad engine that once connected the Mary Harrison Mine to its stamp mills, is on display in front of the history center.

South from Coulterville, most of the chaparral-covered land on either side of Route 49 was once owned by Lieutenant Colonel John C. Frémont, the wandering soldier who made several early exploring expeditions to California. On the second of these he became involved in California politics, fomenting the Bear Flag Revolt and remaining active in the United States seizure of the state. The town of **Bear Valley,** along Route 49, was the center of his 44,000-acre grant, Rancho de las Mariposas.

HORNITOS

West of Bear Valley on Bear Valley Road lies the ghost town of Hornitos, set among dry hills and scattered oaks. Founded by Mexicans driven out of nearby Quartzburg, this once-bustling, placer mining town is built in Mexican fashion around a small square. The church on the hill stands beside a graveyard with small, typical

Mexican tombs raised above the surface of the earth. Hornitos, which means "little ovens" in Spanish, may have been named for these graves. Although the town has been heavily vandalized by curiosity seekers in recent years, there are an **old jail** (High Street) and, on Main Street, a Wells Fargo office and the ruins of a building in which Domingo Ghirardelli operated a general store.

MARIPOSA

An early newspaper editor described Mariposa as "above the fog, below the snow." Indeed, its position in the foothills is higher than the reach of the valley's tule fogs and lower than the mountains' snow line. Its initial prosperity was due to John C. Frémont's Mariposa Mine, opened in 1850 and not finally closed until more than a century later. The area is now important for tungsten mining, and Mariposa is a stop on one of the highways into Yosemite.

As a result of its continuing importance, the town is very well preserved. Among the many notable gold-rush buildings is the wood frame courthouse (Bullion Street), built in 1854 and still in use. **Saint Joseph's Catholic Church,** at the foot of Bullion Street, is a white Gothic Revival church dating from 1862. At Bullion and Fifth streets is the Monterey-style **Schlageter Hotel,** built in 1866. The name "Bullion" refers not to the town's gold strikes but to John C. Frémont's father-in-law, Missouri senator Thomas Hart Benton, whose nickname was "Old Bullion." Charles and Jessie streets are named for Frémont (his middle name was Charles) and his wife; all are reminders that the town lies on what was once his land grant.

Mariposa Museum

One of the best museums in the gold country, the Mariposa Museum dramatically demonstrates the history of mining techniques with a full-size working stamp mill. The museum also includes a reconstructed Miwok village and an intriguing group of period interiors: a general store, a newspaper office, a schoolroom, and a facsimile of Jessie Frémont's parlor, all with period furnishings.

LOCATION: 5119 Jessie Street. HOURS: February through March: 10–4 Saturday–Sunday; April through October: 10–4:30 Daily; November through December: 10–4 Saturday–Sunday. FEE: None. TELEPHONE: 209–966–2924.

THE SIERRA NEVADA

The Sierra Nevada stretches 400 miles from Lassen Peak in the north to Tehachapi Pass in the south. The High Sierra begins at Yosemite, stretching south in ranks of alpine peaks from 12,000 to over 14,000 feet high, with more than 1,200 lakes scattered beneath them. Mount Whitney is the second highest peak in the continental United States. The name Sierra Nevada means "snowy mountains" in Spanish; the mountains were named by Franciscan missionaries who first saw the mountains from the Sacramento Valley in 1776. But another traveler almost a century later, beholding the same view, gave them the name that sticks in the mind of everyone who has spent time among their bright peaks. The great naturalist John Muir wrote: "One glowing April day, from the summit of the Pacheco Pass . . . the luminous wall of the mountains shone in all its glory. Then it seemed to me the Sierra should be called not the Nevada, or Snowy Range, but the Range of Light." Much of the glory of those mountains is found in Yosemite Valley, where the John Muir Trail begins, which follows the Sierra Nevada crest south 200 miles to Mount Whitney. Despite their beauty, the Sierra proved a formidable obstacle to early immigrants. Just north and south of Lake Tahoe, roughly following Interstate 80 and Highway 50, respectively, were two of the chief trails that brought early settlers and gold-rush miners to California. Walkers in the region are still likely to come on the ruts carved by wagons on the forest floor or even in the rock.

DONNER PASS

North of Lake Tahoe, Interstate 80 follows a trail favored by early settlers because it was a fairly direct route to Sacramento. The route crosses the crest at Donner Pass, where walls of steep granite look down onto Donner Lake. The first band of immigrants to use this crossing, led by Elisha Stevens in 1844, was caught by early snows and forced to leave some wagons under guard until spring. Parts of the trail were too steep to be negotiated by ox-drawn wagons; instead, the travelers had to lead the oxen up first, then haul the wagons over the sheer rock faces with ropes and chains.

The most harrowing experience, however, took place in the summer of 1846 when the Donner Party headed west along the newly opened Hastings Cutoff. This trail, which ran south of the Great Salt Lake through the mountains and deserts of Utah and Nevada, was

Yosemite's Bridal Veil Fall, photographed by Ansel Adams, for whom the park was "always a sunrise, a glitter of green and golden wonder in a vast edifice of stone and space."

unexpectedly rugged, and the party did not reach the Sierra cross-ing until November. Trapped in the mountains by early snows, they were forced to make a winter encampment near Donner Lake. In the ensuing months, despite repeated rescue and escape attempts, thirty-five of the party died, and survivors were at one point com-pelled to eat their dead companions' flesh. It was April 1847 before the last of the survivors was brought out. In **Donner Memorial State**

Park (Donner Pass Road off Interstate 80, west of Truckee, 916–587–3841) the **Emigrant Trail Museum** has artifacts of the pioneers who crossed the mountains and exhibits tracing the history of the railroad. A monument stands near the spot where one of the Donner Party families spent the winter. Only two decades later, the Central Pacific Railroad followed this route over the Sierra. The tracks and snowsheds snaking along the mountainside north of Donner Lake were laid mainly by Chinese labor, blasting a path through the rock. Amtrak's California Zephyr still follows this route.

Nestled in a Sierra basin over 6,000 feet above sea level and surrounded by glacier-sculpted peaks, **Lake Tahoe** is more than 20 miles long and covers 193 square miles. Tahoe, which means "lake" or "water" in the language of the Washo Indians who once occupied the area, was seen by John C. Frémont on his 1844 exploring expedition.

ECHO SUMMIT AND CARSON PASS

South of Lake Tahoe are Echo Summit (Route 50) and Carson Pass (Route 88), two alternate crossings for the most popular immigrant trail into California. Although Kit Carson went this way in the 1840's carving his name on a tree at the pass that bears his name, the trail was really opened in 1848 by a party of Mormons heading east to Salt Lake City. Immigrant names can still be found scrawled on the rocks around Carson Pass, near which Sarah Royce—an early immigrant and the mother of the philosopher Josiah Royce—described her first sight of California in 1849: "I looked, down, far over constantly descending hills, to where a soft haze sent up a warm rosy glow that seemed to me a smile of welcome . . . and I knew I was looking into the Sacramento Valley."

YOSEMITE NATIONAL PARK

Lying between sheer walls of granite rising thousands of feet from the valley floor, Yosemite Valley was originally inhabited by the Ahwahneechee, a subtribe of the southern Miwok. These valley dwellers fished and hunted, gathered acorns, and traded with the Paiute, their neighbors across the mountains. They built no permanent structures but slept outdoors in summer and in cone-shaped huts of wood and bark in winter.

When miners began appearing in the area the Ahwahneechee and other Miwok, led by Chief Tenieya, resisted the intrusion and carried out a series of attacks against the settlers. In retaliation the Mariposa Battalion, a volunteer militia recruited from the mining camps, attempted unsuccessfully to remove the Indians to a reservation. As part of this campaign, on March 27, 1851, Major James Savage led a party into Yosemite Valley, the first documented exploration by non-Indians. Later, many Indians were removed to reservations. Some escaped, but on their return to Yosemite they found that the valley's isolation had been breached by tourists.

Word had spread quickly of the breathtaking beauty of the seven-mile-long valley. James M. Hutchings, publisher of *Hutchings' California Magazine,* did much to publicize the area and in 1859 opened the valley's first hotel to accommodate the growing stream of visitors. In 1864, concerned about the danger of overdevelopment, Congress passed a bill requiring the state to protect the valley and the Mariposa Grove of giant sequoia. At the urging of naturalist John Muir, Congress set aside the surrounding area as Yosemite National Park in 1890, and in 1905 the state-owned areas were incorporated into the national park.

There are three museums of note currently operating in the valley. The **Indian Cultural Museum,** located near the visitor center, contains dioramas about Miwok life and exhibits of Miwok basketry, feather work, and other crafts. The **El Portal Transportation Exhibit** at the El Portal park entrance (Route 140) contains rolling stock and a restored station and roundhouse. Most of the material is from the Yosemite Valley Railroad, which first reached the park in 1907. The locomotive is from the Hetch Hetchy Railroad, the line built to serve the builders of the dam that flooded nearby Hetch Hetchy Valley, transforming it into a mammoth lake. John Muir's inability to block the building of this dam was one of the great defeats of his life.

Outside the valley but inside the park, near the Mariposa Grove, is the **Pioneer Yosemite History Center** (Route 41). A number of buildings have been moved to this site, including a pioneer's cabin, a ranger's cabin, a Wells Fargo office, a jail, and a wooden chapel. Also on the site are the Wawona Covered Bridge, constructed in 1858, and the wooden Wawona Hotel, dating from 1885.

LOCATION: Routes 41, 140, or 120, off Route 99, or Route 120, off Route 395. HOURS: *Visitor Center:* 9–5 Daily. FEE: Yes. TELEPHONE: 209–372–0264.

Bridgeport's 1880 Italianate **Mono County Courthouse** (Route 395) is one of the best examples of the style in California and is very well preserved despite being made entirely of wood. The **Mono County Historical Museum** (School Street, 619–932–7911), housed in an 1880 school building, has collections of Paiute basketry and artifacts from the nearby ghost towns of Bodie, Masonic, and Boulder Flat. Seven miles south of town, near the cliff along Dogtown Creek, are the crumbling remains of **Dogtown,** site of the first gold rush on the east side of the Sierra. The town's name is miners' slang for a place of poorly constructed temporary huts, and the ruins are by no means imposing.

BODIE

A striking contrast to Dogtown is Bodie, one of the West's most complete ghost towns, with buildings still standing from the 1870s and after. Named for Waterman S. Bodey, who first discovered gold here in 1859, the town prospered and eventually accounted for $100 million in gold. By 1879 Bodie had a population of 10,000, sixty-five saloons, and a reputation for wickedness—killings and robberies were common, and the phrase "bad man from Bodie" was known throughout the West. Most of the town's buildings are wooden, and

So remote that it escaped the depredations of vandals and souvenir hunters, the ghost town of Bodie was acquired virtually intact by the California state park system in 1962.

its many false-front stores give it a Wild West look. The Methodist church, built in 1882, is particularly charming, and there are also a number of residences, a sawmill, a firehouse, and a schoolhouse. The old jail and the morgue (complete with caskets) stand as reminders of the days when Bodie was a wide-open town. A museum in the old Miners' Union Hall contains artifacts of the town's heyday.

LOCATION: Route 270, off Route 395, southeast of Bridgeport. HOURS: June through August: 9–7 Daily; September through May: 9–4 Daily. FEE: Yes. TELEPHONE: 619–647–6445.

Mono Lake, south of Bodie, is a desolate body of alkaline water that once covered the whole Mono Basin as an inland sea. As barren as it may seem, it is an important breeding ground for sea gulls, and moves are afoot to preserve and protect it, as the water level has been dropping. Mark Twain was not complimentary about the lake, but he did find a novel use for it: "Its sluggish waters are so strong with alkali that if you only dip the most hopelessly soiled garment into them once or twice, and wring it out, it will be found as clean as if it had been through the ablest of washerwomen's hands. While we camped

Bodie's Boone Store, which remained in business until the 1930s, appears today as it did when the state of California acquired it.

there our laundry work was easy. We tied the week's washing astern of our boat, and sailed a quarter of a mile, and the job was complete, all to the wringing out."

From the Mono Lake region Route 395 leads southward to Owens Valley, where ranches and farms sprang up and thrived in the late nineteenth century. When growing Los Angeles began the first of its many efforts to secure more water in 1908, it bought a considerable amount of the valley's land and water rights, transporting the water through an aqueduct and effectively destroying local agriculture. The surviving towns are now mainly trade centers and takeoff points for campers venturing into the Sierra Nevada.

To the north, in **Independence,** the **Eastern California Museum** (155 Grant Street, 619–878–2411) contains an exhibit, developed and maintained by a former internee, describing life in the nearby Manzanar Japanese relocation camp through photographs, artifacts, and eyewitness accounts. The museum also has exhibits on other aspects of local history, including an outstanding collection of Paiute and Shoshone basketry, and maintains the **Commander's House** (303 North Edwards Street), an 1872 Victorian wood frame house built as a residence for the commander of Camp Independence and now furnished with period pieces. Also in town is the ca. 1900 wood frame **home of Mary Austin** (Market Street, private). Austin, a writer, lived here at the turn of the century and wrote *The Land of Little Rain,* a collection of essays about the region.

Halfway between Independence and Lone Pine is the **site of Manzanar** (Route 395), the first of the Japanese relocation camps of World War II. Following the attack on Pearl Harbor, nearly a century of anti-Asian sentiments came to a head in California with the forced relocation of 110,000 Japanese-Americans, both citizens and Asians, to concentration camps in remote areas. Over 10,000 internees lived in Manzanar's pine-and-tarpaper barracks. All that remains of the camp is the gymnasium, the foundations of the other buildings, and the two stone guard stations that once marked the entrance.

The town of **Lone Pine** is the gateway to **Mount Whitney,** at 14,495 feet the tallest peak in the "Lower Forty-eight" of the United States. Also near Lone Pine are the jumble of weathered and eroded rocks called the **Alabama Hills,** last remnant of a mountain range that long preceded the Sierra. It has been a frequent locale for shooting Westerns and other films.

KAWEAH

Visitors to Sequoia National Park may wish to stop briefly at
Kaweah, three miles north of Three Rivers on North Fork Road. A
post office is the only survivor of an ambitious utopian colony
founded there in 1885. This mountainous and heavily forested area
had been the subject of contention between sheep ranchers, who
brought their flocks here from the San Joaquin Valley for the summer, and conservationists, who wanted the land protected from
overgrazing and other abuses. Suddenly, in a single day, fifty-three
people filed contiguous land claims on the Kaweah River and the
Giant Forest. The claimants were all members of the Kaweah
Cooperative Commonwealth, a leftist utopian experiment that eventually attracted up to 400 colonists to what was to become a cooperative lumbering venture. The founder was Burnette Haskell, editor
of the radical paper *Truth,* which bore as its motto: *"Truth* is five
cents a copy and dynamite is forty cents a pound." Nevertheless, the
colonists were peaceful and in the main well liked by the few people
already in the area. They logged only smaller trees, naming the
giants for their heroes. General Grant Tree was called by them
"Karl Marx." The community died in 1892, in part due to internal
strife, but mostly due to the law that created Sequoia and General
Grant national parks, which effectively evicted them.

THE SAN JOAQUIN VALLEY

The San Joaquin Valley, which comprises the southern two-thirds of
California's Central Valley, is named for its principal river, which
runs northward for 100 miles before emptying into San Francisco
Bay. The Sacramento–San Joaquin Delta contains over 1,000 miles
of waterways and some of the richest soil in the world.

Below the Tehachapi Pass, at the southern end of the Sierra
Nevada, is the **Tehachapi Loop,** one of the great feats of railroad
engineering. Completed in 1876, this huge, mountainside spiral of
track is so long that the engine of an eighty-five-car freight train
moving along the loop will pass directly over its caboose in the

OVERLEAF: *Sawtooth Ridge, at the northern boundary of Yosemite National Park, shows
the derivation of the Spanish word sierra, which means both "mountain ridge" and
"saw."*

tunnel seventy-seven feet below. A good vantage point and a state **marker** are about seven miles west of Tehachapi on Woodfield–Tehachapi Road.

FORT TEJON

Across the mountains and near Tejon Pass stands this partial reconstruction of a U.S. Army outpost established in 1854 to control Grapevine Pass and manage Indian reservations and mining sites in the area. The army experimented with camels for desert transport here, without great success—although the camels were hardy desert beasts, neither horses nor mules could abide the sight or the smell of them. Originally the fort comprised twenty-seven adobe structures; the three surviving have been restored as a museum of nineteenth-century outpost life, with costumed mannequins, furniture, and firearms of the period.

LOCATION: Off Route 5, 10 miles north of Gorman, in Lebec. HOURS: 10–4 Daily. FEE: Yes. TELEPHONE: 805–248–6692.

The restored Fort Tejon barracks, active from 1854 to 1864.

BAKERSFIELD

The city is named for one of its founders, Colonel Thomas Baker; the land on which it stands was originally a large corral known as Baker's Field, and the name was simply contracted into one word when Baker plotted the town site in 1868. Set on the Kern River, which provided water for irrigation, the town prospered; in 1874 the county seat was moved here. The railroad came through the same year, and Bakersfield became an important agricultural center. The discovery of oil along the river in 1899 gave the region another economic boost. The town was severely damaged by an earthquake in 1952 and has been rebuilt since that time. In downtown Bakersfield, a statue of Father Francisco Garcés (Chester Avenue) commemorates the Franciscan priest and explorer who passed through the area in 1776.

The Kern County Museum

This is one of the nation's best efforts to preserve an area's heritage by moving historic buildings to a single site. There are more than

Equipment issued to nineteenth-century soldiers, inside the Fort Tejon barracks.

sixty restored or re-created structures from Kern County on the sixteen-acre property, including a Wells Fargo stage stop, an 1891 Queen Anne home, vintage professional offices, a jail, a saloon, and even an early oil rig. Smaller artifacts and natural history displays are exhibited in the main museum.

LOCATION: 3801 Chester Avenue. HOURS: 8–3 Monday–Friday, 10–3 Saturday–Sunday. FEE: Yes. TELEPHONE: 805–861–2132.

Just north of **Maricopa,** on Petroleum Club Road between Cadet and Kerto roads, is a **marker** commemorating the Lakeview Number 1 Well, California's most spectacular gusher, which at one time spouted over 100,000 gallons of crude oil daily.

Oil was discovered on the Kern River in 1899, and the region's first commercial oil well was drilled a few months later. In the town of **Taft,** the history of the petroleum industry is chronicled in the **West Kern Oil Museum** (Route 33 and Wood Street, 805–765–6664), which has original oil-drilling equipment, displays describing the Lakeview gusher and other important oil wells, fossils unearthed from the McKittrick tar pit, and rotating exhibits on local history.

Named for an early settler, **Glennville** is the site of the oldest house in Kern County, the **Glennville Adobe** (Route 155). Built before the Civil War as a trading post, it was an important stop on the road to the Kern River mining district. The whitewashed wood frame **Glennville Community Church** (Route 155), dating from the 1860s, is reminiscent of the simple village churches of New England.

COLONEL ALLENSWORTH STATE HISTORIC PARK

An escaped slave who joined the Union army during the Civil War, Colonel Allen Allensworth later served as an army chaplain during the Spanish–American War and retired from the army as a colonel in 1906, the highest ranking black officer of his day. Two years later, with four other prominent black men, he established the California Colony and Home Promotion Association, which purchased land for a town that would be settled and governed by African-

OPPOSITE: *Other-worldly tufa formations and squirrel-tail barley at Mono Lake, the remnant of a vast inland sea.*

Americans. The site was well chosen, for it offered cheap farmland, proven artesian wells, and proximity to a Santa Fe Railroad station. As a result, the community became an important shipping point for farmers in the area. It prospered until 1918, when a lack of water due to the drawdown of the water table occasioned the town's decline. The school, three homes, and two stores, all from the period 1908–1918, have been restored and furnished, and more buildings are being restored. The visitor center has interpretive exhibits and a thirty-minute video telling the story of the park.

> LOCATION: Route 43, off Route 99, 7 miles northeast of Earlimart. HOURS: 10–4 Daily. FEE: None. TELEPHONE: 805–849–3433.

PORTERVILLE

Founded as a stage stop and named for its founder, Porter Putnam, the town of Porterville thrives as an agricultural market center. The **Porterville Historical Museum** (257 North D Street, 209–784–2053) is housed in the 1913 Hispanic Revival railroad station, which once belonged to the Southern Pacific Railroad. The museum has a good collection of basketry and other materials created by the Yokuts Indians, the premier basket makers of the region, as well as pioneer artifacts and farm equipment, a restored 1880s blacksmith shop, and a stuffed California condor.

FRESNO

Fresno, the largest city of the San Joaquin Valley, owes its prominence to its location in the center of a fertile agricultural area and its position on the Southern Pacific Railroad. The name is Spanish for ash tree, a variety of which is native here. Information about Fresno's Victorian architecture is available from the **chamber of commerce** (2331 Fresno Street, 209–233–4651). The best example is the restored **Mieux Home Museum** (1007 R Street, 209–233–8007), an ornate, towered and gabled house of the 1880s, furnished as it was originally. The **Kearney Mansion Museum** (7160 Kearney Boulevard, 209–441–0862) preserves the house of M. Theodore Kearney, a land developer and pioneer in the local raisin industry. The mansion was built between 1900 and 1903 in the French

Chateau style but using local materials: adobe brick plastered over and painted light gray and white wood trim. Inside are many original furnishings, including French wallpaper and Kearney's collection of Art Nouveau and Art Deco pieces. The **Fresno Metropolitan Museum** (1555 Van Ness Avenue, 209–441–1444) features rotating and permanent exhibits on art, science, and history, including a collection of Chinese snuff bottles. A fine permanent collection of still-life and trompe l'oeil paintings is also on display.

South of Merced, Route 152 crosses the mountains via **Pacheco Pass,** the chief link between coast and valley since it was discovered by Gabriel Moraga in 1805. It was from here that John Muir experienced the spectacular view of the Sierra Nevada that inspired him to call it the "Range of Light."

MODESTO

Modesto was laid out by the Central Pacific Railroad in 1870, and its position on the railroad made it an important shipping and supply center for this part of the valley. Originally the railroad wanted to name the town for banker William C. Ralston, but he declined the honor, so they named it Modesto, Spanish for "modest," instead. The **McHenry Museum** (1402 I Street, 209–577–5366), housed in a 1912 Classic Revival building, contains exhibits on the area's material culture, including a doctor's office, a blacksmith's forge, and a general store.

STOCKTON

Stockton owes its continuing prominence to the deep-water channel, ninety-five miles long, that connects it with San Francisco. It was a natural route for miners and their supplies on their way to the southern mines during the gold rush; later, when wheat farming ruled the valley, the channel made Stockton an important shipping port, and it remains so today, for both produce and manufactured goods.

From 1832 to 1845 the Hudson's Bay Company quartered a group of French Canadian trappers here, at a place then called

French Camp. In 1847 Captain Charles M. Weber arrived and founded the town, which he named Stockton in 1848, in honor of Commodore Robert F. Stockton. The town's earliest industry was shipbuilding, and it was later the home of the Stephens Brothers Company, builders of yachts and other luxury craft. Benjamin Holt of Stockton played an important role in mechanizing American agriculture: He developed the Caterpillar tractor and manufactured the first mass-produced harvesters here in 1876. Holt also developed harvesters with adjustable wheels to follow the contours of hills, opening up previously unarable terrain to mechanized agriculture.

Haggin Museum

This regional museum records Stockton's history and its industries and displays a fine collection of American and French paintings. There are exhibits devoted to the life of Charles M. Weber as well as period rooms and buildings. The American Indian Gallery contains a large basketry collection. The Historic Vehicles Gallery focuses on firefighting equipment, with a steam fire engine (the second oldest on display in the country) that was shipped around the Horn from the East in 1862. Holt Memorial Hall showcases the work of Benjamin Holt, including a large early tractor and an even larger 1904 harvester. The Storefronts Gallery is a re-creation of a turn-of-the-century California town, with a drugstore, blacksmith shop, harness maker, saloon, and a Chinese herb store that was saved from demolition in the 1960s, with nearly all of its items intact. The California Room includes exhibits about shipbuilding, notably a 1926 luxury pleasure craft built by Stephens Brothers. The museum's collection of American paintings includes works by Albert Bierstadt, George Inness, Thomas Moran, William Bradford, Thomas Hill, and E. L. Henry.

LOCATION: 1201 North Pershing Avenue. HOURS: 1:30–5 Tuesday–Sunday. FEE: None. TELEPHONE: 209–462–4116.

A **monument** on East Weber Street in downtown Stockton pays tribute to Mexican War hero John Brown, nicknamed Juan Flaco (Lean John), who is believed to be buried nearby. In September 1846, Brown rode 500 miles from Los Angeles to San Francisco in five days to summon help from Commodore Robert F. Stockton for an American garrison under attack. (Brown concealed the message, written on cigarette paper, in his long hair.) The reinforcements soon arrived by sea.

The residential districts of Stockton preserve some Victorian architecture and early cemeteries. At **Stockton Rural Cemetery** (Cemetery Lane) is the Reuel Colt Gridley Monument, dedicated to a man who raised $275,000 for the Union's sanitary fund during the Civil War by selling and reselling a single sack of flour. The **Temple Israel Cemetery** (Acacia and Union streets), which opened in 1851 on land donated by Stockton's founder, is the oldest Jewish cemetery in continuous use west of the Rocky Mountains.

LODI

Lodi is a typical valley town, with broad tree-lined avenues; much of the surrounding area is given over to vineyards. At Pine and Sacramento streets is the 1907 **Lodi Arch,** a ceremonial arch in the Mission Revival style topped with a statue of a brown bear. The **San Joaquin County Historical Museum** (11793 North Micke Grove Road, 209–368–9154) displays an excellent collection of hand tools, tractors dating from the first half of this century, an original blacksmith shop, a re-created harness shop, period rooms, a one-room schoolhouse, and exhibits on viticulture and ranching.

Near Lodi two smaller towns also retain the look of the last quarter of the nineteenth century. **Woodbridge**, two miles northwest of Lodi, began in 1852 when a man named Woods operated a ferry across the Mokelumne River here; six years later he installed a bridge, and the town was born and named. On lower Sacramento Road are several brick Victorian buildings, notably the tall, slender **Masonic Hall,** built in 1882. On Route 12, about eight miles east of Lodi, is **Lockeford,** named after its original settler, Dean Jewett Locke, who operated a river ford. (It is said that when the Locke brothers arrived in 1851, they spent their first night in the trees, terrorized by grizzly bears.) Of particular note are the 1869 **Lockeford Seventh-Day Adventist Church** on Elliot Road and a brick house and barn farther up the same street, built in 1865 by the Locke family. The brick **Harmony Grove Methodist Church** (Locke Road, two miles west of Lockeford), completed in 1861, shows Gothic and Greek Revival influences.

CHAPTER THREE

THE
CENTRAL
COAST

OPPOSITE: *William Randolph Hearst's grandiose mansion at San Simeon, now owned by the state.*

T he California coast between the Los Angeles County border and San Simeon in northern San Luis Obispo County has been developed at a less hectic pace than it has around the major metropolitan centers. The southernmost part of this region is the agriculturally important Oxnard Plain, which embraces most of Ventura County. The discovery of oil nearby kept the city of Ventura prosperous. The middle section of the region consists of the narrow strip of Santa Barbara coast where the coastal plain is nowhere more than ten miles wide and the chaparral-clad mountains seem on the verge of plunging into the sea. To the north, the land is of varied character, its inland section containing fertile ranchlands and oak-dotted valleys along with such smaller cities as San Luis Obispo and Paso Robles.

The whole region was populated by Chumash Indians before the Spanish arrived. Skilled boatmen, the Chumash were accustomed to canoeing along the coast and out to the Channel Islands. To convert and govern them, the Spaniards established missions along the coast at San Buenaventura, Santa Barbara, La Purísima Concepción, Santa Inés, San Luis Obispo, and San Miguel. Following the missions came the Mexican rancheros, and then the Yankee ranchers whose successors still work the land today. Among the latecomers to the region was William Randolph Hearst, who used his 240,000-acre ranch at San Simeon as the site of a great fantasy castle.

This chapter begins north of Los Angeles County and travels along the coast, then proceeds inland through the missions and agricultural towns of the valleys to San Simeon. The tour of the Monterey coast follows the curve of the Monterey peninsula to Carmel, and ends in Santa Cruz, at the northwestern end of the bay.

In the town of **Thousand Oaks** is the **Stagecoach Inn** (51 Vento Park Road, 805–498–9441). This reconstruction—the original, built in 1876, burned in 1970—of a major stagecoach stop on the great Butterfield Stage contains period rooms, including a kitchen, and a stagecoach. Nearby are re-creations of a Chumash dwelling, a farmer's cabin, and a rancho-style adobe house.

VENTURA

The city's name is derived from the name of the mission, San Buenaventura, around which it grew. Though it has since grown much larger through commerce in agriculture and nearby oil

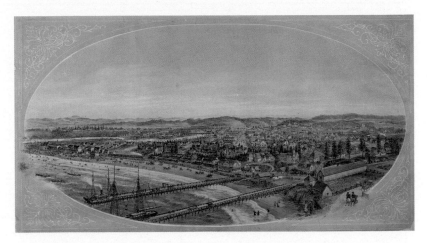

Santa Cruz in 1878, shown in a lithograph by Henry Steinegger, a San Francisco artist who published views of several California cities during the 1880s land boom.

strikes, the town still offers surprising glimpses of its Hispanic past. **Mission San Buenaventura** (211 East Main Street, 805–648–4496), the ninth mission in the twenty-one-mission chain, was founded by Father Junípero Serra in 1782. Only the restored church building (1809) survives from what was an extensive complex. A small museum features, among other items, one of the mission's original wooden bells.

The **Albinger Archaeological Museum** (113 East Main Street, 805–648–5823) has a rich store of Chumash artifacts from the area, as well as memorabilia from the successive waves of settlers on the coastal plain. The nearby **Ventura County Historical Museum** (100 East Main Street, 805–653–0323) contains artifacts and dioramas representing the Indian, Spanish, Mexican, Anglo-American, and Chinese cultures that have contributed to Ventura's history. Two restored adobe houses, the 1857 **Ortega Adobe** (215 West Main Street, 805–658–4726) and the 1847 **Olivas Adobe** (4200 Olivas Park Drive, 805–644–4346) are maintained by the city; rooms in both display furnishings typical of various periods during which the houses were occupied.

OJAI

Ever since Charles Nordhoff began promoting the inland Ojai Valley north of Ventura as a resort in the 1870s, people have been drawn to Ojai to enjoy its tranquil beauty. (When *Lost Horizon* wa filmed in 1937, Ojai was the setting for Shangri-La.) The town ·

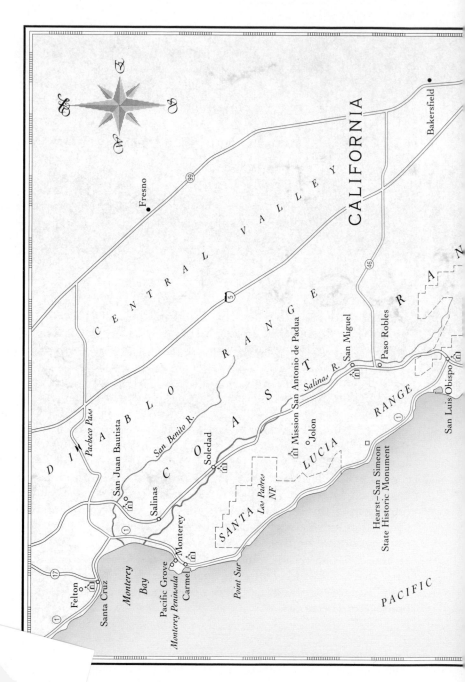

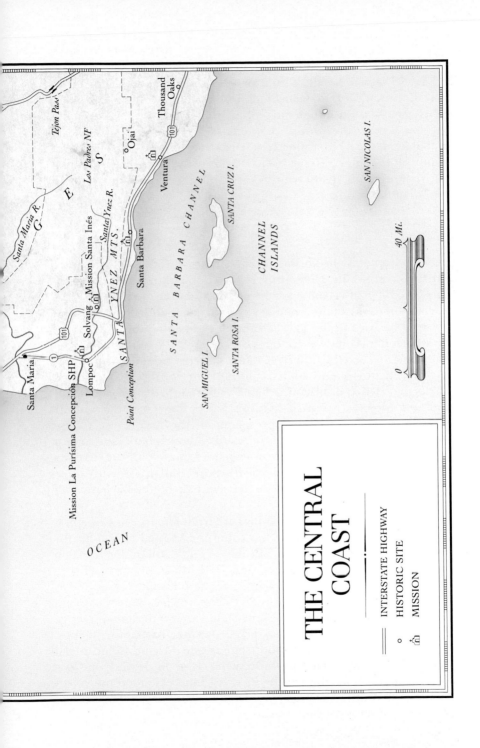

THE CENTRAL COAST

― INTERSTATE HIGHWAY

o HISTORIC SITE

⌂ MISSION

OCEAN

Santa Maria R.

Tejon Paso

Los Padres NF

Santa Maria

Mission La Purísima Concepción SHP

Lompoc

Solvang Mission Santa Inés

Santa Ynez R.

SANTA YNEZ MTS.

Point Conception

Santa Barbara

SANTA BARBARA CHANNEL

SAN MIGUEL I.

SANTA ROSA I.

SANTA CRUZ I.

CHANNEL
ISLANDS

Ventura

Ojai

Thousand
Oaks

SAN NICOLAS I.

0   40 Mi.

originally named Nordhoff, but in 1917 the name was changed to that of the valley. *Ojai* means moon in a Chumash dialect. Orange trees greatly outnumber citizens in this valley with its arcaded Mission Revival downtown. A fine survey of the area's history is available at the **Ojai Valley Historical Society and Museum** (109 South Montgomery Street, 805–646–2290), where exhibits depict native American history and crafts, pioneers, and the natural history of the region.

SANTA BARBARA

Juan Rodríguez Cabrillo was the first European to see the site of Santa Barbara, in 1542, but it was Sebastián Vizcaíno who christened it half a century later in 1602. Settlers arrived in 1782, when Father Serra and a military contingent founded the presidio of Santa Barbara in the middle of what is now the downtown area. The mission was established four years later on the hills overlooking the presidio. Together the two establishments oriented the future city at the north end of its bay, looking south. Few cities in California have so distinguished and well preserved a Hispanic past, and few look as Spanish as does Santa Barbara. Part of its appearance is due to active preservation; the rest is due to the construction of layer after layer of Spanish Revival buildings since a major earthquake in 1925 demolished many of the earlier downtown facades. George Washington Smith, the premier architect of the style, worked extensively in Santa Barbara and surrounding towns.

The Americans took Santa Barbara from Mexico on Christmas Day 1846, but members of the two cultures coexisted peacefully for some years thereafter. The sale of cattle to gold rush miners became a lucrative business for Yankee and Hispanic rancheros. "Every bullock was a skinful of silver," one wrote, "and his marrow as fine as gold." In earlier days vaqueros used to discard the carcasses, saving only the hides for trade with passing ships. After a decade of plenty, however, droughts in the 1860s plagued Santa Barbara's ranches, impoverishing many of the older settlers and forcing them to sell out. The Southern Pacific Railroad arrived in 1887 from Los Angeles, and within two decades its Coast Line extended up to San Francisco. With these connections Santa Barbara became accessible, and its rise as a tourist center began.

Santa Barbara Historical Society Museum

The museum houses a good collection of fine art, artifacts, and decorative arts from Santa Barbara's past. Particularly impressive is a magnificent gold-leaf Chinese tong shrine. This masterpiece of the woodcarver's art was at the spiritual center of the Santa Barbara branch of the Chee Kung Tong, a secret political society that existed at the turn of the century. On the museum grounds stand two historic adobes: the **Covarrubias Adobe,** built here in 1817 and thought by some to be the site of the last congress of Mexican California; and the 1836 **Historic Adobe,** twice moved before coming to rest here. A mile from the museum is a complex that includes the 1854 **Trussell-Winchester Adobe** and the fourteen-room Victorian **Fernald House,** built in 1862.

LOCATION: 136 East De la Guerra Street. HOURS: 10–5 Tuesday–Saturday, 12–5 Sunday. FEE: None. TELEPHONE: 805–966–1601.

The **Santa Barbara Museum of Art** (1130 State Street, 805–963–4364) contains a selective but high-quality assemblage of fine arts from all periods, with particularly good groups of American and Oriental art and ancient statuary. Among the American pieces are works by George Inness, Winslow Homer, Edward Hopper, and Robert Henri.

El Presidio de Santa Barbara State Historic Park

On this site stands the reconstructed adobe chapel and several outbuildings from the original settlement of Santa Barbara, dating from 1782. Soldiers' and priests' quarters have been restored with appropriate furnishings, as has the simple chapel that served the garrison. **El Cuartel,** a small two-room adobe structure on the site, is the last vestige of an original wing of the presidio that probably dates from 1782, making it the oldest adobe building in the city. It has been refurbished and given historically accurate furnishings.

LOCATION: 122–129 East Cañon Perdido. HOURS: 10:30–4:30 Daily. FEE: None. TELEPHONE: 805–966–9719.

The fanciful Santa Barbara County Courthouse, completed in 1929, uses the motifs of Spanish Colonial architecture in an exaggerated scale.

The 1929 Spanish Revival **Santa Barbara County Courthouse** (1100 Anacapa Street), a masterpiece of the style, typifies the image Santa Barbara chose for itself after the 1925 earthquake. Second-floor murals depict local events such as the discovery by Cabrillo and the building of the mission. The structure resembles a grandee's palace as much as it does a courthouse. **Casa de la Guerra** (13 East De la Guerra Street), a U-shaped adobe with a semi-enclosed courtyard, was begun in 1819; expansions of the original building continued through the 1820s. Don José de la Guerra was commander of the presidio, and his home, known for many years simply as "La Casa Grande," was the social center of the town. Today, the home is restored and open to the public, although it has been made part of a Spanish-style shopping mall called El Paseo.

Mission Santa Barbara

This mission is among the most dramatic works of mission architecture and one of the best preserved. The mission was founded in 1786, but the present church and outbuildings (the

The Santa Barbara County Courthouse murals, showing important scenes in early California history, were painted by Dan Sayre Groesbeck, a self-taught local artist.

fourth group erected on the site) were completed in 1820. Composed of native sandstone, the church is beautifully proportioned, with twin arcaded and domed masonry towers and regular buttressing to either side. The design for the church was taken from an eighteenth-century Spanish illustration in a translation of the work of the Roman architect Vitruvius (who did not supply his own illustrations). The book that inspired the architecture still reposes in the mission library today. A fine garden is maintained in the cemetery area beside the church, where some 4,000 converts were buried.

LOCATION: 2201 Laguna Street. HOURS: 9–5 Daily. FEE: Yes. TELEPHONE: 805–682–4149.

Originally established to house an ornithology collection, the **Santa Barbara Museum of Natural History** (2559 Puesta del Sol, 805–682–4711) has broadened its scope to include exhibits of the mammals, marine animals, insects, plants, and minerals of the region; displays of Chumash artifacts; and a plantetarium.

Set in the foothills of the Santa Ynez Mountains, the **Santa Barbara Botanic Garden** (1212 Mission Canyon Road, 805–682–4726) emphasizes the native flora of California with plantings that include stands of full-grown native trees. Over 1,000 species of plants are represented in the sixty-five-acre preserve. Five miles of trails wind through meadows and woodlands and along Mission Creek.

SOLVANG

Hidden in the Santa Ynez Mountains thirty miles west of Santa Barbara, the community of Solvang, known for its Danish Culture and architecture, was founded in 1911 as an experiment in folk education by Danish settlers from Iowa. Buying a tract of ranchland near Mission Santa Inés, the stockholders established both a school and a town. The latter survived and prospered, while the former did not. Among the few buildings in town that predate the Danish purchase is **Mattei's Tavern** (Route 154, off Route 101), built in 1888, the year after a rail line pushed into the area, and still operating as a restaurant today.

Mission Santa Inés

The nineteenth mission to be founded, Santa Inés was first raised in 1804 in this comparatively remote spot. The first church, destroyed in an 1812 earthquake, was replaced by 1817. The present structure on the site consists of the 1817 church and part of the convent; it houses a small museum. After Mexico gained its independence from Spain, the new authorities determined that the missions themselves should finance the garrisons of soldiers that "protected" them. Since enmity between the Indians and the soldiers was already long established, it took only the beating of a neophyte by a sergeant to set off a destructive conflict both here and at Mission La Purísima Concepción some twenty miles to the west. Hardly had Santa Inés recovered from the revolt when Mexico secularized the missions and ordered most of the mission lands to be sold off. The Franciscans finally abandoned Santa Inés in 1849.

LOCATION: 1760 Mission Drive. HOURS: June through August: 9–5:30 Daily; September through May: 9–4:30 Daily. FEE: Yes. TELEPHONE: 805–688–4815.

OPPOSITE: *The two bell towers of Mission Santa Barbara, the only California mission that has remained continuously in the hands of the Franciscan order.*

MISSION LA PURISIMA CONCEPCION

Founded in 1787, the eleventh of the Franciscan missions, La Purísima Concepción grew and prospered, especially during the tenure of Father Mariano Payeras, who is buried beneath the altar. Earthquake damage in 1812 became irreparable when a flood followed the tremor, and the mission had to be moved to a spot four miles away on the other side of the river. The present far-reaching restoration includes the church, the monastery, and workshops built between 1815 and the early 1820s. Like Mission Santa Inés, Purísima suffered a revolt of its neophytes in 1824; here they succeeded in holding the mission for over a month, at the conclusion of which at least seven of the Indian leaders were executed. Father Payeras, who might have prevented the revolt, had died the year before. The mission, like San Antonio de Padua far to the north, has been well restored and remains in a rural

Mission La Purísima Concepción, which fell into ruin after it was abandoned in the 1840s, was extensively restored by the Civilian Conservation Corps beginning in 1934.

setting—offering a remarkably vivid picture of mission life in the early nineteenth century. Purísima is now a state historic park, complete with appropriately garbed guides who demonstrate the crafts and daily routines of the period.

LOCATION: 2295 Purisima Road, Lompoc. HOURS: 9–5 Daily. FEE: Yes. TELEPHONE: 805–733–3713.

SAN LUIS OBISPO

In this town, the **San Luis Obispo County Historical Museum** (696 Monterey Street, 805–543–0638) displays a variety of items, from historic photographs to a period parlor to a mail wagon, detailing the early history of the area. They operate the **Dallidet Adobe** (1185 Pacific Street), the restored late-1850s home of one of the area's pioneer viticulturists.

The main chapel at Mission La Purísima Concepción, with its handsome pulpit, was restored using evidence from other missions.

Mission San Luis Obispo de Tolosa

Founded in 1772, this was the fifth Spanish mission in upper California and one of the first to make extensive use of the red roofing tiles so intimately associated with the Mission style today. Local Indians were receptive to the missionaries, but a neighboring group, envious of their prosperity, set fire to the mission's thatched roofs with flaming arrows; roof tiles were the answer. The Mission-style adobe church has been restored to its original appearance, and the Spanish paintings that hang inside have also been restored. A museum exhibits the original altar and other mission and Indian artifacts. The gardens are also open to the public.

> LOCATION: Chorro and Monterey streets. HOURS: May through September: 9–5 Daily; October through April: 9–4 Daily. FEE: Yes. TELEPHONE: 805–543–6850.

PASO ROBLES

Almost due north of San Luis Obispo, the pretty town of Paso Robles is set among oak copses, almond orchards, and grain ranches. Although it was not founded until 1886, its name goes back more than a century. "El paso de los robles"—the pass of the oaks—was first named by Pedro Font to commemorate the path that Juan Bautista de Anza's party found through the oak woodlands here in 1776. The town was noted for its sulfur springs both before and after Europeans occupied the area; padres of Mission San Miguel were the first to dam the warm stream, using a rude log barricade to create a rustic hot-springs resort. The restored **Call-Booth House** (1315 Vine Street, 805–238–5473) gives an idea of what houses in the town looked like just before the turn of the century. The **Pioneer Museum** (Riverside Avenue) is an eclectic mix of Indian and pioneer artifacts, together with donated collections, such as one of different varieties of barbed wire.

SAN MIGUEL

The restored **Ríos-Caledonia Adobe** (700 Mission Street, 805–467–3357) was built in 1846 by Petronilo Ríos, a local rancher. Its comparatively grand and symmetrical two-story construction shows the influence of the Monterey style introduced by Thomas Larkin.

Mission San Miguel Arcángel

Eight miles north of Paso Robles, San Miguel, founded by Father Lasuén in 1797, was the sixteenth mission, filling the gap between San Antonio de Padua to the north and San Luis Obispo to the south. Its surviving colonnaded outbuildings have a somewhat comical aspect, owing to the fact that the arches are of different sizes.

The church's interior, however, is the best preserved and one of the most elaborate of any mission church in California. The painting and decoration, executed in colors extracted from flowers and minerals and held in a matrix composed of bone marrow, are remarkably intricate, including geometric designs as well as representational and trompe l'oeil patterns. The reredos, centered on a beautiful image of San Miguel, features marbled columns and delicate floral tracery topped by a radiant Eye of God. Spanish painter Esteban Munras contributed to the design and execution, although Indian neophytes did much of the actual painting. The work dates from the 1820s, just after the present church (the third to be built on the site) was completed.

LOCATION: 801 Mission Street. HOURS: 9:30–4:30 Daily. FEE: None. TELEPHONE: 805–467–3256.

HEARST–SAN SIMEON STATE HISTORICAL MONUMENT

William Randolph Hearst's dream castle—stuffed with his various collections and constructed in the Mediterranean Revival style—rose over a period of almost three decades, between 1919 and 1947. Designed by the newspaper magnate's favorite architect, Julia Morgan, the remarkable complex is now owned by the state and open for tours.

The castle—known to the family as La Cuesta Encantada, or the Enchanted Hill—stands on a vast estate that originally comprised almost 250,000 acres. The grounds included a private zoo, and the merest picnic organized for guests inevitably took on the character of a safari. Casa Grande, the main building, is constructed of poured concrete with limestone reliefs incorporating thirteenth- to sixteenth-century motifs. Elaborate twin bell towers, embellished

OVERLEAF: *Hearst Castle's enormous indoor pool, known as the Roman pool, is constructed of hand-set blue glass Murano tiles fused with gold leaf.*

with blue and gold tiles, hold a thirty-six-bell carillon made in Belgium. Inside, the mansion's 130 rooms display Hearst's expansive art collection, including Gothic and Renaissance furniture, sixteenth-century tapestries, Greek pottery, Roman mosaics, medieval paintings, and Neoclassical statuary. The estate also includes three guest houses and the Neptune Pool, a Greco-Roman fantasy surrounded by colonnades and a temple facade. The place is so huge that visitors have a choice of tours, since no single tour could be comprehensive.

> LOCATION: Route 1, San Simeon. HOURS: April through October: 8–5 Daily; November through March: 8–3 Daily. FEE: Yes. TELEPHONE: 805–927–4621.

THE   MONTEREY   COAST

Monterey Bay is overlooked by the redwood-covered Santa Cruz Mountains to the northeast and by the drier Gabilan and Santa Lucia ranges to the southeast. The Santa Lucia range runs close to the Pacific shore, creating the famous **Big Sur** coast between San Simeon and Carmel. The Big Sur is known for groves of redwoods and rocky beaches, and has been the retreat of artists and writers such as Ansel Adams and Henry Miller. The dramatic scenery is visible along Route 1. The Salinas River drains into the bay between these ranges. The bay itself is a remarkable marine habitat, from its tidal fringes to the kelp beds along the continental shelf to the deep-sea submarine canyon that penetrates the bay along the line of its pre-Pleistocene contours. The richness of the littoral may have attracted the Indian population to the spot over 10,000 years ago. Until the Spanish arrived, the Indians followed a nomadic life-style, subsisting on what the ocean offered, from limpets to otters. The explorer Jean-François de Galaup, comte de La Pérouse, saw the last vestiges of this culture on his visit to the area in the 1780s.

In 1770 the Spanish established the presidio of Monterey and the great mission of San Carlos Borromeo del Río Carmelo. The padres also expanded into the inland valleys, establishing the missions of San Antonio de Padua, San Miguel Arcángel, Soledad, and San Juan Bautista. By 1775 Monterey was the capital of Spanish California—a position it retained under Mexican rule until July 7,

OPPOSITE: *Along Big Sur, one of the most spectacular seacoasts in the world, the mountains seem to plunge violently into the sea.*

1846, when Commodore John D. Sloat sailed into the bay and took Monterey for the Americans.

California's constitutional convention was held in the ex-capital in 1849, but thereafter Monterey passed into relative obscurity until it began to be rediscovered as a resort. Already in 1879, Robert Louis Stevenson lamented the passing of the Hispanic town with the arrival of the first hotel. Nevertheless, Monterey did experience a boom of a different sort in the twentieth century, when it became a major center for sardine fisheries, as well as for the processing of other ocean fish. The cannery row that John Steinbeck described in his novel of that name, however, has long since given way to the tourist trade, and the unmistakable odor produced by an annual catch of 200,000 tons of sardines has vanished. Meanwhile, the surrounding agricultural areas—the coastal plains, the alluvial basins, and the great Salinas Valley—have prospered, as farmers grow artichokes and Brussels sprouts on the coast and lettuce, broccoli, and other vegetables inland.

MISSION SAN ANTONIO DE PADUA

The best restored of all the Franciscan missions, San Antonio is set in an area about thirty miles north of San Simeon and about thirty miles south of Soledad that still resembles the land as it was when the padres came. The aptly named Valley of the Oaks remains pristine because William Randolph Hearst had a ranch here, which he eventually gave to the government for use as Fort Hunter-Liggett. Among a cluster of buildings on a hill near the mission is **Las Milpitas,** the Mission Revival building created by Julia Morgan for Hearst early in this century. So faithful a revival is it that the ranch headquarters (now an army headquarters) is often mistaken for the real mission beyond. San Antonio de Padua is typical of the Spanish missions; its simple but dramatic church has been fully restored, and the quadrangle beside it still serves religious functions. Scattered about the grounds are a tannery, some waterworks, and other evidence of the Spanish presence. The museum is first-rate, with exhibits on topics from music to winemaking, all illustrated with authentic artifacts. The mission was founded in 1771, making it the third of the missions, but the surviving church dates from 1813.

LOCATION: Jolon Road, Fort Hunter-Liggett, Jolon. HOURS: 10–4 Monday–Saturday, 11–5 Sunday. FEE: None. TELEPHONE: 408–385–4478.

MISSION NUESTRA SENORA DE LA SOLEDAD

Today Soledad is a prosperous agricultural town twenty-six miles southeast of Salinas, but in 1791, when Father Lasuén founded Mission Nuestra Señora de la Soledad, the thirteenth mission, the building was an outpost in the middle of nowhere, well deserving the name Soledad, which in Spanish means solitude. The windy, isolated locale was wearisome and mentally draining to the monks. Disease decimated the Indian converts, and the mission property suffered from floods. The original building collapsed in 1831; one chapel is now reconstructed on the site, together with a small museum and the crumbling remains of the old church's walls.

LOCATION: Route 1, Fort Romie Road, Soledad. HOURS: 9–4 Wednesday–Monday. FEE: None. TELEPHONE: 408–678–3197.

Three miles south of Soledad, at the Los Coches Rancho Wayside Campground, is the **Los Coches Adobe** (408–678–3963), a house built by an American immigrant in 1843 and later used as a stage station and post office. John C. Frémont stopped here in 1846 and 1847, as his small force of sharpshooters marched and countermarched around California.

SALINAS

The commercial center of the rich Salinas Valley, Salinas was founded in 1856 and soon became the base for the area's cattle ranching. It preserves two outstanding older homes that show the life of Mexican and Yankee immigrants. The **Boronda Adobe** (333 Boronda Road, 408–757–8085) was raised by the land grantee José Eusebio Boronda between 1844 and 1848. Although it is only one story tall, it shows the influence of Larkin's Monterey style in its hipped roof and symmetrical proportions. The Boronda family at one time had thirteen children living under this roof. The house has been carefully restored to reflect its appearance in the Borondas' day. The **Harvey-Baker House** (238 East Romie Lane, 408–757–8085) is a redwood frame home built by the first mayor of Salinas in 1868 from planks dragged all the way from Moss Landing on the coast. The original furnishings are still in the house.

The **Steinbeck House** (132 Central Avenue), now a restaurant, is the 1897 turreted Victorian house where Nobel-prize-winning author John Steinbeck was born in 1902. He describes life in the Salinas Valley in his collection of stories entitled *The Long Valley,* and the region is the setting for much of his work, including the novels *East of Eden, Of Mice and Men,* and *Tortilla Flat.*

CARMEL

At the beginning of the twentieth century, the Carmel Development Company established an artists' colony here to attract the affluent who would want to live among painters and writers. The firm offered special low rates to artists, including such minor literary lights as poet George Sterling and author Mary Austin. The colony was noted for its life-style, not its production, but it did lure a number of well-to-do residents who built a harmonious town of tasteful cottages, most of which are difficult to see from the road. Perhaps the best of these is the **Charles Greene Studio** (between 13th and 14th avenues

Mission San Carlos Borromeo del Río Carmelo, an exquisite architectural creation wrought by unskilled hands.

on the west side of Lincoln Street, private), built in 1918 by a principal of the California architecture firm Greene & Greene. The studio is unlike the other Greene & Greene wooden homes in the area, with their overhanging eaves; rather, it suggests a medieval chapel done in differing tones and courses of brick.

Mission San Carlos Borromeo del Río Carmelo

This mission church is the quintessential monument to the hearts and hands of Franciscan California: The combination of unskilled labor and high artistic aspirations resulted in an architectural achievement of poignant beauty. A professional stonemason from Mexico probably participated in designing the sandstone church, completed in 1797: The tower with its Moorish elements, the star window, and the stone catenary arches of the interior (the only stone ceiling arches in any California mission) all bear witness to the anonymous mason's efforts. The star window is tilted slightly to the right; the dome of the tower is practically ovoid; and variations in thickness make the walls curve.

Efforts to restore the church and its quadrangle, which deteriorated after the mission was secularized, began in the 1870s, spurred by the concern of Robert Louis Stevenson, who wrote in 1879, "The United States Mint can coin many millions more dollar pieces, but not a single Indian, and when the Carmel church is in the dust, not all the wealth of the states and territories can replace what has been lost." Both church and quadrangle are now restored, including the marvelous painted decorations on the interior of both the sanctuary and the side chapel. In the latter stands a statue of the Virgin Mary brought from Spain by Father Junípero Serra.

Three of the notable re-created rooms in the quadrangle are Serra's own spartan cell, a kitchen, and the first library in California. Mission Carmel, as the place is commonly known, is also the burial place of three of the most important California Franciscans: Father Serra, who was beatified by the Roman Catholic church in 1988; Father Lasuén, Serra's able successor and the man who had the present church constructed; and Father Crespi, a diarist who recorded a great deal of important information about the early Spanish exploration and settlement of upper California.

LOCATION: 3080 Rio Road. HOURS: 9:30–4:30 Monday–Friday, 10:30–4:30 Sunday. FEE: None. TELEPHONE: 408–624–3600.

Tor House and Hawk Tower

Beside the gaggle of minor literati who settled in Carmel in its days as an art colony lived one poet of major distinction, Robinson Jeffers. He built his stone Tor House here, beginning in 1919, paying for it in part by working for the building's contractor. Later, in 1924, he built Hawk Tower—inspired by the Irish poet William Butler Yeats and named for a sparrow hawk that perched on the rising stones—with his own hands. Jeffers wanted a universal residence, so some of the stones used in the house came from England and the tower contains Hawaiian lava, a stone from the Great Wall of China, and a porthole from the ship on which Napoléon emerged from exile on the island of Elba. The house and tower, with much of the furniture that he and his wife, Una, gathered or had made, are now a museum commemorating Jeffers's life and work.

Jeffers wrote of his perch on this edge of the world: "I could see people living . . . essentially as they did in the Idyls or the Sagas, or in Homer's Ithaca. Here was life purged of its ephemeral accretions. Men were riding after cattle, or plowing the headlands, hovered by white seagulls, as they have done for thousands of years, and will for thousands of years to come." Much of his poetry concerns these people and this setting.

LOCATION: 26304 Ocean View Avenue. HOURS: 10–3 Friday–Saturday. FEE: Yes. TELEPHONE: 408–624–1813.

North of Carmel begins the famous **Seventeen Mile Drive,** which runs through the Del Monte Forest, with its distinctive stands of wind-twisted Monterey cypress, along the coast to Pacific Grove. There is a fee charged to drive along this private road, which originated in the 1880s, when it was used for carriage rides by guests at the Hotel Del Monte. The drive passes some of the world's most famous golf courses, including Pebble Beach, and many elaborate private houses. **Pacific Grove,** at the northern tip of the Monterey peninsula, was founded in 1875 as a Methodist retreat center, the Chatauqua of the West; indeed, it was known as Chatauqua-by-the-Sea. The town still retains some Victorian houses, but perhaps the biggest attraction is the **Point Piños Light** (Asilomar Boulevard, 408–372–4212), the oldest continuously operating lighthouse on the West Coast, in service since 1855.

OPPOSITE: *Tor House, on Carmel Point, was built by the poet Robinson Jeffers largely from stones gathered from a small cove below the site.*

MONTEREY

Capital of both Spanish and Mexican California, Monterey is graced by many well-preserved sites that tell the story of early California in a language of adobe, tile, and wood. Many of the buildings are open to the public and are stocked with authentic furniture and artifacts of their times.

Larkin House

The greatest and most influential of the American-designed adobes is the Larkin House, begun in 1835 by Thomas O. Larkin, who appeared in California in 1832 and was soon a prominent merchant with a trade stretching as far as Hawaii. Because Larkin was one of the few early immigrants not to take Mexican citizenship, he was available to serve as the first and only American consul to Mexican California. What is often regarded as the ultimate flowering of Mexican adobe style—the Monterey style, with its two-story wraparound verandahs and low hipped roofs—was in fact Larkin's invention. True Spanish and Mexican houses, like the 1817 Casa Boronda (Boronda Lane, off Major Sherman Lane, private), were one-story edifices, often with earthen floors and cowhide windows. Larkin introduced not only the widespread use of glass but also the symmetrical, two-story plan of New England colonial homes. As various architectural writers have noted, the only thing Spanish about the Monterey style is the use of adobe. Mexican merchants both in Monterey and elsewhere imitated the style for their own homes. The Larkin house is beautifully restored and contains period antiques, some of which once belonged to Larkin himself.

LOCATION: 510 Calle Principal. HOURS: 10–5 Daily. FEE: Yes. TELEPHONE: 408–649–7118.

The nearby **Casa Amesti** (516 Polk Street, private) is an excellent example of the Larkin influence. Originally a one-story affair built in 1825, it was later remodeled into its archetypal Monterey-style form. It is now occupied by a men's club. Across the street, the two-acre **Cooper-Molera Complex** (408-649-7118) includes several restored buildings put up by John Rogers Cooper, a dealer in hides, tallow, and sea otter pelts who arrived here in 1823.

OPPOSITE: *The Lone Cypress, along the Monterey Peninsula's famous Seventeen-Mile Drive, is said to be the most frequently photographed tree in the world.*

Colton Hall Museum

Superficially different from earlier houses in its use of stone and its symmetrical exterior staircase, Colton Hall also exemplifies the Yankee tradition of symmetrical, two-story facades. It was built between 1846 and 1849 as the first town hall of American-conquered Monterey by Walter Colton, a Vermonter and Yale graduate who had come West as a Navy chaplain. Named the first American *alcalde* (chief magistrate) of the town, he was very proud of his achievement in getting this hall built—with money provided by liquor taxes and gambling fines and labor provided by convicts. "The scheme was regarded with incredulity by many," he wrote. "But the building is finished, and the citizens have assembled in it, and christened it after my name, which will now go down to posterity with odor of gamblers, convicts and tipplers." The convention that drafted California's first constitution was held here in September and October 1849; one of its acts, however, was to move the capital immediately to San Jose, abandoning Monterey. The restored hall is open to the public, with exhibits of artifacts and re-creations devoted to the state constitutional convention and to the history of the city. The **Old Monterey Jail,** an 1854 granite addition to the hall when it served as the county courthouse, was in use for more than a century.

LOCATION: Pacific Street between Madison and Jefferson streets. HOURS: 10–5 Daily. FEE: None. TELEPHONE: 408–375–9944.

The **Allen Knight Maritime Museum** (550 Calle Principal, 408–372–2608) displays a Fresnel lens from Point Sur Lighthouse, ship models, a re-creation of a ship's cabin, and other artifacts, as well as a large photo collection.

The **Stevenson House** (530 Houston Street, 408–649–7118) was begun as a simple adobe in the 1830s. Later owners added the Italianate detailing and opened it as a boardinghouse, where writer Robert Louis Stevenson stayed in 1879, working for local newspapers. The articles he wrote on Monterey were published in the collection *From Scotland to Silverado.* The house, now a museum of Stevenson memorabilia, includes the desk at which he wrote *Treasure Island.* The **Royal Presidio Chapel of San Carlos de Borromeo** (550 Church Street) has served Monterey since 1770. The current building on the site dates from 1795 and is distinguished by its scalloped Neoclassical facade.

Old Custom House

This adobe and wood structure, located across from Fisherman's Wharf, is the oldest public building in California. Begun in 1814, it served from the 1820s as the custom house for the hide-and-tallow export trade that enabled Mexican landowners to buy imported luxuries. Commodore Sloat raised the first American flag over California here on July 7, 1846, upon capturing the town. A museum inside houses artifacts and exhibits related to its history.

LOCATION: 1 Custom House Plaza. HOURS: 10–5 Daily. FEE: Yes. TELEPHONE: 408–649–7118.

Two other early houses nearby—the 1847 **Pacific House** (10 Custom House Plaza, 408–649–7118) and the 1845 **Casa de Oro** (Olivier and

The Monterey Custom House appears today as it might have in the 1830s, when ships cargoes were declared to customs agents here.

Scott streets, 408–649–3364)—are now museums. The former contains exhibits devoted to early Monterey history and a good collection of Ohlone artifacts; the latter has been re-created as the store it once was in the mid-nineteenth century and displays the original safe in which miners stored the gold (*oro* in Spanish) from their strikes.

California's First Theatre (Pacific and Scott streets, 408–375–4916), a wood and adobe single-story house, was opened as a boardinghouse in 1846. In 1847 it was used as a theater by American veterans discharged after the Mexican War. The **First Brick House in California** (Heritage Harbor, 408–375–5356) was started in 1846 by a settler who had come West in an overland wagon train. To build it, he had to create his own kiln and fire his own bricks.

The U.S. armed forces have been important in the area since Commodore Sloat landed his invading force in 1846. Within the present army **Presidio** (Pacific Street, north of Scott Street), housing advanced schools for intelligence services and linguists, is the **Defense Language Institute** (408–647–5000), which contains artifacts relating to the army's presence in Monterey from the 1840s on. A walking tour of the Presidio leads through the ruins of Fort Mervine, the first American fort on the site; a site of Indian grinding and ceremonial rocks; and the place where both Sebastián Vizcaíno (in 1602) and Father Junípero Serra (in 1770) first touched land in Monterey.

SAN JUAN BAUTISTA

Some twelve miles east of Monterey Bay and a slightly shorter distance northeast of Salinas, San Juan Bautista is a remarkably well-preserved small town that shows the evolution of a California locale from mission to American town. Set on a hill overlooking a fertile valley, San Juan owes its excellent state of preservation to the fact that it was bypassed by the railroad in 1876, providing little occasion for redevelopment. Now a popular tourist attraction, it retains the flavor of a nineteenth-century village.

Mission San Juan Bautista

The fifteenth mission, San Juan Bautista was initiated by Father Lasuén in 1797; the present church was completed in 1812. It has

Plaza Hall, an 1860s building in San Juan Bautista State Historic Park, has a ground floor made of old adobe bricks and an upper story of wood. Its builder, Angelo Zanetta, hoped that it would become the county courthouse. Instead it served as his residence, and the second floor became a noted dance hall.

been restored inside and out and contains a reredos painted by Thomas Doak, one of the first American residents of California, who came here in 1818 after jumping ship in Monterey and did the work in exchange for room and board. Also preserved on the site are several period rooms showing aspects of the work and life of the mission, including Father Estevan Tapis's music room, with instruments and arrangements used by mission Indians. According to legend, Father Tapis once calmed an advancing war party of Tulare Indians by playing to them on his barrel organ.

LOCATION: San Juan Bautista Plaza. HOURS: 9:30–5 Daily. FEE: None. TELEPHONE: 408–623–4528.

San Juan Bautista State Historic Park

When the missions were secularized by Mexican decree in 1834, crowds of land grabbers appeared, vying for portions of their grants, and many set their homes right beside the former missions. Such was the case here, where the town of San Juan de Castro—named for founder José María Castro and later renamed San Juan Bautista—grew up around a plaza fronting the mission church. All of the historic structures on this plaza are part of San Juan Bautista State Historic Park. The Monterey-style **Castro House,** built in 1840 by the founder's son, was occupied by the Breen family, survivors of the Donner Party, in the third quarter of the nineteenth century; the current furnishings reflect the home as they lived in it. The **Plaza Hotel,** built in 1858, has been restored to the style of that time. A stable and meeting hall dating from the 1860s are also restored on the plaza.

LOCATION: San Juan Bautista Plaza. HOURS: 10–4:30 Daily. FEE: Yes. TELEPHONE: 408–623–4881.

SANTA CRUZ

Set against the redwood-covered Santa Cruz Mountains at the northern end of Monterey Bay, Santa Cruz should have been a jewel of Spanish California. When Father Fermin Francisco de Lasuén founded Mission Santa Cruz in 1791, many Indians are said to have attended Mass, portending a rich supply of converts. Six years later, however, the secular authorities decreed the establishment of the village of Branciforte nearby. In theory, it was to be everything that the already-established ones at Los Angeles and San Jose were not: well governed, adequately provisioned, and with adobe houses instead of huts. But a number of the settlers who were sent to the pueblo were ex-convicts, and the settlers built right next to the mission instead of the customary one league away. Continual friction between the town and the mission drove away many potential converts. Then, when a pirate attack was rumored in 1818, the padres fled to the hills only to find upon returning that the townspeople had made off with all of the mission's supplies. The mission was the first in California to be secularized (1834), and it soon fell into ruins.

Through much of the nineteenth century, the town's fortunes depended on the redwood lumber shipped from its port and on the pickaxes it manufactured for forty-niners. In the last quarter of the century, tourism became a major industry. The resort town of Capitola, just east of Santa Cruz, got its start in the 1880s. A major casino on the beach in town opened in 1904 and gave rise to the still-active Santa Cruz Boardwalk, the only beachfront amusement park that continues to operate in the state. Santa Cruz is also the seat of a campus of the University of California. The town is surrounded by pockets of productive farming, particularly of fruit and berries; the loganberry was developed here in 1881.

The current **Mission Santa Cruz** (Emmet and High streets, 408–426–5686) is a one-third-scale, latter-day reconstruction of the adobe church that was raised on the site in 1794. Its domed square tower is quite charming, and among the original treasures to be found inside is a statue of Our Lady of Sorrows donated to Father Lasuén by the earlier mission at Carmel. The only original mission building extant is the **Santa Cruz Mission Adobe,** located in **Santa Cruz Mission State Park** (134 School Street, 408–688–3241). The one-story structure was built in 1824 to serve as housing for neophyte Indian families.

Santa Cruz has many interesting small museums. The **Octagon Museum** (118 Cooper Street, 408–425–2540), housed in an 1882 octagonal house, contains changing exhibits relating to such topics as the Chinese in the Monterey Bay area and the local dairy and lumbering industries. The museum also offers information about walking tours of historic houses and public buildings in Santa Cruz and nearby Davenport. The **Santa Cruz City Museum** (1305 East Cliff Drive, 408–429–3773) has exhibits on local natural history—including a hands-on tidepool—and a room dedicated to the artifacts and culture of the Ohlone, the native people of the Monterey Bay region.

In the redwoods seven miles north of Santa Cruz is the town of **Felton,** which contains a **covered bridge** built in 1892 to span the San Lorenzo River. The **Roaring Camp and Big Trees Railroad** (5355 Graham Hill Road, 408–335–4484), an 1880s narrow-gauge steam train that originally served the lumber industry, now services the tourist trade. The railroad has also purchased the rights to run trains from Felton down to Santa Cruz.

CHAPTER FOUR

SAN
FRANCISCO
AND
NORTHERN
CALIFORNIA

OPPOSITE: *San Francisco's Transamerica Pyramid, one of the city's most distinctive modern buildings, forms an unexpected echo to a pagoda in neighboring Chinatown.*

Geologically, San Francisco was made possible toward the end of the last great Ice Age, when melting glaciers raised the level of the oceans and what had been a coastal valley became a great bay extending forty-five miles inland and varying from three to thirteen miles in width. To the south of the bay's entrance loomed a peninsula on which the spine of the Coast Ranges broke into a scattering of barren hills. Where the peninsula reached the bay, the land consisted of shifting sands, marshes, and mud flats. On those flats and on the forty-three hills around them, the city of San Francisco would rise. Of all the possible sites to settle along the coast, it was among the poorest. Water and wood were scarce; the gap in the Coast Ranges allowed fog to roll unhindered over the area on days when, just a few miles north, south, or east, the countryside basked in sunshine. For centuries, the area was chiefly used as a gathering ground for the Tamal Indians of what is now Marin; they took salt from the marshlands.

The indigenous peoples had the bay to themselves until the autumn of 1769, when Sergeant José Francisco Ortega led a detachment of Gaspar de Portolá's expedition to the summit of Sweeney Ridge in what is now Pacifica. From there, the Spaniards first saw the "estuary" that, diarist Father Juan Crespi surmised, "could shelter not only the King's navy, but all the navies of Europe." No Spanish settlers reached San Francisco Bay until 1776, when Mission San Francisco de Asís and the Presidio were founded. The small settlement of Yerba Buena, established near the mission, became a significant trading port in the mid-1830s. In 1846 Captain John B. Montgomery put into the bay in the sloop *Portsmouth,* immediately claiming the whole area for the United States and renaming the town square Portsmouth Square in honor of his ship. Included in the claim was a settlement of little more than 100 Spaniards and Americans, plus an equal number of Indians. The population tripled when Sam Brannan arrived later that year with over 200 Mormon colonists.

From Father Crespi onward, almost every visitor recognized the potential of the bay as the great harbor of the West Coast. In American hands the population had almost tripled again by the end of 1847, numbering 800 souls and 200 buildings. However, all prospects for an orderly expansion of the town ended on May 12, 1848, when Sam Brannan, now a merchant and editor of the *California Star,* returned from the Sierra foothills town of Coloma with a bottle full of gold dust. (Gold had been discovered there by James W. Marshall, who was building a saw mill for his employer, John

In this painting of San Francisco during the gold rush, the tents of newly arrived miners dot Telegraph Hill, atop which stands the telegraph station that signalled the approach of ships.

Augustus Sutter.) "Gold!" he cried, rushing through the streets of San Francisco. "Gold! Gold from the American River!" He had carefully stocked his store with the necessary equipment before he made the dramatic announcement.

The immediate effect of his proclamation was to empty the town of able-bodied men, who shouldered whatever pans and picks they could find and headed east for the hills. Thanks to Brannan's publicity in the *California Star,* the news spread quickly across the nation and the world, inciting a mass migration toward San Francisco. By 1860 the city's population had swollen to 56,000. Settlement spread from Portsmouth Square to Union Square, Jackson Square, North Beach, Chinatown, and South Park. "There has never been anything to parallel San Francisco," wrote Bayard Taylor, "nor will their ever be. Like the magic seed of the Indian juggler that sprouted, blossomed and bore fruit before the very eyes of the onlooker, so San Francisco seems in one day to have accomplished the growth of half a century." This instant urbanism did not come without problems. Twice citizens had to form vigilance committees to control crime and political corruption by means of the noose. (The word *hoodlum* was coined in San Francisco.)

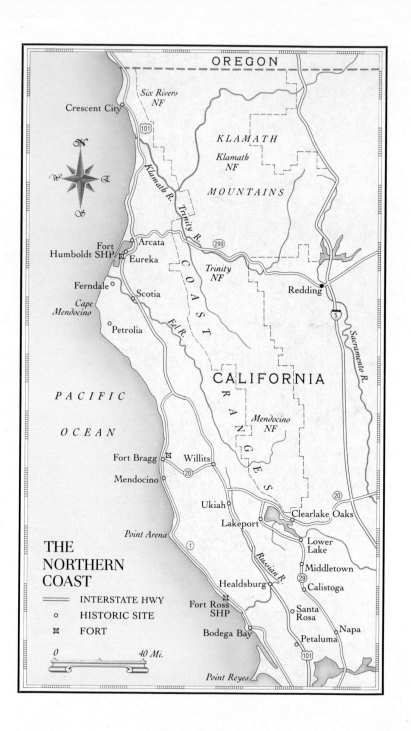

OREGON

Crescent City

Six Rivers NF

101

Klamath R.

Trinity R.

KLAMATH

Klamath NF

MOUNTAINS

Arcata
Fort Humboldt SHP
Eureka

299

Ferndale

Scotia

Trinity NF

Redding

5

Sacramento R.

Cape Mendocino

Petrolia

Eel R.

C O A S T

CALIFORNIA

R A N G E S

PACIFIC

Mendocino NF

OCEAN

Fort Bragg   Willits

20

Mendocino

Ukiah

20

Clearlake Oaks

Lakeport

Point Arena

1

Lower Lake

Middletown

Russian R.

29

Calistoga

Healdsburg

THE
NORTHERN
COAST

Fort Ross SHP

Santa Rosa

Napa

═══   INTERSTATE HWY

o   HISTORIC SITE

Ⱶ   FORT

Bodega Bay

Petaluma

101

0   40 Mi.

Point Reyes

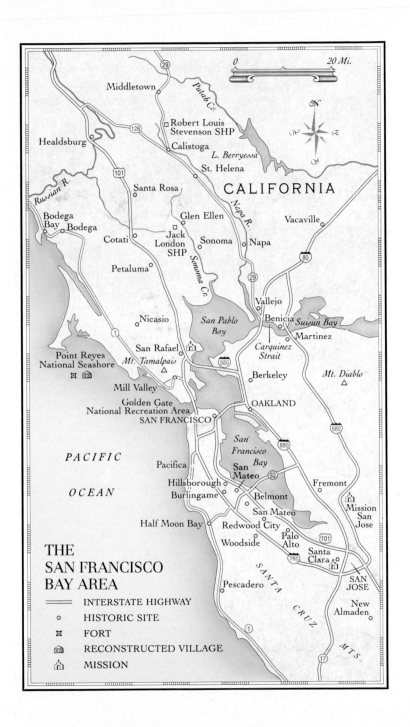

THE
SAN FRANCISCO
BAY AREA

━━━━━ INTERSTATE HIGHWAY
○ HISTORIC SITE
⊠ FORT
🏚 RECONSTRUCTED VILLAGE
⛪ MISSION

The city also acquired an instant aristocracy. The men who would become known as "the Big Four"—Leland Stanford, Collis P. Huntington, Mark Hopkins, and Charles Crocker—all made their initial fortunes as merchants to gold rush miners. As a group they won the right to build the western half of the transcontinental railroad, an endeavor that made them barons of finance and political influence. Others, such as George Hearst, William Ralston, and James C. Flood, grew wealthy on the mines of Nevada's Comstock Lode, first discovered in 1859; and after Andrew S. Hallidie's invention of the cable car in 1871 and its extension two years later, ostentatious homes began to rise on Nob Hill. The best that one English commentator could find to say about the houses was that "they might be swept off by a breath, and leave no trace of their existence." Except with respect to the Flood mansion, his wish was granted.

By 1902 San Francisco—then known from Acapulco to Vancouver simply as the City—had a population of well over 400,000 and so little town planning that the National Board of Fire Underwriters complained, "San Francisco has violated all underwriting traditions and precedents by not burning up." A group of prominent citizens commissioned noted city planner Daniel H. Burnham to create a master plan for San Francisco, which was released on April 17, 1906. One day later, at 5:12 AM, the city began to shake. The first quake lasted two minutes, but fire caused the real damage. Toppling chimneys ignited a blaze that burned uncontrolled for three days, destroying 497 city blocks and 28,000 buildings, about a third of the city. Only when the fire department and the army dynamited the buildings along the west side of newly fashionable Van Ness Avenue was the conflagration checked.

Much of old San Francisco perished during those three days. Will Irwin, a local journalist, eulogized what had gone: "It is as though a pretty, frivolous woman had passed through a great tragedy," he wrote. "She survives, but she is sobered and different." Daniel Burnham, at least, was not displeased about such a future. Immediately after the fire, he rushed to San Francisco, intending to transform his master plan from drawings to reality on the blackened foundations of the demolished city; but for better or worse, he was already too late. Ashes were hardly cold before signs sprouted in rubble-strewn lots proclaiming the imminent construction of new buildings. The only place where Burnham's plan was actually used—albeit in modified form—was for the new Civic Center, whose harmonious proportions and ornate City Hall survive to this day.

The ultimate symbol of the city's resurrection appeared almost a decade later. Opening on February 4, 1915, the Panama–Pacific International Exhibition simultaneously celebrated the completion of the Panama Canal—an event certain to increase San Francisco's importance as the great port of the Pacific—and proclaimed the emergence of San Francisco as a major urban center. The exhibition melded the Beaux-Arts planning principles of Burnham and others with a sensitivity to color and to the interplay of indoor and outdoor spaces, producing the distinctive architectural form that has become the hallmark of the Bay Area. Bernard Maybeck's Palace of Fine Arts, built of stucco to house an exhibit of California painters, was rebuilt of more durable concrete in the 1960s and survives today as the architectural epitome of the exhibition.

This chapter begins in downtown San Francisco and moves through the city, its famous hills and waterfront, its parks, and the island of Alcatraz. It then travels across the bay to Berkeley, Oakland, and the communities of the East Bay, followed by the towns of the Peninsula south of San Francisco, from Pacifica to San Jose. The narrative continues north from the Golden Gate Bridge to Marin County, followed by the Wine Country of the Napa and Sonoma valleys.

S A N   F R A N C I S C O
THE EARLY TOWN CENTER

The original plaza of San Francisco, **Portsmouth Square** lies on Kearny Street between Washington and Clay, with the Financial District to the south, Jackson Square to the east, Chinatown to the west, and North Beach a few blocks to the north. Since John B. Montgomery's arrival on the *Portsmouth*, the shore has been pushed back into the bay to add about five blocks to the east. In the gold rush era, the square was the city's buzzing hub: It was the site of the Parker House, whose windows were imported from Hawaii and whose second story was rented to gamblers in 1849 for $60,000, and of the notorious El Dorado, a gambling den whose first incarnation was a tent where women dealt cards and porters swept up fallen gold dust from the floor. The lone **monument** on the square today is dedicated to Robert Louis Stevenson, who spent parts of 1879 and

OVERLEAF: *The skylines of Victorian and modern San Francisco form a gracious architectural tableau that few American cities can match.*

1880 in San Francisco, waiting to marry his beloved Fanny Osbourne. He often sat here, admiring "the power and beauty of the sea architecture" lying at anchor in the bay.

Originally the waterfront began just east of Montgomery Street, a scant block from Portsmouth Square. At that time Commercial Street, just southeast of the square, was the famous Long Wharf, extending 2,000 feet into the bay, where great ships were moored and everyone from preachers to pickpockets practiced their professions. Montgomery Street was so boggy that, during the wet winter of 1850, a sidewalk was built of strategically sunk pianos, cooking stoves, and tobacco boxes. The main constituent of the landfill that eventually added 100 acres to the city, however, was the ships abandoned by their crews at the height of the gold fever. On part of that fill rose the brick stores, assay offices, and warehouses now known as **Jackson Square**—not really a square but a few urban blocks—located just northeast of Portsmouth Square in the area bordered by Washington, Montgomery, Gold, and Sansome streets. One of the first buildings erected here used unopened boxes of Virginia tobacco for its foundation. So unsettled were the times, however, that before the building was finished the rising price of tobacco had made the foundation worth more than the structure. The sturdy brickwork of the buildings helped them survive the great earthquake of 1906, but only because the navy extended hoses from their tugboats all the way up Telegraph Hill and down Montgomery Street did the area survive the ensuing fire. The district still provides a glimpse of how commercial San Francisco looked in the decade following the gold rush.

The handsome **Ghirardelli Building** (415–417 Jackson Street), constructed in 1853, served as the Ghirardelli chocolate factory until the business moved to Ghirardelli Square in 1894. Two ships were used for the foundation of the 1862 building at **441 Jackson Street.** The 1866 **Hotaling Building** (451 Jackson Street), once the home of the A. P. Hotaling & Company whiskey distillery, also survived the great earthquake and fire, inspiring the ditty:

> If, as they say, God spanked the town
> For being over-frisky,
> Why did He burn His churches down
> And spare Hotaling's whiskey?

OPPOSITE: *Atop one of San Francisco's hills, two women mug for the camera as others watch the destruction of their city in this photograph taken by Arnold Genthe on the morning of the 1906 earthquake.*

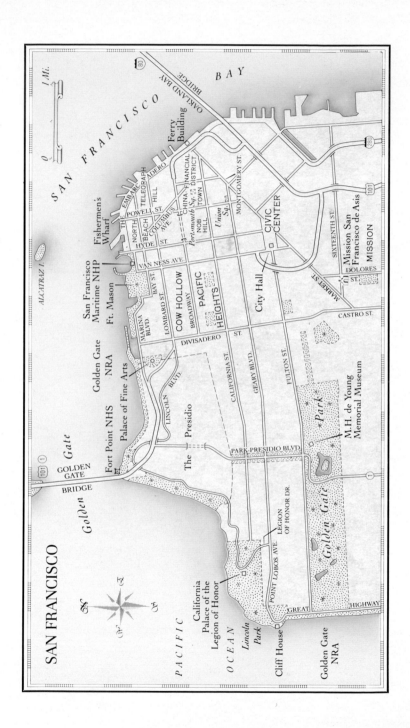

At **498 Jackson Street** stands an Italianate structure built to house the bank of Lucas, Turner & Company in 1854. The bank's managing partner was William Tecumseh Sherman, who a decade later would be marching from Atlanta to the sea as a general in the Union army.

THE FINANCIAL DISTRICT

The Financial District is the one part of San Francisco that suggests an Eastern city, with tall buildings rising on all sides, including such modern landmarks as the **Transamerica Pyramid** (600 Montgomery Street) and the **BankAmerica Corporation's World Headquarters** (555 California Street). The **Old Federal Reserve Bank Building** (400 Sansome Street), built in 1924, is a late example of the pervasive Beaux-Arts influence in San Francisco public buildings. The structure has undergone several remodelings, but it retains the remarkable murals by Jules Guerin.

During the gold rush, the Wells Fargo Company operated a depository for the gold excavated by prospectors, either buying it outright or holding it for safekeeping. The **Wells Fargo History Room** (420 Montgomery Street, 415–396–2619), located in the bank's modern headquarters, features memorabilia from those days, including "wanted" posters and a 130-year-old stagecoach.

Museum of Money of the American West

Housed in the Bank of California building, this museum displays gold ore, silver and gold ingots, and gold rush–era coins valued at more than $1 million. The great variety of privately minted coins and ingots gives a sense of the sudden transformation of San Francisco from a small settlement to a busy city that, almost overnight, had to create everything necessary for its survival, including its own coinage. The museum also displays the pistols used in the Broderick–Terry duel at Lake Merced in 1859. David C. Broderick made a fortune in early San Francisco by privately minting gold coins whose actual gold content was far less than their face value; he was a U.S. senator when California Chief Justice David S. Terry challenged him to a duel, in the course of which Broderick was shot to death. The Classical Revival Bank of California building was built in 1908 on the site of the original Bank of California, founded by William Ralston and Darius Ogden Mills with the then

Clipper ships adorn an elaborate bronze teller's station in the Bank of San Francisco, originally constructed as the headquarters of the Bank of Italy.

astonishing capital of $2 million. The bank was forced to close its doors in 1875, leading to financial panic and Ralston's death—probably by suicide.

LOCATION: 400 California Street. HOURS: 10:30–2:30 Monday–Friday. FEE: None. TELEPHONE: 415–765–2400.

Just across the street, at 465 California Street, stands the **Merchants Exchange** building, whose banking hall is currently occupied by First Interstate Bank. The building, designed in 1903 by San Francisco architect Willis Polk, was once the hub of the city's commercial life. The opulence and pride of turn-of-the-century San Francisco are embodied in William A. Coulter's remarkable eighteen-foot-high murals, among the finest in the city. His depictions of the sailing ships of gold rush San Francisco are both accurate and stirring.

Farther south along Montgomery Street, at number 220, stands the **Mills Building.** In 1891 Daniel Burnham, who later created San Francisco's urban plan, and his partner, John Wellborn Root, designed this understated block with its arched entryway and windows. The **Hallidie Building** (130 Sutter Street, just off Montgomery), created by Willis Polk in 1917, is named for Andrew S. Hallidie, inventor of the cable car. A work of ingenuity and graceful precision, it was the first glass curtain–walled structure ever built—making it a predecessor of the modern skyscraper—although its glass wall was simply affixed to the front of an ordinary wall.

THE EMBARCADERO

The foot of Market Street is now as well known for the Hyatt Regency Hotel and the Justin Herman Plaza as for the **Ferry Building,** once the monumental symbol of San Francisco. Completed in 1898, it was for many years the gateway to the city both for overland rail passengers who had reached the terminus in Oakland and for anyone coming from the East Bay by ferry. In its heyday it handled 50 million passengers per year, a number topped only by London's Charing Cross station. The 235-foot tower is derived from the Giralda Tower in Seville. Though it survived the great earthquake, its clock face was stuck at 5:17 for a year after that

The tower of the Ferry Building, completed in 1898. Every day 170 ferries docked here until the construction of the city's bridges and freeway made auto travel more convenient.

disaster, and its lovely buff-gray sandstone facing fell off, to be replaced by concrete. After many years of disuse, the building is again an embarcation point for ferries serving the Marin County communities of Sausalito, Larkspur, and Tiburon.

A brief walk south along the Embarcadero leads to the **Audiffred Building** (11–21 Mission Street), another survivor from California's turn-of-the-century waterfront. Hypolyte d'Audiffred built the mansard-roofed structure in 1889, and it was reportedly saved from the dynamite brigade—which destroyed numerous buildings nearby in an effort to check the 1906 fire—by an alert bartender, who offered the crew a cart full of wine and two bottles of whiskey per man in return for sparing the structure that housed his bar, the Bulkhead.

Rincon Center (101 Spear Street) preserves the structure of the old Rincon Annex Post Office and houses a series of murals rivaling those of Coit Tower in beauty and scope. The twenty-nine frescoes, executed in the 1940s by Russian-born artist Anton Refregier, represent scenes out of California history from the Indian period through the early 1940s.

MARKET STREET

Market Street breaks up the regular street geometry that defines the downtown area, skewing the grid by bisecting it at a 45-degree angle. Although the name Market Street dates back only to 1847, when it reminded a nostalgic surveyor of a busy thoroughfare in his native Philadelphia, the track it defines has served the city since mission days as the main route from Mission Dolores to the port and its hide-and-tallow trade.

At Market and Battery streets, nestled among the skyscrapers of various banks and service industries, stands the **Mechanics Monument,** a fountain topped by a sculpture of three muscular men forcing a punch through a sheet of metal. Executed in 1899 by Douglas Tilden—the first California sculptor to achieve international fame—it is a memorial to Peter Donahue, who founded the first ironworks in San Francisco. Donahue began by making mining equipment, but his shop was also responsible for the first locomotive, the first government steamer, and the first printing press built in California. The monument also marks the original shoreline of the bay. A block beyond, a **plaque** (406 Market Street) marks the site of the invention of the slot machine by Charles Fey.

Just across Market at the junction with Montgomery Street stands the 1909 **Sheraton Palace Hotel** (2 New Montgomery Street), a structure only slightly less grand than the original Palace, which opened in October 1875. Built by William Ralston, who died before the grand opening, the old Palace was immense: It covered two-and-a-half acres and comprised 800 rooms and a huge, glass-covered central atrium that extended through all of the structure's seven stories. Ralston was so obsessed with his grand project that he bought whole furniture companies to make the furnishings and whole ranches for lumber; he ordered so much carpeting from W. & J. Sloane that the company opened a branch in San Francisco. Among the accessories were 9,000 cuspidors. The old hotel entertained the likes of King David Kalakaua of Hawaii (who died there), Emperor Dom Pedro II of Brazil (who commented, "Nothing makes me ashamed of Brazil so much as the Palace Hotel"), President Ulysses S. Grant, generals William T. Sherman and Philip Sheridan, the charming Oscar Wilde, and the irascible Enrico Caruso. On the morning of the earthquake Caruso, with a towel wrapped about his sensitive throat, fled the hotel carrying a portrait of President Theodore Roosevelt. In the words of one survivor, "The hotel's myriad bay windows on both sides shot out flames at once like a last blaze of glory." The old Palace was through, but it yielded some 15,000 truckloads of landfill debris for new developments at Aquatic Park.

The new Palace Hotel recalls some of the old Palace's grandeur. The present glass-roofed Garden Court is a landmark in its own right: The official opening banquet of the United Nations was held here in 1945. A Pied Piper mural by Maxfield Parrish can be seen in the restaurant that bears its name, and the Happy Valley Cocktail Lounge contains elegant mural portraits of the entertainer Lotta Crabtree and of "Emperor" Norton, the city's favorite eccentric. In its postquake incarnation, the Palace continued to attract the great and near great, and it maintained its dubious tradition of famous deaths: Warren G. Harding died here in 1923.

Just east of the Palace, at the intersection of Kearny, Geary, Market, and Third streets, stands **Lotta's Fountain,** a decorated iron pillar given to the city in 1875 by Lotta Crabtree, a child star who began singing, dancing, acting, and playing the banjo at the age of 8; at 17, she was performing in New York, on her way to amassing a fortune of $4 million before retiring at 44. On Christmas Eve 1910, the great opera singer Luisa Tetrazzini performed here before a crowd of more than 100,000 eager listeners. By the turn of the century, the fountain was surrounded by buildings housing newspapers such as the *Chronicle,* the *Examiner,* and the *Call,* and the noisy corner was called Newspaper Square. The **American Savings Building** (690 Market Street) went up in 1889 (its facade is modern) and for many years was occupied by the *Chronicle.* Cartoonist Rube Goldberg got his start here in 1899. The **Call Building** (southwest corner of Third and Market streets) was built in 1898 and has also received a new facade. Harold Ross, who later founded *The New Yorker,* was on the staff of the *Call* here. The 1909 **Hearst Building** (691–699 Market Street), home of the *Examiner,* still stands as well.

The massive, anachronistically late Greek Revival **Old Mint** (88 Fifth Street, 415–974–0788) was built in 1874. At one time it contained a full third of the nation's gold reserves, and much of the silver from the Comstock Lode was coined here. Employees and soldiers rescued the building during the 1906 fire, working with the aid of a single small fire hose. The mint houses a fine **monetary museum,** displaying early gold coins, gold rush memorabilia, and a $4 million pyramid of gold bars.

UNION SQUARE AND DOWNTOWN

Bordered by Stockton, Post, Powell, and Geary streets, **Union Square** has long been at the center of the city's shopping district, one of the most pleasant in America. Nearby are such old San Francisco firms as the clothiers **Bullock & Jones** (350 Post Street) and the Oriental goods and international gift store **Gump's** (250 Post Street). Construction of the central **obelisk** commemorating the victory of Commodore Dewey at Manila Bay in 1898 involved two presidents: William McKinley, who broke the ground for it in 1901; and Theodore Roosevelt, who dedicated it two years later.

The modern **Neiman Marcus building** (150 Stockton Street) retains the beautiful interior rotunda of the old City of Paris building, a Beaux-Arts structure (1909) that was demolished. It had been the last home of the Verdier family's department stores, founded in 1850 when Felix Verdier sailed into San Francisco on the brig *Ville de Paris,* which was laden with French stockings, lace, shawls, bonnets, liquors, and wines. The surviving rotunda is topped with the original glass dome, adorned by the city crest of Paris, a sailing ship, and the motto of Paris, "Fluctuat nec Mergitur"—"It floats and never sinks."

On the Powell Street side of Union Square stands the **Saint Francis Hotel** (335 Powell Street), among the city's grandest. Although the hotel has been extensively expanded since its opening in 1904, its core remains the Italian Renaissance-influenced block that burned but did not fall during the 1906 inferno. It was built by the Crocker family—heirs to a railroad and banking fortune—as a thoroughly modern alternative to the original Palace Hotel. The vaulted lobby with its Corinthian columns and great Austrian clock is a prominent reminder of the city's grandeur. Glass-walled exterior elevators on the 1972 addition to the Saint Francis provide breathtaking panoramic views of the downtown area.

The **Bohemian Club** (624 Taylor Street, corner of Post, private), perhaps the most prestigious club in San Francisco, was founded in 1872 by journalists looking for a gathering place other than a saloon. Always a club where artists and businessmen might meet on common ground (it nevertheless rejected such nabobs as William C. Ralston in its early days); it counted among its members Mark Twain, economist Henry George, writer Joaquin Miller, and photographer Arnold Genthe. The bronze bas-relief on the Post Street facade of the 1934 clubhouse hints at its literary past, picturing characters from the stories of Bret Harte, another early member.

CIVIC CENTER

San Francisco's Civic Center, backed into the corner of Market and Van Ness, marks the far southwestern corner of the downtown area. The 1906 earthquake, which demolished most of the area, gave the city fathers the opportunity to build what has become one of the most harmonious centers for public administration and entertainment in the nation. The opera, ballet, symphony, and modern art museums are all located here. **City Hall,** a domed Classical Revival structure, occupies two full blocks bounded by Van Ness Avenue, Grove, Polk, and McAllister streets. Completed in 1915 by architect Arthur Brown, Jr., the building is immense; the dome alone weighs 90,000 tons.

Completed in 1932, the **War Memorial Opera House** (301 Van Ness Avenue) and the **Veterans Building** (401 Van Ness Avenue) across from City Hall were the setting for the historic signing of the United Nations Charter in 1945. Six years later, the opera house was again a diplomatic forum—the signing of the final peace treaty with

Japan, ending the American occupation and signaling Japan's reentry into the world community. The buildings enclose a formal garden with pollarded trees. The **San Francisco Museum of Modern Art** (415–863–8800), located in the Veterans Building, exhibits a broad-based collection of modern paintings, drawings, photography, and sculpture. The collection is particularly strong in the works of artists associated with the West Coast, including Clyfford Still, Mark Rothko, Philip Guston, Sam Francis, and Richard Diebenkorn.

The **Society of California Pioneers** (456 McAllister Street, 415–861–5278) maintains a museum of nineteenth-century California art and the Wells Fargo Children's History Gallery, with special exhibits featuring costumes, toys, and tools of the gold rush era. Occupying the block bordered by McAllister, Larkin, Fulton, and Hyde streets, the grand Renaissance Revival **San Francisco Public Library** (415–558–3191) was completed in 1917. Home to a collection of over 1.5 million books, it also houses local history exhibits. The bronze bust in the vestibule is of Edward Robeson Taylor, an archetype of the California Renaissance—physician, lawyer, poet, and mayor of San Francisco from 1907 to 1909. Murals adorn the reading and reference rooms, including Frank Vincent Du Mond's *Pioneers Arriving in the West* and *Pioneers Leaving the East*, created for the Panama–Pacific International Exhibition.

NOB HILL

Along California Street west of Powell Street are several of the city's finest hotels, the Stanford Court, the Fairmont, and the Mark Hopkins, whose names commemorate the ostentatious homes of the three millionaires who first built atop Nob Hill. The **Fairmont Hotel** (California and Mason streets) is an opulent Renaissance Revival building, raised on the site of the mansion that bonanza king James G. Fair never managed to complete. The hotel was ready to open in 1906 when the great earthquake and fire gutted its interior. New York architect Stanford White was called in to create a new interior, and his remarkable marble-columned lobby opening onto adjacent ballrooms preserves the sense of a grand hotel.

Across the street stands the only nabob mansion that remained standing (albeit gutted) after the fire, now housing the **Pacific–Union Club** (1000 California Street, private). Silver tycoon

OPPOSITE: *San Francisco's exquisitely detailed City Hall, focal point of its Civic Center, is one of the foremost monuments of the early-twentieth-century City Beautiful Movement.*

*The famed photographer Eadweard Muybridge took this view of mansions on Nob Hill in
1877. He was a friend of one of the hill's richest moguls, Leland Stanford.*

James C. Flood spent over $1.5 million of his arguably ill-gotten
gains in 1886 to build this palace of Connecticut brownstone and
Eastern timber. After the fire, the structure was redesigned by Willis
Polk, who added the two wings and a third floor.

   A block to the west is the Gothic Revival **Grace Cathedral** (1051
Taylor Street). Its cornerstone was laid in 1910, but it was not
completed until 1964. Though medieval in aspect, it is composed of
poured-in-place concrete. The doors of the main portals were cast
from molds of Lorenzo Ghiberti's "Gates of Paradise" at the
Baptistry in Florence. The east rose window is the creation of a
modern workshop in Chartres; at night it is often illuminated from
within. The interior of the cathedral displays unusually good
examples of religious artwork, including a fifteenth-century Flemish
altarpiece and a thirteenth-century crucifix from Catalonia. The
forty-four-bell carillon in the north tower is played daily.

San Francisco Cable Car Museum

The museum demonstrates the inner workings of the contraption
that made Nob's high life possible, including the huge wheels

responsible for moving all the cables that run along the hill's streets. The gripman who drives each car starts and stops it by connecting the car to (or disconnecting it from) the constantly moving cable. The museum also displays portions of some of the earliest cable cars (the earthquake demolished the existing cable cars, leaving only segments), including Hallidie's prototype car, together with a collection of vintage photographs. A film shows how the system works.

LOCATION: 1201 Mason Street. HOURS: April through October: 10–6 Daily; November through March: 10–5 Daily. FEE: None. TELEPHONE: 415–474–1887.

CHINATOWN

The first Chinese in California were two servants who arrived in San Francisco in 1848 aboard the brig *Pilgrim*. Within six years 25,000 more had followed, driven out of their home provinces by famine and drawn to California by the lure of gold (their name for California was the Gold Mountain). From the first, the Chinese settled on the lower eastern slopes of Nob Hill, just west of Portsmouth Square—land that was deemed relatively undesirable because the east-west grade was too steep for horse-drawn transport.

It soon became obvious, especially to moguls such as Charles Crocker, that these people could be induced to work extremely hard for very little money. He employed 10,000 Chinese immigrants to build the Central Pacific Railroad, and the worst problem he encountered was an 1867 strike in which the workers demanded that their working days be reduced to twelve hours and that they be paid forty dollars per month. By the time of the financial panic of 1875, Chinese laborers held approximately half the factory jobs in San Francisco, and nearly 50,000 people were living in Chinatown.

White workers blamed the Chinese for the low wages San Francisco's factory owners and businessmen were willing to pay. Their long-smoldering resentment (not without a component of racial prejudice and scapegoating) exploded during the late 1870s: Mobs looted homes, harassed Chinese, and even tried to burn the steamship docks at which most Asian immigrants disembarked. When Chinatown burned in the 1906 fire, Boss Ruef, the city's power broker, decided not to allow its denizens to return to the now-desirable land they had occupied. Ruef's land-grab was foiled, however, by the fact that more than a third of the land in the neighborhood was already owned by Chinese. In the rapid reconstruction that followed the fire, Chinatown acquired the picturesque Oriental facades that many buildings exhibit today. It is estimated that 75,000 Chinese now occupy the small area of city blocks surrounding Grant Avenue between the Chinatown Gateway to the south and Columbus Avenue to the north.

On Grant Avenue the first building of note is Chinese only in its granite foundation. **Old Saint Mary's Church** (660 California Street) was consecrated as the seat of the Catholic bishop of the Pacific coast on Christmas Eve in 1854. The structure is composed of brick and iron brought around Cape Horn from the East Coast and of granite shipped from China. This simple Gothic Revival church served as the bishop's seat until 1891, and although the shell has burned twice, in 1906 and 1969, the sturdy brick framework has survived intact since 1854. Its ninety-foot-high square tower was among the tallest structures in the early town.

Just east on California Street, **Saint Mary's Square** opens to the right. The stainless-steel and rose-granite **statue of Sun Yat-sen** that stands on the square commemorates the several visits to San Francisco of the founder of modern China. Sun launched the newspaper *Young China* and created the second overseas office of his new party, the Kuomintang, here. The statue is the work of Beniamino Bufano, a prolific sculptor whose figures of animals and people can be found in public places throughout the Bay Area. Bufano was a noted pacifist—a devotee of St. Francis, Gandhi, and Sun Yat-sen—who, upon the announcement of the American entry into World War I, is said to have cut off his trigger finger and mailed it to President Woodrow Wilson.

On tiny Waverly Place, the **Tien Hou Temple** (125 Waverly Place) reflects the lovely Oriental-Baroque character of post-1906 rebuilding. The temple itself is located on the fourth floor and is dedicated to Tien Hou, the Queen of the Heavens and Goddess of the Seven Seas; among the altars is one said to have been brought to San Francisco in 1848.

The **Chinese Consolidated Benevolent Building** (843 Stockton Street), a fine example of the "Chinatown Renaissance" style, is the long-time headquarters of the Six Companies, the organization under whose auspices Chinese laborers came to San Francisco in the middle of the nineteenth century. The Six Companies, which represented six separate regions of China, mediated controversies within the Chinese community and defended Chinese interests in the surrounding metropolis.

Just off Grant Avenue is a branch of the **Bank of Canton** (743 Washington Street), an elaborate, pagodalike structure completed in 1909 and once occupied by the Chinese Telephone Exchange. For many years the operators of the Chinese-language exchange memorized the names of the more than 2,000 subscribers, since callers in the days before dial phones would often ask to be connected by name instead of by number. The headquarters building of the Bank of Canton of California houses the **Pacific Heritage Museum** (608 Commercial Street, 415–398–6199). Rotating exhibits cover such topics as Chinese contributions to the industries of early San Francisco and American influence on China and Japan.

At the north end of Chinatown proper, the **Chinese Historical Society of America** (17 Adler Street, off Grant Avenue, 415–391–1188) houses a substantial permanent collection of photographs, artifacts, and memorabilia on the Chinese presence in the United States.

The facade of the Chinese Consolidated Benevolent Building, a colorful example of the "Chinatown Renaissance" style that emerged in Chinatown's rush of construction after the fire of 1906.

NORTH BEACH

North Beach really was a beach in the 1850s. Columbus Avenue, the diagonal artery of the district, lies mainly on landfill that converted an inlet of San Francisco Bay between Telegraph Hill and Russian Hill into a thriving and frequently infamous community. Among the earliest residents were Australian ex-convicts who settled on the south slopes of Telegraph Hill and a group of Chilean and Peruvian settlers who colonized the west slopes. Among the former were the "Sydney Ducks," a gang of hoodlums whose methods included setting buildings afire prior to looting them. Later, Italian and Irish immigrants came in large numbers.

The turn of the century, the 1920s, and the 1950s witnessed three influxes of bohemians into and around what was long called "the Latin Quarter." Artists, writers, and hangers-on of the first wave tenanted the flanks of both Telegraph and Russian hills. *Les Jeunes*, a group of aesthetes that grew around Gelett Burgess's magazine, *The Lark*, lived on Russian Hill, where Burgess himself penned the immortal doggerel, "I've never seen a purple cow / I never hope to see one / but I can tell you anyhow / I'd rather see than be one." The bohemians of the 1920s left fewer traces, but the mark of the beatniks of the 1950s remains highly visible on the quarter.

San Francisco's oldest Catholic parish church, **Saint Francis of Assisi** (621 Vallejo Street), dates from 1860. Its simple Gothic Revival style closely resembles that of Old Saint Mary's. A **plaque** at 202 Green Street marks Philo T. Farnsworth's Green Street lab. At this spot in 1929, Farnsworth transmitted the first television picture ever broadcast. When James J. Fagan, a Crocker First National Bank vice-president, first heard of Farnsworth and his ideas in 1926, he supposedly remarked, "It certainly is a darn fool idea, but somebody should put money into it who could afford to lose it." Fagan and others did supply the capital, and before long Farnsworth was in Philadelphia developing pioneering television devices for Philco.

Washington Square, a green oasis formed at the intersections of Columbus Avenue and Union, Stockton, and Filbert streets, is still an informal gathering place for North Beach. The statue of Benjamin Franklin in the middle of the park is one of twenty erected by Henry D. Cogswell, a dentist and real estate speculator, to honor famous teetotalers (including himself); all but the statue of Franklin have disappeared. The monument here is marked with an inscription instructing the historical society to open a box inside in the year 1975. When the society members did, they found

The National Maritime Museum's sailing ships moored at the Hyde Street Pier, with Coit Tower, atop Telegraph Hill, in the background.

newspapers, photographs, buttons, and objects of the sort that those who witnessed the sealing of this time capsule had in their pockets. The other prominent statue on the square is the Volunteer Fireman's Monument, donated by Lillie Hitchcock Coit, whose far grander salute to the city rises from the top of nearby Telegraph Hill.

TELEGRAPH HILL

The hill was named for the telegraph system that by 1853 connected it to Point Lobos on the edge of the Pacific in what is now Lincoln Park. The wire was intended as an improvement on an earlier semaphore system, in which a man stationed at the summit would signal the imminent arrival of a ship through the Golden Gate by holding his arms out in a particular manner; for example, holding both arms out at right angles signaled the appearance of a mail-bearing side-wheel steamer.

Coit Tower

Telegraph Hill today is best known for Coit Tower, built with a $125,000 bequest from Lillie Hitchcock Coit and designed by Arthur Brown, Jr., the architect responsible for City Hall. A notable San

Francisco character, Coit had been the adopted mascot of Knickerbocker Fire Company Number 5 during her early youth. When the tower was dedicated in 1933, the old Number 5 firetruck was taken from a museum and stationed beside it. Stretching to 540 feet above the bay, Coit Tower still provides wonderful panoramic views of bay and city, and it is unquestionably the best place to go for a visual record of the aspirations of Depression-era San Francisco. The sixteen Public Works of Art project murals on the first and second floors, painted by twenty-five artists, vividly depict scenes of California life, industry, agriculture, sports, and labor unrest.

LOCATION: No. 1 Telegraph Hill. HOURS: 10–5:30 Daily. FEE: Yes. TELEPHONE: 415–362–8037.

WEST OF VAN NESS

North of the Civic Center, a broad slice of San Francisco to the west of Van Ness Avenue epitomizes the city's traditional private life. Before the 1906 earthquake, Van Ness itself had been a fashionable residential boulevard, but following the dynamiting of many of its residences in an effort to contain the fire, the avenue was rebuilt as a commercial strip—the city's auto row. Just to the west, however, in an area once known as the Western Addition (the term now refers to a limited area even farther west), are many of old San Francisco's premier residences. North of California Street in the districts of Pacific Heights and Cow Hollow are opulent palaces and fine gingerbread Victorians, as well as the halls of such religious organizations as the Swedenborgians and the Vedanta Society.

The **British Motor Car showroom** (901 Van Ness, 415–776–7700) is a palace for the display of automobiles. Its columns and ornate capitals bear some resemblance to those of the Palace of Fine Arts; both building were designed by the leading pioneer of the Bay Area style of architecture, Bernard Maybeck. Completed in 1928, the showroom was originally a Packard dealership.

The stone Romanesque Revival **First Unitarian Church** (1187 Franklin Street) was erected in 1888 (the old site of the First Unitarian was at Stockton and Geary streets). Inside, the winged angels flanking the pulpit were sculpted by Arthur Putnam, whose prodigious output included light fixtures for Market Street, sculptures of mountain lions, and a set of naked ladies for a Barbary

Coast bar. In the churchyard lies the white marble sarcophagus of Thomas Starr King, the pastor from 1860 until his death in 1864. A man with little formal but enormous informal education, King had held a prominent pulpit in Boston and consorted with the likes of Ralph Waldo Emerson. In San Francisco he was viewed as culture incarnate, the new city's leading exponent of higher ideals. Up and down the Pacific coast and all over the mining camps, he lectured on every topic from Shakespeare to gardens to God's hieroglyphics in Yosemite. During the Civil War he was a staunch advocate of the Union. He died of diphtheria and pneumonia at the age of 40, just four years after his arrival, but the whirlwind of his ministry helped transform the gold rush town.

Haas–Lilienthal House

With gables and dormers, a tower reachable only via an attic stairway, art-glass windows, and various shingles, the Haas–Lilienthal House is one of the most striking examples of Victorian architecture still standing in California. Built in 1886 for Bavarian merchant William Haas, it has exterior ornamentation reflecting widely varying styles. The same family occupied it continuously until 1972, and it preserves their furnishings, gathered over almost a century. The interior's mahogany and oak woodwork, tiling, and marble are also noteworthy. Walking tours of the Pacific Heights district depart from here.

LOCATION: 2007 Franklin Street. HOURS: 12–4 Wednesday, 11–4:30 Sunday. FEE: Yes. TELEPHONE: 415–441–3004.

Two blocks west of Franklin Street a mansion of opposite character, the Baroque Revival **Spreckels House** (2080 Washington Street, private), commands a fine view from Pacific Heights. The house was erected in 1912 by George A. Applegarth, the same architect who later designed the Palace of the Legion of Honor for the Spreckels family. His client for this house was Adolph Spreckels, second son of sugar king Claus Spreckels. The elder Spreckels started in San Francisco as a grocery clerk in 1848, later learned sugar refining, and eventually established control over most of the state's refining plants and most of Hawaii's sugar cane production. Adolph was active in the family business—so much so that he shot M. H. de Young, editor of the *Chronicle*, when that paper questioned the company's finances in 1884.

The grand Spreckels House, located in the aptly named Pacific Heights section. Alcatraz Island is in the distance.

Swedenborgian Church of the New Jerusalem

Here, as at the First Unitarian, New England-born ideas in the hands of San Francisco artists produced startlingly beautiful results. The sketch on which the church's design was loosely based was executed by Bruce Porter, a member of *Les Jeunes* who excelled as a muralist, stained-glass artist, and landscape designer. While traveling in Italy, Porter had sketched a village church in the Po Valley near Verona. To this he later added elements of the California Mission style, such as a low tile roof supported by rough-hewn logs of madrone. The principal designer of the church was probably A. C. Schweinfurth, and the young Bernard Maybeck contributed a sketch for the client. A combination of many talents under the unifying influence of the church's minister, Joseph Worcester, with his respect for nature, produced a wholly integrated church and garden of moving simplicity. The church, its ornamentation, and its grounds remain intact—the garden planted with trees from many nations, Porter's stained-glass window of St. Christopher with the Christ child, four murals of the California seasons painted by William Keith (one of

California's first notable landscape painters, and himself a Swedenborgian), and eighty original chairs for the congregation. The chairs, made of maple and caned with rushes from the Sacramento River delta, are regarded by some as predecessors of Mission-style furniture.

LOCATION: 2107 Lyon Street. HOURS: 9–4 Monday–Saturday, 11–4 Sunday. TELEPHONE: 415–346–6466.

The **California Historical Society Museum** (2090 Jackson Street, 415–567–1848) is housed in the **Whittier Mansion,** one of the finest surviving examples of late-nineteenth-century residential architecture in the city. Completed in 1896, it features a facade of red sandstone behind a columned central portico flanked by two towers. The remarkable interior panelling was executed in oaks and mahogany. Rotating exhibits of paintings, drawings, and other representations of pre-earthquake San Francisco are on display. A few blocks north and west stands the brick Georgian Revival **William Bourn Mansion** (2550 Webster Street, private), designed in 1896 by Willis Polk. At his father's death in 1874, Bourn was called back from his studies at Cambridge University to take charge of the Empire Mine, which he shrewdly developed into one of the state's great producers. Another block west is the simple frame **Leale House** (2475 Pacific Avenue, private), among the oldest in the area, dating from 1852 (its Italianate detailing was probably added during the 1880s). For years it was the residence of dairy farmers, whose cattle gave their name to Cow Hollow.

COW HOLLOW

During the third quarter of the nineteenth century, more than thirty dairies operated in Cow Hollow—an area roughly bounded by Vallejo Street, Van Ness Avenue, Lombard Street, and the Presidio. In the 1870s and 1880s, the area was transformed by the building boom that created San Francisco's trademark Victorian "lace house" architecture. Such houses were constructed quite cheaply, using standardized plans, but were embellished with a galaxy of machine-made ornamental details. Their outthrust bay windows became as characteristic of San Francisco as brownstones are of New York, though opponents lambasted the style as "a carpenter's frenzy" and advocated that their makers be "skewered with antique pins upon one of their so-called Eastlake elevations."

Some of the city's most graceful late-nineteenth- and early-twentieth-century residences are to be found in the Pacific Heights district. Elaborate scrolls, foliage, and cartouches surround one window, top right, and a dragon rears its head below another, bottom.

Octagon House

Now owned by the National Society of the Colonial Dames of America in California, the Octagon House is perhaps the best surviving example on the West Coast of a type created and popularized during the 1850s by Orson Squire Fowler, an architectural theorist and a vociferous exponent of phrenology. Fowler advocated the octagonal form for houses not only because it provided more floor space using the same wall area but also because the shape approximated nature's perfect sphere. He also gave proofs that an octagon would save the family steps in its daily chores. But despite the articulated advantages of octagonal living, San Francisco architect Henry Cleaveland opined that it "was the most ridiculous plan that ever came into the head of a noodle." The house is the state headquarters of the Colonial Dames, who maintain a museum here of colonial and Federal-period antiques.

LOCATION: 2645 Gough Street, near Union Street. HOURS: 12–3 second and fourth Thursdays, second Sunday of every month. FEE: None. TELEPHONE: 415–441–7512.

Vedanta Old Temple

Elaborately domed and towered, the temple was erected between 1905 and 1908 under the supervision of Swami Trigunatitananda and his American followers, who followed a religious doctrine emphasizing the validity of all religions as ways to the divine. The Vedantists expressed their eclectic beliefs in their building's components: Moorish columns, Mughal arches, a castle tower, a Bengalese onion dome, an octagonal dome like those on temples of Shiva, and a dome that pays homage to the Taj Mahal.

LOCATION: 2963 Webster Street at Filbert. HOURS: By appointment only. FEE: None. TELEPHONE: 415–922–2323.

The **San Francisco Fire Department Memorial Museum** (655 Presidio Avenue, 415–558–3981) houses a collection of historical photographs and fire equipment. The earliest fire engine on display dates from 1810 and the latest from 1937. Especially strong are the exhibits of material from gold rush days and from the 1906 earthquake and fire, as well as the coverage of Lillie Hitchcock Coit, the builder of Coit Tower.

Farther west, where Geary Boulevard crosses Parker Avenue, the unprepossessing house at **167 Parker Avenue** was built as a refugee shack after the 1906 earthquake. A number of such houses, since remodeled, survive in the residential districts of the city.

THE WATERFRONT

Although much of the international shipping trade has moved across the bay to the Oakland shipyard, the San Francisco waterfront maintains an active shipping industry along the piers of the Embarcadero on the east side of the peninsula's tip. Even-numbered piers start to the south of the Ferry Building, and odd-numbered piers start to the north. The historic waterfront begins where the peninsula rounds to the north, just at the tip of the Embarcadero.

Toward the end of the last century, fishermen of Genoese and Sicilian extraction established **Fisherman's Wharf** (at the foot of Taylor Street) as a humming port full of brightly painted boats laden with catches of Dungeness crab, sole, salmon, and sardines. With the Marin headlands and Alcatraz Island rising in the background out of the deep blue bay, the wharf has a view that inspired artist and author Ernest Peixotto to write, "If you want to behold a bit of the Bay of Naples, go some misty morning to Fisherman's Wharf." Only about thirty fishing vessels still make the wharf their home—fewer than one-tenth of the number that once moored here.

Alcatraz—which means pelican in Spanish—is not the only island in the bay. The Bay Bridge crosses **Treasure** and **Yerba Buena** islands, and boats travel to bucolic **Angel Island** used before World War II as a processing center for Asian immigrants. But Alcatraz is the most famous, because of the federal prison—nicknamed "the Rock"—that operated there between 1933 and 1963. The somewhat dilapidated structures are still standing. Among the Rock's unwilling tenants were "Machine Gun" Kelly, Al Capone, and convicted murderer Robert Stroud, known as the "Birdman of Alcatraz" because he kept and studied canaries while incarcerated. He was transferred to Alcatraz in 1942, the same year he published his natural history classic, *Stroud's Digest of the Diseases of Birds*. The island is accessible by ferry from Pier 41 (415–546–2805).

OPPOSITE: *The deck of the 256-foot full-rigged ship* Balclutha, *seen from the foredeck. She was built for a full complement of twenty-eight sailors but frequently sailed with a smaller crew.*

An abandoned cellblock at Alcatraz, for thirty years a maximum-security Federal penitentiary.

San Francisco Maritime National Historic Park

The National Maritime Museum, across Beach Street from Ghirardelli Square, has one of the best collections of ships' models in the world, as well as rotating exhibits of photographs and memorabilia on Pacific maritime life. Other items of note are artifacts pertaining to early shipping in the region (including the tiny vessel in which a Japanese sailor made the first recorded solo crossing of the Pacific) and fine WPA murals by Hilaire Hyler and Sargent Johnson. The museum has expanded beyond its original building and now includes a number of vintage ships along the waterfront.

Most of the museum's historic ships are located just west of Fisherman's Wharf on the Hyde Street Pier. Many of the vessels moored here played important roles in Pacific coast maritime commerce. The stately, steel-hulled square-rigger *Balclutha* was built near Glasgow, Scotland, in 1886. For years the ship carried coal from Britain to California and then returned around Cape Horn with loads of grain. Later she was pressed into service for the Alaska fishing trade, carrying workers to the fisheries and bearing canned salmon back to San Francisco. She lies at the pier fully rigged, and her cabins are fitted out as they would have been for a voyage. The scow-schooner *Alma* is the sole survivor of more than 300 flat-bottomed, light-draft vessels of her kind. Able to operate under sail or power—or even to be towed along riverbanks by her sweating crew—the *Alma* was built in 1891 to transport hay, coal, and other necessities to small, shallow ports around the bay and along the Sacramento River. The design of these ships is native to the bay.

Another rare survivor, the *C. A. Thayer*, is one of two remaining ships from a fleet of more than 900 schooners that carried lumber from the Pacific Northwest—hard and dangerous work that sometimes required ships' captains to put in at tiny, unprotected ports, ready to move fast at the first change in the weather. The *Thayer* was built in 1895, and after its lumber days, it carried on for many years in the fishing trade, transporting salmon from Alaska and cod from the Bering Sea. Before it went out of service in 1950, it was the last active commercial sailing vessel on the Pacific coast. Built in 1890, the side-wheel ferry *Eureka* was the largest bay ferry of her day, housing a steam engine four stories tall. A rare surviving paddle-wheel tug, the 1914 *Eppleton Hall*, once worked the River Clyde in Great Britain.

Two historic vessels are docked at Fort Mason's Piers 1 and 3. The *Hercules*, built in 1907 in New Jersey, was one of the best tugs of her day and was among the few to make the journey around Cape Horn. She earned her keep as an oceangoing tug, towing ships in and out of the bay and hauling lumber barges along the coast. Docked at Pier 3 is the SS *Jeremiah O'Brien* (415–441–3101), the only unaltered survivor of the 2,751 Liberty ships mass-produced during World War II to meet the urgent need for cargo vessels. Constructed in Maine and named for a Revolutionary War hero, the *O'Brien* brought supplies from the United States to Britain, ferried troops during the Normandy invasion of occupied France, and also served in the South Pacific.

LOCATION: Foot of Polk Street, in Aquatic Park. HOURS: January through April: 10–5 Tuesday–Sunday; May through June: 10–6 Tuesday–Sunday; July through October: 10–6 Daily; November through December: 10–5 Daily. FEE: None for museum; yes for ships. TELEPHONE: 415–556–8177.

Near the San Francisco Maritime Historic Park is another historic vessel open to the public. Operated by the National Maritime Museum Association, the World War II fleet submarine USS

Pampanito (Pier 45) was commissioned in 1943 and ran six patrols in the Pacific theater, sinking five enemy ships and damaging four more. A self-guided audio tour describes the working of the sub, from torpedo tubes to crew quarters.

Two of the nation's best examples of adaptive reuse of historic structures are nearby, both housing shops and eateries. **The Cannery** (at Hyde, Jefferson, and Beach streets just east of Aquatic Park) was a sardine warehouse before its conversion in 1968 into a market complex. **Ghirardelli Square** (North Point, Beach, and Larkin streets) is named for pioneer chocolatier Domingo Ghirardelli. The chocolate maker moved its operations to an 1864 building here in 1897, adding new structures over the next two decades, including a clock tower modeled on a wing of the Château Blois in France's Loire Valley. When the outmoded factory was offered for sale in 1962, it was transformed into one of the premier urban shopping malls in the nation.

Another noteworthy museum in the area is the **American Carousel Museum** (633 Beach Street, 415–928–0550), which contains excellent examples of the woodcarver's art as represented in carousel figures created between 1875 and 1927. Exhibits include vintage photographs and two working carousel band organs. Demonstrations of restoration techniques occur throughout the day.

A block west of Ghirardelli Square, **Fort Mason** was first occupied by the Spanish in 1797 as a secondary battery of six cannon to support the guns of the Presidio. Today it has been demilitarized and houses a number of interesting small museums, studios, performance spaces, and restaurants. In the 1850s, it became San Francisco's first suburb when a number of families squatted on what was then named Black Point for the dense laurel and scrub that overgrew it. The area was later established as an army base and eventually became a major transport hub for soldiers heading to the Pacific theater during World War II. The major buildings surviving today, however, are the same structures (much remodeled and with second stories added) that the squatters built around 1855. When Senator David C. Broderick was mortally wounded by Justice David S. Terry near Lake Merced in 1859, the dying man was brought here to the house of his friend, Leonidas Haskell, now Quarters Three.

Fort Mason is now the administrative headquarters (415–441–5705) for the entire **Golden Gate National Recreation Area,** embracing most of the city's undeveloped waterfront and the

Marin headlands across the mouth of the bay. Maps and informational brochures are available here.

Fort Mason Center hosts periodic cultural events and is the permanent location of four museums. The **Museum of the San Francisco African-American Historical and Cultural Society** (415–441–0640) contains a small permanent collection of African artifacts and features rotating exhibits on subjects ranging from black history in California to current events. The **Mexican Museum** (415–441–0445) focuses on Mexican and Mexican-American art from pre-Hispanic to modern times. The collection includes 500 pieces from the Nelson A. Rockefeller Collection of Mexican Folk Art, as well as substantial pre-Hispanic material and examples of the work of such noted Mexican artists as Rufino Tamayo and Francisco Zuñiga. The **San Francisco Craft and Folk Art Museum** (415–775–0990) devotes its galleries to periodic temporary shows on specific themes; past topics have ranged from Hopi crafts to the work of modern craftspeople to the folk art of Japan. The **Museo ItaloAmericano** (415–673–2200) displays a permanent collection of contemporary Italian and Italian-American art in addition to offering lectures, classes, and movies on Italian culture.

West of Fort Mason, at the edge of the Presidio, stands Bernard Maybeck's great Neoclassical rotunda, the **Palace of Fine Arts** (Baker and Beach streets). It is the last remnant of the 1915 Panama–Pacific International Exhibition, whose buildings and gardens once stretched in an unbroken line from Fort Mason to the Presidio. Most of the exhibition's buildings were in the Classical Revival, or "Beaux-Arts," style, although the exhibits of visiting states and nations included everything from a Turkish mosque to a New York mansion, and the overall tone was one of economic and technological promotion. Structures included Festival Hall; the 432-foot Tower of Jewels; the palaces of Agriculture, Liberal Arts, Horticulture, and Fine Arts; and the courts of Flowers, Abundance, Palms, and the Four Seasons. Most were executed in a *faux* travertine marble composed of gypsum and hemp, elaborately ornamented and detailed. The Palace of Fine Arts stood out among its fellows for its restraint, its simple buff-colored Corinthian colonnades reflected in the lagoon laid out beside it. Maybeck said he had designed this picturesque structure with an elegiac quality so that it would resemble "an old Roman ruin, away from civilization." After a major renovation, the palace today is reconstructed in durable concrete, its detail and color preserved intact. During the exhibition, the sheds

behind the palace displayed the work of over fifty painters. Today
they contain a theater and a "hands-on" science museum called the
Exploratorium (3601 Lyon Street, 415–563–3200).

The Presidio

Farther to the west, where the peninsula rounds the corner from the
bay to the ocean, is the Presidio, the oldest continuously occupied
army base in the western United States, established by the Spanish in
1776. Treeless and windswept then, it is now forested with cypress
and eucalyptus, thanks to plantings made by army engineers
beginning in the 1870s. Although the Presidio remains the
headquarters of the Sixth Army, most of the base is open to the
public, including a nature trail and a history trail. The Presidio was a
refugee camp after the 1906 earthquake, and during World War II
troops were billeted here before embarking for the Pacific theater.

The **Presidio Army Museum** (Lincoln Boulevard at Funston
Avenue, 415–561–4115) displays armaments and uniforms used by
the succeeding generations of troops quartered on the base. Also

*Bernard Maybeck's Palace of Fine Arts, the last remnant of San Francisco's 1915 Panama-
Pacific Exposition.*

preserved here are two reconstructed refugee cottages that housed San Franciscans after the 1906 disaster, along with many photographs and documents illustrating the army's role in controlling the damage. The simply colonnaded frame museum building, constructed in 1864, is the oldest structure in the Presidio. It served as the post hospital for more than a century. The only tangible remains of the Spanish presence at the Presidio is what is now the **Officers' Club.** Despite having been extensively remodeled in the Mission Revival style, the building preserves parts of the old commandant's house, probably built in 1791 or 1792.

LOCATION: Lombard Street. TELEPHONE: 415-561-3870.

Fort Point National Historical Site

The sturdy three-tiered brick fortress, built between 1853 and 1861, stands on the site of the Castillo de Joaquín, finished by the Spanish in 1794. The fort is now situated beneath the Golden Gate Bridge, which was built over it. Neither the old Spanish nor the newer American fort ever fired a shot at an enemy. As early as 1796, a Spanish report complained that the castillo's guns were worn out and that the walls "crumbled at the shock whenever a salute was fired." When the Russian explorer Otto von Kotzebue entered at the bay in 1823, he commented, "I found St. Joachim on his rocky throne, truly a peaceful and well-disposed saint, not one of his cannons in condition to fire a single shot." The subsequent American fortification was more formidable, and its 126 cannons were primed for action. But no enemy ever appeared before the cannons, and the fort itself was rendered obsolete by advances in gunnery. The structure is nevertheless imposing, the walls from within resembling a gigantic honeycomb, each of whose cells contained a cannon. Civil War memorabilia including exhibits of artillery, uniforms, personal effects, medicine, and historical photos of the fort are on display.

LOCATION: Marine Drive, under the south end of the Golden Gate Bridge at the Presidio. HOURS: 10-5 Daily. FEE: None. TELEPHONE: 415-556-1693.

Golden Gate Bridge

Two towers, each 746 feet high, support a great red arc more than three miles long—a load of more than 240 million pounds—but this magnificent structure looks as light as an angel's wing. The project was entrusted to Joseph Strauss, a bridge builder who had earlier proposed bridging the Bering Straits. Although the Golden Gate Bridge would be comparatively modest, many people, upon seeing Strauss's plan in 1922, said it could not be done. Years of squabbling and the onset of the Depression delayed the start of construction until 1933. Strauss was in charge, but the final design was not the ugly cantilevered structure he had proposed but a far more elegant plan worked out by one of his employees. When the bridge finally opened in 1937, 200,000 people were on hand to celebrate by walking across it. In 1987, when the bridge's fiftieth anniversary was observed, city officials expected approximately the same number to show up on the day when the bridge would again be reserved for pedestrians. Instead, 800,000 people walked the bridge that day, testifying to its exalted place in the popular imagination and to its extraordinary strength: The central span sank more than two feet under the weight of the densely packed throng. It is the third-longest suspension bridge in the world, connecting San Francisco with Marin County.

California Palace of the Legion of Honor

Since 1972, the museum has been devoted largely to French fine and decorative arts. Examples of the work of virtually every French master from the sixteenth through the twentieth century are on display, with particular strength in the eighteenth and nineteenth centuries. The displays include medieval tapestries, period rooms, and French furniture. The only exhibits not exclusively French are the works of the remarkable Achenbach Foundation for the Graphic Arts, whose huge collection embraces artists from the fifteenth century to the modern period. The museum, a grand cream-colored palace that is entered via a Roman arch, was erected in 1924 at the behest of sugar magnate Adolph Spreckels and his wife.

LOCATION: Lincoln Park, Thirty-fourth Avenue and Clement Street. HOURS: 10–5 Wednesday–Sunday. FEE: Yes. TELEPHONE: 415–750–3659.

Lincoln Park also contains an impressive though unremarked tribute to the power of seismic events in this region of the state: An abandoned one-lane blacktop road curves around a hill above the coast before, after a few hundred yards, it begins to undulate as

The famous entrance to San Francisco Bay, the Golden Gate, photographed by Ansel Adams in 1932 before the construction of the bridge.

though it were mimicking the troughs and swells of offshore waves; and just as suddenly it breaks off altogether, reappearing two feet below the miniature bluff of the fault line and continuing into the distance in a smooth straight line.

Perched on the headlands where Point Lobos Avenue becomes the Great Highway, which fronts the western beaches from Lincoln Park to Lake Merced, is the latest rendition of the **Cliff House** (1090 Point Lobos Avenue, 415–556–8642). The views up and down the coast are spectacular, sometimes including schools of gray whales offshore. The history of the Cliff House is tied to that of Adolph Sutro, a Prussian who arrived in California during the gold rush. Sutro founded his fortune on the great tunnel he engineered and built for miners of the later Nevada Comstock silver strike; investments in San Francisco real estate made him richer still. In 1879 he purchased the original Cliff House, built in 1863, along with 1,000 oceanfront acres on which he later built his own mansion and the famous Sutro Baths, a series of six huge indoor pools (some with fresh, some with saltwater) in a structure stuffed with art objects and exotic palms. Both the mansions and the baths are long gone, although the nearby ruins may still be visited. Photos from their glory days are preserved in the visitor center. The original Cliff House also suffered a grim fate, being blown to bits in 1887 when a schooner loaded with 80,000 pounds of dynamite exploded against the rocks beneath the building. Sutro immediately rebuilt it, creating a grand chateau on stilts that burned to the ground in 1907 and was replaced by the present, more modest structure (now much remodeled) in 1909.

GOLDEN GATE PARK

Stretching from the Pacific coast halfway across the peninsula and occupying an area of almost two square miles, Golden Gate Park, today perhaps the finest urban park in the West—studded with groves, lawns, lakes, ponds, and cultural amenities—was an assemblage of sand dunes when the city bought it in 1868. Over the succeeding years, it was transformed through the work and vision of one man, Superintendent John McLaren, who had arrived in San Francisco after training at the Edinburgh Botanical Gardens. The Bay Area's combination of mild, wet winters and cool, dry summers provides it with one of the most hospitable horticultural climates in the world—one that allows Canadian spruce and mountain laurels from northern latitudes and semitropical bougainvillea and birds-of-paradise to thrive virtually side by side. **Strybing Arboretum** (Martin Luther King Drive and Ninth Avenue, 415–661–1316), begun by McLaren, demonstrates the extraordinary breadth of plant life that can flourish here.

Surrounded by ornamental flower beds and filled with a permanent tropical garden plus changing exhibits of different groups of ornamental plants, the **Conservatory of Flowers** (Conservatory Drive, 415–386–3150) is the oldest building in the park. San Francisco real estate mogul James Lick had the glass house shipped around Cape Horn from England in 1879. Its design is derived from that of the royal conservatories at Kew Gardens.

The **California Academy of Sciences** (415–221–5100), roughly midway between the conservatory and the arboretum, has been a mecca for generations of San Francisco children—owing largely to the **Steinhart Aquarium,** one of the largest aquariums in the world. In addition to endless fish exhibits, it also includes a large tank of marine mammals, a penguin habitat, a tidepool, and a fine collection of reptiles and amphibians,' including an alligator pit. Also housed within the open quadrangle of the academy is the **Wattis Hall of Man,** a traditional natural history museum containing many dioramas illustrating human evolution and animal habitats. Across the quadrangle, among numerous physics and mechanics exhibits (including a huge pendulum clock), is the **Morrison Planetarium,** which offers astronomy programs and a laserium show.

M. H. de Young Memorial Museum

The current building, which dates from the 1920s, houses both the general museum and the **Asian Art Museum of San Francisco.** The general museum is vast and miscellaneous, with collections of European paintings, American fine and decorative arts, and folk and primitive art from around the world. All works date from the mid-nineteenth century or earlier. The Asian Muscum is almost entirely composed of the collection of one man, Avery Brundage, who for two decades served as president of the International Olympic Committee and who throughout his life collected Oriental art. The museum is strongest in Chinese art and weakest in Japanese, but it contains pieces from virtually every major Asian

Albert Bierstadt's California Spring, *painted in 1875, from the collection of the M. H. de Young Memorial Museum.*

civilization. The Chinese jade collection is the finest anywhere outside China. Space limitations restrict the portion of the collection on view at any one time to only a fraction of the whole.

LOCATION: Golden Gate Park. HOURS: 10–5 Wednesday–Sunday. FEE: Yes. TELEPHONE: 415–750–7636.

Near the art museums stands the pleasant **Japanese Tea Garden** (415–752–1171), created in 1894 as the Japanese Village exhibit of the California Midwinter Exposition. Inside, beyond the Japanese gate, are stone bridges, a pagoda, and a teahouse set in a Japanese stroll garden. Makoto Hagiwara, the garden's creator, lived and worked here for more than three decades. In 1952 the garden was rededicated as a specifically Japanese one. Since then, renovations have emphasized the virtues of restraint, a contrast to the Victorian flamboyance of the original buildings.

MISSION SAN FRANCISCO DE ASIS

Founded in 1776, Mission San Francisco was the sixth mission of twenty-one built by the Franciscans in California. As often happened, however, the site for the original building was ill chosen, and the mission had to be moved. The present church structure is all that remains of the once extensive quarters constructed on the second site. The simple white facade, with its harmonious Corinthian columns, is the most dramatic feature of the church completed in 1791. Within can be seen the restored geometrical designs painted on beams and ceiling, possibly by Indian neophytes. The ornate wooden reredos was imported from Mexico in 1796; behind it survives the original reredos, painted directly on the wall. The mission—known colloquially as Mission Dolores on account of the lake called Laguna de Nuestra Señora de los Dolores that once lay nearby—was never very prosperous or successful, owing to a climate that favored neither agriculture (in the absence of irrigation) nor the health of the Ohlone Indians who lived and worked there.

LOCATION: Sixteenth and Dolores streets. HOURS: April through October: 9–4:30 Daily; November through March: 9–4 Daily. FEE: Yes. TELEPHONE: 415–621–8203.

T H E   E A S T   B A Y

Originally known as the Contra Costa—meaning the "opposite coast"—almost the entire East Bay is within Alameda and Contra Costa counties. Since the turn of the century, and especially since the construction of the Bay Bridge in 1936, the area's population has exploded. A series of regional parks nestled in the hills overlooking the urban sprawl of the coastal flatlands preserves the natural environment of live oaks, California bay laurels, manzanitas, and grasslands that once swept down from the hills to the mud flats at the edge of the bay. Privately held land further inland, however, continues to be converted into housing tracts and industrial parks at a rapid rate.

Prior to the American occupation, the East Bay was a patchwork of twenty Spanish and then Mexican land grants, including those of the Peralta family (whose home survives in San Jose) and the Vallejos. The region's rolling hills and relatively dry climate invited the grazing of large herds of cattle. When statehood was granted to California in 1850, the East Bay's population soon increased. Oakland was settled by squatters in 1850; the University of California created the eastern section of Berkeley by moving there in 1873; and towns such as Livermore and Pleasanton grew up along the right-of-way of the Central Pacific Railroad, which opened in 1869. For half a century, however, growth was slow. Oakland had no deep-water port, and the prospects for dredging one were hindered by the fact that much of the coastline was owned by Horace W. Carpentier, an ally of the railroad barons of the Big Four and a steadfast supporter of his friends' desire to maintain a monopoly on bay crossings. The area's first sudden influx of residents came after the 1906 earthquake and fire, when displaced San Francisco families moved across the bay. When the San Francisco-Oakland Bay Bridge opened in 1936, the East Bay region finally came into its own as a population center. The following entries begin with Oakland and proceed north to Vacaville.

OAKLAND

In the East Bay proper, south of the Bay Bridge crossing, stands Oakland, the East Bay's largest city and industrial magnet. Once a minor economic force in the Bay Area, Oakland has now

outstripped San Francisco as a port. Oakland's main surviving historical sites recall the literary figures who lived here. The **Bret Harte Boardwalk** (569–579 Fifth Street) is a small group of attractive and simple clapboard houses built in the early 1870s. Harte, the celebrated author of gold rush stories and poems, lived nearby. More elaborate is **Jack London Square,** at the waterfront end of Broadway, where the rough-hewn little **First and Last Chance Saloon**—a favorite haunt of prolific author Jack London—is now surrounded by eateries and shops, together with part of London's Klondike mining cabin, brought from Alaska and reconstructed on the site.

The Oakland Museum

Designed by Kevin Roche, this museum has as its centerpiece a California history exhibit examining the changing aspirations of both immigrants and native Californians, with displays of artifacts ranging from tools, clothing, and wagons to a restored gold rush assayer's office to the first low-rider motorcycle. The area's natural history is presented in a simulated walk across the state, with exhibits of the flora and fauna that inhabit each of its eight biotic zones. The museum also has an outstanding and comprehensive collection of works by California painters and photographers, among them Albert Bierstadt, Richard Diebenkorn, and Ansel Adams.

LOCATION: 1000 Oak Street. HOURS: 10–5 Wednesday–Saturday, 12–7 Sunday. FEE: None. TELEPHONE: 415–273–3401.

Located in **Joaquin Miller Park** (Joaquin Miller Road and Sanborn Drive, 415–531–2205), **the Hights** was the home of Joaquin Miller, an extravagant poet and dramatist who lived in various parts of the Pacific Northwest. He achieved his literary breakthrough in England, where he affected western garb and a sombrero, became known for such tricks as smoking three cigars at once, and was celebrated as "the Byron of Oregon." Upon returning to America he moved to the East Bay, settling at the Hights—so written because he was an advocate of simplified spelling—in 1886. Here he erected statues to his heroes, Moses, Robert Browning, and John C.

OPPOSITE: *Oakland's First and Last Chance Saloon was located near the landing of the Oakland–Alameda ferry. In the 1920s Alameda was a dry town, and this bar was the commuter's "first and last chance" for a drink.*

Frémont, and a dramatic funeral pyre. Although he built several small residences on the property—believing that each individual needed a separate home—he lived in one called "the Abby," which was equipped with a water tower and sprinkler system to enable him to listen to "rain" on his roof during bouts of writing. The **Northern California Center for Afro-American History and Life** (5606 San Pablo Avenue, 415–658–3158) has exhibits on the history of the black community in the Bay Area.

BERKELEY

The **Judah L. Magnes Museum** (2911 Russell Street, 415–849–2710) has the third-largest collection of Judaica in the country, including both ceremonial objects and fine arts. Although specializing in the artifacts of Sephardic and Middle Eastern Jews, it also includes such European treasures as Moritz Daniel Oppenheim's 1856 painting *Lavater and Lessing Visit Moses Mendelssohn.*

Two churches located just south of the UC campus were key buildings in the emerging Bay Region style of architecture. A. C. Schweinfurth's 1898 **Unitarian Church** (Bancroft and Dana streets) is a beautiful wood-shingled structure with corner porches and amber glass windows. Whole redwood tree trunks were used as columns on the front portico. It is now used as a dance studio. The **First Church of Christ, Scientist** (Dwight Way and Bowditch Street), is Bernard Maybeck's masterpiece. Built in 1910, the church is simultaneously playful, harmonious, and even majestic. Maybeck was never afraid to overscale or to use Gothic, Neoclassical, and Oriental motifs in whimsical juxtaposition.

University of California at Berkeley

Facing San Francisco across the bay, Berkeley has its own light-industrial sector near the bayside and its own enclave of upper-crust homes on the first line of steep hills east of town, but its character is defined by the mammoth university—the centerpiece of the University of California system—that opened its doors here in 1873. The name of the town was bestowed by a university trustee in honor of the Irish philosopher George Berkeley (Berkeley had said, "Westward the course of empire takes its way"). Over the years, such prominent figures as geologist Joseph N. Le Conte, anthropologist Alfred Kroeber, physicist E. O. Lawrence, and architect Bernard Maybeck taught here.

Sather Gate and Tower at the University of California at Berkeley. They were designed by John Galen Howard, who later founded the university's Department of Architecture.

John Galen Howard's campanile, **Sather Tower,** rises high over the campus. The view from the top affords an overview of the huge campus with its Thomas Church landscaping as well as a vista of the Golden Gate and the bay. Built in 1914, it is based on the bell tower on the Piazza San Marco in Venice. From the centrally located tower, it is an easy walk to most of the small museums scattered among the university's buildings (for visitor information about the campus: 415–642–5215). The **Robert H. Lowie Museum of Anthropology** in Kroeber Hall (Bancroft Way, at the end of College Avenue, 415–643–7648) draws its exhibits from a huge collection of Native American, Eskimo, and Polynesian artifacts. The Earth Sciences Building houses a seismograph and a **Museum of Paleontology** (415–642–1821) with fossils dating back to the Jurassic period.

Just off campus is the **University Art Museum** (2626 Bancroft Way, 415–642–1207). Founded at the instigation of painter Hans Hofmann, who taught at Berkeley and donated forty-five of his paintings to the museum, it is a leading modern art museum, although individual pieces in the collection were executed by

artists as historically remote as Rubens. Attached to the museum is the **Pacific Film Archives** (2621 Durant Avenue, 415–642–1124), whose stock of over 5,000 movies is shown on a rotating basis.

Beyond the Richmond–San Rafael Bridge, the bay opens out again and is known as San Pablo Bay. Fresh water from the Sacramento River flows into San Pablo Bay on the eastern side by way of the Carquinez Strait. A surprising amount of early California history is preserved in sites on either side of the strait and on Suisun Bay.

MARTINEZ

This town is named for Ignacio Martínez, a commander of the Spanish Presidio at San Francisco who had part of his ranch here. Conservationist John Muir lived here and made a small fortune as a fruit grower nearby, and the legendary baseball player Joe DiMaggio was born here. Both the Muir House and the two-story adobe residence of the elder Martínez son, Vicente, are preserved at the **John Muir National Historic Site** (4202 Alhambra Avenue, 415–228–8860). Muir's home is a two-story Italianate mansion finished in 1882 by his in-laws, who left the house to Muir and his wife in 1890. The Martínez house, in the Monterey style, dates from 1849 and was occupied early in this century by Muir's daughter. Family memorabilia and a film put Muir into context as a naturalist and walker who was largely responsible for the establishment of Yosemite National Park.

BENICIA

Robert Semple, a leader in the "Bear Flag Rebellion" that helped free California from Mexican rule, founded the town of Benicia in 1847 in partnership with Thomas O. Larkin and the Mexican grandee Mariano Vallejo. The town has an unusual number of fine early buildings. The 1852 **Old State Capitol** (First and West G streets, 707–745–3385) is a simple temple-form Greek Revival structure restored, inside and out, to its design when California's legislators met there. Next door is the **Fischer-Hanlon House** (117 West G Street, 707–745–3385), originally built as a hotel in the 1840s, but with an interior that has been restored with original furnishings as the residence of the local butcher.

OPPOSITE: *Legislators' desks at the Old State Capitol, which has been restored to its appearance during the year when Benicia was California's capital, from February 9, 1853, to February 24, 1854.*

Though these are the only buildings open to the public as museums, a walk through Benicia's streets is an architectural tour in itself. The oldest house in town dates from 1790. Now the rectory of **Saint Paul's Episcopal Church** (122 East J Street), it originally stood in Torrington, Connecticut, before being dismantled and shipped around the Horn in 1868. Other buildings prefabricated in the East and sent to California by ship are the 1848 **store** (123 West D Street), the 1850 **saltbox house** (145 West D Street), and the 1850 **Frisbie-Walsh House** (235 East L Street). The **Old Masonic Temple** (110 West J Street), built in 1850, is the oldest Masonic building still standing in California. Also notable are the fine old buildings of the **Benicia Arsenal and Barracks** (at the end of East M Street). The stone work of the 1859 **Clock Tower Building** is particularly impressive.

VALLEJO

Located west of Benicia on the same side of the strait, Vallejo was the preferred choice of Mariano Vallejo to become the state capital. Though in 1852 the legislature agreed to do so, it reversed its decision after only a week. Instead the town became the site of the Mare Island Shipyard. Purchased by the U.S. Navy in 1853, the shipyard became the first naval station in the Pacific. The **Vallejo Naval and Historical Museum** (734 Marin Street, 707–643–0077) explores both the town and its naval history through many historical and maritime artifacts, including a working periscope providing a skipper's-eye-view of Vallejo, Mare Island, and as far away as San Francisco.

VACAVILLE

The town of Vacaville was named for Juan Manuel Vaca, who settled in the area around 1842. Two miles south of town on Peña Adobe Road stands the 1843 **Vaca-Peña Adobe** (off Route 80, 707–449–1830), the lone memorial of Vaca's time. The town itself has a well-preserved collection of mainly Victorian houses. Information about walking tours can be obtained at the **Vacaville Museum** (213 Buck Avenue, 707–447–4513), whose permanent collection focuses on agriculture, with antique farm tools, fruit-crate labels, and other artifacts, and articles of daily life, including a collection of antique clothing.

T H E   P E N I N S U L A

On the western side of San Francisco Bay, bordered by San Francisco to the north and the rich Santa Clara Valley to the south, the Peninsula might be said to occupy all of its thumb of land except the thumbnail—the city of San Francisco itself. Until the Americans arrived, its territory was divided into irregular parcels of Spanish land grants. Climate has determined its pattern of settlement since then, with the land on the bay side of the coastal mountains comparatively sunny and warm, while the coast side is considerably cooler and foggier. It is often possible, standing on the ridge of the Coast Ranges, to observe a sunny vista of bayside communities to the east and a sea of fog to the west.

On the bay side of the central ridge ran **El Camino Real,** a Spanish road connecting the missions from one end of California to the other. (Markers topped by mission bells still mark this route.) By the early 1850s, San Francisco's newly rich were building country homes on the bay side, a process facilitated by the opening of the San Bruno Turnpike in 1855 and of a San Francisco–San Jose rail line nine years later. Subsequently their estates were subdivided into the string of communities now filling the space from the bay to the Coast Ranges, with the exception of large preserves for San Andreas and Crystal Springs reservoirs (San Francisco's water supply), Stanford University, and the high-tech industrial complexes between Stanford and the city of San Jose at the Peninsula's base. The coast side, on the other hand, has until recently been a sparsely populated, undulating ribbon of land on the edge of the continent.

PACIFICA

An agglomeration of subdivisions straddling the Coast Ranges, Pacifica contains two of the most important historic sites on the coast side. Over 1,000 acres of open space has been preserved at **Sweeney Ridge** (Fassler Avenue), the vantage point from which the Spanish first saw San Francisco Bay on November 4, 1769. The **Sánchez Adobe** (1000 Linda Mar Boulevard, 415–359–1462) is the best preserved of the few Hispanic-period adobe houses surviving on the Peninsula. This two-story house was completed in 1846 by Francisco Sánchez, thrice *alcalde* (chief magistrate) of Yerba Buena (soon to be renamed San Francisco) and son of the Presidio's first commander. In later years it was used as a speakeasy, a brothel, and an artichoke warehouse. It has since been carefully restored with a mixture of Spanish and Victorian furnishings.

The route south on Route 1 winds along the tops of dramatic headlands, past secluded beaches, and through eucalyptus forests to **Half Moon Bay,** the oldest town in San Mateo County. First settled in 1840, the town got a boost from Mexicans fleeing the Yankee occupation of San Francisco and later briefly challenged Redwood City's claim to be the largest town in the county. The downtown area is still remarkably picturesque, with a number of surviving Victorian frame houses. The headstones at **Pilarcitos Cemetery** (San Mateo Road and Main Street) reveal how many different nationalities have populated the town.

Also notable for its collection of Victorian frame architecture is the village of **Pescadero**, a bit farther south and a few miles east of Route 1. The town got its start around 1853, when a Missourian named Eli Moore brought his family and other settlers to the area to farm. Of all the coastside towns on the Peninsula, Pescadero, full of white houses, most nearly resembles a New England village.

HILLSBOROUGH AND BURLINGAME

South of San Francisco on the bay side, these two neighboring towns have a shared history. The town of Burlingame owes its name to a brief visit by Anson Burlingame, the American ambassador to China, to William Ralston's country estate in 1868. The ambassador's host suggested naming a town for him, and on paper at least, Burlingame was born. A few years later, a railroad stop created in the vicinity of the Burlingame Country Club began to attract a community around it. To maintain a suitable distance between themselves and their less affluent neighbors, the wealthy incorporated Hillsborough in 1910, thereby preserving the quiet of the club. To this day, Hillsborough has no sidewalks, streetlights, or businesses, and it is one of the nation's most beautiful suburbs. In the somewhat less opulent town of Burlingame stands the **Burlingame Depot** (California Drive and Burlingame Avenue), built by the club members in 1894. The depot is a simple building with a low-slung tile roof whose tiles came from surviving mission structures in San Mateo and at Mission San Antonio de Padua.

OPPOSITE: *The balcony inside Ralston Hall, the enormous Italianate mansion where William C. Ralston sometimes entertained 120 guests for the weekend.*

BELMONT

The town of Belmont owes most of its development to post-World War I suburban construction, but its centerpiece is one of the nabobs' great country homes: William Chapman Ralston's **Ralston Hall** (1500 Ralston Avenue, 415–593–1608). Founder of the Bank of California, Ralston purchased Count Leonetto Cipriani's canyonside home in 1864. With the help of architect John P. Gaynor, he had it enlarged and transformed into an imposing Italianate villa of more than eighty rooms. Its spacious interiors, elegant parquet floors, silver fixtures, chandeliers, and mirrors make it one of the finest surviving mansions in California. The ground-floor rooms and the second-floor gallery have been restored and painstakingly preserved. Since 1922 the mansion has been an integral part of the campus of the College of Notre Dame.

WOODSIDE

Farther south and abutting the Coast Ranges, Woodside retains the rural charm of an earlier time, though it is now mainly a suburb. The **Woodside Store** (Kings Mountain Road, 415–851–7615), built in 1853 and for many years the general store for the logging community, now houses a small historical museum. The town also possesses Filoli, a mansion that rivals Belmont's Ralston Hall.

Filoli

At the base of the Coast Ranges and just south of Crystal Springs Reservoir stands William B. Bourn's estate, Filoli (the name is a sort of acronym for its owner's motto: Fight, Love, Live). Bourn, who ran both the Empire Gold Mine and the Spring Valley Water Company, was among the most powerful citizens of turn-of-the-century San Francisco. Willis Polk completed Filoli for his patron in 1916. Built of glazed terra-cotta and white stone according to a modified Georgian design, the house is surrounded by one of the best-preserved estate gardens in the nation. The gardens—modeled on French and Italian ideas, with both formal and informal areas—were created by Bruce Porter, who turned his hand with equal success to gardening, stained-glass, murals, and humorous writing.

LOCTION: Cañada Road. HOURS: Mid-February through mid-November: Tours by reservation only. FEE: Yes. TELEPHONE: 415–364–2880.

STANFORD UNIVERSITY

The Palo Alto campus of Stanford University has been greatly expanded over the century since it was founded, but the core of its plan and buildings is still intact, despite the necessity to rebuild some of the latter after the 1906 earthquake. The rustic setting in acre after acre of eucalyptus groves is the result of a landscape design created by Frederick Law Olmsted, who had earlier planned the layout of the original quadrangle. Its buildings are built of locally quarried sandstone in Romanesque Revival forms designed by Sheply, Rutan & Coolidge—a Boston firm carrying on the office of Henry Hobson Richardson—and completed in 1891. Leland Stanford's wife, Jane, had the **Memorial Church** added in 1903 in memory of her husband. The figural mosaics on both the exterior facade and the interior walls represent biblical scenes.

The university owes its existence to the untimely death of the Stanfords' son, Leland, Jr., at the age of 15. The presumptive heir to

Stanford University's Memorial Church, viewed through the arches of the Quadrangle. When the buildings were leveled by the 1906 earthquake, their pieces were re-erected on the site.

a huge fortune, he appeared after death in a half-waking vision to his father with the message, "Live for humanity!" The university was his parents' response to this command. Information on campus tours is available by calling 415–725–3335.

The **Leland Stanford, Jr., Museum** (Lomita Drive and Museum Way, 415–723–4177), just east of the quad, was also dedicated to the younger Stanford's memory. Among the wide-ranging collections of European, American, Asian, and African art are the extensive photographic studies of animal locomotion commissioned from Eadweard Muybridge by Stanford; a group of Rodin sculptures; and the original golden spike driven into the rail at Promontory, Utah, on May 10, 1869, marking the completion of the first transcontinental railroad.

SAN JOSE AND ENVIRONS

South of Stanford University, the once pastoral countryside has in the last decade become dotted with industrial parks, sites of the multitudinous high-tech ventures of Silicon Valley. The development stretches all the way to San Jose, the oldest town in California and the vertex of the Peninsula and the East Bay. Founded in 1777, it was the first secular Spanish settlement in California; later it was briefly the state capital and from 1849 to 1851 hosted the roistering meetings of what came to be known as the Legislature of 1,000 Drinks.

Sarah L. Winchester, heir to a munitions fortune, built a rambling and strange Victorian mansion now known as the **Winchester Mystery House** (525 South Winchester Boulevard, 408–247–2000), beginning in 1884 and continuing until her death in 1922. A psychic told her she would never die so long as she kept building the house; she responded by having workers add on a welter of towers and staircases, some leading to nowhere.

The **Rosicrucian Egyptian Museum** (Park and Naglee avenues, 408–287–2807) is set in Rosicrucian Park, a full city block of Egyptian-style buildings. The museum is operated by the Rosicrucian Order, AMORC, a mystical and educational organization that traces its roots back to the mystery schools of ancient Egypt. It contains a collection of Egyptian, Babylonian, and Assyrian pieces, including mummies, plus a life-size replica of an Egyptian tomb.

San Jose Historical Museum

This excellent and wide-ranging museum of the history and culture of San Jose and the Santa Clara Valley occupies twenty-five acres in Kelley Park. Although the collection focuses on the Spanish/Mexican period, it also contains considerable material dating from the 1790s to the present century. The outdoor exhibits include a number of authentic or re-created houses and public buildings, including stables, fruit barns, period houses, a bank, and a firehouse. The museum also offers periodic walking tours of historic San Jose.

LOCATION: 635 Phelan Avenue. HOURS: 10–4:30 Monday–Friday, 12–4:30 Saturday–Sunday. FEE: Yes. TELEPHONE: 408–287–2291.

Luis María Peralta Adobe

Operated by the San Jose Historical Museum but located in downtown San Jose, the Peralta Adobe is the oldest remaining monument to San Jose's Spanish past. Its extreme simplicity shows what adobe construction was like before the influx of American ideas that resulted in the more elaborate two-story Monterey style. It is thought to have been constructed before 1800 by an Indian who was among the first settlers of the village; later it was occupied by the family of Luis María Peralta, a veteran of the Anza expedition who held a large land grant in the area. Furnishings are replicas of originals from the early Mission period.

LOCATION: Saint John and Terraine streets. HOURS: By appointment. FEE: None. TELEPHONE: 408–287–2291.

The **San Jose Art Museum** (110 South Market Street, 408–294–2787) is located in a Richardson Romanesque-style building that earlier housed a post office and a library. The museum contains an interesting collection of regional artwork, including a good collection of American prints.

New Almaden Quicksilver County Park and Museum

Thirteen miles south of San Jose, the New Almaden Mine was America's premier source of mercury for well over a century. Prior to American occupation, Indians had gathered cinnabar here and Mexicans had begun to mine for mercury. Since mercury was needed to extract gold from ore, the mining operation was crucial to the extensive exploitation of Mother Lode gold deposits after the gold rush had exhausted the readily available placer gold. The museum on the site contains mining artifacts.

LOCATION: Almaden Road, New Almaden. HOURS: 12–4 Saturday. FEE: Yes. TELEPHONE: 408–268–7192.

Mission Santa Clara de Asís

Founded in 1777, the eighth of California's twenty-one missions, Santa Clara enrolled and served more Indians than any other California mission. The original buildings have not survived the ravages of the years, but the present replica, built in 1929, is a faithful copy of the 1825 church, which was itself the fifth church to bear the mission's name. Particularly impressive are the ceiling designs, copied from the originals done by Mexican painter Augstin Dávila.

LOCATION: The Alameda, Santa Clara University campus, Santa Clara. HOURS: 7–7 Daily. FEE: None. TELEPHONE: 408–984–4545.

Mission San Jose de Guadalupe

Located in the suburb of Fremont about ten miles north of San Jose, this replica of the fourteenth California mission was completed in 1985. Founded by Father Lasuén in 1797, the mission later became famous for its Indian orchestra, led by Father Narciso Durán, who headed the mission for twenty-seven years and served as president of all the missions. The mission buildings were destroyed by an earthquake in 1868. The reconstructed church is a simple, narrow structure like most of the mission churches, but the meticulous recreation of the original interior gives a good idea of how these houses of worship must have looked when new. Like Mission Santa Clara, Mission San Jose was uncommonly successful at attracting Indian converts. An adjacent museum displays artifacts of the mission days.

LOCATION: 43300 Mission Boulevard, Fremont. HOURS: 10–5 Daily. FEE: Yes. TELEPHONE: 415–657–1797.

WINE COUNTRY

North of San Francisco, the swells of the Pacific Ocean seem mirrored in the successive ridges of the Coast Ranges. Near the Russian River in Sonoma County, the westernmost ridges are covered with redwoods; eastward, the mountains show patches of scrubby chaparral and stretches of grassy slope, green in winter and golden brown in summer. Between the ridges lie a series of fertile valleys, radiating northward from the Bay Area like a hand's fingers. Although at least four major valleys run through the region, two have given their names to the surrounding counties: Napa and Sonoma.

Two figures—one military and one oenological—loom large in the history of the area. General Mariano Guadalupe Vallejo, commander of the northern frontier of Mexican California, parlayed land grants into control over most of the property from Napa and Sonoma to the Carquinez Strait at the northern end of

The Napa Valley reemerged as an important wine-producing region after Prohibition had forced many vineyards out of business.

San Pablo Bay. The Mexican government knew that it needed a strong leader in the north, since the Russians had signified their interest in the area by building Fort Ross on the coast; but the general proved to be both strong and adaptable. When the Bear Flag Revolt—the opening rebellion in the struggles that eventually put upper California under American control—broke out at the town of Sonoma in 1846, Vallejo was taken prisoner, but when freed he took an active role on behalf of American annexation. Consequently, unlike most of his fellow Californios, he preserved much of his fortune following the American takeover.

The second figure is Agoston Haraszthy. Although not the first man to plant a vineyard in the valleys (that distinction goes to George C. Yount, who started one in 1838), this peripatetic Hungarian—who first emigrated to Wisconsin and then moved successively to San Diego, San Francisco, Sonoma, and finally Nicaragua—was the real founder of the wine industry now almost synonymous with Napa and Sonoma. In 1858 he created the state's first large-scale vineyard, near Sonoma, and soon thereafter went on a state-sponsored tour of Europe to collect appropriate grapes for the California climate. He was the first to import the Zinfandel grape, among other varieties. Before leaving for Nicaragua to become a sugar planter, he saw his two sons marry daughters of Mariano Vallejo.

The region also attracted two distinguished writers. In 1880 Robert Louis Stevenson honeymooned with his bride, Fanny Osbourne, in an abandoned mining shack on the slopes of Mount Saint Helena and wrote a book about the area, *The Silverado Squatters.* Among other things, he predicted the bright future of the wine industry, claiming, "The smack of Californian earth shall linger on the palate of your grandson." Three decades later, Jack London settled in more grandly, buying over 1,400 acres near Glen Ellen for his Beauty Ranch.

NAPA

The town of Napa had a gridiron pattern of streets before it had any houses. The first of the town's grids was laid out in 1848, but an 1849 settler commented that there was really no town at all: "The name had got there somehow, but the city hadn't." By the late nineteenth century, however, Napa had become a processing and shipping center for wine and produce. The town retains a core of Victorian buildings and the **First Presbyterian Church** (Randolph and Third streets), a dramatic wooden building in the Gothic Revival style.

SONOMA

Among the smaller towns of California, only Monterey can rival the town of Sonoma in the number and importance of its historic sites. Sonoma was founded in the unsettled times between the end of Spanish rule and the beginning of the American period, and its history is a microcosm of that transition. The last of the Franciscan missions was established here and was quickly followed by the pueblo of Sonoma, many of whose original structures survive. The town's founder, Mariano Vallejo, first lived in a now-destroyed house on Sonoma's plaza but later moved to a house nearby that has been restored.

Sonoma State Historic Park

On June 14, 1846, the Sonoma plaza was the scene of the chief act of the Bear Flag Revolt, the rebellion that started California on the way to American control. On that date, twenty-four Americans living in California stormed the plaza, taking the garrison at the **Sonoma Barracks** and making General Vallejo, his brother, and his brother-in-law their prisoners. Apparently the Americanos had feared expulsion from the territory, and they had been encouraged to take preemptive action by Colonel John C. Frémont, then in the area with a U.S. surveying expedition. Immediately they proclaimed California an independent republic, named William B. Ide its president, and created the Bear Flag, whose main features were a star and a bear roughly rendered in blackberry juice. (Local people said the bear more closely resembled a pig than a grizzly.) In less than a month, events elsewhere brought all of California under U.S. control, and the independent republic ceased to exist. The Bear Flag, however, formed the basis for the design of the current state flag.

    Mission San Francisco Solano, on the plaza, a simple, gabled adobe, is a much-restored version of the second building created to serve as the mission church. When near completion in 1833, it was severely damaged in a heavy rain and was not fully repaired until the early 1840s, by which time it had ceased to be a mission and was instead a parish church. It was founded in 1823 by Father José Altimira, who left in the autumn of 1827 after a fire started by troublemakers destroyed the adjacent Indian village. His successor established the mission on a firm foundation and began to build the present church, only to have his efforts nullified when the entire mission system was secularized by Mexican decree in 1834. That same year, General Mariano Vallejo—put in charge of the northern frontier by Mexican Governor Figueroa—founded the pueblo of Sonoma around a plaza adjacent to the mission church. He informed the padres that the mission system had been abolished and took most of its supplies and Indians to use on his own large land grant.

At the end of Third Street, half a mile northwest of the Sonoma plaza, is **Lachryma Montis,** the elaborate Carpenter-Gothic home of Mariano Vallejo. His "Casa Grande" on the Sonoma plaza burned in 1867. Vallejo built this mansion in the early 1850s in what was then the most modern style, perhaps as a symbol of his conversion to faith in Yankee progress. It was lavish both inside and out, complete with imported chandeliers, lace curtains, and a rosewood grand piano. The name Lachryma Montis is a translation of the Indian name for the spring by which Vallejo built the house: Chiucuyem, or "crying mountain." The house has been restored and stocked with a collection of Vallejo's personal effects. A map and guide to the park are available at park headquarters, located in an 1870s wood-frame building on the plaza.

LOCATION: East Spain and First streets. HOURS: 10–5 Daily. FEE: Yes. TELEPHONE: 707–938–1519.

A few miles east of the plaza stands the **Buena Vista Winery** (18000 Old Winery Road, 707–938–1266), with its stone buildings and hand-hewn limestone cave cellars set in a wooded valley. This is the vineyard founded by Agoston Haraszthy in 1857, making it the oldest premium winery in the state and the progenitor of the industry.

PETALUMA

Thirteen miles west of Sonoma by car, Petaluma has a fine array of Victorian houses and Italianate iron storefronts (Petaluma Boulevard to Kentucky Street, on the south side of Western Street). Set in the broad Petaluma Valley, the town was an important farming center as early as the 1850s, supplying the Bay Area with produce, particularly potatoes. In 1878 Lyman Rice appeared in Petaluma with an invention—an incubator—that was to revolutionize the poultry and egg industries and make Petaluma, for a time, the egg capital of the world.

Petaluma Adobe

About four miles east of town stands the extensive and well-restored adobe that Mariano Vallejo began to build in 1834 as the headquarters for a 64,000-acre land grant dedicated mainly to the hide-and-tallow trade. The large and beautiful surviving structure, with its surrounding verandah, represents only one of the two great wings of the original complex. The ranch produced everything it needed for self-sufficiency, from furniture and tools to oil and candles. The state park system has gathered Mexican-period artifacts to demonstrate the ways in which many of these items were created and used.

> LOCATION: Casa Grande and Old Adobe roads. HOURS: 10–5 Daily. FEE: Yes. TELEPHONE: 707–762–4871.

North of Petaluma, the town of **Cotati** is notable for its hexagonal grid street pattern, arranged with an attractive plaza in the center. Its plan reflects novel city-planning ideas formulated during the 1890s, and it is one of only two such existing systems in the United States.

SANTA ROSA

One of the largest cities in the region of California north of the Bay Area, Santa Rosa preserves several interesting Victorian homes along McDonald Street, including the ornate **McDonald Mansion** (private), which covers the whole block between Sixteenth and Spencer streets. The 1874 **Baptist Church,** now located on Sonoma Avenue between A Street and Santa Rosa Avenue, is an interesting Gothic Revival structure said to have been constructed in its entirety from a single redwood log.

Luther Burbank Home and Gardens

The modified Greek Revival home and a two-acre memorial garden belonging to the noted horticulturalist Luther Burbank have been restored and opened to the public in Santa Rosa. The house contains many original furnishings, and the garden demonstrates some of Burbank's plant developments, including the spineless cactus. A museum devoted to his life and work is located in the Carriage House. Arriving in Santa Rosa from Massachusetts in 1875 with no planting stock other than a few of his Burbank potatoes, Luther Burbank succeeded in breeding and introducing hundreds of new plant varieties, many of which are still grown today. He introduced more than 100 new varieties of plums and prunes alone. Burbank died in 1926 and is buried under the huge cedar of Lebanon he had planted near the greenhouse.

LOCATION: Santa Rosa and Sonoma avenues. HOURS: *House and Museum:* April through mid-October: 10–3:30 Wednesday–Sunday; *Gardens:* 8–7 Daily. FEE: For house tours. TELEPHONE: 707–576–5115.

JACK LONDON STATE HISTORIC PARK

North of Sonoma and a mile northeast of Glen Ellen are the charred remains of a mansion Jack London built and the surviving stone house that his widow, Charmian, built after his death. The latter is now a museum, containing the Londons' furniture and other personal effects as well as exhibits on London's life as a writer, adventurer, and farmer. London's grave is on the site, as are the remains of his numerous projects in scientific agriculture, including the "Pig Palace," designed according to the latest efficiency principles.

London first came to Glen Ellen in 1903, shortly after the success of his novel *The Call of the Wild.* By 1911 he owned a 1,400-acre ranch and had begun construction of the elaborate stone mansion he called Wolf House, designed by noted San Francisco architect Albert Farr. On the eve of its completion, Wolf House burned, possibly as a result of arson. The Londons continued to live in the Cottage, a wooden house already standing on the ranch, until the author's death in 1916.

LOCATION: London Ranch Road, one mile from Glen Ellen. HOURS: *Grounds:* 8–Dusk Daily; *Museum:* 10–5 Daily. FEE: Yes. TELEPHONE: 707–938–5216.

SAINT HELENA

Sixteen miles north of Napa, the **Silverado Museum** (1490 Library Lane, 707–963–3757) is dedicated to the life and work of Robert

OPPOSITE: *Jack London's roll-top desk and other memorabilia are preserved in the study of the house built by Charmian London after her husband's death in 1916.*

Louis Stevenson, the great Scots writer who honeymooned nearby on Mount Saint Helena. The museum features a fine collection of Stevenson manuscripts, first editions, and memorabilia—over 8,000 items in all.

Clustered at the northwest end of Saint Helena are three of the valley's oldest and most prolific wineries: Beringer Vineyards, Charles Krug Winery, and Christian Brothers Winery. All offer tastings and tours. The **Beringer Vineyards** (2000 Main Street, 707–963–7115) preserves the unusual house and cellars created by German immigrants Frederick and Jacob Beringer after founding their winery in 1876. The imposing **Rhine House,** built as their residence in 1883, pays homage to the castles of the German Rhine. Its well-preserved Eastlake and Queen Anne interior is striking. The 1,000-foot-deep wine cellar, dug into the hillside by Chinese labor, is still in use.

The current winery building of the **Charles Krug Winery** (2800 St. Helena Highway, 707–963–2761) dates from 1874, but Charles Krug founded the business in 1861, making it the oldest winery in the Napa Valley. Krug had been a newspaperman in San Francisco before meeting Agoston Haraszthy, the father of the California wine industry, who prompted Krug to learn winemaking and to purchase the vineyard in which he labored for the rest of his life.

What is now one of three Christian Brothers' wineries in the Napa Valley was created by San Francisco magnate William Bourn as **Greystone Cellars** (2555 Main Street, 707–963–0763) in 1889. The harmonious and extensive stone winery was built in a style that recalls Richardsonian Romanesque, especially in its arched entrance. It cost Bourn $2 million to erect it, but not long afterward the phylloxera plague attacked the valley's vines, forcing Bourn to sell out. The present owners are a lay order of the Catholic Church, part of whose profits go to support the order's schools.

A few miles north of Saint Helena stands the striking, well-preserved **Bale Grist Mill State Historic Park** (Route 29, 707–963–2236), with its towering overshot mill wheel. The structure, made entirely of local redwood and Douglas fir, was built in 1846 by Edward Bale, an English surgeon stranded by his ship in Monterey, where he became a physician to the army of the Californios. He married a niece of Mariano Vallejo and acquired a grant in the Napa Valley for a parcel of land with the unappetizing name of Rancho Carne Humana (literally, Human Flesh Ranch—the true meaning and origin of the name are unknown).

CALISTOGA

The tireless Sam Brannan—who ran California's first newspaper and its first gristmill and who promoted the gold rush in San Francisco—virtually conjured up the now quaint and picturesque resort town of Calistoga, nestled in the shadow of Mount Saint Helena. The local Indians called this hot-springs area Colaynomo, or "oven place." Brannan combined the names California and Saratoga (the popular New York resort) to create Calistoga. The hotel and cottages he built there in 1859 sustained a brisk resort business through the next two decades. The chief remains of Brannan's era are clustered around the small but intriguing **Sharpsteen Museum** (1311 Washington Street, 707–942–5911), featuring a diorama of the Calistoga Brannan built, along with artifacts. Next door is one of the cottages from Brannan's spa, its interior restored to its appearance during the resort's heyday. Nearby, on Wapoo Avenue at Grant Street, is the simple building (now a private home) that was Brannan's store.

Robert Louis Stevenson State Park

The upper parts of 4,500-foot Mount Saint Helena have been set aside as a state park in honor of Robert Louis Stevenson, who in 1880 spent his honeymoon here in an abandoned silver miner's shack. Only a monument remains to mark the spot where Robert and Fanny shared the romantic idyll he would later describe in *The Silverado Squatters*. Nonetheless, a hike to the summit is rewarded with the view that Stevenson described as follows: "From its summit you must have an excellent lesson in geography. . . . Three counties, Napa, Lake, and Sonoma, march across its cliffy shoulder. . . . Its sides are fringed with forest, and the soil where it is bare, glows warm with cinnabar."

LOCATION: Route 29, five miles north of Calistoga. HOURS: Dawn–Dusk Daily. FEE: None. TELEPHONE: 707–942–4575.

HEALDSBURG

Healdsburg, in the heart of northern Sonoma County's wine country and near the foot of Fitch Mountain, preserves many Victorian buildings and some earlier homes. The **Healdsburg Museum** (221 Matheson Street, 707–431–3325) is an unusually good small museum, with a fine collection of artifacts, from Pomo Indian basketry to antique firearms, documenting many of the cultures of the area.

THE NORTH COAST

California's northwest is rugged and heavily forested, with a welter of middle-sized mountain ranges whose rivers drain into the Pacific. Coastal highlands offer dramatic interactions of land and ocean: Redwood-covered slopes descend to grass-covered headlands whose sheer faces front the roaring Pacific. Along the coast, the climate is cooler and wetter than in most of the state; behind the Coast Ranges, however, in the narrow interior valleys and on the inland Klamath Mountains, summer temperatures can be extremely warm. The rough character of the country was not attractive to the Spanish, who never established a land grant north of Ukiah. The California Indians, on the other hand, found the north coast a very congenial habitat, rich in everything from acorns and game to salmon that run up the swift rivers. A dozen tribes belonging to five separate linguistic groups had territories along the coast and in the inland valleys.

The Russian presence in the area began when Count Nikolay Rezanov sailed down the coast to San Francisco in 1806. A temporary Russian base was established on the Sonoma coast in 1809, and three years later the more elaborate Fort Ross was created as a base for the sea otter trade and as an agricultural settlement. The Spanish, alarmed by this penetration, established Mission San Francisco Solano at Sonoma in 1823 and subsequently consolidated control of the Napa and Sonoma valleys under the leadership of General Mariano Vallejo. Eventually, however, with the otter trade overburdened and in decline, the Russians simply lost interest, selling Fort Ross to John Augustus Sutter in 1842.

Gold provided the occasion for the area's first real influx of American settlers. Mines were opened on the Trinity River as early as 1848, attracting gold seekers who later abandoned their claims to create the base of the region's present economy: lumbering and agriculture. The timber industry was important from the early 1850s onward. At Humboldt Bay in 1869, for example, 75 million board-feet of redwood were produced. Soon afterward, a specialized agriculture based on dairy cattle and such fruits as pears and apples was developed; but many of the towns still depend on the timber trade.

OPPOSITE: *The Point Cabrillo Lighthouse, built in 1909 north of Mendocino, was an important beacon for the lumber schooners that traded along the Northern California coast.*

MARIN COUNTY

The peninsula whose southern tip forms the north post of the Golden Gate is home to some of the finest suburban housing in the nation, set in an incomparable landscape of hills, forests, and grasslands. Farther north, the suburbs and parklands give way to small towns and placid dairy farms.

The Spanish made some early incursions here, building Mission San Rafael Arcángel near San Pablo Bay in 1817. Later the territory was subdivided into Mexican land grants. In the American period, settlement remained sparse until the building of the Golden Gate Bridge prompted an influx of commuter residents. During the two decades following the bridge's construction, the population of the county more than tripled.

The most densely settled part of the county lies to the east of the abruptly rising Coast Ranges, giving the area a warmer, sunnier climate than San Francisco's. From the Marin headlands to Tomales Point in Point Reyes National Seashore thirty-five miles to the northwest, an unbroken chain of national, state, and municipal parklands preserve the beauty and variety of natural habitats in western Marin County. The **Golden Gate National Recreation Area** (off Route 101, 415–556–0560) manages the Marin headlands, whose winding roads, open hills, and narrow beaches offer views of the city across the mouth of the bay. The park contains the remains of three twentieth-century forts—Fort Cronkhite, Fort Barry, and Fort Baker—and their numerous gun batteries, buried in bunkers carved out of the headlands' hills.

Mill Valley

Northeast of the Maria headlands, Mill Valley, an early exercise in suburban development whose lots were sold at auction in 1890, was dedicated from the outset to preserving its superb natural setting. Foremost among the many interesting structures is the **Outdoor Art Club** (1 West Blithedale Avenue, private), designed as a women's club in 1904 by the great Bernard Maybeck. The elegant building has one whole wall almost entirely made of glass, emphasizing the indoor/outdoor focus of the club's life; four interior trusses pierce the roofline and stand above it, indicating the building's structure. The town's other landmark is the restored 1836 **sawmill** (Throckmorton Avenue) from which Mill Valley derives its name.

Muir Woods National Monument

Here, three winding miles west of Mill Valley, is the best place near San Francisco to see the giant redwood tree (*Sequoia sempervirens*). The largest trees in this 550-acre preserve are 14 feet in diameter and over 253 feet high. Set aside as a national monument in 1908—as part of the wave of conservation efforts inspired by Muir himself—the park was named at the request of Congressman William Kent, who also donated the land. Simultaneously, however, Kent was opposing Muir's campaign to stop the flooding of stunning Hetch Hetchy Canyon—now Hetch Hetchy Reservoir—in the Sierra.

LOCATION: Off Route 1, 9 miles north of San Francisco. HOURS: 8–5 Daily. FEE: None. TELEPHONE: 415–388–2595.

Located on the shores of San Pablo Bay near San Rafael, **China Camp State Park** (off Route 101, five miles east of San Rafael, 415–456–0766) preserves the last remnant of the more than two dozen Chinese shrimping villages that once dotted San Francisco Bay. A few wharf buildings and some machinery survive, now being protected, restored, and interpreted by state park rangers. The village outlasted decades of anti-Chinese persecution and declining revenues until pollution in the bay effectively closed it after World War II.

MISSION SAN RAFAEL ARCANGEL

This mission, named for the patron saint of health, was first created as a hospital auxiliary for Mission San Francisco in 1817. The original structure was razed in 1870, but the star window and the bells hung from a cross beam of the reconstructed mission are original. The next-to-last mission to be established, it was meant only to provide a refuge for Indians sickened by San Francisco's climate and by various European diseases. But so successful was the auxiliary mission in its healing work—it counted among its padres the only one in all of California who had medical training—that it began to receive the sick from other missions too, and in 1823 it attained full mission status.

LOCATION: 1104 Fifth Avenue, San Rafael. HOURS: 11–4 Daily. FEE: None. TELEPHONE: 415–456–3016.

POINT REYES NATIONAL SEASHORE

Point Reyes National Seashore preserves woodland, grassland, and beaches on a peninsula jutting north into the Pacific. Information is available at the **Bear Valley Visitor Center,** which is also the location of a reconstructed **Miwok Indian village,** showing the dugout shelters used by this people, and the **Earthquake Trail,** a short trail with explanatory signposts, showing a rift in the earth along the San Andreas fault. (The epicenter of the great 1906 earthquake was not far from this spot.) Farther out on the peninsula are the 1870 **Point Reyes Lighthouse** and **Drake's Beach.** The latter is protected in a notch of the peninsula and may be the place where the English privateer Sir Francis Drake grounded the *Golden Hind* in order to make repairs in June 1579.

LOCATION: Bear Valley Road, off Route 1. HOURS: *Park:* Always open; *Visitor Center:* 9–5 Monday–Friday, 8–5 Saturday–Sunday. FEE: None. TELEPHONE: 415–663–1092.

FORT ROSS

Most of the fort, located eleven miles or so up the coast from Jenner, consists of accurate reconstructions of the Russian buildings and palisades erected here in 1812 as the settlement called Rossiya. Like the outpost at Bodega Bay, it was established to supply the Alaskan settlements with wheat and to engage in the lucrative sea otter trade. Only the house of the last commander, Aleksandr Rotchev (who had married a princess and was himself a poet and bon vivant), is an original building. Raised in 1836, it is far more elegant than the two-story log **Kuskov House,** originally erected in 1812 as quarters for earlier fort commanders. Also on the site are reconstructions of the original **Russian Orthodox Chapel** and other period buildings, furnished as they would have been during the period of Russian occupation. The nearby 1867 **Call House,** ranch headquarters for the American farm that covered 15,000 acres, is furnished as it was during its heyday.

LOCATION: 19005 Pacific Highway, Jenner. HOURS: 10–4:30 Daily. FEE: Yes. TELEPHONE: 707–847–3286.

OPPOSITE: *A reconstruction of the Russian Orthodox Chapel at Fort Ross. The original, built in 1812, burned to the ground in 1971.*

Just south of Lake Mendocino in **Ukiah** the **Grace Hudson Museum** (431 South Main Street, 707–462–3370), in a 1911 Craftsman-style house, displays a collection of artifacts from the local Pomo culture. Back on the coast, forty-five miles north of Fort Ross, a lighthouse has stood at **Point Arena**—*arena* is Spanish for sand—since 1870; however, the current structure (Lighthouse Road, 707–882–2777) was erected after the 1906 earthquake toppled the original one.

MENDOCINO

Mendocino, a picturesque coastal town, resembles a New England village with its many fine wooden structures reflecting its past as a prominent lumbering town until local resources were exhausted. The 1865 **Masonic Hall** (Lansing and Ukiah streets) has on its tower a peculiar statue of Father Time standing over a young woman. The **Mendocino Presbyterian Church** (44831 Main Street) is a singularly handsome white-painted redwood church done in the Gothic Revival style; built in 1868, it is still in use. The **Kelley House Museum** (47500 Albion Street and Main Street, 707–937–5791), the small 1861 home of pioneer William Kelley, exhibits artifacts and photographs relating to local lumbering and shipping industries and to the town's Victorian architecture.

EUREKA

Eureka is the largest city in California north of Sacramento; in comparison to it, neighboring Ferndale is just a village. But both are among the best places in the state to find examples spanning the full range of California Victorian architecture.

Eureka was founded in 1850 as a result of the gold rush. Its name probably comes from the then recently adopted state motto, meaning "I have found it!" While the town's gold rush enthusiasm was short-lived, the void was filled almost instantly by the enduring if cyclical prosperity of the lumber industry. North of Fourth Street, **Old Town Eureka** preserves many fine business buildings once dedicated to shipping, but adjacent to the business district are dozens of blocks covered with fine Victorian architecture. The **Carson House** (southwest corner of M and Second streets, private) is one of the most exuberant houses built in nineteenth-century America. Created for lumber grandee William Carson in 1885, it flaunts a strangely harmonious welter of styles. The **Clarke Memorial**

Museum (Third and E streets, 707–443–1947) contains period rooms and other artifacts from the town's Victorian area, as well as a collection of Indian basketry and exhibits relating to Eureka's port and to its natural history.

Fort Humboldt State Historic Park (Highland Avenue, off Route 101, 707–445–6567) protects the remains of the isolated fort established near Eureka in 1853. When Ulysses S. Grant was stationed at this lonely post in 1854, he wrote home, "You do not know how forsaken I feel here!" The only original building still standing in the park is the redwood-frame hospital, which dates from the mid-1800s; it now houses the visitor center and interpretive exhibits. Plaques mark the sites of the other fort buildings.

Like Eureka, **Ferndale,** twenty miles to the south, is a living museum of Victoriana. The **Ferndale Museum** (Shaw and Third streets, 707–786–4466) displays furnished Victorian rooms and period artifacts such as a working crank telephone. The museum also provides information about walking tours of the well-preserved town.

Loggers in Humboldt County pose with the chunks of a felled redwood that measured twelve feet in diameter at its base. The photograph was taken some time in the 1890s.

CHAPTER FIVE

OREGON

Oregon has always claimed a special place in the American imagination. To this country of wild forests, raging rivers, fertile valleys, volcanic mountains, and Pacific-swept shores came thousands of immigrants in the mid-nineteenth century, determined to start their lives anew. They traveled in wagon trains from Independence, Missouri, where the Oregon Trail began, to a land they had heard and read about 2,000 miles away. One pioneer described the trip as "a long picnic" in which "the changing scenes of the journey . . . just about sufficed to keep up the interest, and formed a sort of mental culture that the world has rarely offered." Although the rigorous trip left others less enthusiastic, the precedent for westward migration had been established, and with it the future of the state of Oregon.

For many Oregon meant the fertile rolling hills of the Willamette Valley, which remains the state's most densely populated and developed region. Yet, as with Washington, with which it shares much of its early history, Oregon has an enormously varied topography. The lush vegetation and wetness that characterize the coast, on the west side of the Cascades, stand in contrast to the eastern part of the state, which includes the Columbia lava flow, the sagebrush plains of the semiarid Snake River region, and the high desert of southeastern Oregon.

This landscape was home to an equally diverse population of Indians—among them the Clatsop, Multnomah, Klamath, Modoc, and Nez Percé—whose complex cultures were irrevocably altered by the arrival of white settlers in the Pacific Northwest. From 1542, when Bartolome Ferrelo caught the first glimpse of Oregon's fog-shrouded coast, to George Vancouver's coastal probings of what is now Washington in 1792–1794, the British and the Spanish devoted some of their imperial energies to the search for the Northwest Passage. Toward the end of the eighteenth century, the quest for the passage was replaced by the search for furs.

In the first half of the nineteenth century, the Americans and the British vied for supremacy in the Oregon Country, which included what is now Oregon, Washington, Idaho, and portions of Wyoming, Montana, and Canada. This vast region extended from the Pacific Ocean to the Continental Divide. Thomas Jefferson, hop-

OPPOSITE: *A page from Lewis and Clark's journals, which President Thomas Jefferson had instructed them to keep "with great pains and accuracy," contains a careful drawing of a white salmon trout.*

This is a likeness of it; it was 2 feet 8 inches long, and weighed
ten pounds the eye is moderately large, the puple black
with a small admixture of yellow and the irs
of a silvery white with a small admixture
of yellow and a little ——: terbed near
its border with a yellowish brown.
the position of the fins may be seen
from the drawing, they are small
in perpotion to the fish. the fin
are boney but not pointed
eacept the tail and back
which are a little so, the
fin and venteral ones,
ten rays; those of the
and the small fin
the tail above ha
but is a tough flea
covered with smooth
perpotion to its
Salmon. the
best one each
subutale teeth
the kett
before
fish
with

fins
prone back
contain each
gills twelve,
placed near
no long rays,
-able substance
thin. it is thicker in
wedth than the
tongue is thick and firm
border with small
in a single series.
of the mouth are as
discribed. neither this
nor the Salmon. are coucght
the hook, nor do I know on
what they feed. —— -
now began to run. a t

<u>Monday March 17th 1806</u>

ing to gather scientific data and to strengthen the U.S. claim to the Columbia watershed, sent Lewis and Clark on what would become this nation's most celebrated expedition. Starting in Saint Louis, Missouri, they traced the Missouri River to its source, crossed the Rocky Mountains, and followed the Columbia River to the Pacific, where they set up camp at Fort Clatsop on Oregon's northern coast. In 1811, five years later, fur trader John Jacob Astor attempted to capture his share of the lucrative fur trade by sending two parties— over land and by sea—to the Pacific Northwest. Although the casualties were great on both trips, his men managed to establish the first permanent American settlement in the Oregon Country. However, Astor's operation was acquired by Britain's North West Company, which in turn was absorbed by the Hudson's Bay Company, which dominated the region from its headquarters at Fort Vancouver, Washington, until the Treaty of 1846 established U.S. sovereignty below the 49th parallel.

Loads of wheat, packed in bags, being hauled through Rufus, Oregon, about 1880.

The germs of "Oregon Fever" spread through the United States in the 1820s and 1830s as tales of this Eden were told. The Great Migration began in the 1840s, inspired by reports of the fertile valley, anticipation of trade with the Orient, and the promise of free land. Methodist missionary Jason Lee founded the city of Salem in 1840, and other missionaries of his faith settled at Oregon City a year later, joining the Hudson's Bay Company's chief factor of the Columbia department, John McLoughlin, who located a land claim there in 1829 and laid out a town in 1842. By 1843, with the British influence waning, the Americans established a provisional government in Champoeg. In 1848 Oregon became a territory and a decade later a state.

The second half of the nineteenth century saw the development of Oregon's major cities: Portland, Salem, Corvallis, Albany, Eugene, and Ashland. Settlement east of the Cascades was slower. The rugged terrain discouraged even the most stalwart pioneers, and those who took up the challenge—including gold seekers and cattle ranchers—were shaken by a series of Indian wars that racked central and eastern Oregon from the early 1850s until the late 1870s. Among those who were particularly resistant to the seizure of their lands by settlers and, thereafter, to the federal government's policy of segregation on reservations were the Modoc and the Nez Percé, whose protracted struggles to maintain their lands were fierce and heroic. The removal of the Indians to reservations and the coming of the railroads spurred greater growth east of the Cascades, which in turn brought more conflict in the late 1880s and 1890s when competition among sheep ranchers, cattle ranchers, and wheat farmers resulted in range wars in some areas.

This chapter moves northward along the coast from Port Orford to Fort Clatsop, at the mouth of the Columbia River, then over to Portland, Oregon's largest city. After a side trip along the Columbia, the narrative moves south along Route 5 through the fertile Willamette Valley—the destination of many pioneers—and then eastward through three early towns, Grants Pass, Jacksonville, and Ashland. Across the Cascade Range, in central Oregon, the entries lie along Route 97, running northward from Klamath Falls. Shifting over to the eastern border of the state, the chapter follows the Oregon Trail (which roughly parallels Route 84) northward to Pendleton before turning southward again along Route 395 to Lakeview and the California border.

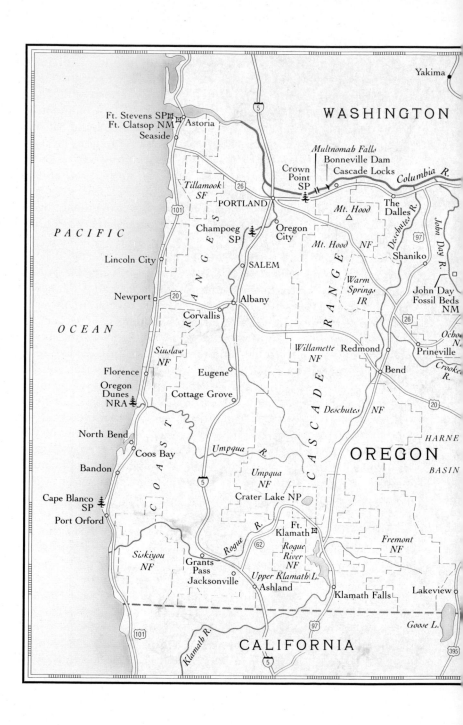

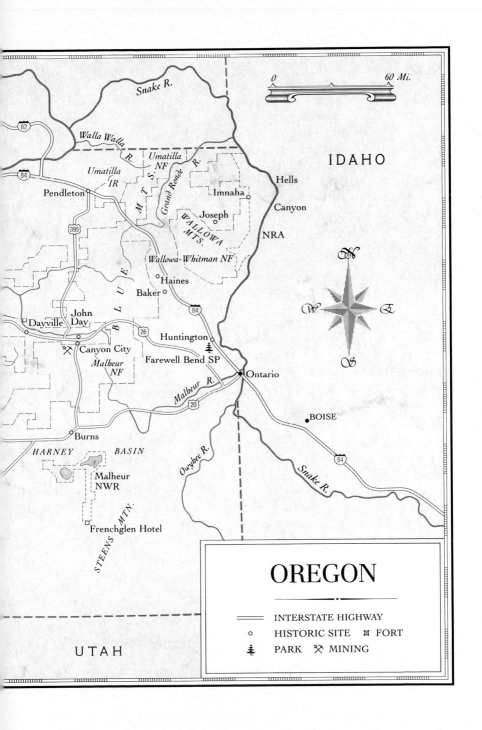

Snake R.

IDAHO

82

Walla Walla R.

84

Umatilla NF

Umatilla IR

Pendleton

Hells

Grand Ronde R.

Imnaha

Canyon

395

Joseph

WALLOWA MTS.

NRA

Wallowa-Whitman NF

BLUE

Haines

Baker

John Day

84

Dayville

Huntington

26

Farewell Bend SP

Canyon City

Malheur NF

Ontario

Malheur R.

20

BOISE

Burns

HARNEY   BASIN

Owyhee R.

84

Malheur NWR

Snake R.

Frenchglen Hotel

STEENS MTN.

OREGON

─────── INTERSTATE HIGHWAY

○   HISTORIC SITE   ⊞ FORT

🌲   PARK   ⚒ MINING

UTAH

0   60 Mi.

THE   OREGON   COAST

Thanks to forward-thinking legislators and a protective populace, Oregon's coast remains, for the most part, as startlingly beautiful as when Spanish explorers navigated its treacherous waters in the sixteenth century. State parks outnumber towns and cities; forty-four miles of mammoth sand dunes line the shore between Florence and Coos Bay; and virgin coniferous forests have been preserved. For centuries the region was inhabited by the Clatsop, Tillamook, Coquille, Siuslaw, and other coastal tribes, who lived on a rich store of salmon and traveled the rivers in graceful canoes carved from cedar and spruce. Although British and Spanish sea captains probed the coast in the seventeenth and eighteenth centuries, the wilderness remained relatively undisturbed until the arrival of Lewis and Clark. Their camp at Fort Clatsop, occupied during the winter of 1805–1806, was the first U.S. outpost in the Pacific Northwest, followed just five years later by the Pacific Fur Company's Fort Astoria. Hostilities between the Indians and the newcomers, including the massacre of Indians near the site of Bandon in 1854, slowed settlement, but by the second half of the nineteenth century the region was awash with fishermen, lumber barons, and vacationers.

PORT ORFORD

The town of Port Orford began inauspiciously in 1851 when a group of gold seekers landed here against the wishes of a band of Coquille Indians. **Battle Rock** (off Route 101), on the southern edge of town, marks the site of their fierce fight, which forced the white men to flee to nearby settlements. But they returned the following year, and by 1856 Port Orford was the seat of Curry County. The town has several houses dating to the late nineteenth century. The Victorian Gothic **Hughes House,** built by architect Per Johan Lindberg in 1898, has been restored and may be seen eight miles northwest in **Cape Blanco State Park** (503–332–6774), in **Sixes.** Cape Blanco, the coast's westernmost point, was first noted in 1603 by the Spanish explorer Martín de Aguilar, whose cocaptain named it for its chalky appearance.

BANDON

The region surrounding the lower Coquille River, upon which Bandon is situated, was home to the Coquille Indians who reacted

OPPOSITE: *The Marshfield* Sun *Printing Museum in Coos Bay.*

violently to the first white settlers in the early 1850s. As gold drew more prospectors to the region tensions heightened, and in January 1854 seventeen members of another tribe were murdered by a gang of forty miners. It is thought that part of the massacre took place in what is today **Bullards Beach State Park** (Route 101, two miles north of Bandon, 503–347–2209). The **Bandon Historical Society Museum** (Southwest First Street, 503–347–2164) contains exhibits on the area's maritime history, photographs of a devastating town fire, and a collection of Indian artifacts.

THE COOS BAY AREA

Founded in the early 1850s, **Empire City** was the first community on Coos Bay, the largest natural harbor between Puget Sound and San Francisco. It was soon followed by Coos Bay and North Bend, twin towns that later absorbed Empire City and became the great lumber capitals of the coast. By the late nineteenth century the company town of **North Bend,** founded by the New Englander Asa Simpson, was flourishing, its mill and shipyard well on their way to forming one of Oregon's major lumber empires. The **Coos County Historical Society Museum** (Simpson Park, 503–756–6320) has exhibits on pioneers, logging, and regional Indian crafts. In Coos Bay, originally named Marshfield, the **Marshfield *Sun* Printing Museum** (North Front Street) is housed in the five-sided building where the city's weekly newspaper, the *Sun,* was printed from 1911 to 1944. Marble-top tables, typecases, and platen and hand presses are among the equipment on view.

Also noteworthy is **Shore Acres State Park** (off Route 101, twelve miles southwest of Coos Bay, 503–888–3732). The park features gardens that were part of the estate of Asa Simpson's son, Louis, who followed his father into the lumber business and played a prominent role in the development of the bay area. The ocean views are spectacular, but they did not impress the elder Simpson: When Louis finished his three-story home on its bluff, his father, having passed it by schooner, asked what fool had built on such a site.

Stretching forty-four miles from North Bend to Florence, the **Oregon Dunes National Recreation Area** (off Route 101, 503–271–3611) preserves dunes formed after a glacial retreat some 15,000 years ago. The dunes evolved through the force of erosion and the movement of sediment from rivers and streams, pushed by the ocean's currents into their present form.

FLORENCE

Florence was home to the Siuslaw Indians, who relinquished 2.5 million acres of land to the federal government in 1855, retaining only small homesteading tracts. Remnants of the fishing town that the white settlers created in the second half of the nineteenth century may be seen in the **Old Town area,** which runs along Bay Street; information is available at the town's **visitor center** (270 Route 101, 503–997–3128). Florence's elegant **Siuslaw River Bridge** (Oregon Coast Highway), constructed in the 1930s by a WPA crew, boasts Gothic piers with metal finials and archways with Art Deco designs. Just south of the bridge, the **Siuslaw Pioneer Museum** (Route 101, 503–997–7884) contains Indian artifacts, early logging equipment, and furniture and clothing from early settlers.

NEWPORT

Wedged between the ocean and Yaquina Bay, Newport was settled in 1855 by traders and fishermen. In the 1860s and 1870s it became a favorite resort for Willamette Valley residents, who vacationed at the town's hotels or set sail on five-day coastal voyages to San Francisco. Clamming and crabbing have flourished on the bay since the late nineteenth century. The Lincoln County Historical Society maintains the **Burrows House Museum** (545 Southwest Ninth Street, 503–265–7509) and the **Log Cabin Museum** (579 Southwest Ninth Street, 503–265–7509), containing Native American artifacts, maritime displays, and pioneer furnishings and clothing. The region's natural history is explained in exhibits at the aquarium and museum of the **Mark O. Hatfield Marine Science Center** (2030 Marine Science Drive, 503–867–3011), run by Oregon State University.

North of Newport, Route 101 winds along Oregon's rugged coast, which is protected from development by a series of state parks. Just below **Lincoln City** is **Cape Foulweather,** named by Captain James Cook, who sighted it in 1778 but was unable to land because of bad weather. A **marker** (Route 101, just north of Otter Rock) commemorates the naming of the cape.

Farther north on Route 101 is **Tillamook,** from an Indian name meaning "land of many waters." The town has long been a

OVERLEAF: *The Oregon Dunes National Recreation Area preserves forty-four miles of sand dunes.*

dairy center, with cheese as its major product. The **Tillamook County Pioneer Museum** (2106 Second Street, 503–842–4553), housed in the town's 1905 courthouse, contains exhibits on early logging and cheesemaking operations, photographs of the county's settlers, and a replica of a pioneer home.

SEASIDE

Members of the Lewis and Clark expedition spent part of the winter of 1805–1806 here extracting salt from the ocean: They boiled approximately 1,400 gallons of water in five brass kettles to produce three and a half bushels of salt. The town was developed as a beach resort in the 1870s by transport magnate Ben Holladay, whose racetrack and hotel lured Portlanders to the ocean, and Southerner W. G. Grimes, who owned several local hotels. The **Seaside Historical Museum** (570 Necanicum Drive, 503–738–7065) features an exhibit of Clatsop Indian artifacts excavated from two local middens by the Smithsonian Institution during the 1970s.

ASTORIA

Astoria figured prominently in the early settlement of the Pacific Northwest. The first white person to see the site was Captain Robert Gray, whose discovery of the mouth of the Columbia River in 1792 attracted U.S. maritime traders to the region. Lewis and Clark made their Pacific camp seven miles southwest of the present city in the winter of 1805–1806. In 1811 representatives of John Jacob Astor's Pacific Fur Company founded the first permanent American settlement in the Oregon Country here. After clearing some land, marking the sites for a residence, storehouse, and powder magazine, and sowing some vegetable seeds, the men named their post in honor of "the projector and supporter of the whole enterprise." Due to poor management and a series of mishaps, the settlement was already failing by the outbreak of the War of 1812, when it was sold to Britain's North West Company. The trading post remained in British hands until the 1830s, although sovereignty was nominally returned to the United States by the Treaty of Ghent. With the arrival of the first overland immigrants in the mid-nineteenth century, Astoria prospered, establishing itself as a center of trade for the lower Columbia region. It is often said that the fur trade was the basis of the Astor fortune, but the family earned much more in New York real estate.

Columbia River Maritime Museum

Situated on the river whose name it bears, the museum is divided into seven galleries that depict different aspects of the Columbia's heritage. Included among the displays and exhibits are models, nautical instruments, naval weapons, photographs, boats, and marine engines. The 128-foot *Columbia*, which was the last active lightship on the West Coast, is moored outside and may be boarded.

> LOCATION: 1792 Marine Drive. HOURS: April through September: 9:30–5 Daily; October through March: 9:30–5 Tuesday–Sunday. FEE: Yes. TELEPHONE: 503–325–2323.

Astoria's seafaring families have left a legacy of Victorian homes, and the **chamber of commerce** (503–325–6311) provides detailed maps for walking tours. One of the finest houses is the restored **Flavel House** (441 Eighth Street, 503–325–2203), a Queen Anne mansion built in 1885 by a Columbia River bar pilot for his family, members of whom lived in it until 1933. The house, now a museum run by the

The lightship Columbia, *built in 1950 in East Boothbay, Maine, stood at the entrance of the Columbia River for thirty years. She now is moored at the Columbia River Maritime Museum in Astoria.*

Clatsop County Historical Society, contains six fireplaces, Eastlake woodwork, and period furniture. The historical society is headquartered at the **Heritage Museum** (1618 Exchange Street, 503–325–2563), a 1904 Classic Revival building that formerly served as Astoria's city hall. Recently restored, this museum contains exhibits on the history of the region. A block away, at Fifteenth and Exchange streets, is a replica of the **blockhouse** built by Astor's traders in 1811 (private).

Fort Clatsop National Memorial

Fort Clatsop is a reconstruction of Lewis and Clark's camp on the Pacific from December 7, 1805, to March 23, 1806. Although overjoyed to see the ocean after their arduous transcontinental journey, the members of the expedition put in a hard winter making salt, writing reports, and preparing maps—one of the most important contributions of the expedition. The site includes a replica of the fort (built after the floor plan drawn by William Clark), the canoe

Fort Clatsop, built by the Lewis and Clark Expedition for shelter during the winter of 1805–1806, was named to honor the hospitable Clatsop Indians.

landing, and a visitor center featuring a slide show and exhibits about the celebrated trek. During the summer the National Park Service sponsors a living history program.

> LOCATION: Off Route 101, 5 miles southeast of Astoria. HOURS: Mid-June through September: 8–6 Daily; October through mid-June: 8–5 Daily. FEE: Yes. TELEPHONE: 503–861–2471.

Ten miles west of Astoria, off Route 101, **Fort Stevens State Park** (Ridge Road, 503–861–2000) is the site of a military reservation that guarded the mouth of the Columbia River from the Civil War until World War II. The fort has the distinction of being the only coastal installation in the lower forty-eight states to be attacked by a foreign enemy since the War of 1812: On June 21, 1942, a Japanese submarine fired a few shells in the fort's vicinity, causing no damage. Though most of the guns and buildings are gone, a museum on the grounds displays maps, photographs, and artifacts that tell the history of the fort. Also within the park is the wreck of the iron-hulled British schooner *Peter Iredale,* which ran aground in 1906, a fate shared by many ships that have approached Oregon's treacherous rocky shores.

PORTLAND AND ENVIRONS

Perhaps epitomizing the state of Oregon, Portland has grown slowly and cautiously, ever protective of its natural riches and its independent citizens. The state's largest city sits on the banks of the Willamette River, just south of its junction with the Columbia. To the east are the Cascade Mountains and Mount Hood (at 11,239 feet, Oregon's highest point) and to the west is the Coast Range.

It was on the west bank of the Willamette, in a place the region's Indians called "the clearing," that William Overton and Asa Lovejoy stopped in 1843. Although headed for Oregon City, they were impressed by the fir-lined hills, the snow-capped peak in the distance, and the land, punctuated by buttes, that lay across the river to the east. Encouraged by the promise of free land—a proposal soon to be approved by Congress—the two filed a claim in early 1844, each receiving 340 acres of what would shortly become downtown Portland. Overton, who was known for his reputation as a wanderer, quickly sold his share to Francis Pettygrove, a New England merchant. Left to their Yankee devices, Lovejoy and Pettygrove began plotting a town, arguing over what to call it as they went.

A night view of Portland with Mount Hood in the distance.

Pettygrove, a native of Maine, wanted Portland; Lovejoy, from Massachusetts, preferred Boston. Flips of a copper coin determined the outcome.

Portland possessed a lovely landscape, but it was not suited for farming. Many of the state's earliest immigrants bypassed the new settlement for the more fertile lands of the Willamette Valley. The city began to develop in the late 1840s, however, nurtured by the efforts of such entrepreneurs as John Couch, a New England sea captain who had seen the site's potential as early as 1840, when he first came to explore the possibility of a salmon fishery. "To this point," he remarked, "I can bring any ship that can get into the mouth of the Great Columbia River." He kept his word, helping to transform the village into a major port. In 1845 another enterprising settler, Daniel Lownsdale, established a tannery—reputed to be the first in the Pacific Northwest—exchanging his leather for rawhides, furs, wheat, or cash. He was also a guiding force behind the development of the fertile Tualatin Valley to the west: The Great Plank Road he and others constructed (known today as Canyon Road) connected the ships and shops of the river port with the fields and granaries of the valley.

In its second decade the city prospered, fueled by California's gold rush, which created a demand for lumber, wheat, and farm products. By 1851, the year the city was incorporated, Portland's population had reached a respectable 800, nearly 200 buildings lined its streets, and a newspaper, the *Oregonian,* had begun publication. Portland also launched its first steamboat, the *Lot Whitcomb,* on Christmas Day 1850. The Columbia and its tributaries, which wound their ways among the various communities of the Pacific Northwest, were ripe for exploitation. Among those who saw the commercial potential and benefited from it was John Ainsworth, a Mississippi River captain who came to Oregon in 1850. "The sensation to me," he wrote in his memoirs, "of entering water that had never before been divided by the prow of a steamer, was beyond description." Ainsworth went on to build his own boats and became one of the founders of the Oregon Steam Navigation Company, a highly successful monopoly whose investors belonged to the city's ruling elite and were behind many of its cultural institutions.

Thanks to the discovery of gold in Idaho and the eastern part of the Oregon Territory, Portland continued to flourish in the 1860s and 1870s, despite a number of setbacks. The business district was moved inland to escape recurrent river flooding. The city was also struck by two fires—in December 1872 and August 1873—that leveled thirty blocks and inspired a flurry of rebuilding. Residential Portland was coming into its own as well. In the town's southwestern part, known by the unseemly appellation "Stumptown," Italianate villas, elm-lined streets, and spacious gardens replaced the early pioneer cottages. Ordinances were passed to encourage decorum: No logs were to be dragged down the streets, the only wheeled vehicles to use the sidewalks would be baby carriages, and anyone caught shooting a gun within the city limits would be fined.

Turn-of-the-century Portlanders were proud of their civilized city, one in which "social austerity," the legacy of their New England forebears and civic leaders, prevailed. They also treasured their natural habitat, enjoying mountain climbs, river excursions, hunting, fishing, and swimming. This carefully balanced combination of nature and urbanism drew more immigrants, who were, by the 1880s and 1890s, aided in their journey west by the transcontinental railroad. In response, the city expanded. East Portland, originally a separate town, was annexed in 1891. The wealthy and fashionable left their neighborhood in southwestern Portland for the hills—now called "the heights"—to the west. The city's population was rising quickly, but not quickly enough—Seattle, that upstart to the north, was exploding, and Washington's Puget Sound seemed to be the terminus of choice for the new transcontinental railroads. Harvey Scott, editor of the *Oregonian*, lamented Portlanders' "indifference, inertia, self-sufficiency," and their "wish to be alone." However, the Lewis and Clark Centennial Exposition of 1905, landscaped by John Olmsted, brother of Frederick Law Olmsted and a member of his firm, managed to arouse the city's residents as well as the interest of the outside world. Three million outsiders visited the fair, and Portland's population increased from 90,000 to nearly a quarter of a million in the first decade of the twentieth century.

Portland did not surpass Seattle, which became the Pacific Northwest's major metropolis, but it did become an eminently livable, if not always welcoming, city. During World War I patriotic Portlanders routed out dissidents and changed German street names, and during the 1920s, as the city's shipping and lumber industries boomed, the "Invisible Empire" of the Ku Klux Klan was busy recruiting members. In recent decades, however, conservative Portland has been forced to reassess its historic claims to self-sufficiency and isolation as some of its traditional industries, such as lumber and fishing, have declined. The influence of high technology, an influx of newcomers, and the city's potential to participate in the commerce of the Pacific Rim are working to induce change.

DOWNTOWN

Portland's downtown—a place of flowers, parks, cafés, and public squares—reflects its citizens' love for the great outdoors. Fountains dominate the landscape, the most famous being the twenty identical drinking fountains dedicated to the city in 1912 by lumber baron Simon Benson. Recognizable by their four-spigoted heads, they were allegedly conceived by Benson as a means of discouraging loggers from imbibing stronger stuff.

Near the waterfront the **Old Town Historic District,** site of Portland's original settlement in 1844, extends for several blocks on either side of West Burnside Street. In the 1860s and 1870s the harbor bustled with ships, steamboats, and sailors, and construction had begun on one of the country's largest collections of cast-iron buildings. As in Seattle, the wharf was dubbed "Skid Road" for the logs

OPPOSITE: *The New Market Theater, which opened in 1875. The theater fell into disrepair, was used as a parking garage, and has recently been renovated as the New Market Block with commercial tenants.*

that rolled down the timber tracks; the pejorative connotation of that term arose at the turn of the century, when the port moved downriver and the area went into decline. More recently the district has been gentrified, and though still a haven for the city's down-and-out, it boasts some fine architectural relics as well as the mile-long **Waterfront Park,** which runs along the Willamette River from the River Place Marina to the Steel Bridge.

Once the centerpiece for a lively new city, the **Skidmore Fountain** (Southwest First Avenue at Ankeny) was created by Olin Warner, known for the bronze doors at the Library of Congress in Washington, DC. The sculpture, a group of maidens atop a fluted basin, was named for Stephen Skidmore, one of six commissioners Portland sent to the Paris Exposition in 1878. So impressed was Skidmore by Europe's plazas and fountains that he willed money to the city to build a similar refreshment stop for the "horses, men and dogs" of Portland. The facade of the restored **Poppleton Building** (83 Southwest First Avenue) is particularly noteworthy with its lovely combination of cast-iron pilasters and truncated arches. It was built in 1871. The **New Market Theater** (50 Southwest Second Avenue), built in 1875, is a structural hybrid where vendors hawked produce on its main floor from twenty-eight marble-countered arched stalls, while upstairs Portland's polite society was entertained in an elegant crimson theater lit by 100 gas jets.

Dominating central Portland is the Mall, an eleven-block brick artery that extends along Fifth and Sixth avenues between Madison and Burnside streets. Here the city's eclectic mix of architecture provides some intriguing juxtapositions. Many of the buildings on **Pioneer Courthouse Square** (701 Southwest Sixth Avenue), the city's major public plaza, date to the first quarter of this century, but the **Pioneer Courthouse** (555 Southwest Yamhill, 503–221–2256) was constructed in 1869. At that time it was far enough from the town's center to prompt jokes about the need for a pony express to deliver the mail. Restored in 1973, it now houses the Ninth Federal Circuit Court of Appeals. Also on the mall is Michael Graves's controversial **Portland Building** (1120 Southwest Fifth Avenue), a Postmodern creation of pink, blue, and cream concrete and tile that has been both reviled and hailed by the architectural establishment and by Portlanders themselves. The 1895 **City Hall** (1120 Southwest Fifth Avenue), designed by William Whidden and Jon Lewis with a balustraded roof, long loggia, and pilasters on its east facade, stands in contrast to its glass-and-steel neighbors.

Oregon Historical Center

The Oregon Historical Society, the oldest statewide cultural institution in Oregon, is headquartered in the block-square Oregon Historical Center west of the Mall. The museum in the south wing of the complex features a major permanent exhibition documenting the state's history from prehistoric times to the present. New galleries in the north wing have exhibits on the settlement of the Willamette Valley, North Pacific maritime history, and Western art, as well as changing exhibits; this wing also contains two enormous architectural murals by the trompe l'oeil artist Richard Haas.

LOCATION: 1230 Southwest Park Avenue. HOURS: 10–4:45 Monday–Saturday. FEE: None. TELEPHONE: 503–222–1741.

The **Portland Art Museum** (1219 Southwest Park Avenue, 503–226–2811), designed by Pietro Belluschi in 1930, features a fine exhibit of Northwest Coast Indian art, including masks, textiles, and sacred objects; European painting and sculpture; and a respectable Asian collection. To the south are the **South Park Blocks,** set aside by the town founders in 1852 as a respite from fledgling urban woes.

Auguste Renoir's 1873 painting The Seine at Argenteuil, *in the collection of the Portland Art Museum.*

Planted with elms and grass, the area spawned town houses, a gentlemen's club, and churches. More recently it has attracted **Portland State University** (Southwest Broadway, 503–464–3511) and a lively student population.

South of the Mall is Portland Center, the outgrowth of the city's urban renewal project, begun in 1963. Previously, the district had been home to Jews who had migrated to Portland from Germany, Eastern Europe, Turkey, and Spain. Part of the Portland Center for the Performing Arts, the **Civic Auditorium** (222 Southwest Clay, 503–248–4335) is an ornate building overlooking the **Forecourt Fountain.** This fountain and the **Lovejoy Fountain** in **Lovejoy Park,** just south of the auditorium, were designed by the renowned landscape architect Lawrence Halprin, who envisioned them "as waterfalls echoing the natural water qualities of many of the magnificent cascades along the Columbia River and in the High Sierra."

SOUTHWEST PORTLAND

Just a few miles from downtown, reaching up into the western hills, southwest Portland is marked by wooded residential neighborhoods accessible by scenic roads. Vista Boulevard winds through Portland Heights, one of the city's first hillside suburbs, and leads to Council Crest, the city's highest point, which offers views of the Cascades, the Willamette Valley, the Coast Range, and the Columbia River. Dominating the district is **Washington Park** (Park Place, off Vista Boulevard), another gift of the city's foresighted civic leaders, who purchased the land in 1871. The park remained undeveloped until the 1880s, when a zoo was established, plantings were started, and a group called the German Songbird Society encouraged starlings, nightingales, thrushes, and finches to nest here. Today some four of the park's one hundred acres are devoted to the International Rose Test Gardens, founded in 1917 by the Portland Rose Society. Another five-and-a-half acres are formal Japanese gardens (503–223–1321) with a splendid variety of flowers, shrubs, and trees. In the park's southern end is the **Oregon Museum of Science and Industry** (4015 Southwest Canyon Road, 503–222–2828). OMSI, as it is known, originated in the collections of the Portland Free Museum, which displayed fossils, stuffed animals, skeletons, and other artifacts

OPPOSITE: *An elaborate staircase in the Pittock Mansion, Portland's most lavish home, built in 1914.*

contributed by local residents with a passion for the natural sciences. The push for a separate science museum came after World War II, but it wasn't until 1957 that OMSI was built. Today the museum includes a planetarium as well as varied exhibits on the natural sciences, industry, and agriculture. Next door is the **World Forestry Center** (4033 Southwest Canyon Road, 503–228–1367), with exhibits on forest management, resources, and products. The main hall resembles a traditional Oregon round barn and is designed with an appropriately rich variety of woods, including redwood, pine, cedar, fir, birch, walnut, and oak.

NORTHWEST PORTLAND

Home to elegant villas, mini-chateaus, and mini-castles in the late nineteenth century, northwest Portland has taken on an increasingly industrial character in recent decades. Nevertheless, it has its own nature preserve: the 1,000-acre **Forest Park.** A striking remnant of the district's residential past is the restored **Pittock Mansion** (3229 Northwest Pittock Drive, 503–248–4469). Situated on forty-six of the park's acres, the twenty-two-room French Renaissance Revival house was built in 1914 by Henry Pittock, the owner and publisher of Portland's *Daily Oregonian* (later known simply as the *Oregonian)* from 1861 to 1919. Considered self-consciously opulent in its time—some say Pittock was determined to impress the New York Fricks and San Francisco Spreckels—the house is graced with hardwood floors and panelling, polished marble, and period furniture, as well as spectacular views of the city's two rivers and five peaks of the Cascade Range.

THE EAST SIDE

Portland's East Side was slow in developing. While a city grew up on the west side of the Willamette River, small numbers of farmers crossed over it, followed by ferries. With the arrival of the railroads and the construction of a bridge in the late nineteenth century, residential development took off, producing the neighborhoods of Brooklyn, Sunnyside, Irvington, and Mount Tabor. By the 1920s the East Side—bounded by Milwaukie on the south and Eighty-second Avenue on the east—housed many of the city's residents, and today most of the city lies east of the river. Eastmoreland, a pleasant residential district described in an early promotional pamphlet as "Portland's standard-bearer for gracious living," is the home of **Reed College** (3203 Southeast Woodstock Boulevard, 503–777–7591). This small but prestigious liberal arts college, the legacy of Portland transport baron Simeon Reed and his wife, Amanda, opened in 1911 in a 40-acre cow pasture. The present 100-acre campus, which encompasses a wildlife refuge and lake, is distinguished by its ivy-covered buildings, including Hauser Library and the Gothic Revival Eliot Hall.

SAUVIE ISLAND

Just north of Portland, Sauvie Island (across the Sauvie Island Bridge, off Route 30) is a marvelous rural retreat of farms, wildlife sanctuaries, prairies, and quiet country roads. The island's first inhabitants were the Multnomah Indians, whose "scarlet and blue blankets Sailor Jackets, overalls, Shirts and hats" were noted by Lewis and Clark, the first white explorers to visit the island, on November 4, 1805. Outbreaks of malaria, scarlet fever, and small-pox reduced the population, and by the time Nathaniel Wyeth established a trading post in 1834, there was, he wrote, "nothing to attest that they ever existed except their decaying houses, their graves and their unburied bones." The island takes its name from a trapper, Jean Baptiste Sauvé, who was sent to establish a dairy here by the Hudson's Bay Company.

With the resolution of the boundary dispute between Britain and the United States in 1846, U.S. citizens were free to settle on the island, which they did in great numbers during the 1850s. A reminder of that era is the Greek Revival **James F. Bybee House** (Howell Territorial Park, 503–222–1741), restored and maintained by the Oregon Historical Society. The Greek Revival style was popular in the Northwest in the 1840s and 1850s as the region progressed beyond the pioneer period into an era of more sophistication. In many towns the first substantial houses and public buildings to be put up were designed in the Greek Revival style. Bybee, a county commissioner and horse breeder, built the nine-room dwelling in 1858, selling the property in 1873 to John Howell, a successful dairy farmer and promoter of agricultural development on the island. In addition to the house, the site, known as **Howell Territorial Park** (Tabor Road), includes an early orchard with 115 varieties of apple trees and a children's agricultural museum featuring horse-drawn equipment.

COLUMBIA RIVER GORGE

The 3,000-foot-deep, 75-mile Columbia River Gorge marks, with spectacular beauty, the passage of the river through the Cascade mountain range. As it approaches this basaltic channel the river gains great force and then flattens out for the final stage of its 1,243-mile journey from the Canadian Rockies to the Pacific Ocean. With the construction of the Columbia River Scenic Highway along the crest of the gorge in 1915, this natural wonder was opened to motorists from Portland and the surrounding areas. Two sections of the road remain, traveling parallel to Route 84, which runs the length of the gorge. The first section stretches from the Sandy River to Ainsworth State Park, the second from Mosier to The Dalles.

Crown Point State Park (Columbia River Scenic Highway), 725 feet above the river, is the site of **Vista House,** the brainchild of Samuel Lancaster, the consulting engineer for the highway. Construction began in 1916 and the building was dedicated in May 1918. A memorial to Oregon's pioneers, its dome contains eight panels, each inscribed with the name of a prominent settler. To the east of Crown Point is a series of splendid waterfalls, including Latourell, Shepperds Dell, Bridal Veil, Wahkeena, and the celebrated Multnomah, 620 feet high. A **visitor center** at the base of Multnomah Falls includes exhibits about the region's geology.

Forty-four miles from Portland, off Route 84, is the **Bonneville Dam,** authorized in 1933 and completed in 1939. Its **visitor center** (503–374–8820) features exhibits on the history of the gorge and the dam and provides views of the fish ladders used by salmon migrating to their spawning grounds. Four miles east are the **Cascade Locks,** built in 1896 to tame the treacherous rapids that were crossed, often at great peril, by early immigrants to the Oregon Country. Now unused, the locks are commemorated in the **Cascade Locks Museum** (503–374–8619), located in the town of Cascade Locks. The museum features the *Oregon Pony,* the Northwest's first steam locomotive, and photographs of steamboats, railroads, and portaging operations. Visitors can tour the river on the *Columbia Sightseer,* a paddle-wheeler, and the *Columbia Gorge Sternwheeler.*

The Dalles was named by the Hudson's Bay Company's French Canadian voyageurs, who thought the basaltic rocks lining the Columbia resembled flagstones *(les dalles).* Lewis and Clark stopped

OPPOSITE: *Multnomah Falls, the most spectacular of eleven waterfalls in an eleven-mile stretch of the Columbia River Gorge east of Crown Point.*

here in the fall of 1805 on their journey westward and made note of the vigorous trading among the Indians of the lower river and the tribes from the Columbia Plateau, who came "for the purpose of purchasing fish." The explorers were followed by fur traders; the first white settlement, a Methodist mission, was founded in 1838 by Daniel Lee. In 1849 a fort was established to protect Oregon Trail emigrants, who loaded their wagons onto rafts here and continued down the Columbia to Oregon City. Information about historical sites is available at the town's **visitor center** (406 West Second Street, 503–296–4798), located in the original Wasco County Courthouse, a frame building constructed in 1859. The **Fort Dalles Historical Museum** (Fifteenth and Garrison streets, 503–296–4547), housed in the fort's restored surgeon's quarters (1856), contains Indian and pioneer artifacts, including an original covered wagon and a collection of other horse-drawn vehicles.

MOUNT HOOD NATIONAL FOREST

Oregon's highest peak, Mount Hood has fascinated the region's inhabitants for centuries. According to one Indian legend, a warrior thought he could stop the lava flows by throwing boulders into the mountain's crater. Enraged, Mount Hood spit them back into the vil-

A 1913 climbing expedition up Mount Hood, Oregon's highest peak.

lage below. The warrior, distressed by the destruction that ensued, dropped to his knees in despair and was engulfed by lava. No major eruptions have been recorded, but the state's early settlers often claimed that they had witnessed some volcanic activity. The Portland *Oregonian* reported on September 18, 1859, that a man driving cattle over Barlow Road had seen "intermittent columns of fire erupting from the crater for two hours." The mountain's summit was first reached by whites when a group of Portland climbers ascended it in 1857. Now ski lifts travel part of the way up. The imposing **Timberline Lodge** (off Route 26, 800–452–1335), built in 1937 by the WPA, was the setting of Stanley Kubrick's film *The Shining.*

LOCATION: Route 26, off Route 35, 45 miles east of Portland. HOURS: Always open. FEE: None. TELEPHONE: 503–666–0700.

WILLAMETTE RIVER VALLEY

For most emigrants heading west to Oregon in the mid-nineteenth century, the Willamette River valley was the destination of choice. After the rigors of the Oregon Trail its prairies, fertile soil, moderate climate, and the access to markets provided by the Columbia and Willamette rivers made the region seem like Eden. "Here we find all of the conveniences of civilized life and we are able for the first time to appreciate them," wrote one pioneer who had just crossed the treacherous road around the base of Mount Hood.

The "civilization" these immigrants found began amid the struggle between the United States and Great Britain for domination of the Oregon Country. John McLoughlin, head of the Columbia department of the Hudson's Bay Company, established the region's first settlement near the site of present-day Oregon City in the winter of 1828–1829. Close behind the British were American missionaries, who started out in hopes of converting the Indians and found themselves involved in the more secular task of claiming Oregon for the United States. In 1843 the U.S. settlers established a provisional government at Oregon City, and by 1846 the U.S. title to Oregon was secured in a treaty with Great Britain.

In the past century the valley has attracted Midwestern farmers, New England merchants, journalists, educators, politicians, and more recently, high technology. Today the region remains a lovely combination of small river towns, gracious larger cities, dense evergreen forests, verdant fields, and abundant water.

OREGON CITY

Situated on the falls of the Willamette River, Oregon City was born of the struggle by the United States and Great Britain for supremacy in the Oregon Country. From his base at Fort Vancouver, Washington, John McLoughlin of the Hudson's Bay Company ordered three log cabins built next to the falls in the winter of 1828–1829. Although they were burned by Indians, McLoughlin would not be deterred; in 1832 he established a sawmill and flour mill on the site. The next decade saw the arrival of small groups of U.S. settlers, including Methodist missionaries who founded a milling company in 1841 opposite McLoughlin's property. To forestall them, McLoughlin named the town and sent a group of settlers to survey house lots in 1842. In 1843, however, the U.S. settlers voted at Champoeg to establish a provisional government, with Oregon City as its seat.

The city sits on two levels. The lower level, site of the original settlement, retains a number of late-nineteenth- and early-twentieth-century commercial buildings along Main Street, most noteworthy among them the terra cotta and brick Classic Revival **Bank of Commerce** (702 Main Street), designed by the prominent Portland architect A. E. Doyle in 1922. Residential development began on the upper level, in the **McLoughlin Neighborhood** (Tenth Street to Fourth Street, between High and Van Buren streets), in the 1850s. Today it contains a mixture of Queen Anne, Colonial Revival, Georgian Revival, and English cottage styles of architecture. After the United States claimed the Oregon Country with the Treaty of 1846, McLoughlin settled in Oregon City and became a U.S. citizen. The Georgian Revival **John McLoughlin House** (713 Center Street, 503–656–5146) has been restored with period furniture, much of it original to the house. The white clapboard **Barclay House,** on the same site, dates from 1849. The flat-roofed **Ermatinger House** (619 Sixth Street), built in 1845, was the home of Francis Ermatinger, chief trader for the Hudson's Bay Company and a member of the provisional government; it contains early-nineteenth-century furnishings. Also in the neighborhood are the Clackamas County Historical Society, which maintains the restored **Stevens-Crawford House Museum,** a 1908 Classic Revival house (603 Sixth Street, 503–655–2866), and the **End of the Oregon Trail Interpretive Center** (500 Washington Street, 503–657–9336). The center contains exhibits on the pioneers who journeyed the arduous 2,000 miles from Independence, Missouri, to the Pacific Northwest, stopping at the falls of the Willamette River before heading out to Fort Vancouver or the Willamette Valley.

In 1848 President James K. Polk established the Oregon Territory, with Oregon City as its capital. The first territorial legislature met in the second-floor ballroom of the **Rose Farm** (Holmes and Rilance lanes, 503–657–7804) in 1849, and Joseph Lane, the newly appointed governor, gave his inaugural address there. Built in 1847, the house has been restored with period furnishings, including a square piano brought around the Horn of South America in 1859. The original land grant, signed by Abraham Lincoln, is also on display. The rose garden that gave the house its name is being re-established.

Information about the city's historic districts is available from the **Oregon City Civic Improvement Trust** (320 Warner Milne Road, 503–657–0891) and the **chamber of commerce** (500 Abernethy Road, 503–656–1619).

CHAMPOEG STATE PARK

This park marks the site of the village of Champoeg, an important political center in the early 1840s. It was here in May 1843 that the region's French Canadian and U.S. settlers voted to organize a provisional government for Oregon. When Oregon City was designated the home of this government Champoeg's political importance declined, but the town thrived as a commercial and transportation center until 1861, when it was destroyed by a flood. The park's visitor center tells Champoeg's history with paintings, photographs, films, and lectures.

LOCATION: 8239 Champoeg Road NE, Saint Paul. HOURS: 8–4:30 Monday–Friday, 1–4 Saturday–Sunday. FEE: Yes. TELEPHONE: 503–678–1251.

SALEM

Oregon's capital was founded in 1840 by Methodist missionary Jason Lee. Discouraged by his failure to convert the region's Indians, he devoted his energies to the white immigrants, who were taking to the Oregon Trail in increasing numbers, and to the secular task of building a city. Salem grew slowly, and nearly half of its population left to mine California's Mother Lode in the late 1840s. Nevertheless, in 1851, at the urging of a prominent group of Democrats called the "Salem Clique," the territorial legislature voted to move the capital to Salem. Still in its infancy, the town had little to offer the legislature in the way of proper lodgings. They voted to move to Corvallis in 1855 but were stopped by the appropriation of money for a capitol building by Congress. Salem's position was firmly established in 1859 when Oregon was admitted to the Union.

The city's centerpiece is the **State Capitol** (Court Street, 503–378–4423). Built in 1938, the modern white structure boasts a sharp, symmetrical facade and a fluted, cylindrical central dome topped by a twenty-four-foot gold-leaf statue, *The Pioneer.* The upper walls of the capitol's rotunda, which is handsomely finished in rose travertine marble, are decorated with murals depicting the history of the state.

Across the street is **Willamette University** (900 State Street, 503–370–6300), which claims to be the oldest institution of higher learning west of the Missouri River and north of New Mexico.

Carding machines at the 1889 Thomas Kay Woolen Mill, part of Salem's Mission Mill Village. The mill's original water-power system has been restored and is used to generate electricity.

Established by Jason Lee in 1842 as the Oregon Institute, it was chartered in 1853. Among the buildings on the red-brick campus is **Waller Hall,** built between 1864 and 1867 in the form of a cross and named for one of the state's early missionaries.

South and east of the capitol, Salem marks its past with a number of interesting landmarks. The **Mission Mill Village** (1313 Mill Street SE, 503–585–7012) is a complex of restored buildings that includes the Jason Lee House and the Methodist Mission Parsonage, both built in 1841; the John D. Boon House (1847); and the Thomas Kay Woolen Mill (1889). Aaschel Bush, a member of the "Salem Clique," who founded the *Oregon Statesman* newspaper and the Ladd and Bush Bank (both still in operation), spent part of his fortune on a twelve-room Victorian Italianate house, completed in 1878. Now restored, the **Bush House** (600 Mission Street SE, 503–363–4714) has ten fireplaces of Italian marble and is furnished with period pieces. Down the block is **Deepwood** (Twelfth and Mission streets, 503–363–1825), a late-nineteenth-century estate that has been home to several prominent Salem families. The Queen Anne house has been restored, and the gardens (landscaped in 1929), the back pasture, and the greenhouse are open. **Mahonia Hall** (533 Lincoln Street South, 503–378–3111), the governor's residence, is named in honor of the state flower, the Oregon Grape *(Mahonia aquifolium).* A Tudor mansion built in 1930 and given to the state in 1988 by private citizens, it is open for tours by appointment.

ALBANY

Founded in 1848 by two brothers from New York's state capital, this small town is known as the birthplace of Oregon's Republican party. Here, in 1856, Free State men drafted a platform that called for "free speech, free labor, [and] a free press." Albany's graceful center, with its many Carpenter Gothic, Italianate, Queen Anne, and Eastlake houses, is a testament to the town's prosperity in the second half of the nineteenth century, when it served as a major processing center for forest and agricultural products. The **Monteith House** (518 Second Avenue SW, 503–926–1517), home to the town's founders and then a community center, is now a museum in the process of being authentically restored.

In the Albany vicinity, particularly to the east around Scio, are ten covered bridges, all built in the early decades of this century. Information is available at the **chamber of commerce** (435 West First Avenue, 503–926–1517).

CORVALLIS

Latin for "heart of the valley," Corvallis is well named. Although it lost to Salem the chance to be territorial capital in 1855, the city went on to achieve prominence as a distribution point for the fertile valley's fruit and dairy industries. Today Corvallis is one of the world's largest grass-seed-growing areas, supplying approximately 90 percent of the nation's grass seed. It is also the home of **Oregon State University** (Fourteenth and Jefferson streets, 503–754–3733), founded in 1856. It became an agricultural college in 1862, and today produces engineers for Corvallis's growing high-tech community, presided over by Hewlett Packard. The university's **Horner Museum** (in the Gill Coliseum near Southwest Western and 26th streets, 503–754–2951) features exhibits on the region's history and natural history. The **Benton County Historical Museum,** housed in an 1865 Georgian Revival brick building in the nearby lumber town of **Philomath** (1101 Main Street, 503–929–6230), is another source of information on the area's past.

EUGENE

With the Willamette National Forest to the east, the Coast Range to the west, and the river's rich fields in between, Eugene is a mixture of the urban and the pastoral. The seat of Lane County, the city was founded in 1846 and prospered with wheat, fruit, dairies, and lumber in the 1870s. In 1872 the University of Oregon was established here.

The **East Skinner Butte Historic Landmark Area** (High to Pearl streets, between Second and Fifth streets), the site of the city's first settlement, contains a collection of residential architecture—including Queen Anne, Bungalow, Colonial Revival, and Classic Revival styles—dating from the 1850s to the 1920s. Particularly noteworthy is the **Shelton-McMurphey House** (303 Willamette Street, 503–687–4239), on the south slope of Skinner Butte. A fine example of the late-Victorian villa style, the house was known as "the Castle on the Hill," though lumber was so inexpensive in 1888 that it only cost $8,000 to build.

The boundaries of the city's downtown correspond roughly to the city limits of 1876, when the railroad's arrival inspired confi-

OPPOSITE: *Saint Mary's Roman Catholic Church, Albany, a Gothic Revival structure put up in 1898. The church has more than 100 stained-glass windows.*

dence in the future. The Georgian Revival **Oregon Electric Depot** (27 East Fifth Avenue), designed by the prominent Oregon architect A. E. Doyle, is a landmark from the early nineteenth century; it is now a restaurant. The Italianate **Smeede Hotel** (767 Willamette Street), with round arches over its windows, dates from 1885 and is one of the region's oldest surviving hotel buildings. Today it houses retail businesses, restaurants, and professional offices.

On the **University of Oregon** campus (13th Avenue and Kincaid Street, 503–686–3014), among the fir, spruce, and redwood trees, there are several architectural gems including the Second Empire **Deady Hall,** built in 1876 as the university's first building. Its recessed surfaces and cast-iron keystones and window sills add richness to the exterior. **Villard Hall** was built in 1885 in a style similar to that of Deady Hall but more thickly stuccoed. It was named for Henry Villard, the railway magnate and university benefactor. Villard came to the United States from Germany at the age of eighteen, reported on the gold rush and the Civil War as a newspaper correspondent, and in the 1870s took charge of building the Oregon and California Railroad. He bought out other companies until he virtually controlled transportation in the Northwest, then took over the faltering Union Pacific Railroad. He completed that line, which linked the Northwest with the rest of the country, in 1883.

The **Lane County Historical Museum** (740 West 13th Avenue, 503–687–4239) chronicles the region's history through the 1920s. The experiences of pioneers who arrived via the Elliot Cutoff from the Oregon Trail prior to 1860 are recounted in an exhibit that includes artifacts, photos, maps, and a covered wagon. Exhibits and photographs are also housed in the 1853 **Lane County Clerk's Office,** adjacent to the main museum building.

COTTAGE GROVE

A major lumber center today, Cottage Grove was filled with miners in the 1860s, when gold-bearing quartz was discovered in the neighboring Bohemia Mining District. The **Cottage Grove Historical Museum** (Birch Avenue and H Street), housed in a late-nineteenth-century Roman Catholic church, contains antique mining equipment and working models of a stamp mill and sawmill from the late nineteenth century.

OPPOSITE: *Eugene's elaborate Shelton-McMurphey House, a fine example of craftsmanship in wood.*

S O U T H W E S T   O R E G O N

Southwest Oregon is dominated by the Rogue River, which begins at Boundary Springs north of Crater Lake National Park, flows through a valley past Ashland, Medford, and Grants Pass, cuts through the Coast Range, and empties into the Pacific at Gold Beach. Among the region's first inhabitants were the Takelma Indians and related bands, whose lives were irrevocably changed by the discovery of gold in the 1850s. As white miners and farmers set down roots, tensions between the newcomers and the Indians grew. The ensuing Rogue River Wars raged from 1851 to 1856—interrupted only by one peace agreement and the 1853 Treaty of Table Rock, negotiated by former Oregon territorial governor Joseph Lane. In a pattern typical of the entire Pacific Northwest, the problem was resolved by the removal of the Indians to reservations (Siletz and Grand Ronde in northwestern Oregon), opening up the area for further white settlement. In the second half of the nineteenth century, logging towns, dairy farms, cattle ranches, and pear orchards sprung up in southern Oregon. This rural region also welcomed city culture: Vaudeville acts filled the saloons of Jacksonville in its earliest days and the Chautauqua movement brought lectures and entertainment to Ashland.

In the late 1800s Peter Britt of Jacksonville photographed his daughter, son, and stepson pouring wine produced at the family's vineyard. An avid gardener, Britt kept such exotic plants as the banana tree in his conservatory over the winter.

GRANTS PASS

Grants Pass began as a stop on the California stagecoach route that connected Portland and Sacramento from the 1850s until the two states were linked by rail in the late 1880s. Today the lumber industry dominates the town, nestled in a small valley on the west bank of the Rogue River. It is also a center for recreational activities. The **Visitor and Convention Bureau** (1501 Northeast Sixth Street, 800-547-5927) provides information on boat and pack trips, many of which cover old mining territory. Among the first people to run the river for sport was writer Zane Grey, who in 1925 hired local guide Claude Bardon to shepherd his party of wooden boats down the river's white water. The **Schmidt House** (Fifth and J streets, 503-479-7827) was built around the turn of the century by Claus and Hannchen Schmidt, German immigrants who homesteaded on the Rogue River in the 1880s and later opened a grocery store in town. The house is preserved almost intact with some original furnishings and a collection of antique toys.

JACKSONVILLE

The early history of Jacksonville, settled by gold miners in the 1850s, resembled that of other gold towns. The lawyer and politician Orange Jacobs, later mayor of Seattle, wrote in 1853, "there were but few women, and most of them not angelic. The mines were rich, money was abundant, and gambling rampant." An epidemic of smallpox, a flood, and a fire devastated the city in the late 1860s and 1870s, but the rebuilt community, created in anticipation of the railroad that would never come, has survived; the entire city is a National Historic Landmark. The **Jacksonville Museum of Southern Oregon History** (206 North Fifth Street, 503-899-1847) contains exhibits on the impact of railroading in the Rogue Valley; stoneware made in the local Hannah family pottery; and displays on Peter Britt, a frontier Renaissance man who photographed Jacksonville and southern Oregon from 1852 to 1905, farmed, mined gold, kept bees, and was a financier. The museum is operated by the Southern Oregon Historical Society, which also maintains the 1880 **U.S. Hotel** (125 East California Street), the 1863 **Beekman Express and Banking Office** (110 West California Street), the 1891 **Rogue River Valley Railroad Depot** (185 North Oregon Street), and the 1873 **Cornelius C. Beekman House** (470 East California Street) and sponsors walking tours.

The Jacksonville merchant Jeremiah Nunan built this eclectic Victorian house in 1893 using a plan book issued by George Barber, an architect from Tennessee.

ASHLAND

Ashland was founded in 1852 on Bear Creek, at the southernmost end of the Rogue River valley. Mining, logging, wool production, and agriculture became the town's main industries, and in the early twentieth century a group of Ashland businessmen tried to promote the city as a mineral springs resort, capitalizing on the lithia water that flowed nearby. Although the venture failed, mineral water rich in lithium, sulfur, sodium, and chlorine still bubbles from fountains in the city's main plaza and in **Lithia Park,** to the west of the plaza off Main Street. The park was the site of Chautauqua meetings in the 1890s and early 1900s and is now home to the Oregon Shakespeare Festival. The wall surrounding the seating area of the festival's Elizabethan theater was the foundation of the Chautauqua's mammoth beehive-shaped tabernacle, demolished in 1916.

The Southern Oregon Historical Society runs a museum in the restored Colonial Revival **Chappell-Swedenburg House** (1250 Siskiyou Boulevard, 503–488–1341), which was built in 1904–1905. Exhibits focus on the history of the region's development and its residents, and the society sponsors guided walking tours of the area.

C E N T R A L   O R E G O N

People are scarce, distances are long, and landscapes are dramatic in this part of the state. The number of sizable towns can be counted on one hand. Surrounding them, however, are the pine trees of the Fremont, Deschutes, and Ochoco national forests; mountains and high desert; many deep lakes; hundreds of species of flora and fauna; and lands that were shaped into caves, tubes, dams, and other fascinating features by the great Columbia lava flows during the Miocene epoch. Among those who explored this forbidding, sometimes startlingly beautiful territory were the Hudson's Bay Company's Peter Skene Ogden in 1825 and John C. Frémont, whose journeys in 1843 and 1846 are approximately followed by the course of present-day Route 97. Settlement proceeded slowly in Oregon's center. From 1856 to 1858, recognizing the firmness of Indian resistance, the U.S. Army prevented immigrants from settling east of the Cascades. The Modoc War of 1872–1873, distinguished by the campaigns of Modoc chief Kientpoos (known as "Captain Jack"), left white homesteaders uneasy, but during the following decade they shifted the focus of their hostility from the Indians, by then banished to reservations, to one another. Range wars between cattlemen and sheepherders raged, with beatings and murder bloodying the land.

Central Oregon today is still home to cows and sheep as well as antelope and deer, who are protected in the Hart Mountain National Antelope Refuge, not far from Lakeview. Lumbering is a major industry, as is tourism. From the ghost towns of the northern prairies to the shores of Upper Klamath Lake, the region's wild beauty and history make for interesting travels.

KLAMATH FALLS

The region around Klamath Falls was settled in the 1860s. The Klamath and Modoc Indians resisted the white newcomers by launching a series of attacks. In 1872 and 1873, northern California's Modoc left the reservation and clashed with the U.S. Army in the Modoc War. Klamath Falls, originally called Linkville for the river that flowed through it, is the center for the area's lumber, cattle, and agricultural industries. The **Klamath County Museum** (1441 Main Street, 503–883–4208) features exhibits on local geology, history, and wildlife. Also notable is the museum's annex, the restored **Baldwin Hotel Museum** (31 Main Street, 503–883–4207). This four-story brick structure, built in 1904, first housed the hardware business of one of the city's civic leaders and was converted into a hotel in 1911. Among the guests were presidents Theodore Roosevelt, Taft, and Wilson. Many of the hotel's original furnishings remain. At the **Favell Museum of Western Art and Indian Artifacts** (125 West Main Street, 503–882–9996), the works of Western artists are displayed along with Native American artifacts, including an extensive collection of arrowheads.

North of town is the **Fort Klamath Museum** (Route 62, south of Crater Lake, 503–883–4208) on the site of a fort established in 1863 to protect white settlers. A replica of the guardhouse contains military clothing, equipment, firearms, and exhibits on the Modoc War.

CRATER LAKE NATIONAL PARK

Crater Lake was formed nearly 7,000 years ago after Mount Mazama erupted, showering the region with fiery ash. Following the eruption, the top of the mountain collapsed, creating a caldera, or basin, that filled with rain and melted snow to form a lake. The eruption was witnessed by local Indians and the lake came to be regarded by many as sacred—so much so that they were forbidden to look upon it or even speak of it. Thus the first white explorers in the region were unaware of its existence. A group of prospectors stumbled upon the lake in 1853, while searching for a rumored gold mine in the region; they reported their discovery, but public interest was not aroused until 1865, when soldiers from nearby Fort Klamath began bringing in parties of sightseers. The lake quickly became a tourist attraction, and in 1902, following a seventeen-year campaign by conservationist William Gladstone Steel, it was made a national park.

LOCATION: Route 62, sixty miles north of Klamath Falls. HOURS: Varied according to season. FEE: Yes, in summer. TELEPHONE: 503–594–2211.

The **Lava Lands Visitor Center** (Route 97, 503–593–2421), situated at the edge of Lava Butte, ten miles south of Bend, contains dioramas depicting the volcanic activity that created the Cascade peaks and has trails that wind through the lava beds. Three miles north on Route 97 is the **High Desert Museum** (503–382–4754), which features exhibits on the ecosystems of the Oregon Plateau and the geology of the area.

Between Redmond and Bend, two-and-a-half miles west of Route 97, are the **Petersen Rock Gardens** (503–382–5574), where local petrified wood, thunder eggs, malachite, lava, and obsidian have been fashioned into statues and castles. In nearby **Prineville,** the **Bowman Museum** (246 North Main Street, 503–447–3715), run by the Crook County Historical Society, features artifacts and exhibits on local history.

SHANIKO

Shaniko was named for August Scherneckau (pronounced "Shaniko" by the Indians), whose house in nearby Cross Hollow served in the 1870s as a station on the stage route from The Dalles to the more isolated settlements in central Oregon. The town boomed in the early 1900s when it was made the terminus of the Columbia Southern Railroad. It was also the site of skirmishes between sheep-herders and cattlemen, who vied for domination of the range. The sheepherders persevered, and Shaniko became a central shipping point for wool and other goods from the surrounding region. A number of buildings survive from the town's heyday, including the **Shaniko Hotel** (Fourth and E streets), built in 1900 and still in busi-ness. Across the street are the city hall and the post office, and the old water tower and schoolhouse are two blocks north of the hotel.

Shaniko preserves many evocative remnants of its days as an important wool-shipping center. Sections of it have the look of a ghost town. OVERLEAF: *Crater Lake.*

EASTERN OREGON

The first assessments of eastern Oregon by early pioneers were dismal. One emigrant wrote, upon reaching the mouth of the Walla Walla River in 1843, "If this is a fair specimen of Oregon, it falls far below the conceptions which I formed of the country. . . . The whole country looks poverty stricken." The Nez Percé, northeast Oregon's native inhabitants, knew better. Nomadic and mountain-bred, they spent winters in the canyons of the Grand Ronde, Imnaha, and Snake rivers and summers in the Wallowa Valley and near Wallowa Lake. They fished for trout and salmon, hunted for elk, deer, and bighorn sheep, and gathered different kinds of berries. The land had much to offer, but its mountains, rugged canyons, and deserts were a challenge to settlement.

By the second half of the nineteenth century, the Nez Percé found themselves on the defensive. Gold strikes in Idaho, Montana, and eastern Oregon in 1860 and 1861 brought a stream of fortune seekers. In the 1870s cattlemen had begun to stake their claim, lured by the region's acres of meadows and bunch grass. Pressured by increasing white settlement, the government negotiated with the Nez Percé, who were adamant about keeping their land in the Wallowa Valley. Treaties and executive orders from 1855 through the mid-1870s alternately honored the Indians' demands and ignored them. The wrangling culminated in the tragic 1877 Nez Percé War, in which Chief Joseph and his people, after an 1,800-mile-long trek battling with the U.S. Army, surrendered in the Bear Paw Mountains of Montana. The 1878 "Bannock War" was fought by a small group of Bannock and Paiute Indians who resisted settlement on reservations. The Indians were suppressed by General O. O. Howard's troops and placed on the Yakima reservation in Washington.

Today eastern Oregon's natural attractions—the John Day Fossil Beds, Hells Canyon National Recreation Area, Malheur National Wildlife Refuge, and others—draw naturalists, hikers, white-water enthusiasts, and skiers. The region's towns are small and scattered, centers for the local industries of cattle raising, lumber, and agriculture.

THE OREGON TRAIL

Parts of the route that John Jacob Astor's fur traders took during their overland expedition in 1811–1812 would later become known

as the Oregon Trail. For the next several decades, sections of the
trail were used by mountain men, missionaries, scientists, and sports-
men. When the Great Migration from Independence, Missouri, to
the Oregon Country began in the 1840s, thousands of settlers traveling in covered wagons braved deserts, mountains, difficult water
crossings, and occasional harassment by Indians in the six-month
journey to the Willamette Valley. Later the home-seekers were out-
numbered by Mormons, gold-seekers, and others bound for
California, Utah, and Idaho as well as Oregon. The trail, rarely a single track, was ten miles wide in some places and diverged in others
to accommodate the destinations of different parties.

Those going to the Willamette Valley and points farther west
passed through northeastern Oregon. Along Routes 84 and 30,
which roughly parallel the old Oregon Trail, are monuments and
signs marking this historic migration and towns that sprouted up in
its wake. Just south of **Huntington,** a stagecoach station and railway
division point in the late nineteenth century, is **Farewell Bend State
Park** (Route 30, 503–869–2365). Hard by the Idaho border, the park
marks the site where the wagons left the Snake River for the arduous
journey to the Columbia. To the northwest is **Baker,** which sprang
up with the discovery of gold nearby in 1861 and prospered through
the early 1900s. The **Oregon Trail Regional Museum** (Campbell and
Grove streets, 503–523–9308) contains displays of period clothing
and artifacts of such early regional industries as mining and ranching. At the **Eastern Oregon Museum** (Third and Wilcox streets,
503–856–3233), nine miles northwest of Baker in **Haines,** turn-of-
the-century agricultural equipment (including manure spreaders,
threshing machines, and hay balers) is on display along with a collection of restored antique dolls and rooms furnished with period
furniture.

JOSEPH

This town north of Wallowa Lake was named for the two great Nez
Percé chiefs, Old and Young Joseph, whose bands inhabited Wallowa
County before the arrival of white settlers. The town, which was
known by three different names (Lake City, Silver Lake, and Joseph
Town), was incorporated as Joseph in 1887. The **Wallowa County
Museum** (Main Street) is housed in an Eastlake-style building that
originally served as the First Bank of Joseph. It contains displays on
Nez Percé and early pioneer history. Old Chief Joseph's grave is

marked by a stone shaft in the **Nez Percé Indian Cemetery** (Route 82) at Wallowa Lake. Information is available at the town's **visitor center** (102 East First Street, 503–432–1015).

Thirty miles northeast of Joseph lies the tiny town of **Imnaha,** from which County Road 350 leads to the **Nee-Me-Poo Trail** in the **Hells Canyon National Recreation Area** (503–426–3151). The Wallowa band of the Nez Percé followed this 3.7-mile route from the Inmaha River to the Snake River in 1877, the year they were finally forced from the Wallowa Valley by the U.S. Army. With 750 Indians and 2,000 head of horses and cattle, Young Chief Joseph and other tribal leaders began a roundabout 1,200-mile flight, which ended with their surrender in the Bear Paw Mountains of Montana, just forty miles from their goal, the Canadian border. Had the Nez Percé been able to cross into Canada, they might have remained free.

PENDLETON

On the route of thousands of emigrants on the Oregon Trail, Pendleton became a town in the 1860s, when it was recognized as a fine place to grow wheat. By the time of its incorporation in 1880, it had become the seat of Umatilla County and the center of eastern Oregon's cattle industry. Wool is a major industry today, and the processes of carding, spinning, weaving, and dyeing may be seen at **Pendleton Woolen Mills** (1307 Southeast Court Place, 503–276–6911). Five miles east of town on Route 30 is the **Umatilla Indian Reservation,** established in 1855. It contains one of the Pacific Northwest's oldest Catholic missions.

JOHN DAY

This town was named for John Day, a scout of John Jacob Astor's overland expedition in 1811, who fell ill and was found on the Columbia River in May of 1812. He later died insane in Astoria. The town, however, prospered as a pony express station on the route from The Dalles to Canyon City during the gold strikes in Idaho, Montana, and eastern Oregon in 1860 and 1861 and became a ranching center, which it remains today. The **Kam Wah Chung & Co.**

OPPOSITE: *Young Chief Joseph photographed in Bismarck, Dakota Territory, after the surrender of the Nez Percé in 1877. His Indian name meant "Thunder Traveling to Loftier Mountain Heights."*

Museum (Canton Street, 503–575–0028), in a restored building that served as a trading post in the late 1860s, records the history of the town and the Chinese community drawn here in the gold rush days.

The **John Day Fossil Beds National Monument,** which encompasses more than 14,000 acres, contains fossils of vegetation and animals that flourished in the region up to 45 million years ago. Among the first to take note of the area's rich store of fossils was Thomas Condon, a Congregational pastor from The Dalles, who shipped some of his specimens to the Smithsonian Institution in 1870. In the late nineteenth century many major expeditions were mounted here by paleontologists. Fossil specimens are on display in the **park headquarters** (Route 395, 503–575–0721) in the town of John Day. In the park's Sheep Rock Unit seven miles northwest of Dayville, the **visitor center** (off Route 19, 503–987–2333), housed in a ranch house dating from the early 1900s, has exhibits on fossils and the geology of the area. Artifacts of the Cant family, the Scottish immigrants who lived on the ranch, are also on display.

Employees of the Pendleton Woolen Mills proudly drape themselves in their products for the camera in 1910.

CANYON CITY

This tiny town was the hub of gold-rush activity in the John Day Valley during the 1860s, when some 10,000 miners camped in the vicinity and conducted business on the town's main street. The **Grant County Historical Museum** (Route 395, 503–575–0362) marks this era with artifacts and displays of the period. The restored **Joaquin Miller Cabin** is also on the museum grounds. Miller, who came to Canyon City in 1864 after a stint in the Willamette Valley, was an eccentric and peripatetic writer, whose works about the West—including *Life Among the Modocs*—were popular at the turn of the century.

BURNS

Burns, southeastern Oregon's major city and livestock center, was settled by cattle ranchers in the 1880s and named for the Scottish poet Robert Burns. The **Harney County Historical Museum** (18 West D Street, 503–573–2636) contains displays of arrowheads, quilts, furniture, clothing, and other artifacts from the region's early days.

Sixty miles south of Burns, at the southern end of the **Malheur National Wildlife Refuge** (off Route 205, 503–493–2612) and the terminus of a popular tour route through the Harney Valley, is the restored **Frenchglen Hotel** (Route 205, 503–493–2825). Built in 1916 and still open for business, it is located on land that belonged to cattle baron Peter French, who was killed in 1897 by another rancher. To the southeast lie the Steens Mountains, a spectacular range that steeply drops 5,000 feet on its eastern side to the Alvord Valley.

LAKEVIEW

Founded in 1876 in the peaceful era that followed the Indian wars, Lakeview was the commercial center for south-central Oregon's sheep and cattle ranches. Today cattle ranching and the lumber industry are still important to the economy of the area. The **Schminck Memorial Museum** (128 South E Street, 503–947–3134), operated by the Daughters of the American Revolution, has an extensive collection of pioneer artifacts dating from the mid-nineteenth century, including quilts, children's toys, furniture, glassware, china, tools, and clothing.

WASHINGTON

OPPOSITE: *Point Wilson Lighthouse, erected in 1879 at the entrance to Puget Sound near Port Townsend.*

From the earliest days of its discovery, Washington has inspired awe. The most hard-bitten traders and explorers waxed eloquent, driven to poetic descriptions of its lofty trees, stupendous peaks, and bountiful rivers filled with salmon. The trade-off for these natural gifts, however, was best expressed by Lewis and Clark. Though ecstatic at their first glimpse of the Pacific on November 7, 1805—"O! the joy," wrote William Clark in his journal—they could not help but comment on the weather: "We passed a disagreeable night, the rain during the day having wet us completely, as indeed we have been for some days."

Such wetness, to this day associated with the state–indeed, the entire Pacific Northwest—is characteristic of only part of Washington's diverse geography. The state's major topographical features—the Olympic, Cascade, and Blue mountains, the Willapa Hills, Puget Sound, the Okanogan Highlands, and the Columbia Plateau—define regions of vastly different climates and resources. The Cascades are the dividing line: To the west are the rain forests of the Olympic Peninsula and Puget Sound, which includes Seattle; to the east are the drier ponderosa forests of the Okanogan Highlands, the semiarid lands of the Columbia River basin, and the rich volcanic soils of the Palouse. The great river of the Columbia Plateau, the Columbia, is the spawning place for Pacific salmon.

There is evidence that the Indians of the region may have been fishing for salmon in the Columbia as long as 11,000 years ago. Prehistoric Washington State was the home of several distinctive Indian cultures from at least four different linguistic groups. The coastal tribes—among them the Makah, Quinault, Salish, Puyallup, Nisqually, and Skokomish, who lived in the vicinity of Puget Sound, and the Chinook, Cowlitz, and Klickitat along the Columbia River—comprised one of the most prosperous groups of hunter-gatherer cultures known. Their main source of food was the salmon that spawned in Washington's many rivers. Some tribes were highly proficient whalers, using ocean-going canoes made of the abundant local cedar. Near Cape Alava on the Olympic Peninsula are the remains of Ozette, a Makah hunting and fishing village that was buried in a mud slide 500 years ago. It had been occupied for at least 2,000 years, and archaeologists have found over 50,000 artifacts there, including a remarkable effigy of a killer whale. Another excavation at a fishing station near the mouth of the Hoko River in the northern Olympic Peninsula has turned up artifacts from three millennia ago.

The Canadian artist Paul Kane, who witnessed Mount Saint Helens venting steam in the 1840s, based this painting of a nighttime eruption on accounts of the moutain's volcanic activity during 1842–1844 (detail).

Many of the region's Indians were highly skilled makers of ceremonial masks, decorated boxes, and other objects. The tribes to the south concentrated on trade, using the Columbia River as a highway to the tribes located east of the Cascade Mountains in the interior plateau, a region made up of high desert and rolling hills extending east to the Rockies. These tribes—the Sanpoil, Yakima, Wenatchee, Spokane, Palouse, and Wallawalla among them—lived in less permanent settlements than their coastal counterparts. Instead, they established camps where they found food—salmon in the Columbia River, elk and deer in the expanse of the plateau.

European explorers and traders began arriving in the late sixteenth century. The Spanish and English came first, intent upon finding a Northwest Passage from the Atlantic to the Pacific. However, Juan Cabrillo's expedition in 1542 was stymied by wind and fog, and his lieutenant, Bartolomé Ferrelo, just caught sight of Oregon before turning back. In 1774 Bruno Heceta passed the mouth of the Columbia River, obscured by waves and fog at a hazardous sandbar. Captain Cook, on his last voyage in 1778, also missed

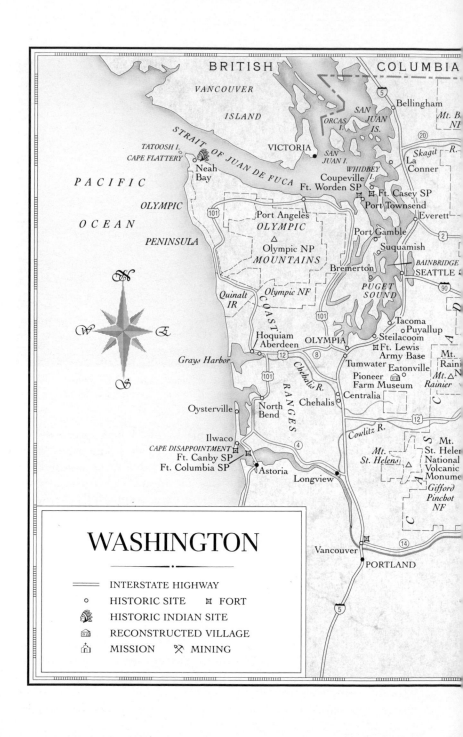

WASHINGTON

INTERSTATE HIGHWAY
- o   HISTORIC SITE   ⊞ FORT
- 🪶 HISTORIC INDIAN SITE
- 🏛 RECONSTRUCTED VILLAGE
- ⛪ MISSION   ⛏ MINING

BRITISH COLUMBIA

VANCOUVER

ISLAND

Bellingham

Mt. B.
NI

ORCAS
I.

SAN
JUAN
IS.

20

STRAIT

TATOOSH I.
CAPE FLATTERY

VICTORIA

Skagit R.
La
Conner

OF JUAN DE FUCA

SAN
JUAN I.

Neah
Bay

WHIDBEY
I.

PACIFIC

Coupeville
Ft. Worden SP

⊞ Ft. Casey SP

OLYMPIC

Port Townsend

OCEAN

101

Everett

Port Angeles

PENINSULA

OLYMPIC

Port Gamble

2

△
Olympic NP
MOUNTAINS

Suquamish

Bremerton

BAINBRIDGE

SEATTLE

Quinalt
IR

Olympic NF

COAST

PUGET
SOUND

90

Tacoma
Puyallup
Steilacoom

Hoquiam
Aberdeen

OLYMPIA

⊞ Ft. Lewis
Army Base

Mt.
Rain

Grays Harbor

12

8

Tumwater Eatonville

Mt. △
Rainier

101

RANGES

Chehalis R.

Pioneer 🏛
Farm Museum

Centralia

Oysterville

North
Bend

Chehalis

12

Cowlitz R.

Ilwaco

4

Mt.
St. Helen
National
Volcanic
Monume

CAPE DISAPPOINTMENT
Ft. Canby SP
Ft. Columbia SP

⊞

Mt.
St. Helens

△

Astoria

Longview

Gifford
Pinchot
NF

14

Vancouver

PORTLAND

5

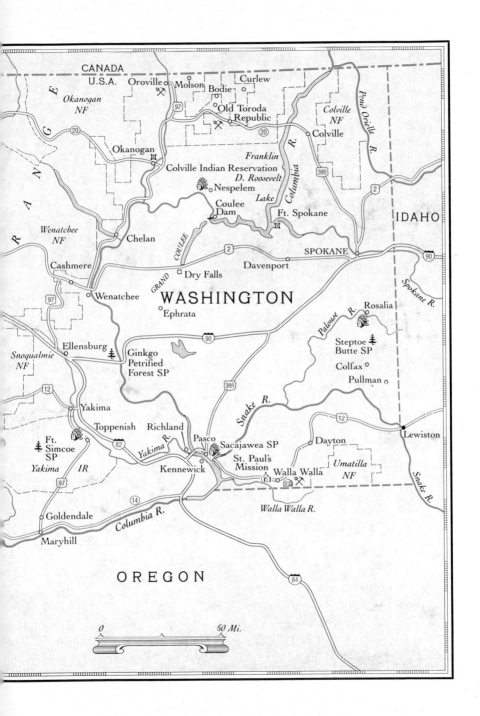

CANADA
U.S.A.

Okanogan
NF

Oroville Molson Bodie Curlew
97 Old Toroda
Republic
20
20 Colville

Colville
NF

Pend Orielle R.

IDAHO

Okanogan

Franklin
Colville Indian Reservation
D. Roosevelt
Nespelem
Coulee Lake
Dam Ft. Spokane

Columbia R.

395

2

Wenatchee
NF Chelan

90

Cashmere Dry Falls Davenport SPOKANE Spokane R.

97 Wenatchee WASHINGTON

Ephrata

Rosalia

Palouse R.

Snoqualmie
NF Ellensburg Ginkgo
Petrified
Forest SP

90

Steptoe
Butte SP

Colfax

Pullman

12

395

Yakima
Toppenish Richland

Snake R.

Dayton

12

Lewiston

Ft.
Simcoe
SP

82 Pasco Sacajawea SP

Yakima IR

Yakima R.

St. Paul's
Mission Walla Walla

Umatilla
NF

Snake R.

97 Kennewick

14

Goldendale

Columbia R.

Walla Walla R.

Maryhill

OREGON

84

0 60 Mi.

the mouth of the river. By the late 1780s the quest for the ever-elusive Northwest Passage was replaced by the search for furs, which the Russians had been selling to the Chinese at an excellent profit. In 1792 England's George Vancouver explored Puget Sound and an American fur trader, Robert Gray, managed to cross the bar at the mouth of the Columbia, which he named after his ship. Gray collected a cargo of sea otter pelts and sailed on to China, where he sold them at a great profit.

In 1804 President Thomas Jefferson dispatched Meriwether Lewis and William Clark to make their way across the continent to the river that Gray had found, in order to gather scientific information and to strengthen American claims to the Northwest. British and American fur traders were competing for the rich harvest of otter and beaver pelts, the British represented by two companies—the North West Company and the Hudson's Bay Company, which eventually merged under the latter name—and the Americans by John Jacob Astor's Pacific Fur Company. (It is often said that the great Astor fortune was made in the furs of the Northwest; in fact, Astor's operations here failed and the basis of his wealth was huge holdings in New York City real estate.) In 1811 Astor's company established a post at the mouth of the Columbia at the site of present-day Astoria, Oregon, and then ventured up the river to found Fort Okanogan. From 1825 to 1860 the Hudson's Bay Company flourished from its headquarters at Fort Vancouver. The fort's chief factor, John McLoughlin, encouraged American settlement by making supplies and credit available to newcomers spreading the "Oregon Fever" that swept the country from the 1840s to the 1860s. During the first half of the nineteenth century, England and the United States jointly controlled what was then called the Oregon Country. President James K. Polk, elected in 1844 on a platform of territorial expansion, had campaigned with the bellicose cry of "Fifty-four forty or fight!"—demanding a U.S.–Canada border along that line—but settled in 1846 for a boundary along the 49th parallel.

In the 1840s, as the fur trade was declining due to changes in style and overtrapping of beaver, American families were emigrating in ever larger numbers. Among the earliest were two Protestant missionaries from New York, Marcus and Narcissa Whitman. When Cayuse Indians killed the Whitmans in 1847, a violent punitive expedition of militia led by Colonel Cornelius Gilliam aroused all of the

OPPOSITE: *Goat Rocks Wilderness in Gifford Pinchot National Forest. Mount Adams rises in the distance.*

tribes of the Columbia River basin: Walla Walla, Palouse, Umatilla, and Nez Percé. Before a full-scale war could erupt, however, the militia abandoned the field. Subsequently, the Indians who killed the Whitmans surrendered to the authorities and were tried and hanged in 1850. In that same year the Oregon Donation Land Act was passed by Congress, allowing open settlement in the territory regardless of any Indian land claims.

In the early 1850s the residents of the northern Oregon Territory felt their interests were being ignored by the territorial legislature, dominated by the more numerous settlers to the south of the Columbia River. In August 1852 a convention at Cowlitz Landing (now called Toledo) prepared a petition to Congress requesting northern Oregon be made a separate territory and in November 1852 members of the Monticello Convention (held at modern-day Longview) asked that the "area lying north of the Columbia and west of the great northern branch thereof be organized as a separate territory under the name and style of the 'Territory of Columbia.'" Congress approved the division on March 2, 1853, but chose to name the new territory after the country's first president and doubled its size by extending the eastern boundary to the Rockies.

In May 1855 the newly appointed territorial governor, the devious and politically ambitious expansionist Isaac I. Stevens, summoned the Nez Percé, Walla Walla, Yakima, Umatilla, Cayuse, and others to a conference to inform them that they must move to reservations. (This was preceded by similar conferences in western Washington.) Most of the chiefs agreed to cede their lands in return for houses, schools, livestock, and cash. Nothing was to be done until the agreement was ratified in Washington, DC, but Stevens announced that the Indian lands were immediately available for settlement. A few months later war erupted in the Rogue River area of southern Oregon and in eastern Washington. The Yakima War, which took place to the east of the Cascades, began when six white settlers were killed in September. Militia units (the U.S. Army officers in the area were generally sympathetic to the Indians and held back from the local punitive expeditions) were unable to find the perpetrators but managed to murder the chief of the Walla Walla after sitting down with him for peace talks. The war petered out without any real resolution, only to flare up again when gold miners flocked to Colville, prompting Chief Kamiakin of the Yakima to urge violence against the newcomers. An expedition from Fort Walla Walla to Colville, led by Lieutenant Colonel Edward Steptoe, was intended to calm the Indians but had the opposite effect. On May16, 1858, hundreds of warriors followed and encircled Steptoe; he barely managed to escape. In two battles in September, at Spokane Plain and Four Lakes, the Indians were defeated. Subsequently the militia and army units hanged, shot, or imprisoned a score or so of Indians, breaking the Indian resistance. Brutalities were committed by both sides, but the most brazen act was the murder of an Indian leader in Governor Stevens's own office in Olympia.

Gold seekers headed up through central and eastern Washington to Republic, Oroville, and other towns to make their fortunes. Pioneers with names like "Swearing Jack" and "Wild Goose Bill" ventured into the scablands of the sagebrush-filled Big Bend Country, where the Columbia winds through central Washington. William Lewis sang their praises in an address he gave to the Lincoln and Adams counties pioneer association picnic in 1919: "[They] were good examples of that sturdy, self-reliant and courageous race of stalwart men who made the West . . . who could neither be discouraged by hardships nor deterred by disaster." They were joined by other entrepreneurs who, encouraged by the westward push of the Northern Pacific Railroad, built towns and lumber empires. Seattle and Tacoma, the state's major Puget Sound cities, flourished on the strength of the lumber business.

The wondrous rain forests of western Washington had attracted scientific attention as early as 1792, when the naturalist Archibald Menzies, sailing aboard George Vancouver's vessel *Discovery* as it explored Puget Sound, catalogued trees previously unknown to Europeans. In the 1820s the Scottish naturalist David Douglas found specimens of the immense tree that bears his name, the Douglas fir, which can reach 300 feet in height after a century and a half of growth. The region's colossal supply of timber attracted the notice of agents for the railroad: "Oh! What timber!" exclaimed the report of a Northern Pacific Railroad agent in 1869. He described Washington's forests as "surpassing the woods of all the rest of the globe in the size, quantity and quality of the timber." John McLoughlin built the region's first sawmill in 1828. Seattle was the site of the area's first steam-powered sawmill, built by Henry Yesler in 1852. But it was not until the 1880s, with the coming of the Northern Pacific Railroad, that the lumber business really boomed. The railroad received enormous land grants from the federal government, sold them to small logging operations at moderate prices, and then reaped huge profits by charging the highest possible rates for hauling the trees. In 1900

James J. Hill's Northern Pacific Railroad sold 900,000 acres in Oregon and Washington to Frederick Weyerhauser, whose company had previously logged in the Great Lakes region. Weyerhauser introduced land-management techniques designed to ensure a permanent supply of timber, whereas previous loggers had operated on the "cut and run" principle. The consolidation of logging led to the exploitation of laborers, who turned to radical organizations such as the Industrial Workers of the World for relief. Labor relations remained difficult for decades; a major strike occurred in 1935. Logging remains one of Washington's most important industries.

Another great natural resource, the Columbia River, has been the key to the success of agriculture in the semiarid region east of the Cascades. Irrigation projects have allowed profitable farming, notably the production of apples. Massive dams such as the Grand Coulee harnessed the Columbia's power for the production of hydroelectricity. The waters that carried Lewis and Clark on the final leg of their journey to the western sea now power the lights of the Space Needle in Seattle.

This chapter is arranged in several sections, beginning with Seattle and Puget Sound, proceeding southwest along the Olympic Peninsula to the mouth of the Columbia, and then inland to central and eastern Washington.

SEATTLE AND PUGET SOUND

Geologists claim that Puget Sound's inlets, bays, indentations, and islands were carved by glaciers during the last Ice Age. According to an Indian legend, however, the region was created when Ocean, hoping to keep his children Cloud and Rain close to home, carved a trough and molded the dirt into a mountain range. His children never strayed east of this range, the Cascades. The sound extends eighty miles from the Strait of Juan de Fuca to Olympia, the capital, and reaches depths of 900 feet. First inhabited by the Coast Salish Indians—including the Lummi, Swinomish, Suquamish, and others—the region was explored in 1792 by George Vancouver, James Whidbey, and Peter Puget. Port Townsend, which was founded in 1851, a few months before Seattle, hoped to be the sound's major port, but its lack of a rail connection left it to languish.

The region's strategic location has made it a natural home for the navy. Wedged between the foothills of two great mountain ranges, Puget Sound has also been an important transportation nexus for Washington's lumber industry. Although some of the region's pastoral towns and rural enclaves are increasingly giving way to urbanization, there are still villages where history is palpable.

SEATTLE

From its inception, Seattle had great expectations. One of the city's first settlers, Charles Terry of New York, arrived on the shore near the mouth of the Duwamish River in 1851 and christened the settlement New York, to which the Indian term *Alki,* or "by and by," was added in a small concession to modesty. That point of land, today known as Alki Point, was part of a landscape whose splendor could only inspire. Puget Sound, an arm of the Pacific Ocean, lay on three sides, and many lakes gleamed between forested hills to the east. A stand of evergreens occupied the hilly site of present-day Seattle, and in the distance to the west and east were the snow-clad Olympic and Cascade mountain ranges.

Arthur Denny of Cherry Grove, Illinois, landed at Alki Point in the fall of 1851. By February 1852 Denny, Carson Boren, and William Bell had staked claims on the east side of Elliott Bay, which

Seattle's Space Needle, built for the 1962 Century 21 Exposition. It has since been joined by a number of skyscrapers.

offered deeper water and more protection from the winds than the Alki site. In May 1853 a town was platted, its hillside divided among Denny, Boren, and Dr. David Maynard, an Illinoian who had been en route to the California gold fields but instead followed an attractive widow to Puget Sound. Maynard started a salmon-packing business and named the settlement Seattle after the Puget Sound Indian chief, who had befriended the new white settlers. The chief's good will toward the white settlers did not preclude exile to a reservation. At the signing of the Treaty of Port Elliott in January 1855, his words reflected, eloquently, the fate of his fellow native Americans at that moment in time: "The Indian's night promises to be dark. Not a single star of hope hovers above his horizon." In January 1856 a band of Yakima and Klickitat Indians attempted to destroy the fledgling town. The inhabitants took shelter in a blockhouse as a naval vessel bombarded the attackers, forcing them away.

Presided over by Denny, a taciturn six-footer of great entrepreneurial ingenuity, the new town grew. Denny started a real-estate company and a brick factory and was a partner in a bank. He also encouraged other newcomers and, together with his fellow founders, relinquished a mill site on the waterfront and some of the hill's best forestland to Henry Yesler, who came to Seattle from Ohio and built the first steam-powered sawmill in Washington Territory. Timber was skidded down from the forested slopes to the mill, processed, and then loaded aboard ships.

As the Northern Pacific Railroad moved west from Minnesota in 1870, Seattle hoped to be its terminus. In 1873 the city offered the railroad $250,000 in cash and bonds, 7,500 town lots, 3,000 acres of undeveloped land, and half the waterfront. The offer was rebuffed by the Northern Pacific, which chose Tacoma instead. Nonetheless, Seattle's population leapt from 3,553 to 42,837 in the 1880s. In 1893 the Great Northern Railway linked Seattle with the East, and the population continued to grow, reaching more than 200,000 by 1914.

So bent was this city on success that even the action of a careless assistant in Victor Clairmont's paint and cabinet shop could not stop it. More than thirty blocks of what is now the Pioneer Square Historic District were destroyed by Seattle's great fire on June 6, 1889. Within a few years, however, the city was rebuilt—just in time for the Alaskan gold rush of 1897 and an influx of new settlers and business.

OPPOSITE: *A totem pole erected by the Pacific Novelty Company on Seattle's Pioneer Square, photographed by Asahel Curtis in 1924.*

Pioneer Square and International Districts

The enclave of restored, late-nineteenth-century, low brick buildings in the **Pioneer Square Historical District** was inspired by the work in Chicago of the architects Louis Sullivan, Daniel Burnham, and Henry Hobson Richardson. These buildings replaced the wooden shantylike structures that burned in the great fire of 1889. They stand on the pleasantly irregular grid created when the city's founders, Arthur Denny and David Maynard, could not agree on whether the streets should parallel the shore of Elliott Bay or run directly north and south by the compass. The triangular **Pioneer Square** (First Avenue and Yesler Way) contains a restored pergola of ornate ironwork and glass (1909) that protects wooden benches from sun and, more often, rain. There are also a sixty-foot Tlingit Indian totem pole and a bust of Chief Seattle.

Fronting the square is the **Pioneer Building** (606 First Avenue), built in 1889—1890, whose crowning central tower was destroyed by an earthquake in 1949. Nearby, along First Avenue South, are the **Yesler Building** (Yesler Way and First Avenue South), built between 1890 and 1895 and designed by the Scottish architect Elmer Fisher, who designed fifty buildings in the year after the fire, and the 1892 **Maynard Building** (119 First Avenue South). The forty-two-story **Smith Tower** (1914), at Yesler Way and Second Avenue, is claimed locally to have been the highest building west of the Mississippi when it was built and was the highest in Seattle for half a century. Erected by the typewriter magnate L. C. Smith, it was intended to keep the city's businesses in the original downtown area, but by 1905, at the end of the Alaskan gold rush, the area south of Yesler Way had become a magnet for gamblers, prostitutes, and transients.

After Seattle's fire, First Avenue was raised to reduce the incline of the hill. Since rebuilding had already begun, the first story of some commercial buildings ended up below the street level, accessible by stairs. The shops that remained below ground level were condemned in 1907—a technicality that did not greatly impede the area's commerce, for this below-ground boulevard had become the domain of brothels and gambling houses. An underground tour beginning at **Doc Maynard's Public House** (610 First Avenue, 206–682–4648) offers walks through this subterranean sin city, which operated until the 1930s. Seattle was the jumping-off point for the Alaskan gold rushes, and a unit of **Klondike Gold Rush National Historic Park** (117 South Main Street, 206–442–7226)—less a park than an interpretive center—features a slide show depicting the life and adventures of the miners. This is the southernmost post of the park, which commemorates the route to Skagway, Alaska.

East of Pioneer Square on King Street and the surrounding blocks is the **International District,** cultural and commercial center for Seattle's Asian population. A slide presentation at the restored **Nippon Kan Theatre** (628 South Washington Street, 206–624–8801), a community venture built in 1909, depicts the experience of Asians in Seattle. The **Wing Luke Asian Museum** (407 Seventh Avenue South, 206–623–5124) is a memorial to Wing Chong Luke, who migrated to Seattle in the late 1920s and went on to become Washington State assistant attorney general, Seattle city councilman, and an ardent champion of the Chinese community. The museum features exhibits on the history of Asian-Americans in Seattle and King County as well as collections of Asian folk art.

Downtown and the Waterfront

Seattle's central business district, bounded by Yesler Way, Route 5, Stewart Street, and the waterfront, has among its sleek glass monoliths smaller buildings with gargoyles and other lively early-twentieth-century decorations that give it an interesting texture. The restored **Arctic Building** (1917), on the corner of Third Avenue and Cherry Street, is a Renaissance Revival palazzo in terra-cotta decorated with a set of walrus heads. Eight Indian heads distinguish an upper-story frieze of the brick-and-terra-cotta **Cobb Building** (1910), on the corner of Fourth Avenue and University Street, which reflects the Beaux-Arts orientation of its New York architects, Howells and Stokes. The **Seattle Tower** (1928–1929), 1218 Third Avenue, has a lobby of dark marble walls and a gilt ceiling.

West of the commercial district, beyond the Alaskan Way Viaduct (Route 99), is Seattle's waterfront. The **Pike Place Market,** which sprawls over three blocks at the foot of Pike Street between First and Western avenues, was established in 1907 to allow farmers to sell their produce directly to consumers. The centerpiece of the renovated waterfront, which lies south of the market, is **Waterfront Park,** a multilevel wood-and-concrete platform that extends from Piers 57 to 59.

The blocks northwest of Pike Place Market, the commercial district, and the area inland from Pier 70 form **Denny Regrade,** a former hill that was leveled (one half between 1902 and 1911 and the remainder in 1929 and 1930) following the ambitious plans of city engineer R. H. Thomson. With hydraulic power provided by millions

The Arctic Building, designed by A. Warren Gould in 1917, is appropriately decorated with a row of walrus heads.

of gallons of water from Lake Union and Elliott Bay, the hill was sluiced into the bay. In 1911 a civic center was proposed at Fourth Avenue and Blanchard Street, but it never materialized. Among the generally undistinguished architecture in the Regrade are several noteworthy structures, including two that were part of the sprawling Pike Place Market; the 1909 **Alaska Trade Building** (1915–1919 First Avenue), one of the first steel structures to replace the farmers' wagons, and the 1910 **Pike Place Market Livery Stable** (2200 Western Avenue), once the largest stable of its kind west of the Mississippi. Also in the Regrade is the legacy of the 1962 World's Fair, **Seattle Center,** site of the city's **Space Needle,** which was designed by Seattle architect Victor Steinbrueck. The 500-foot-high observation deck at the top gives a 360-degree panoramic view.

The Hills

First Hill, a suburb for the city's wealthy at the turn of the century (now less affluent and referred to locally as "Pill Hill" because of its six hospitals and various medical facilities), retains a few landmarks from this period. The **Stimson-Green Mansion** (1204 Minor Avenue,

206–624–0474), designed in 1899 by Kirtland Cutter, was inspired by the European Arts and Crafts movement. The interior features several fine fireplaces designed by Cutter. Also noteworthy are the Neo-Baroque **Saint James Cathedral** (Ninth Avenue and Marion Street), built in 1907 by Heins & LaFarge, and the 1891 **Trinity Episcopal Church** (609 Eighth Avenue), which, with its rough-cut stone, resembles an English country parish church. The **Charles & Emma Frye Art Museum** (704 Terry Avenue, 206–622–9250) houses a collection of 230 nineteenth- and early-twentieth-century American and European paintings. The Fryes, who moved to Seattle in 1888, established a trust to administer their collection in a free public art museum. The highlights include an important number of paintings of the Munich School (1850–1900) and works by Edouard Manet, Johann Barthold Jongkind, and Childe Hassam.

    Capitol Hill, named by a hopeful Arthur Denny before Olympia had permanently secured the territorial capital, succeeded First Hill as the neighborhood of choice for wealthy Seattlites in the late nineteenth and early twentieth centuries. Restored mansions in a wide range of revival styles—including Tudor, Baroque, Renaissance, and Georgian—as well as Craftsman, Prairie, and Mediterranean, are throughout the district. On the hill's northern crest is **Volunteer Park,** named to honor soldiers who fought in the Spanish-American War. Originally established as Lakeview Park in 1887, it was redesigned in 1903 according to the City Beautiful principles of the Olmsted brothers. The **Seattle Art Museum** (206–625–8900) in the park at Fourteenth and East Prospect streets contains an excellent collection of Asian art, including sculpture, paintings, screens, lacquer, ceramics, and jade carvings from 4000 B.C. to the present. Other collections include the Katherine White Collection of African Art, and Baroque, Renaissance, pre-Columbian, and American paintings and sculpture.

    Queen Anne Hill, named for the many towered villas that were built on its slopes at the turn of the century, also housed the wealthy in their flight from downtown. Still a residential area, it retains only a few of its namesake houses, such as those at 912 and 918 Second Avenue West and 520 West Kinnear Place.

    West of Queen Anne Hill is the Magnolia neighborhood and 500-acre **Discovery Park** (3801 West Government Way, 206–386–4236). This property was ceded by the citizens and city of Seattle to the secretary of war in 1895 to be the site of Fort Lawton, an active military base from the Spanish-American War until 1970.

The **Indian Cultural Center** (206–285–4425), located on Discovery Park land that has been leased for ninety-nine years to the All Tribes Foundation, features a collection of native American art and crafts. Jutting into Elliott Bay across from Magnolia Bluff is **Alki Point,** the site of Seattle's original settlement. The **Alki Lighthouse** (1916) at the western point is still in operation.

Northern Seattle

The settlements of Ballard, Fremont, Eastlake, and Cascade, once separate towns, are now annexed Seattle neighborhoods. Fishing remains an important industry in the Scandinavian enclave of Ballard on Salmon Bay. The bay forms the western entrance to the **Lake Washington Ship Canal,** which connects Puget Sound with Lakes Washington and Union. The **Chittenden Locks,** finished in 1917, are the second-largest locks in the Americas (those of the Panama Canal are the largest). They can be seen from Seaview Avenue NW or Northwest 54th Street. With its specially constructed streetscapes, ships, houses, and logging and fishing camps, the **Nordic Heritage Museum** (3014 Northwest 67th Street, 206–789–5707) re-creates the experience of a typical Scandinavian immigrant departing from Europe, reaching Ellis Island, moving across America, and finally settling in the Northwest. There are also displays of artifacts brought by Nordic immigrants to the New World and exhibits showing the contribution of each Nordic group to the history of the Northwest.

In the neighborhood of **Montlake** is the **Museum of History and Industry** (2700 Twenty-fourth Avenue East, 206–324–1125). Operated by the Historical Society of Seattle and King County, the museum features exhibits on the history of local pioneers and the aviation and maritime industries. Displays include a re-creation of an 1880s Seattle street scene, a fashion gallery, and mementoes of the Alaskan gold rushes and the Alaska-Yukon-Pacific Exposition.

University of Washington

The Pacific Northwest's first territorial university, originally located downtown, moved in 1895 to its current 690-acre campus north of Portage and Union bays. The university agreed to have the 1909

OPPOSITE: *This room in the Stimson-Green House features a profusion of Classical ornamentation. The fireplace is decorated with griffins, a speeding chariot, and a pair of faces in the style of ancient Greek funerary masks.*

Alaska-Yukon-Pacific Exposition on campus in exchange for an upgrading of the grounds and some new buildings. For the exposition J. C. Olmsted, son of the famed designer of New York's Central Park, had the site cleared of its dense fir and cedar forest and replaced it with walks, pools, fountains, and gardens. Among the elements of his design that remain are the Rainier Vista with the Drumheller Fountain, part of the rose garden, Campus Parkway, which led to the Expo grounds, and the curving paths on the east side of the campus. Olmsted later designed the Academic and Science quadrangles. A map of the campus is available at the visitor information center (4014 University Way NE, 206-543-9198).

Thomas Burke Memorial Washington State Museum

The Burke Museum, affiliated with the university since 1880, was the brainchild of the Young Naturalists' Society, a group of amateurs and university faculty devoted to the study of natural history. By 1899 the Young Naturalists had evolved into a professional institution, known as the Washington State Museum, which was designated as Washington's official scientific and historical museum. The museum settled into its present home in 1962. It features anthropology, geology, and zoology, with collections of artifacts—including twenty-five-foot totem poles and seagoing vessels—from the Pacific Rim cultures of the Northwest Coast, Alaska, Polynesia, Australia, the Philippines, Southeast Asia, and Indonesia.

> LOCATION: Seventeenth Avenue NE and Northeast 45th Street in the northwest corner of the University of Washington campus. HOURS: 10–5:30 Monday–Friday, 9–4:30 Saturday–Sunday. FEE: None. TELEPHONE: 206-543-5590.

On Lake Washington's eastern shore the towns of **Kirkland** and **Renton** sprang up in the late 1870s and 1880s with the establishment of the King County coal mines. Still standing in Kirkland is the 1891 **Peter Kirk Building** (Seventh Avenue NE and Market Street), a turreted commercial structure built by one of the town's founders. **Bellevue,** the eastern shore's largest suburb, was the site of the semi-utopian **Beaux Arts Village** (west of 108th Avenue SE). Founded in 1908 by Alfred Renfro, an architect, and Frank Calvert, a newspaper cartoonist, its Craftsman-style bungalows, beachfront, forest, and

OPPOSITE: *The Suzzallo Library at the University of Washington in Seattle.*

Three examples of the distinctive art of the Northwest Coast Indians, from the collection of the Thomas Burke Memorial Washington State Museum, show the continuity of this artistic tradition: An early nineteenth-century Tlingit shaman's headdress, above; a ca. 1900 Kwakiutl sea monster mask from Vancouver Island, opposite; a Kwakiutl owl mask from ca. 1920, below.

curbless streets were intended to attract artists and their studios; however, the community proved too expensive for artists. About eight miles south of downtown, on Boeing Field and the King County Airport, is the **Museum of Flight** (9404 East Marginal Way South, exit 158 off Route 5, 206–764–5720), displaying thirty-five full-size aircraft, from a 1916 B&W to a late 1960s Apollo command module. The museum also features exhibits on aviation pioneers, the history of the industry, modern flight, and the space age.

TACOMA

Washington's shipping, distributing, and industrial center, Tacoma sits at the tip of Puget Sound on the great harbor of Commencement Bay. In the early 1850s and 1860s lumber lured the city's first settlers, among them Nicholas De Lin, a Swedish immigrant and entrepreneur who built the first water-driven mill and then went on to open a brewery, a barrel factory, and a salmon-packing plant. Tacoma was a tiny village until 1873, when it was chosen as the western terminus of the Northern Pacific Railroad and vied with Seattle for dominance on Puget Sound. From the 1880s to the 1890s Tacoma's population exploded, increasing from 1,000 to 36,000, as the railroad stimulated industrial development. Charles Wright, president of Northern Pacific Railroad, was the town's greatest booster, donating money for schools and parks from his home in Philadelphia. Elegant homes and neighborhoods were built, but the town's prosperity was badly shaken by the depression of 1893. "The commercial universe seemed to be but a house of cards," wrote one local historian. Although Tacoma rallied with the Klondike gold rush, its growth slowed at the turn of the century. In the 1920s the Northern Pacific moved its western headquarters to Seattle.

Downtown, the **Old City Hall Historic District** reflects the activity—both civic and financial—that flourished in this railroad town at the turn of the century. The **Old Tacoma City Hall** (625 Commerce Street) was built in 1893 in a style described by its builders as "Italian Renaissance"; it now houses offices. The nearby **Northern Pacific Headquarters** is a handsome Italianate structure built in 1888. Also notable is the **Elks Temple** (565 Broadway), built in 1916 in the eclectic Classic style. The chamber of commerce (Pacific Street, 206–627–2175) provides information on local museums.

The **Stadium-Seminary Historic District,** named for the two landmarks on its eastern and western boundaries, was one of the city's first wealthy residential neighborhoods. **Stadium High School,** at 111 North E Street, was built in 1891 in the Canadian Pacific Railroad Chateauesque style. It was intended to be a hotel, but the depression of 1893 stopped construction; when work resumed, the building was redesigned and a glorious-looking school emerged in 1906. The **Annie Wright Seminary** (827 Tacoma Avenue North) boasts a fine campus of Collegiate Gothic buildings. **Wright Park Arboretum** (316 South G Street, 206–591–5330), landscaped in 1887 with exotic trees and shrubs and statuary, has one of the three surviving turn-of-the-century glass-and-steel conservatories in the West, the **Seymour Conservatory,** built in 1907. Also in the district is the **Washington State Historical Society Museum** (315 North Stadium Way, 206–593–2830). The Classic Revival building houses an excellent museum with exhibits on state and Puget Sound history and collections of Northwest Coast Indian spirit boards, basketry, and clothing, as well as China trade artifacts. The oldest part of the city, called **Old Tacoma,** lies just to the north of the Stadium-Seminary district. Here, markers point out the sites of the first log house, school, hotel, and hospital, none of which remain today. The only significant landmark still standing is **Saint Peter's Episcopal Church** (1873), a Gothic Revival board-and-batten church on Starr Street.

Fort Nisqually Historic Site

This fort is a reconstruction of a post built in 1833 by the Hudson's Bay Company on the beach in DuPont, seventeen miles south of Tacoma. Dr. William Fraser Tolmie, a surgeon and botanist from Glasgow, was among the group of fur traders. Just 21 years old, he wrote eloquently in his journal of a virgin territory with "stupendous Rainier embosomed in cloud." The fort quickly became a center of trade with the Indians and later between the British and Americans. It was also headquarters for the Puget's Sound Agricultural Company, the ranching and farming arm of the Hudson's Bay Company. Tolmie became factor in 1843 and moved the post to the banks of nearby Sequalitchew Creek. The fort's 255-square-foot stockade was built in 1848 and was purchased by the federal government from the Hudson's Bay Company in 1869 for $650,000. It later fell into disrepair and was reconstructed in the park from 1933 to 1939. There are ten buildings, including the **factor's house** (1854) and the **granary** (1850), the only surviving original example in Washington State of the French Canadian post-and-sill construction used in the Hudson's Bay Company's forts of the period. A museum features exhibits on the role of the fort in Puget Sound history. The

The reconstructed stockade of Fort Nisqually, a Hudson's Bay Company outpost near Puget Sound that was named for a local Indian tribe.

fort is surrounded by the 640-acre Point Defiance Park, which was laid out in 1905 by Kansas City landscape architects Hare & Hare.

LOCATION: Point Defiance Park, North 54th and Pearl streets. HOURS: Mid–June through Labor Day: 12–6 Daily; September through mid-June: 1–4 Wednesday–Sunday. FEE: Yes. TELEPHONE: 206–591–5339.

Also located in Point Defiance Park, **Camp Six Logging Museum** (Five-Mile Drive, 206–752–0047) is a replica of a logging camp of the late nineteenth century. It features a Dolbeer donkey steam engine, a restored water wagon, bunkhouses, and a ride on an original, ninety-ton Shay steam locomotive.

PUYALLUP

Located east of Tacoma in the Puyallup Valley, this town was settled in the 1850s. One of its founders was Ezra Meeker, an upright and energetic pioneer who promoted railroads and highways, and fought against the expulsion of the Chinese. The restored, seventeen-room **Ezra Meeker Mansion** (321 East Pioneer Avenue, 206–848–1770) was built in 1889. Gables, stained glass, and Italianate detail define the exterior of the house; the interior has intricate woodwork, hand-stenciled ceilings, six handmade coal-burning fireplaces that were shipped around the Horn, and the original speaking tubes.

The **Pioneer Farm Museum** just north of Eatonville (7716 Ohop Valley Road, 206–832–6300) is a replica of an 1880s farm with a refurnished cabin of the period, a replica of a one-room school-house, and an interpretive center, designed primarily for children, where visitors may use farming and woodworking tools.

MOUNT RAINIER NATIONAL PARK

Referred to as "the Mountain" by Washington residents, 14,410-foot Rainier presides majestically over its fellow Cascade peaks. George Vancouver named it in 1792 for a friend, Peter Rainier. The first recorded climbers were two men named Stevens and Van Trump, who made the ascent in 1870 and left a marker with their names at the peak. The park has several visitor centers, but the one at **Longmire,** named for a family who settled and promoted the area in

Two carloads of tourists at Mount Rainier National Park, photographed by Asahel Curtis in 1912, fifteen years after the park was established.

the 1880s, has a museum featuring interpretive displays on the mountain's first climbers and the park's most noted naturalists.

LOCATION: Western entrance between Nisqually and Longmire accessible via routes 512, 7, and 706. HOURS: Always open. FEE: Yes. TELEPHONE: 206–659–2211.

STEILACOOM

One of the state's oldest towns, Steilacoom was incorporated in 1854 and is now a historic district. **Fort Steilacoom** (Steilacoom Boulevard) was built in 1849 to protect settlers from the Puget Sound Indians, including the Snoqualmie and Nisqually, who were threatened by growing white colonization. In 1858, the leader of the Nisqually, Leschi, was hanged at the fort by local officials after being falsely convicted of murder. Leschi had been rescued from the noose once before by sympathetic Army officers and federal officials, who arrested him on the gallows—on the federal charge of selling liquor to Indians—and put him into protective custody. However, intense pressure from territorial officials forced Leschi's execution. The U.S. government abandoned the fort in 1868 and leased it to Washington Territory for use as an insane asylum. Four of the officers' houses, dating back to the 1850s, are being renovated and may be seen at the original fort location on the grounds of the Western State Hospital (by appointment, 206–582–8900).

The **Steilacoom Historical Museum Association** (206–584–4133) administers three historic sites. Their **museum** is in the town hall (112 Main Street) and features exhibits on local history, pioneer tools, and furniture from the second half of the nineteenth century. The **Nathaniel Orr House** (1811 Rainier Street), built in 1857 as a wagon- and cabinetmaking shop, displays original furnishings and artifacts. The association's third site is the **Bair Drug & Hardware Store** (1617 Lafayette), built in 1895. Inside are an old post office, a 1906 soda fountain, and other artifacts.

OLYMPIA

Now Washington's capital, Olympia was settled in the 1840s by pioneers who were attracted by the industrial potential of the Deschutes Falls. But **Tumwater** (from the Chinook word *Tum wa ta,* meaning "waterfalls") rose up first, a few miles south of what is today Olympia's city center. The first permanent American settlement on Puget Sound, Tumwater flourished with sawmills and gristmills in the mid-nineteenth century and later with brewing. Olympia, originally called Smithfield after its founder, became the seat of the territorial government in 1853. Beer brewing is still a major industry in the Olympia metropolitan area, along with manufacturing and government.

Capitol Group

Work on the capitol complex (Capitol Way, between Eleventh and Fourteenth avenues) began in 1893 under the supervision of Ernest Flagg, but the depression of the 1890s and the opposition of the governor stopped the project until 1911, when the New York architects Wilder & White took over, aided in landscaping by the Olmsted Brothers. The result combined Classic Revival buildings and handsome landscaping. Later additions in the 1920s, 1930s, and 1950s reflect the styles fashionable in those years. The Doric colonnades of the **Legislative Building** are surmounted by a 287-foot dome encircled by a Corinthian colonnade, and its interior boasts marble, parquet floors, chandeliers by Tiffany and Company, and elegant furnishings. Guided tours of the building, which was completed in 1928, are available when the legislature is in session and by appointment (206–786–7703). Other buildings in the park include the **Governor's Mansion**, the **Temple of Justice**, and **Washington State Library**. The **State Capital Museum**, housed in a 1920 California-style stucco mansion (211 West Twenty-first Avenue, 206–753–2580), contains exhibits on native American culture.

North of the state capitol is a group of nineteenth-century houses and buildings. The headquarters of the **Board of Education** (Franklin to Washington Street), formerly the Thurston County Courthouse and an early state capitol, was designed in the Romanesque Revival style by W. A. Ritchie in 1891–1892. Also notable are the **William G. White House** (1431 Eleventh Avenue, 206–352–3212), a Queen Anne villa built in 1893; and the **Bigelow House** (918 Glass Avenue, 206–357–6198), a fourteen-room Gothic Revival mansion, built in 1854 for Judge Daniel Bigelow. It has been occupied continuously by the family since it was built.

South of Olympia, in Tumwater, is the **Olympia Brewery** (Schmidt Place and Custer Way, 206–754–5252), a complex that includes an Italianate brewhouse (now a warehouse) and the Colonial Revival **Leopold Schmidt House** (private), both built in 1905. Schmidt, the company's German-born founder, moved his operations from Montana to Tumwater after tasting its artesian well water.

The Victorian Parlor in Olympia's State Capital Museum, originally the residence of Clarence J. Lord, a prominent citizen and mayor.

To the north, the town of **Bremerton** is dominated by Puget Sound Naval Shipyard, Kitsap County's largest employer. The **Naval Shipyard Museum** (130 Washington Street, 206–479–7447) features exhibits on naval history, ship models, and an artillery collection ranging from 400-year-old cannon to modern missiles.

Directly across the sound from downtown Seattle, **Bainbridge Island** is a bucolic suburban community. Captain George Vancouver dropped anchor here in 1792. The island was later named after a captain of the USS *Constitution.* **Fort Ward State Park,** on the island's western point, was the site of a military reservation established in 1910 to protect Bremerton's navy yard.

Just across Agate Passage, on the Port Madison Indian Reservation, is the town of **Suquamish.** Before settlement by whites in the early nineteenth century, Puget Sound was inhabited by the Coast Salish tribes, including the Suquamish. The **Suquamish Museum** (Sandy Hook Road, 206–598–3311) displays photographs and a collection of artifacts, including fishing equipment, canoes, and basketry. The museum also features a reconstruction of a portion of the mid-nineteenth-century long house occupied by the Suquamish. Long houses were communal dwellings, large enough to accommodate an entire tribe, with living spaces for individual families. The original long house, 600 by 30 feet, was built as a cooperative effort by several tribes under the direction of Chief Seattle. It was burned by the U.S. Army in 1870 to force the Suquamish to live in the manner of whites, in separate houses. The reconstruction shows a family's living quarters with furniture and household artifacts. The **grave of Chief Seattle** is also on the reservation. It was he who represented the various Puget Sound tribes in the 1855 Treaty of Port Elliott negotiations that sent the region's Indians to the reservation at Suquamish.

PORT GAMBLE

With its sugar maples, salt-box houses, and elegant parish church, Port Gamble resembles East Machias, Maine, the hometown of its founders, Andrew Pope and William Talbot. Pope & Talbot, the forest products and land development firm that evolved from their early enterprise, is still the village's main employer. The company operates a **historical museum** (206–297–3341), which features exhibits on the evolution of Pope & Talbot and has rebuilt and restored more than thirty buildings. The entire town has been declared a historic district. Among the architecturally notable buildings (private) are the **Thompson House,** built in 1859; the **Jackson House,** of 1871; and the **Walker-Ames House,** a Queen Anne villa built in 1887.

WHIDBEY ISLAND

The island is named for Joseph Whidbey, master of Captain George Vancouver's HMS *Discovery,* who in 1792 found the strait at the island's northern end, Deception Pass, and passages that lead south to Puget Sound. His voyage showed that the island was not part of the mainland, as had been thought. White settlement of the island did not begin until the 1840s, but the first settlers were driven off by the Indians. In 1852 Captain Thomas Coupe started a town on Penn Cove, now known as **Coupeville,** which flourished as a center of fishing and farming. The town preserves numerous houses and commercial buildings dating to the 1880s and 1890s. The Central Whidbey Chamber of Commerce (5 Main Street, 206–678–5434) provides information about walking tours. The oldest structure in town is the **Captain Coupe House** (Front and Gould streets, private), built in 1854. In the 1850s the settlers built several blockhouses, fear-

ing Indian attacks that never actually came. Three survive in the area, one on private property; another, the **Crockett Blockhouse,** is located on Fort Casey Road three miles south of town; and the third is the **Alexander Blockhouse** (Alexander Street), which may be visited by arrangement with the Island County Historical Society (206–678–6854). The society also maintains a **museum** (Alexander and Coveland streets, 206–678–3310) with displays of photographs, local historical items, and Indian artifacts such as dugout canoes, baskets, and dolls. The **Ebey's Landing National Historic Reserve** (206–678–6854) at the western edge of town is a twenty-two-square-mile district with some eighty buildings put up by shipbuilders in the 1880s.

Fort Casey, now a state park, looks across Admiralty Inlet at Fort Worden, with which it functioned as part of the coastal defense system in the early decades of the twentieth century. Remnants of some of the fortifications, most of which were built in 1906, and old artillery may still be seen. The **Fort Casey Interpretive Center** (1280 South Fort Casey Road, 206–678–4519), located in the restored, early-twentieth-century **Admiralty Head Lighthouse,** contains exhibits on the history of the coastal forts.

SAN JUAN ISLANDS

Northwest of Whidbey are the San Juan Islands, an archipelago of 172 islands, most privately owned. Only four are accessible to the public (by ferry from Anacortes): San Juan, Shaw, Orcas, and Lopez. The Oregon Treaty of 1846 that established the boundary between Canada and the U.S. contained a geographical ambiguity that left the status of the San Juans open to dispute. Americans shared San Juan Island with farmers employed by the British Hudson's Bay Company. Hostility flared in the summer months of 1859 during the so-called "Pig War," after an American farmer shot a British pig that was rooting in his garden. A U.S. infantry unit was dispatched to the island by the regional commander to prevent Canadian authorities from arresting the shooter. In response the British sent three warships to frighten off the troops. Tensions grew as both sides built wooden blockhouses for defense and sent additional troops. The crisis had been brought on by regional commanders and officials; when senior officials in Washington learned of the confrontation, General Winfield Scott was sent to negotiate the withdrawal of troops and a joint tenan-

OPPOSITE: *Saint Paul's Church in Port Gamble, built in 1870, was modeled after the Episcopalian church in East Machias, Maine, the birthplace of the town's founders.*

cy. It was not until 1872 that sovereignty over the islands was awarded to the U.S. by an arbitrator, Kaiser Wilhelm I of Germany. The remnants of the Anglo-American era are preserved in **San Juan Island National Historical Park,** which maintains a visitor center in the town of Friday Harbor (First and Spring streets, 206–378–2240). Two buildings remain at the **American Camp** (six miles southeast of Friday Harbor), where a self-guided tour begins at an interpretive shelter that explains the history of the Pig War and shows what life was like at the camp. At the **English Camp** (West Valley Road, on Garrison Bay) four original buildings have been restored, including the barracks, which is used as an interpretive center.

In **Friday Harbor,** the island's main town, the **San Juan Historical Museum** (405 Price Street) displays photographs and artifacts from the late nineteenth century. The **Whale Museum** (62 First Street North, 206–378–4710) contains skeletons, sculptures, and exhibits with information on whale research. **Roche Harbor Resort** (Roche Harbor Road, 206–378–2150) is the centerpiece of what was, in the late 1880s, a company town owned by a lime and cement magnate, John S. McMillan. The **Hotel de Haro,** built by McMillan in 1887, still functions, and its grounds are open to the public.

LACONNER

Back on the mainland lies the Skagit River valley. Skagit County's oldest city, LaConner, was first settled in 1864 and was called Swinomish, after the flats on which it was built. In 1869 John Conner, a hotelier and restaurateur from Nevada City, bought the town's trading post and renamed the site after his wife, Louisa. The small fishing town, parts of which resemble a New England village, has been declared a historic district. The restored **Gaches Mansion** (703 South 2nd Street, 206–466–4288) is a half-timbered Victorian fantasy, housing the **Valley Museum of Northwestern Art** (206–466–4446) on the second floor and decorated in period style on the first and third floors. The **Skagit County Historical Museum** (501 South 4th Street, 206–466–3365) displays pioneer clothing, toys, books, and furniture, along with photographs and Northwest Coast Indian artifacts.

BELLINGHAM

Three creeks originally coursed through the site of Bellingham, which inspired the Indian name *Whatcom,* or "noisy waters." Lummi

Tugs hauling a raft of logs down the Swinomish Slough in LaConner.

Island, off the coast of Bellingham, was the fishing and hunting ground for the Lummi Indians, who live today on a reservation on the northwestern side of Bellingham Bay. In 1852 Henry Roeder, the city's founder, built a sawmill on the creek below the bluff that would become the city's downtown. Lumbering, salmon fishing, fur trading, and coal mining flourished. Downtown Bellingham boasts an impressive number of nineteenth- and early-twentieth-century buildings. The oldest, the **George E. Pickett House** (10 Bancroft Street, 206–733–1586), was built in 1856 for Captain Pickett, who erected a stockade in Bellingham to protect against Indian attacks from British Columbia and later went on to fame leading a gallant but futile Confederate charge at Gettysburg. The **Eldridge Avenue Historic District** includes Loggie House (1885), a rustic Eastlake villa; the Lottie Roth Block (1890), a Richardson Romanesque–style commercial block built by Henry Roeder's son-in-law, an owner of the Bellingham Bay Quarry; and the Aftermath Club (1904), a Craftsman- and Mediterranean-style building.

Whatcom Museum of History and Art

This museum, one of the state's finest, is housed in a brick Victorian building built in 1892 in the Second Empire style with a hint of

Romanesque Revival. Bellingham's city hall until 1939, the imposing landmark was converted for the use of the museum in 1940 and restored in the late 1960s. Exhibits on Northwest art and such regional-history themes as early exploration and logging are featured, along with displays of Northwest Coast Indian artifacts and Victorian furniture.

LOCATION: 121 Prospect Street. HOURS: 12–5 Tuesday–Sunday. FEE: None. TELEPHONE: 206–676–6981.

Bellingham's southernmost community, **Fairhaven** built its business district in the early 1890s, anticipating that the Northern Pacific Railroad would choose the site for its terminus. It wasn't to be, but the district's brick and sandstone buildings remain, many of them designed in the Romanesque Revival and Classic Revival styles. Just south of downtown is the **Roland G. Gamwell House** (1001 16th Street, private), an elaborate Queen Anne villa built for Gamwell, a real-estate entrepreneur, who hired the Boston architects Longstaff & Black to build the Fairhaven Hotel (no longer standing) and then had them design his own home.

The Whatcom Museum of History and Art is housed in the former city hall, designed by Alfred Lee, a self-taught local architect who was commissioned to create a building that would be "elaborate, commodious, and elegant."

OLYMPIC PENINSULA

Bounded by the Strait of Juan de Fuca on the north, the Pacific on
the west, and Puget Sound on the east, the Olympic Peninsula is a
fitting culmination of America's westward discoveries of beauty and
wildness. Its small villages retain their charm and remnants of their
past. The peninsula's isolated, windswept beaches, glaciated Olympic
peaks, and rain forests still remind visitors of the primeval Northwest
Coast. For centuries the Quinault, Makah, and Chinook Indians
fished, hunted, and built elaborate plank houses in this region. By
the end of the eighteenth century and into the nineteenth, Spanish,
English, and American explorers—including Bruno Heceta, John
Meares, and Robert Gray—were plying the waters off the coast,
searching for newer and better trade opportunities. Lewis and Clark
reached the Pacific in 1805, confirming the seriousness of America's
interest in the Pacific Northwest. Within several decades emigrants
from all points in the United States were settling along the coast,
establishing sawmills, canneries, and ports.

PORT TOWNSEND

Situated on the northeastern corner of the Olympic Peninsula,
where the Strait of Juan de Fuca meets Puget Sound, Port Townsend
was founded in 1851, a few months before Seattle. It was soon
bustling with lumber mills, gold seekers, and pioneers calling their
settlement the "Key City of Puget Sound." Passed over as the terminus for the Northern Pacific Railroad, the town decided to build its
own line, and by the late 1880s it was in partnership with the Union
Pacific. Between 1888 and 1890, an instant city sprang up in anticipation of the completion of the transcontinental connection. Elegant
commercial buildings rose downtown, Victorian mansions overlooking them from the plateau above. But the Oregon Improvement
Company, the subsidiary of the Union Pacific that had invested in
Port Townsend's railroad and had promised to build twenty-five miles
of tracks, went under, and with it the economy of Port Townsend.
The town, however, was left with a splendid architectural legacy.

   In the last few decades much of the town has been restored by
writers, artists, and other preservation-minded residents. On Water
Street, the center of the old commercial district, are some particularly
impressive Renaissance- and Romanesque Revival–style brick buildings, including the **Pioneer Building** (1889) and **Mount Baker Block**
(1890). The 1891 city hall houses the **Jefferson County Historical**

In Port Townsend at Walker and Washington streets, the turreted Frank W. Hastings House, built in 1890 and now an inn. OPPOSITE: *A handsome spiral staircase in the Starrett House, at Clay and Adams Streets.*

Society (210 Madison Street, 206–385–1003) and its collections of military memorabilia, Indian artifacts, and historical photographs as well as displays of the interiors of period homes.

The upper part of the town has many Victorian houses, some of which are included in Port Townsend's biannual house tours in September and May (for information contact the chamber of commerce, 206–385–2722). The **Rothschild House** (Taylor and Franklin streets, 206–385–2722) has been restored with original furniture and is regularly open to the public. Built in 1868, it is a fine example of the Greek Revival houses that were prefabricated in New England and transported to Pacific Coast settlements during this era. Also uptown is the **Jefferson County Courthouse** (Walker and Jefferson streets), the Chateauesque creation of Willis A. Ritchie, designer of Spokane's county courthouse.

Fort Worden State Park

This park lies northeast of Port Townsend between Admiralty Inlet and the Strait of Juan de Fuca. Captain George Vancouver stopped

here on his Puget Sound voyage in 1792 and gave Point Wilson its name. The Point Wilson Lighthouse was first built in 1879 and rebuilt in 1919. The first fort on the site, Fort Wilson, was built in 1855 during hostilities with the Indians and abandoned in 1856. It was rebuilt in 1900 and renamed in honor of Admiral John L. Worden, commander of the Union ironclad *Monitor* during the Civil War. The fort was one of three—the others were Fort Casey and Fort Flagler—established between 1896 and 1912 to defend Puget Sound and the naval shipyard at Bremerton. When the army left in 1953, the fort was used as a juvenile treatment center; it became a state park in 1972. The remaining barracks and officers' quarters, which were built in 1904–1905 in the Georgian style, have been restored. Also on the grounds is Alexander's Castle, so called because of its turreted tower; it was built around 1882 for a Port Townsend minister. The Coast Artillery Museum features exhibits on the fort and its structures with interpretive text and photographs covering the era from 1897 to the 1950s. Also on display are uniforms, rifles, and other ammunition from the early twentieth century.

LOCATION: One mile north of Port Townsend. HOURS: April through September: 6:30–Dusk Daily; October through March: 8–Dusk Daily. FEE: None. TELEPHONE: 206–385–4730.

OLYMPIC NATIONAL PARK

This 1,400-square-mile wilderness comprises three separate environments—mountain, rain forest, and seashore—in two separate units. The naturalist Roger Tory Peterson described the area as having "the greatest weight of living matter, per acre, in the world." The major section of the park, containing the mountains and the rain forest, is located in the middle of the Olympic Peninsula—one of the rainiest areas of the United States; during heavy rainfalls, rivers have risen six feet in a day. The peninsula was first sighted by the Spanish explorer Juan Perez in 1774. Fourteen years later, Captain John Meares declared the mountains a home fit for the gods and named the highest peak Mount Olympus. As the burgeoning Northwest logging industry cast its eyes on the forests, conservationists lobbied for their preservation and the Olympic Forest Reserve was created in 1897. The region was declared a national park in 1938. Most of the fifty-mile-long coastal strip was added in 1953. Interpretive centers throughout the park have displays on its varied ecology, geology, and history. Also in the park is the **Pioneer Memorial Museum** (3002

Mount Angeles Road, 206–452–4501), which exhibits a turn-of-the-century homesteader's cabin, a logging bunkhouse used in the early 1900s, and a whaling canoe with replicas of harpoons and other whaling equipment of the sort used by the Makah. The Olympic Park headquarters is at 600 East Park Avenue, Port Angeles (206–452–4501).

MAKAH CULTURAL & RESEARCH CENTER

The center contains the world's largest collection of Northwest Indian artifacts predating contact with Europeans, including objects from the Ozette archaeological site at Cape Alava, south of Neah Bay, where a Makah Indian village was buried and preserved by a mudslide 500 years ago. (The site has been filled in and is not accessible to the public.) Among the artifacts on display are baskets, clothing, weavings of bird feathers and animal hair, and a whaling canoe. There are also beautifully crafted totem poles and a replica of a long house.

LOCATION: East Front Street. HOURS: June through mid-September: 10–5 Daily; mid-September through June: 10–5 Wednesday–Sunday. FEE: Yes. TELEPHONE: 206–645–2711.

HOQUIAM AND ABERDEEN

These twin towns on the eastern tip of Grays Harbor were settled in the 1860s. By 1885 the first sawmill had been built, beginning the shipping and milling industries that would grow into the early decades of the twentieth century. **The Aberdeen Museum of History** (111 East Third Street, 206–533–1976) contains collections of historical photographs, displays of logging equipment, and exhibits of furnishings and implements from the 1880s to the 1920s of a kitchen, bedroom, general store, and one-room school. **Hoquiam's Castle** (515 Chenault Avenue, 206–533–2005) is a towered Queen Anne mansion built in 1897 for Robert Lytle, a lumber baron. It has been restored with period furnishings, a panelled and oak-columned entry hall, and a cut-crystal chandelier of 600 pieces. The twenty-six-room, shingled Colonial Revival mansion of Arnold Polson, son of another prominent lumberman, has been converted into a museum. Both the restored house and landscaped garden can be seen at the **Polson Park and Museum** (1611 Riverside Avenue, 206–533–5862).

SOUTHWESTERN WASHINGTON

OYSTERVILLE

Founded in 1854, this small village on Willapa Bay flourished in its early days by marketing *Ostrea lurida,* the region's native oyster, to San Francisco's gold seekers. The industry died out as the beds were depleted but was rejuvenated by the importing of Japanese oyster larvae, which continues today. The late-nineteenth-century homes and churches of this village form a national historic district. Oysterville is the northernmost town of **Long Beach Peninsula,** which was a summer retreat for Portland residents in the late nineteenth century.

Fort Canby State Park

This park was the site of one of the earliest forts in Washington. Built in 1852, it was an essential part of the Northwest Coast defense from the Civil War through World War II. Although many concrete bunkers are to be seen throughout the park, only a few granite slabs remain from the Civil War–era gun emplacements. But the site's history goes back to the summer of 1788, when the British fur trader John Meares sailed down the coast of the Olympic Peninsula and tried, as Spanish explorer Bruno Heceta had done in 1775, to cross the hazardous Columbia River bar. Unable to do so, he named the promontory at the river's mouth Cape Disappointment. He wrote in his journal: "We can now with safety say that no such river . . . exists as laid down in the Spanish chart." There are two **lighthouses** in the park, on North Head and on Cape Disappointment. The one on the cape, built in 1856, is the oldest in the Pacific Northwest. Also here is the **Lewis and Clark Interpretive Center,** with slide presentations and displays of drawings about the celebrated expedition. On November 7, 1805, as they journeyed west toward Ilwaco and Cape Disappointment, Lewis and Clark got their first glimpse of the Pacific. "Great joy in camp," wrote Clark, "we are in view of the Ocian, this great Pacific Octian which we have been so long anxious to see." The exhibit leads to a window framing breathtaking views of the Pacific. There is also an exhibit on the history of Fort Canby.

LOCATION: Two and a half miles southwest of Route 101 at Ilwaco.
HOURS: Dawn–Dusk Daily. FEE: None. TELEPHONE: 206–642–3078.

OPPOSITE: *The Captain Stream House in Oysterville.*

FORT COLUMBIA STATE PARK

Fort Columbia was established in 1895 by the War Department, but in the years it served as a unit of coast defense—from 1904 through World War II—its guns were never fired in anger. Dozens of the fort's buildings remain, providing an accurate glimpse of turn-of-the-century military life. The park's interpretive center, in the former men's barracks, contains displays on daily life at the fort, including a barracks kitchen with a chef's manual that warns that "beans, badly boiled, kill more than bullets." The former commander's quarters houses a museum run by the Daughters of the American Revolution.

LOCATION: Route 101, 1 mile east of Chinook. HOURS: *Park:* Mid-April through mid-October: Dawn–Dusk Daily; mid-October through mid-April: Dawn–Dusk Wednesday–Sunday. *Interpretive Center:* By appointment. FEE: None. TELEPHONE: 206–642–3078.

VANCOUVER

Vancouver was the headquarters for the Hudson's Bay Company's Columbia department, which encompassed present-day British Columbia, Washington, Oregon, and Idaho. Their settlement was founded in the winter of 1824–1825 and flourished until the advent of America's "Oregon Fever" and the Treaty of 1846. The fur-trade capital of the Pacific coast, Fort Vancouver represented Britain's last stand in the Pacific Northwest.

Fort Vancouver

This outpost of the British Empire was presided over by the Canadian-born chief factor, John McLoughlin. At six-foot-four, he was a towering man with a mane of prematurely white hair that earned him the name "White-Headed Eagle" among the Indians. He was also known as "the despot west of the Rockies": His job was to keep peace with the Indians, squeeze the Americans out of the fur trade, and ensure British dominance in the Oregon Territory. His was a cosmopolitan post, employing between 400 and 500 people from all corners of the globe in the business of trapping, trading, and moving merchandise among the inland forts of the Pacific Northwest and then on to England. Sir George Simpson, head of the Hudson's Bay Company's North American operations, described the crew of men on one of their ships as containing "Iroquois who spoke

A room in the reconstructed hospital at Fort Vancouver.

their own tongue; a Cree halfbreed of French origin, who appeared to have borrowed his dialect from both his parents; a North Briton who understood only the Gaellic of his native hills; Canadians who, of course, knew French, and Sandwich [Hawaiian] Islanders, who jabbered a medley of Chinook and their vernacular jargon." In short, he concluded, "you have . . . the nicest confusion of tongues that has ever taken place since the tower of Babel."

McLoughlin managed both the community and the Hudson's Bay Company's fur trade well, but he failed to stem the tide of American migration; in fact, he supported American settlement by extending credit, selling provisions, and offering lodgings at the fort. The decline of his career coincided with the establishment of the Oregon Territory's new boundary at the 49th parallel. Forced to retire, he built a house on property he had capitalized with Hudson's Bay Company money in Oregon City, Oregon, and became an American citizen. Part of his legacy was Fort Vancouver: a stockade surrounding numerous buildings, including warehouses, workshops, the chief factor's house, seventeen hivelike cells called the Bachelor's Range, and a chaplain's residence that occasionally doubled as a schoolhouse. The trading post burned to the ground in 1866, six years after the departure of the Hudson's Bay Company. The stockade and five major buildings—including the chief factor's house, an impressive and well-furnished wood frame house with an ample verandah—have been reconstructed. The visitor center contains a museum with artifacts recovered during archaeological excavations and also features slide shows outlining the history of the fort, interpretive talks, and living history programs.

LOCATION: East Evergreen Boulevard. HOURS: 9:30–5:30 Daily. FEE: Yes. TELEPHONE: 206–696–7618.

MOUNT SAINT HELENS NATIONAL VOLCANIC MONUMENT

Mount Saint Helens had been dormant for 123 years when it stunned the West with two months of violent activity in the spring of 1980. But the mountain's pyrotechnics were well known by the Northwest Indians, some of whom called it *Louwala-Clough*, or "smoking mountain." According to Klickitat mythology, Wy'East and Klickitat, the two sons of Sahale, the Great Spirit, fell in love with a beautiful maiden, Loowit, and proceeded to fight for her attention. After they had wreaked havoc, burning villages and forests, Sahale struck down the three lovers and erected mountain peaks in their places. Loowit became Saint Helens, with its beautiful cone of dazzling white; Wy'East, Mount Hood; and Klickitat, Mount Adams.

When the mountain erupted on May 18, 1980, sixty-five people were killed. The north side of the volcano fell into the north fork of the Toutle River valley, damming Spirit Lake with debris. Floods on the Cowlitz River destroyed bridges, roads, parks, and 160,000 acres of forest. The force of the blast uprooted trees or snapped them at ground level, and ash from the eruption circled the globe.

There is one major visitor center in the park, on the shore of Silver Lake, next to Seaquest State Park, five miles east of Castle Rock. Here a ten-minute slide show illustrates the mountain's past eruptions and present activity, a walk-through scale model simulates volcanic activity, and exhibits describe the area's geology. Certain zones of the monument are restricted for safety reasons.

LOCATION: Route 504, east of Castle Rock. HOURS: April through September: 9–6 Daily; October through March: 9–5 Daily. FEE: None. TELEPHONE: 206–274–4038.

OPPOSITE: *Smoke, ash, and steam billow from Mount Saint Helens during its spectacular eruption in 1980.*

CENTRALIA

Situated midway between Portland and the cities of Puget Sound, Centralia began as a station for stagecoaches en route to Seattle from the Columbia River region and grew into an important lumbering town by the early twentieth century. A free black, George Washington, platted the town in 1852. Hostilities between settlers and Indians in the 1850s prompted the construction of a blockhouse called **Fort Borst,** a structure of hewn-log walls that stands in Fort Borst Park (one mile west of Centralia off Route 5). Also in the park is the **Joseph Borst Home** (206–736–7687), a restored Greek Revival house built by the pioneer Joseph Borst. Both the house and the fort are furnished with period pieces and may be seen by appointment.

Centralia is known for the bloody riot that occurred in 1919 at a time of great tension between labor organizers and anti-union factions. On Armistice Day, during an American Legion parade in the city, legionnaires and members of the Industrial Workers of the World came to blows on Tower Avenue, resulting in the death of four legionnaires and the lynching of "Wobblie" Wesley Everest on the bridge on Mellen Street.

CENTRAL   WASHINGTON

The Columbia River, which flows from its source in British Columbia through central Washington to the Pacific Ocean, is this region's most dominant feature. Woody Guthrie immortalized it in his 1941 ballad "Roll on Columbia." Lewis and Clark wrote of the roar of its white water in their journal. During the last Ice Age, some 10,000 years ago, the river was dammed by ice and forced to find new channels, among them the fifty-mile-long Grand Coulee. After the ice melted, the Columbia reverted to its original course, leaving the coulee dry. The Grand Coulee Dam and the reservoirs that surround it were built on part of the coulee. The glaciers themselves created channels, rock basins, and buttes—which characterize the region's scablands—as they tore basaltic rock from the earth and left it behind.

This geologically dramatic, but rather inhospitable, environment was home to Washington's Plateau Indians—the Yakima, Columbia, Okanogan, Nespelem, and others. Their struggles with the new white settlers were fierce, continuing even after they had signed away their land in treaties with Washington's territorial governor in 1855. Still, amid a shaky peace in the second half of the century, ranchers began to settle the region, joined by gold seekers. The prospectors headed for the dry and pine-forested hills of the Okanogan Highlands up north, where small towns such as Oroville and Molson mark their history. The arrival of the railroads in the 1880s and 1890s fueled the development of Yakima, Wenatchee, and Ellensburg, the region's main cities. And early irrigation projects at the turn of the century began to transform the region into the thriving agricultural center it has now become.

COLVILLE RESERVATION

Created by an executive order of President Ulysses S. Grant in 1872, this 1.3-million-acre reservation is the headquarters of the Wenatchee, Chelan, Anentiat, Methow, Colville, Sanpoil, Okanogan, Moses, Nespelem, Nez Percé, and Lakes peoples, known collectively as the Colville Confederated Tribes.

Nespelem, on the Colville Reservation, is the final resting place of the celebrated Chief Joseph of the Nez Percé, whose life spanned the period of major white immigration to Washington. The **Chief Joseph Memorial,** a monument with his portrait in relief, marks his grave site in a reservation cemetery. Though initially well disposed toward the newcomers—he was educated and renamed by missionaries in his youth—Joseph was later forced into a savage war in 1877 when the younger, more militant members of his tribe in northeastern Oregon's Wallowa Valley refused to be moved from their territory onto a government reservation. Challenging thousands of U.S. cavalrymen with his small force, Joseph fought valiantly, surrendering in October of that year with the words: "I am tired. My heart is sick and sad. From where the sun now stands I will fight no more forever." After a time in Kansas at Fort Leavenworth, he was transferred in 1885 to the Colville Reservation.

GRAND COULEE DAM

A mile long and 550 feet high, the Grand Coulee Dam is one of the world's largest hydroelectric engineering works. By harnessing the swift currents of the Columbia River, it has helped transform the barren deserts of central Washington into rich farmland. Opposition to the construction of the dam was fierce. Farmers, existing power companies, organized labor, and Congress—in the grip of the Great Depression—doubted the nation's need for such a project. President Franklin D. Roosevelt, having embarked on the New Deal, saw the dam as a potential symbol of recovery and opportunity. The Grand Coulee Dam was authorized by Congress in 1935, and its first turbo-generating units were completed in 1941, just in time to power the atomic works at Hanford. The dam's water was not used for irrigation until 1951.

Marcel Breuer, a Bauhaus-trained architect, was consulted on the design of the 1976 extension of the dam along the north wall of the canyon and the new turbine house, both of which display faceted concrete work in the International style. The U.S. Bureau of Reclamation staffs a **visitor center,** which offers self-guided tours of the dam aided by a fifteen-minute film featuring scenes of the dam's construction and modern irrigation methods. The **Coulee Dam National Recreation Area** (509–633–9441), which stretches 151 miles along the lakes and rivers that surround the dam, offers recreational facilities and opportunities for observing wildlife.

LOCATION: Route 155, 2 miles north of the town of Coulee Dam. HOURS: *Visitor Arrival Center:* June through August: 8:30 AM–10 PM Daily; September through May: 9–5 Daily. FEE: None. TELEPHONE: 509–633–9265.

Dry Falls, a chasm located in **Sun Lakes State Park** (Route 17, three miles south of Coulee City, 509–632–5214), is an awesome landmark, the dry bed of an immense prehistoric waterfall created when the Columbia River changed course during the Ice Age. An interpretive center offers splendid views of the chasm and exhibits depicting the history of the area.

EPHRATA

Located at the southern end of the Grand Coulee, Ephrata was so named because its method of irrigation by wells was similar to that of the village in the Old Testament. It was homesteaded in the 1880s. The **Grant County Historical Museum** (742 North Basin Street, 509–754–3334) has exhibits on the evolution of the town and county and a pioneer village with restored buildings from 1902 to 1930.

CHELAN

The small town of Chelan, at the southern end of the 1,500-foot-deep Lake Chelan, was settled late in the nineteenth century. In

1880, when Alexander Brender bought railroad land in one of Chelan's valleys, he found only five settlers. "There was no amusement, month in and month out. I would see no one. . . . My dissipation was newspapers." Today, at 2,802, the population is still small. The **Lake Chelan Historical Museum,** housed in the 1903 Miners & Merchants Bank Building (204 East Woodin Avenue, 509–682–5644), contains collections of apple labels, including stone lithographs from the early 1900s, as well as artifacts from central Washington Indian tribes. Downtown structures include the **Campbell House** (104 West Woodin Avenue), built in 1901 and now a hotel; the **Log Church** (120 East Woodin Avenue), dating to 1898; and the 1890 **Whaley Mansion** (415 3rd Street), now an inn.

WENATCHEE

The self-proclaimed apple capital of the world, Wenatchee sits on the banks of the Columbia River in a landscape of orchard-carpeted terraces and bare yellow hills. Wenatchee and its environs were a challenge to early settlers. Fur traders visiting in 1811 commented in their journals on winds and storms and other natural phenomena. Judge L. B. Nash, a pioneer who lived near Badger Mountain in the 1880s, told of meeting a newcomer on one of the region's trails. "Say mister," the man said to the judge, "I'm a stranger in these parts, but I have traveled some, and I want to say that this is the damned best ventilated country I ever was in." Winds notwithstanding, Wenatchee grew, its settlement fueled by the arrival of the Great Northern Railway in 1892 and the construction in 1903 of the Highline Canal, which irrigated the valley's rich volcanic soil.

The **North Central Washington Museum** (127 South Mission Street, 509–664–5989) features permanent and temporary exhibits on the region's history, geology, archaeology, natural history, and fine arts. The pioneer heritage section includes a furnished replica of a Victorian house. Other exhibits trace the impact of the apple industry and the railroad on the region's development—there is a working model of the Great Northern Railway and its routes over the Cascades. The museum also contains an exhibit on the first nonstop transpacific flight from Japan to the United States, made in 1931 by Clyde Pangborn and Hugh Herndon, Jr. Forty-one hours after they took off from Misawa, Japan, the aviators made a belly landing at Wenatchee.

CASHMERE

Settled in 1856 by the Oblate Fathers, among the region's first Christian missionaries, Cashmere profited in the later decades of the nineteenth century from the discovery of gold in Blewett at neighboring Peshastin Creek and the arrival of the railroad in 1892. Today an apple-growing town, Cashmere marks its heritage at the **Chelan County Historical Museum** (600 Cottage Avenue, 509-782-3230). On the grounds is a pioneer village with nearly twenty mid- to late-nineteenth-century log cabins moved here from different parts of Chelan County. The museum contains an archaeological collection of artifacts from the middle Columbia River and lower Snake River, including carvings and tools that date back 10,000 years.

ELLENSBURG

Situated just east of the Cascades, Ellensburg is the geographic center of the state and the seat of Kittitas County. The city started out with the racy name "Robber's Roost," the name of a trading post established in 1870 on Wilson Creek at the present-day intersection of Third Avenue and Main Street. Ellensburg flourished in the 1880s as the Northern Pacific Railroad's terminal and distribution center for the Kittitas Valley. The town had a fire in 1889, but it went on to rebuild and prosper, aided by the arrival of the Chicago, Milwaukee, & Saint Paul Railroad in 1907.

Known today for ranching, corn and grain production, and Central Washington University, Ellensburg maintains a finely preserved **historic district** (between Third and Fifth avenues and Pearl and Main streets) of nearly twenty buildings, many of them constructed just after the 1889 fire. The **Kittitas County Museum** (114 East Third Avenue, 509-925-3778), housed in the 1889 Cadwell Building, displays dishes, clothing, photographs, and other artifacts of local history.

Olmstead Place State Park

This state park was the site of a homestead built in 1875 by pioneer Samuel Olmstead. A Union soldier who headed west after the Civil War, he initially raised cattle here. His sons later started a dairy, whose butter was shipped as far away as Seattle. On the grounds are Olmstead's original cottonwood log cabin, now restored and furnished with the family's memorabilia; a gambrel-roofed hay barn; a dairy barn and granary; and a wagon shed, all built in the period 1875 to 1908.

LOCATION: Four miles southeast of Ellensburg. HOURS: 8–5 Daily. FEE: None. TELEPHONE: 509–925–1943.

YAKIMA

Sagebrush, brown hills, and wildflowers surround Yakima, which was founded by ranchers in 1858 as the Yakima Indians were being forced onto a reservation. The **Yakima Valley Museum** (2105 Tieton Drive, 509–248–0747) displays baskets, beadwork, clothing, and horse regalia of the Yakima Indian Nation; and a collection of horse-drawn vehicles, including a Conestoga wagon and a Concord stage-coach. The history of the Yakima Indians is told at the **Yakima Nation Museum** (509–865–2800) on their reservation in **Toppenish,** twenty miles south of Yakima. Part of a complex that includes a research library and a theater, the museum traces the evolution of the tribe through films, wall poetry, and dramatic presentations.

FORT SIMCOE HISTORICAL STATE PARK

Situated in the Simcoe Valley where the Toppenish plain meets the foothills of the Cascades, Fort Simcoe was established in August 1856, during the Yakima War. Five of the original structures that faced the fort's 420-foot tree-lined parade ground remain. The Gothic Revival **commanding officer's quarters** was designed by an Army draftsman using A. J. Downing's fashionable pattern book of Gothic country houses. From this fort Major Robert S. Garnett, the fort's commander, attacked the Yakima in 1858.

LOCATION: Route 220, near White Swan, 38 miles southwest of Yakima. HOURS: April through September: 6:30 AM–Dusk Daily; October through March: 8 AM–Dusk Saturday–Sunday. FEE: None. TELEPHONE: 509–874–2372.

South of Toppenish, Route 97 winds through the abundant grass-lands and pine-filled mountain slopes of Horse Heaven Hills, across Satus Pass, and into **Goldendale,** the seat of Klickitat County, and the northeast entrance to the Columbia River Gorge. Goldendale was named after John J. Golden, who homesteaded here in 1863. The **Klickitat County Historical Society** (127 West Broadway, 509-772-4303) is headquartered in a restored, twenty-room Victorian mansion built by Winthrop Presley, a lawyer, in 1902. About ten miles south of Goldendale, looking delightfully out of place on a cliff overlooking the Columbia River, is the **Maryhill Museum of Art** (33 Maryhill Museum Drive, 509-773-3733). The museum, housed in a palatial, poured-concrete mansion built by Samuel Hill, who inherited great wealth from his father, James J. Hill, founder of the Great Northern Railway, was dedicated in 1926 by Hill's friend Queen Marie of Romania during a well-publicized visit to the United States. In addition to a Queen Marie of Romania Room there are a substantial collection of works by Auguste Rodin and other nineteenth- and twentieth-century European and American painters, more than 1,000 native American baskets and artifacts, and 100-plus antique chess sets.

EASTERN WASHINGTON
SPOKANE

Incorporated in 1881, Spokane is a city born of wheat, mining, electricity, and railroads. It stands on an impressive site at the upper falls of the Spokane River, where the first hydroelectric plant west of the Mississippi was built in 1885. In that decade five major railroads linked the city to the East, making it an important shipping hub for the region's wheat as well as gold, silver, copper, and lead taken from mines in eastern Washington and neighboring states. After a fire in 1889 destroyed much of Spokane (only one significant building survived the fire), the city was rapidly rebuilt. However, development was not haphazard: In the early decades of this century Spokane's leading citizens set aside parcels of land for a series of parks, designed by the Olmsted Brothers firm. Another pleasant remnant of the Olmsted plan is the curved stretch of Riverside Avenue, a boulevard faced by a set of handsome Beaux Arts buildings.

Spokane is still a thriving agricultural service center, but its era as a railroad hub has passed. The city's centerpiece is the scenic **Riverfront Park,** built for the 1974 World's Fair Expo, which replaced a network of disused railroad tracks, yards, and stations. In

OPPOSITE: *The elaborate Spokane County Courthouse, designed by Willis Ritchie, who was lavish in his use of Early French Renaissance details.*

the park, reminders of Spokane's boom decades include the **clock tower** from the Great Northern Depot (1902) and a restored early twentieth-century **carousel** that operated in the former Natatorium Park until 1968.

North of the river sits the 1895 **Spokane County Courthouse** (West 1116 Broadway), one of several Washington structures (including the Jefferson County Courthouse in Port Townsend and Stadium High School in Tacoma) designed in a Chateauesque style by Willis Ritchie, who learned his trade in a correspondence course from the superintendent of architecture in the U.S. Treasury Department.

Remains of Spokane's boom years fill a two-mile-square rectangular area of the business district, with Riverside Avenue and the surrounding streets providing a fine architectural review. The sole survivor of Spokane's devastating 1889 fire (Seattle, Ellensburg, and Vancouver were also struck by fires that year) is the **Crescent Building** (1880) at West 919–925 Riverside. A harbinger of the city's postfire renaissance is the **Spokesman Review Building** (927 Riverside Avenue), built in 1891 of red brick and gray Montana granite in the Romanesque Revival style. The **Davenport Hotel** (1914) and the **Matador Restaurant** (1908), designed by the noted Washington architect Kirtland Cutter, enliven Sprague Avenue with an unlikely juxtaposition of Beaux-Arts eclecticism and California Mission style.

Cutter is responsible for much of Spokane's late-nineteenth-century architecture; it has been said he did $568,000 worth of business the year of the fire. His hand is most evident in the **Browne's Addition Historic District** and **The Hill,** elegant residential neighborhoods west and south of the center in which the city's wealthier citizens built their mansions. The **Cheney Cowles Museum** (West 2316 First Avenue, 509–456–3931) is home of the Eastern Washington State Historical Society. The society houses a major thematic exhibition on the history of eastern Washington; sponsors changing exhibitions on such regional themes as mining, native American cultures, and agriculture; and displays textiles and decorative arts from their extensive collection. The adjoining half-timbered Old English–style **Campbell House** was built in 1898 for Amasa B. Campbell, who made his millions from mining in the Coeur d'Alene. Also administered by the historical society, it has been restored and retains its original furniture. The Colonial Revival **John A. Finch House** (2340 First Avenue, private) was built for Campbell's partner Finch in 1898.

The Hill is the site of the city's highest lookout point, Review Rock in Cliff Park. The **Austin Corbin II House** (West 815 Seventh

The Patrick F. Clark House at Cutter and Malmgren streets in Browne's Addition. Clark sent the architect, Kirtland Cutter, on a tour of Europe for inspiration.

Avénue), now converted to offices, is a fine example of the Colonial Revival style, designed by Kirtland Cutter. Corbin, the general manager of the Spokane Falls and Northern Railroad, spent $35,000 on his seventeen-room mansion of buff brick. He was the son of Daniel Chase Corbin, who founded the Coeur D'Alene Railroad and Navigation Company and the Spokane Falls and Northern Railroad. The elder Corbin's house, now the **Corbin Art Center** (West 507 Seventh Avenue, 509–456–3865), was also designed by Cutter. The Teutonic-style **James N. Glover House** (West 321 Eighth Avenue, on the grounds of the Unitarian Church of Spokane, 509–624–4802) was built in 1888. It now houses the offices of the church but is open to the public. None of the original furnishings remain, but the house retains its fine woodwork and fabric wallcoverings.

At Gonzaga University, the **Museum of Native American Cultures** (East 200 Cataldo Avenue, between Division Street and the university, 509–326–4550) is home to a large collection of artifacts of native American peoples from Alaska to South America. Exhibits include clothing, corn-husk work, and beaded flat bags made by Columbia Plateau Indians; baskets, copper drums, totem poles, and ceremonial masks from Alaskan tribes; artwork and artifacts of the

North Plains Indians; and a sizable collection of pre-Columbian ceramics and textiles.

Just outside of Spokane in **Riverside State Park,** early Washington history is marked by the **Spokane House Interpretive Center** (six miles northwest, on Downriver Drive, 509–456–3946). The state's first European fur-trading post and permanent white settlement, Spokane House was built by the British North West Company in 1810. The traders abandoned the site for the better location of Fort Colville in 1826. The center has a small collection of trade items, including weapons and tools.

Fort Spokane (Route 25, in Coulee Dam National Recreation Area, 23 miles north of Davenport, 509–725–2715) was erected in 1882 to protect the settlers of the upper Columbia River and to keep an eye on the newly established Indian reservations of the Colville and Spokane tribes. Four of the fort's original buildings—the quarter-master stable, powder magazine, reservoir, and guardhouse—have been restored by the National Park Service.

REPUBLIC

Amid the pines and firs of the Colville National Forest sits Republic, one of Washington's major mining centers in the late 1890s. Typical of the mining towns of that time, Republic's pattern of growth was one of boom and bust. The town grew quickly—in 1900 it was sixth in population among eastern Washington's cities and had twenty-eight saloons and two dance halls—and then quieted when mining activity subsided in 1901. The **Knob Hill Mine**, which spurred Republic's economy in the mid-1930s, is still one of the Northwest's richest gold producers. The **Ferry County Historical Museum** (509–775–3888), on the town's Courthouse Square, chronicles the early days with a collection of mining equipment and photographs.

North and west of Republic in **Colville National Forest** one can still see remnants of mining settlements at **Old Toroda,** northeast of Wauconda, and **Bodie,** where a stamp mill processed ores from the Golden Reward and Elk (Golconda) mines until the late 1930s. Twelve miles south of the Canadian border on Route 395, Orient pays tribute to its boom period with a small, wooden city hall, local headquarters of the Big Nine Mine and Mining Company. Nearby **Curlew,** a village of 100 people, still has the 1890s **Ansorge Hotel,** a stopover point for travelers on the Great Northern Railway.

In **Rosalia,** thirty-one miles south of Spokane, is the **Steptoe Battlefield Memorial,** a twenty-six-foot-tall granite monument commemorating the site of a battle between the U.S. Army and several Indian tribes. Departing from Fort Walla Walla on May 16, 1858, Lieutenant Colonel Edward J. Steptoe embarked on a fact-finding trip to check reports of hostility among Indians in Colville and to talk with the Spokane. Instead of talking, he ended up fighting when nearly 1,000 Spokane, Palouse, Coeur d'Alene, and other warriors attacked his party near the site of present-day Rosalia. By the end of the day, all except 7 of Steptoe's 158 men had escaped, driven in defeat back to Walla Walla. In retaliation the U.S. Army began a search-and-destroy mission under the direction of Colonel George Wright, burning villages and killing Indians and their horses.

Steptoe Butte, about twenty miles south of Rosalia, a 3,612-foot outcrop of the Selkirk Mountains, was called Pyramid Peak on early maps of the region but was later renamed after Colonel Steptoe. A paved road winds to the top of the butte, providing a marvelous panoramic view across the wheatlands of the Palouse and the Blue, Moscow, Selkirk, and Cascade mountains.

COLFAX

Colfax was founded in 1870 by James Perkins, a pioneer from Illinois. His home, the **Perkins House** (623 North Perkins Street, 509–332–1029), is a Victorian mansion with four balconies, built between 1884 and 1886 to accommodate his growing family. The interior has been restored with turn-of-the-century furnishings by the Whitman County Historical Society. Behind the house is Perkins's squared-log cabin, the first house to be built in Colfax and the site of the first Republican convention in Whitman County.

PULLMAN

Originally known as Three Forks, a favorite watering and camping site for Indians and early homesteaders, Pullman is reputed to have been rechristened in honor of the inventor of the railroad sleeping car in 1881. Pullman was selected as the site for **Washington State University** (509–335–3581), which, with $12,000 in cash and 160 acres, was established in 1891. The campus (now comprising 600 acres) has a number of museums, such as the **Museum of Anthropology** and the **Jacklin Collection of Petrified Wood,** and tours of the university are offered.

Three Forks Pioneer Village Museum (six miles north of Pullman on Anderson Road, 509–332–3889) displays artifacts of the nineteenth and early twentieth centuries in fifteen modestly restored buildings. They include a log cabin, whose parlor has an 1875 pianoforte that was shipped around Cape Horn to the Uniontown Opera House, and a general store with a post office, a potbellied stove, coffee mills, and shelves stacked to the tin ceiling with bottles, boxes, china, tins, and hardware.

DAYTON

An example of a wheatlands market town, Dayton is a distributing point for surrounding dryland farms. Some eighty-five nineteenth- and early-twentieth-century houses grace the town. The restored **Dayton Historical Depot** (Second and Commercial streets, 509–382–4825), the state's oldest existing railroad station, was built by the Oregon Railroad and Navigation Company in 1881. Now a museum, the building is furnished with railroad memorabilia and period benches, lanterns, and a potbellied stove on the first floor. The second floor, formerly the stationmaster's apartment, has a changing exhibition of photographs of the area. The **Columbia County Courthouse,** Washington's oldest courthouse, was built in 1887 and is undergoing restoration. Though its exterior has been altered, the interior woodwork and central staircase still reflect the building's Italianate style.

WALLA WALLA

Walla Walla, which means "many waters" in Nez Percé, was a rendezvous spot for native tribes. The missionaries came here in 1836, and the first wagon trains over the Oregon Trail stopped here in the 1840s. In the 1860s it was a colorful, if rowdy, supply post for mines in Idaho, Montana, and California. After the luster of the gold rush dimmed, the city continued to prosper, albeit more quietly, as an agricultural center, which it has remained to this day. There are some three dozen historic buildings in the city's downtown district, most of which have been put to commercial use. The **Kirkman House** (214 North Colville, 509–525–2840) is a bracketed Italianate villa built in 1880 by William Kirkman, a cattle rancher, meat-packer, and town developer. Still in the process of restoration, the house has a dining room, double parlor, marble fireplaces, ornate brass door-

OPPOSITE: *A view of the town of Steptoe and the surrounding fields from the top of Steptoe Butte.*

knobs, elegant parquet floors, and distinctive fan transom that make it a handsome landmark of Victoriana.

Fort Walla Walla Museum Complex

This museum complex contains a village of fourteen pioneer buildings, dating as early as 1859, that were transported from other points in Walla Walla and the surrounding area. Local heirlooms and artifacts, including an 1859 Osborne spinning wheel, have been used to furnish log cabins, a blockhouse, a doctor's office, a blacksmith shop, and other structures. There are also life-size agricultural displays, including that of a combine wheat harvester harnessed to thirty-three mules (fiberglass models) by means of the "Shandoney" hitch, which allowed one driver to control all the animals.

LOCATION: Myra Road, off Dalles Military Road in the city of Walla Walla. HOURS: June through September: 1–5 Tuesday–Sunday; May and October: 1–5 Saturday–Sunday. FEE: Yes. TELEPHONE: 509–525–7703.

Whitman Mission

In 1836 Dr. Marcus Whitman and his new bride, Narcissa, came from upstate New York and established a mission at Waiilatpu, "place of the people of the rye grass," on the Walla Walla River, among the Cayuse. The mission no longer stands, but the spot, now a National Historic Site, commemorates one of the most crucial incidents in Washington's history. Narcissa was one of the first two white women—Eliza Spalding was the other—known to have crossed the continent overland, and the Whitman's daughter, Alice Clarissa, was the first white child born in the Northwest, in 1837. (She later wandered off from the mission and drowned.) The Whitmans farmed, built a gristmill and sawmill, learned the Indian languages, printed books in Nez Percé and Spokan, and encouraged the Indians to follow their methods. But they had little luck in matters spiritual or agricultural. Like other Protestant missionaries, they came into conflict with the more successful Catholic priests, who displayed greater understanding of the Indians' cultural differences. The Cayuse refused to give up hunting for farming and resented the harsh punishments Marcus Whitman meted out for stealing and other infractions. The influx of new emigrants, who stopped at the mission for food and medical care, further angered the Cayuse. In 1847, after an epidemic of measles brought by the emigrants wiped out half the tribe, the enraged Cayuse, convinced they were being poisoned, attacked the mission, killing the Whitmans and eleven others. The massacre ended Protestant missionary activity in the Oregon Country and sparked a war between the Cayuse and settlers from the Willamette and lower Columbia valleys. In order to save their people from extermination, five Cayuse warriors surrendered to authorities, said that they were the killers, and calmly went to their death by hanging.

The locations of the mission buildings are marked for self-guided tours. Also on the site is a visitor center with displays and artifacts—including the tomahawk used by one of the Cayuse to kill Dr. Whitman—that portray the life of the mission.

LOCATION: Off Route 12, 7 miles west of Walla Walla. HOURS: Memorial Day through Labor Day: 8–6 Daily; September through May: 8–4:30 Daily. FEE: Yes. TELEPHONE: 509–522–6360.

SACAJAWEA STATE PARK

This park, which commemorates Lewis and Clark's arrival at the Columbia River on October 16, 1805, was named after Sacajawea, the young Indian woman who joined the expedition at Fort Mandan in North Dakota with her husband, Toussaint Charbonneau, a trader. Though a new mother—whose delivery was reputedly hastened by a dose of rattlesnake's rattle—she proved to be a valuable member of the expedition. It is often said that she acted as the expedition's pathfinder, but that was not the case. She had been kidnapped by members of another tribe and had little knowledge of geography beyond her homeland in what is now western Montana. She was, however, particularly helpful in negotiations with her tribe, the Shoshone, whose horses carried the expedition over the Continental Divide. The park contains an interpretive center that highlights their journey, the activities at this site, and Sacajawea's role. There is also a room of prehistoric Indian artifacts from the Columbia Plateau, including stone points, mauls, mortars and pestles, and bone tools. Tours and special programs are offered.

LOCATION: At the junction of the Snake and Columbia rivers, off Route 395 in Pasco. HOURS: Late April through Labor Day: 10–6 Wednesday–Sunday. FEE: None. TELEPHONE: 509–545–2361.

CHAPTER SEVEN

ALASKA

OPPOSITE: *The fishing village of Petersburg, settled by Norwegians at the turn of the century, lies at the tip of Mitkof Island in the Alaska Panhandle.*

Alaska may still be considered a last frontier. In 1880, when such far western communities as San Francisco and Sacramento were thriving, Alaska had barely been colonized. Much of the region's great wilderness lay unexplored by non-native Alaskans, while the settled spots were almost as wild, attracting hunters, trappers, speculators, traders, prospectors, and missionaries, but few urbanites. A land unknown or caricatured as "Uncle Sam's stepchild," Alaska in 1880 had only recently been given a civil government. In that year, however, two prospectors seeking gold in present-day Juneau hit pay dirt. Others quickly followed—first in a trickle, then a stream, and ultimately, in 1897, a flood that brought tens of thousands of Americans north by every available boat to join the gold rush. Since then Alaska has truly been a boom state, taking in waves of newcomers lured by a pioneering economy, unparalleled natural wonders, and a spirit of adventure into the untamed.

The first of all native American peoples arrived by way of a land bridge between Asia and Alaska in what is now the Bering Strait anywhere from 50,000 to 10,000 years ago. While many peoples must have passed through Alaska, only four groups made permanent homes here: the Aleut, in the Aleutian Islands; the Eskimo, in the northern and western coastal areas; the Athapaskan, in the Interior along the Yukon River; and the Northwest Coast, including the Tlingit, in the Panhandle of the southeast. Because of Alaska's vast size and short digging season, archaeological evidence is relatively scarce, but it is believed that by A.D. 1000 these four cultures had adapted to the food, climate, and isolation of the regions in which they were found by white explorers in the eighteenth century.

The American Revolution had already been fought and the American colonies sprinkled with towns when the first permanent non-native settlement was established in Alaska. The settlers were not from Spain or America, but from Russia, and their intent was less to settle the land than to exploit it for its natural wealth. The first expedition to reach Alaska was commissioned in 1724 by Peter the Great, who selected Vitus Bering, a Danish sea captain, to explore the northwestern coast of the American continent. In 1728 Bering sailed through the strait that now bears his name. Bering died on a second voyage, in 1741, but his men returned to Siberia with samples of the fur-bearing animals to be found in Alaska, leading to more extensive explorations and the advance of Russian fur traders.

OPPOSITE: *The meeting of three cultures in Saint Michael in 1908, two years after Alaska became a U.S. territory: Eskimo women seated around a Russian blockhouse from the 1830s, holding the U.S. flag.*

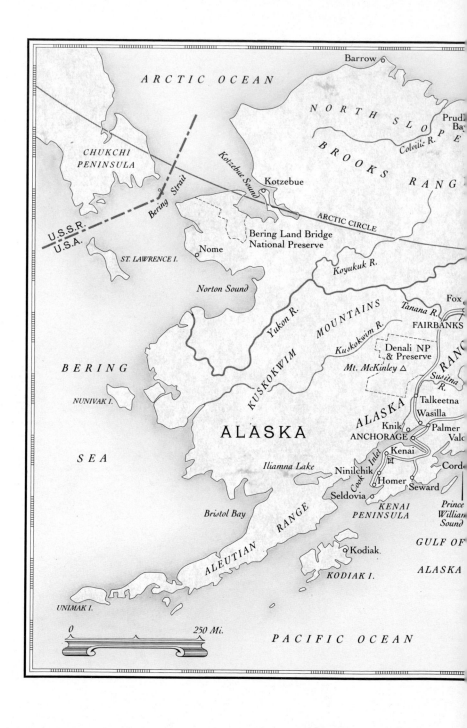

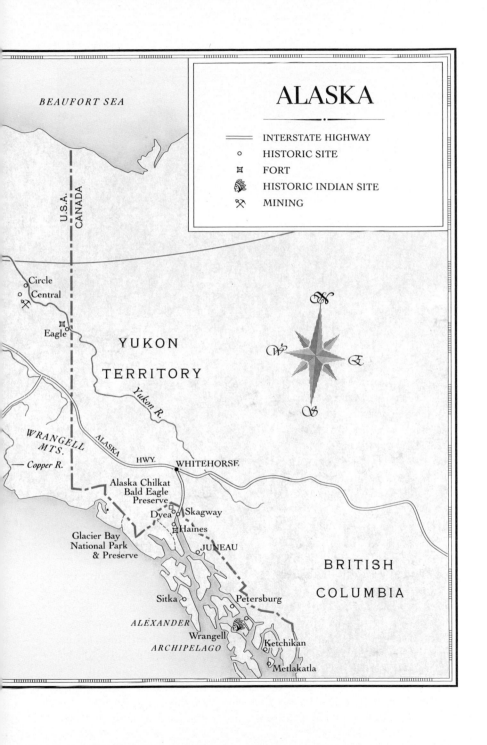

BEAUFORT SEA

ALASKA

	INTERSTATE HIGHWAY
○	HISTORIC SITE
⊟	FORT
🪶	HISTORIC INDIAN SITE
⚒	MINING

U.S.A.
CANADA

Circle
Central

Eagle

YUKON

TERRITORY

Yukon R.

WRANGELL
MTS.

ALASKA

Copper R.

HWY.

WHITEHORSE

Alaska Chilkat
Bald Eagle
Preserve

Dyea Skagway

Haines

Glacier Bay
National Park
& Preserve

JUNEAU

BRITISH

COLUMBIA

Sitka

Petersburg

ALEXANDER

Wrangell

Ketchikan

ARCHIPELAGO

Metlakatla

*Members of the Second Presbyterian Church of Juneau in front of their church build-
ing, a former miner's cabin.*

In their quest for fur seal and sea otter pelts, the Russians came
into conflict with the Aleut, a peaceful people who fished and hunted on the Alaska Peninsula and the Aleutian Islands. The Aleut welcomed the newcomers, but the Russians promptly massacred or
enslaved them, forcing them to hunt furs. The Russians also battled
furiously with the Eskimo, who lived farther north and, like the
Aleut, wrested their living from the sea.

In 1784 the Russians established their first permanent colony
on what had been an Eskimo stronghold, Kodiak Island. From this
outpost, one of the most ambitious traders, Aleksandr Baranov,
expanded Russia's hunting operations and also opened trade with
British, American, and Spanish explorers who had begun surveying
the Alaskan coastline. Exploiting one hunting ground after another,
Baranov founded a trading station in 1799 at Sitka. In the area
around Sitka, however, the Russians had to contend with the Tlingit,
who were far more hostile than the Eskimo or Aleut. From villages
containing solidly constructed communal houses and impressive
totems, the Tlingit sailed the rivers and bays of southeastern Alaska
in war canoes, battling other natives. The Tlingit traded with the
Russians but never submitted to them, and in 1802 they stormed and
captured the fort at Sitka, using firearms probably acquired from the
British. Baranov returned and finally drove the Indians away in 1804.

He established Sitka as a frontier capital from which, as general manager of the Russian American Company, he oversaw virtually all Russian activities in North America. But the Tlingit continued to pick away at the Russians, ambushing them whenever possible.

Also troublesome for the Russians was the rival Hudson's Bay Company, a British concern that sent hunters and traders into territory claimed by the Russians. Unable to fend off this encroachment, the Russians signed an agreement in 1839 leasing all of southeastern Alaska to their rivals. American ships had also begun plying the coastal waters in greater numbers, and the Russians found defending their territory an increasing financial drain with little return. They had not only killed off most of the fur-bearing animals but also failed to engage in farming or to mine any of the territory's immense mineral resources.

Weakened further by their defeat in the Crimean War, the Russians tried to interest the American government in buying the territory in 1859, but the domestic difficulties then facing the United States overrode any interest in Alaska. Once the Civil War was over, Secretary of State William H. Seward, who saw Alaska's strategic importance, began negotiating secretly for its purchase. Possession of Alaska was formally transferred during a flag-raising ceremony at Sitka on October 18, 1867. The purchase price was an astonishingly low $7.2 million—about two cents an acre. At that point, the number of non-native Alaskans, which had never risen above 1,000, had dropped to about 400, most of them Russians. Their only monuments to civilization were a handful of handsome, onion-domed churches, a few of which still survive.

Tradition has it that Seward's purchase was regarded by the American public as a ludicrous mistake deserving the epithets "Seward's Folly" and "Seward's Icebox," but many Americans approved of the purchase, and settlers began pouring into Sitka, turning it into something of a boomtown. The boom was short lived, however, primarily because Congress had not installed a civil government in Alaska. There were no homesteading laws, so settlers could acquire no title to land, and for a time, only a military garrison provided Alaskans any official government.

What finally spurred the federal government to act was gold. After Joseph Juneau and Richard Harris discovered gold in a stream about fifty miles from Sitka, a rude frontier town—which became Juneau, Alaska's capital—sprang up, and in 1884 the federal government passed an act providing for the appointment of a civil governor, a judge, and other officials. The law gave gold prospectors the right to make claims, but the continued lack of homesteading laws provided little impetus to settlers. More compelling was the salmon industry, which started with the erection of the first canneries in 1878. Yet just as traders had depleted the fur seal, fishermen killed off the salmon wholesale. In Alaska, it seemed, nothing lasted long.

The thinning of Alaska's population reversed in 1896, when prospectors struck gold in the Klondike region of the Yukon Territory in northwestern Canada. This gold, easier to mine than the hard-rock gold around Juneau, fired the American imagination. Some 100,000 adventurers from the lower states rushed north, lured by advertisements promising gold so plentiful it clung to the anchors of ships. Gold fever quickly spread from the Yukon fields into Alaska, where strikes were made at Nome in 1898.

Only a few hundred prospectors obtained any real wealth from Alaskan gold, but the gold rush began the state's real growth. The population, reported as 32,052 in the 1890 census, nearly doubled by 1900. With this rise came the demand for more adequate government, and Congress soon provided an expanded criminal and civil code for Alaska. In 1906, during the final phase of exploration and settlement of the American West, Alaska was given status first as a United States possession, then, in 1912, as a territory with its own legislature and governor. However, the federal government still controlled the region's resources, and during this era it enacted the first conservation laws in Alaska, setting aside forest reserves and protecting the fur seals. As gold mining dwindled after World War I, Alaska's population again declined, but World War II and the postwar years saw a tremendous boom in military construction that brought an influx of newcomers. Other industries boomed as well, particularly salmon fishing, the mining of minerals, and oil drilling. As the population surged, Alaskans became aware of their increasing importance and pressed for statehood. On January 3, 1959, when the population stood at 225,000, Alaska became the forty-ninth state.

Newcomers to Alaska must first contend with its vastness, for it is larger than the combined areas of Washington, Oregon, California, Idaho, Nevada, and Utah. It covers some 586,000 square miles and is fully a fifth as large as the other forty-eight continental states. In terms of both geography and weather, there are several Alaskas. The Panhandle of southeastern Alaska, centered on the capital at Juneau, has a cool and damp climate similar to parts of Oregon and Washington. The area supports immense forests of evergreens, mazes of islands and fjords, and, rising behind them, a snow-covered range of coastal mountains. South-central Alaska, the area extending west of the Panhandle, has warm summers and two fertile valleys that are renowned for their dairy products and their huge cabbages and other lush crops. The Interior, cut by the Yukon River, comprises thousands of square miles between the Brooks Range to the north and the Alaska Range to the south. Despite the fact that winter temperatures reach sixty degrees below zero Fahrenheit, Fairbanks, the state's second largest city, has a bearable climate. And far to the west there is Nome, no longer as vital as during the gold-rush days, but still a magnet for modern-day pioneers. To the north lies the Alaskan Arctic, one region in the United States that could defy modernization for some time.

This chapter begins at the southern end of the Panhandle, where visitors coming by boat first enter the state. It proceeds northwest along the coastal waterways to Anchorage and points south—the Kenai Peninsula and Kodiak Island—then turns to the Interior and on to the far-western and northern coasts.

SOUTHEAST ALASKA

The Alaska Panhandle, a 600-mile spur of islands and coastal frontage, extends southeastward from the main body of the state in a narrow zone between the Canadian mainland and the Pacific Ocean. Most communities in the area are located on its over 1,000 islands, the peaks of a once-dry mountain range now known as the Alexander Archipelago, and ships and planes are the chief means of transportation. The region's main water highway, the Inland Passage, follows routes first opened thousands of years ago by the Tlingit and Haida, fishing peoples who traded up and down the Pacific Northwest in their great canoes.

KETCHIKAN

Ketchikan was a gold-rush supply depot before the turn of the century, but its enduring wealth rests on fishing. Earlier in this century the town was one of the leading packagers of salmon, and both fishing and canning remain important to the local economy.

Clinging to the rocky hillside, the wood frame houses of the downtown area are connected by wooden stairways and raised walkways. A variety of styles, including late Victorian and Queen Anne,

can be found in the district, which was settled by the town's more prosperous families between 1900 and 1935. The turreted **Monrean House** (500 Main Street, private) was built in the Queen Anne style in 1904. **Creek Street,** once a red-light district, contains a number of late Victorian wood-frame buildings raised up on pilings over Ketchikan Creek. A **visitor center** (131 Front Street, 907–225–6166) provides information on the town's historic buildings and districts.

The **Tongass Historical Museum** (629 Dock Street, 907–225–5600) provides a view of the Ketchikan Creek salmon run in summer. It has displays on fishing and canning as well as a collection of Haida, Tlingit, and Tsimshian tools, baskets, and ceremonial objects, and exhibitions of the works of local artists. The region has several assemblages of ancient and modern Tlingit and Haida totem poles, and the **Totem Heritage Center** (601 Deermount Street, 907–225–5900) contains thirty–three genuine poles from villages in the area. Carved from red cedar, the poles were used as house supports, memorials, or to denote status and clan relationships.

Ten miles north of Ketchikan is **Totem Bight State Historical Park** (Tongass Highway North, 907–465–4563), where a path leads to a group of fine replica totems. Set among them is the front of the traditional Tlingit community house, carved and painted so the door seems to be the mouth of a gigantic bird. The Tlingit village of **Saxman** (off Tongass Highway, two miles south of Ketchikan, 907–225–8687) has twenty–four modern poles and an open workshop where traditional craftspeople may be seen at work.

About fifteen miles south of Ketchikan, on neighboring Annette Island, is the town of **Metlakatla,** a cooperative that has thrived for many years, chiefly from fishing and lumbering activities. It was founded in 1887 by an Anglican missionary, William Duncan, and 400 Tsimshian Indians from British Columbia. Ousted by the Anglican hierarchy, Duncan and his Tsimshian parishioners moved to the spot, which they named for their village in Canada. Duncan's house, built for the aged pastor by his fellow colonists in 1894, is now the **Duncan Cottage Museum** (Atkinson Street, 907–886–4441), still with its original furnishings, and exhibiting pictures and documents describing the building of the town.

OPPOSITE: *Totem pole and tribal house, Saxman.*

WRANGELL

On Wrangell Island in the shadow of Mount Cote is the small town of Wrangell, a quiet place that looks much as it did when it served turn–of–the–century gold miners on their way to the Klondike. The Russians built a fort here in 1834, largely to hold off the British, but within five years they had leased the land to their opponents.

The **Wrangell Museum** (122 2nd Street, 907–874–3770), housed in the town's first schoolhouse, is notable for its collection of Indian petroglyphs. Other carvings can be seen, most at their original sites, along **Petroglyph Beach** (off Evergreen Avenue). The **Chief Shakes gravesite** (Case Avenue) marks the burial place of a nineteenth-century leader of the local Stikine clan of the Tlingit. He was the fifth Stikine chief to bear that name, which was won by the first Chief Shakes from a Tsimshian warrior as part of the spoils of war. Surrounded by a picket fence the grave is marked by two carvings of killer whales. A more complete evocation of Indian life can be found at the **Tlingit Tribal House of the Bear** (Chief Shakes Island, 907–874–3747). This is a reproduction of a Tlingit community house, great cedar buildings where 50 to 100 people lived together

Saint Michael's Cathedral rises above the rooftops of Sitka in a 1900 photograph. The Seven Sisters Peaks are in the background.

through the cold wet winters before splitting up into families for the summer's fishing and hunting season. Also on the site are reproduction totem poles and a collection of Tlingit carving tools.

SITKA

The abundance of fur seals and sea otters in this area led Aleksandr Baranov, chief manager of the Russian American Company, to establish a Russian outpost, Redoubt Saint Michael, here in 1799. Three years later the Tlingit, who had occupied the site for centuries, destroyed the new colony, but Baranov drove them off in 1804 and moved the company headquarters here from Kodiak Island. The new settlement, renamed New Archangel, quickly became the capital of Russian America and thrived as the shipping point for all the company's products—lumber, ice, and fish as well as furs—and the stopping point for merchant vessels bound for Asia. By the 1850s, however, overtrapping had depleted the otter population and the economy began to falter. When, in 1867, the Russian government sold Alaska to the United States, the official transfer took place in what is now **Castle Hill State Historic Site** (off Lincoln Street, 907–747–6249).

A replica of a Russian blockhouse, at left, and the spire of the reconstructed Saint Michael's Cathedral, at right, are reminders of Sitka's Russian heritage.

The site is marked by interpretive plaques and seven Russian cannon; signs at the foot of the hill describe the history of Castle Hill, where the Tlingit once built their clan houses.

The 106-acre **Sitka National Historical Park** (106 Metlakatla Street, 907–747–6281) marks the spot where the Tlingit made their last stand in 1804. Nothing remains of the fort they built to protect themselves, but there are a number of Tlingit and Haida totem poles on the trail to the fort site, and the visitor center contains a fine collection of native ornamental objects, blankets, and baskets and an area where visitors may see craftspeople at work.

Also part of the park, but located outside of the main area, is the 1842 **Russian Bishop's House** (corner of Lincoln and Monastery streets), a spruce–log structure that served as a bishop's residence for 127 years. The first floor contains interpretive exhibits on Russian America, focusing on the Orthodox church, the Russian American Company, and the history of the house itself; upstairs, the chapel and bishop's quarters have been restored to their 1853

Inside Saint Michael's are Russian icons and other religious articles rescued by the townspeople from the fire that destroyed the original church.

appearance with original and period furnishings. Farther down Lincoln Street is an accurate replica of **Saint Michael's Cathedral,** an onion–domed structure built in 1848. Although the original church burned in 1966, its remarkable collection of icons—including one of Saint Michael that also survived the sinking of the ship that brought it from Russia in 1912—is intact and on display.

The **Sheldon Jackson Museum** (104 College Drive, 907–747–8981), established in 1888, has one of the best collections of artifacts from the four native cultures of Alaska: the Eskimo, Aleut, Athapaskan, and Northwest Coast (which include the Tlingit). Much of the material—basketry, clothing, carvings, necklaces, and masks—was collected by the missionary and educator for whom the museum is named. The **Isabel Miller Museum** (330 Harbor Drive, 907–747–6455) focuses on the period after 1840 with artifacts from Russian and American settlers. The town's **visitor center** (907–747–5940) is located in the same building.

Seven miles north of town, **Old Sitka State Historic Site** (Halibut Point Road, 907–747–6249) marks the location of the original Redoubt Saint Michael with interpretive signs describing the history of the outpost.

JUNEAU

Only the Tlingit lived in this area when prospectors Dick Harris and Joe Juneau arrived in 1880, led by a Tlingit named Kowee to the rich deposits of gold in the stream still called Gold Creek. The great mines created in the next decades operated continuously until World War II, yielding more than $158 million in gold. The **Juneau–Douglas City Museum** (114 4th Street, 907–586–3572) describes the history of the Juneau Gold Belt area with displays of mining equipment and artifacts and nineteenth–century household implements. The museum also has a number of totem poles, which are scattered throughout the city, and provides information about walking tours of two privately owned local gold mines.

In 1906 Juneau wrested the honor of territorial capital away from Sitka, but the first territorial legislature did not convene in Juneau until 1913. The ornate **Governor's Mansion** (716 Calhoun Avenue, private) was completed the following year. The **State Capitol** (222 Seward Street, 907–465–3854) was constructed in 1930 of brick and limestone, with pillars of Alaska marble. A block away is the town **visitor center** (Seward and 3rd streets, 907–465–3854), located in a replica of a nineteenth–century log cabin.

A *totem pole, at right, graces the Alaska Governor's Mansion.*

Being the seat of government has brought money, modernity, and an excellent museum to Juneau. The **Alaska State Museum** (395 Whittier Street, 907–465–2901) is particularly strong in artifacts from all the state's native cultures, and there are displays of fine house posts and carvings, a remarkable Eskimo skin boat, rare Chilkat blankets made of mountain-goat wool and cedar bark, and intricate spruce–root basketry. The exhibits on natural history and early Russian and American occupation are among the finest in the state.

Like a museum itself is the nearby **Saint Nicholas Russian Orthodox Church** (326 5th Street), the oldest Russian church remaining in southeastern Alaska. Built in 1894, this octagonal, onion–domed structure contains splendid icons and other religious relics. The **House of Wickersham** (213 Seventh Street, 907–586–9001) was the last home of Judge James H. Wickersham, one of the state's most active early citizens—a judge, legislator, proponent of statehood, outdoorsman, and amateur ethnologist. The house now serves as a museum featuring original furnishings, books, artifacts, photographs, and correspondence.

When Captain George Vancouver explored the Alaskan coast in 1794, **Icy Strait** was choked with ice and **Glacier Bay** was completely obscured. The glacier had retreated forty-eight miles by the time naturalist John Muir visited the area in 1879 and another twenty-three miles by 1916, the fastest known glacial retreat. No longer shrouded in ice, the bay is now a national park and preserve. To the east is **Lynn Canal,** named by Vancouver for his home in England.

HAINES

Dramatically framed by the snowy peaks of the Chilkat Range, Haines is one of the few Panhandle towns accessible by road as well as by boat and plane. The Russians never succeeded in establishing a permanent post here, owing to the presence of five large and sometimes hostile Tlingit villages in the immediate vicinity. Present-day Haines had its beginnings as a Presbyterian mission established in 1881, on a spot chosen by conservationist John Muir and missionary S. Hall Young, at the request of local Chilkat and Chilkoot chiefs. The town prospered during the gold rush as the jumping–off point for the Dalton Trail, an old Chilkat trade route to the Yukon that was improved and renamed by frontier entrepreneur John Dalton. The **Haines Visitor Center** (Second Avenue near Willard Street, 907–766–2234) provides information about the area. Among the diverse exhibits at the **Sheldon Museum and Cultural Center** (Main Street, just above the Small Boat Harbor, 907–766–2366) are a fine collection of native artifacts, totem poles (including a censorious "Ridicule Pole," meant to shame a debtor), a replica of a Tlingit tribal house, and photographs and documents relating to the gold rush and Fort William H. Seward.

South of the Haines Highway is the first army post in Alaska, **Fort William H. Seward,** which still looks much as it did when it was built in 1903. Deactivated in 1946, the fort is now a historic district, and several buildings have been put to use by local artisans. The **Alaska Indian Arts** workshop (Fort Seward Drive, 907–266–2160), located in a 1904 hospital building, offers demonstrations of traditional crafts such as totem pole, tribal mask, and silver carving. On the parade ground **Totem Village,** a replica of a Tlingit village, contains a community house, totem poles, and a Yukon trapper's cabin. At the **Chilkat Center for the Arts,** the Chilkat Dancers perform traditional Northwest Coast dances in full costume.

SKAGWAY AND DYEA

In 1897 and 1898, when thousands of would–be miners were seeking the quickest way into the Yukon in pursuit of gold, the most popular route led from these two towns over the mountains to lakes Lindeman and Bennett, the Yukon River headwaters. There the stampeders loaded their possessions onto boats for the 560–mile journey downriver to the gold fields. The thirty–three–mile Chilkoot Trail, which began at Dyea, was too steep for pack animals, and early travelers carried their belongings on their backs; a tramway was completed in May 1898. The White Pass Trail, which ran forty–one miles from Skagway to Bennett, was accessible to pack animals and over 3,000 of them died on the trail. In 1899 the White Pass and Yukon Route Railroad was completed along this route. The railroad promptly bought and dismantled the Chilkoot tramway, thus eliminating the competition and ensuring the ascendancy of Skagway and the White Pass route, and Dyea quickly dwindled to a ghost town. Both trails are now units of **Klondike Gold Rush National Historical Park** (907–983–2921). When weather permits, the Chilkoot Trail is open to experienced backpackers; remnants and artifacts of the gold rush can be seen along the way. In 1900 the railroad line was extended to Whitehorse in the Yukon, 110 miles from Skagway. The railroad still operates excursions from Skagway to Frazier, British Columbia, on narrow–gauge trains (Second Avenue and Spring Street, 800–343–7373).

Skagway's rich gold–rush heritage is reflected in its many restored and reconstructed saloons, shops, and hotels. Much of the downtown area is preserved as part of Klondike Gold Rush National Historical Park, including a **visitor center** (Second Avenue and Broadway), located in the former White Pass and Yukon Railroad Depot, restored to its 1900 appearance; **Captain Moore's Cabin** (Fifth Avenue), built in 1887 by the town's original settler; and the 1898 **Mascot Saloon** (Third Avenue and Broadway). Skagway contains a number of historic sites in addition to those maintained by the park. The **Arctic Brotherhood Hall** (Broadway between Second and Third avenues) was built in 1899 with pedimented windows and doors and a facade made of more than 20,000 small sticks of driftwood. The **Trail of '98 Museum** (Seventh Avenue and Spring Street, 907–983–2420) preserves some of the ceremonial parkas and other paraphernalia of the Arctic Brotherhood, together with an assortment of local history and native culture exhibits.

One of Skagway's most notorious local characters was con man Jefferson R. "Soapy" Smith, who reputedly drilled his band of outlaws militia–style on Holly Street—and offered their services to President McKinley at the outbreak of the Spanish–American War.

The false front of Skagway's Arctic Brotherhood Hall is a mosaic of over 20,000 bits of driftwood picked up from local beaches.

Smith was killed in a frontier–style shootout with city surveyor Frank Reid, who was himself mortally wounded in the exchange. Both men are buried, along with other early residents, in **Gold Rush Cemetery** (State Street).

SOUTH-CENTRAL ALASKA

The south–central area of Alaska constitutes a relatively small portion of the state, from Cordova on Prince William Sound northwest to the Anchorage vicinity, then southwest from Anchorage out the Kenai Peninsula to Kodiak Island. The Athapaskan and Aleut were the main inhabitants before Grigori Shelikof established the first European outpost at Three Saints Bay on Kodiak Island in 1784.

ANCHORAGE

Anchorage, at the head of Cook Inlet, is now Alaska's largest city, holding fully one-half of the state's population. Founded in 1915, the town owes its name to its port, which provided good anchorage for ships carrying supplies to build the federally financed Alaska Railway. The oldest building is the **Oscar Anderson House** (420 M Street, 907–274–2336), a simple frame structure that was among the first private dwellings built in the new railroad town in 1915. The **Log Cabin Visitor Information Center** (547 West Fourth Avenue, 907–274–3531) provides information about the town's historic areas. Next door is the **Old City Hall** (524 West Fourth Avenue), now a bank. When the municipal government moved to larger quarters, the bank restored the building to its 1936 appearance, uncovering cornices, banisters, and an old skylight. All additions were made in keeping with the building's depression–era design, and the bank has set aside space for local–history exhibits. **Anchorage Historic Properties** (907–274–3600), also located in the building, provides visitor information and has installed kiosks with historical information at various sites in the downtown area. Specimens of Alaska wildlife can be seen at the **Alaska Wilderness Museum** (844 West Fifth Avenue, 907–274–1600).

The Anchorage Museum of History and Art

The expanded Anchorage Museum devotes an entire floor to Alaska's history and native peoples. The Alaska Gallery features complete house scenes—both interior and exterior—for all native peoples and for the successive waves of white settlers. The fine–arts collection focuses on Far Northern painting and painters, with

Skyscrapers and snowy peaks, Anchorage.

important works by Sydney Laurence, Thomas Hill, Eustace P. Ziegler, Albert Bierstadt, and others, as well as solo shows of works by contemporary Alaskan artists.

LOCATION: 121 West Seventh Avenue. HOURS: June through August: 10–6 Monday–Saturday, 1–5 Sunday; September through May: 10–6 Tuesday–Saturday, 1–5 Monday. FEE: Yes. TELEPHONE: 907–343–4326.

On the south shore of Lake Hood, near Anchorage International Airport, is the **Alaska Aviation Heritage Museum** (4721 Aircraft Drive, 907–248–5325), commemorating the bush pilots who flew settlers and supplies into the vast Alaska interior wilderness and the World War II pilots who patrolled and fought on the Aleutian Islands. The museum has collected more than twenty vintage aircraft dating from 1929 to 1944, which are being restored to flying condition, and maintains an exhibit gallery with models, photographs, and memorabilia.

Five miles south of Anchorage in Chugach State Park, the **Potter Section House Railroad Museum** (Seward Highway, Mile 115, 907–345–2631) traces the history of the Alaska Railroad with exhibits of photos and artifacts. The section house, built in 1929, served as living quarters for the track workers and the section foreman, and the workers' quarters have been restored with period items. Outside are a World War II troop train and a rotary snowplow.

NORTH OF ANCHORAGE

The road to Denali and on into the Interior follows the edge of Knik Arm of Cook Inlet, then proceeds through the lovely Susitna River basin. A number of the small towns along it contain sites or museums of note. **Palmer,** a town founded during the Great Depression by a federal project to resettle Dust Bowl farmers, is something of an agricultural success in a state not known for growing much of anything. The University of Alaska's agricultural experiment station is now located here, and it produces such crops as sixty-pound cabbages. The four–acre complex at the **Museum of Alaska Transportation & Industry** (Glenn Highway, Mile 40.2, at the fairgrounds, 907–745–4493) contains a miscellany of buildings and exhibits documenting the development of roadways, aviation, railroading, fishing, farming, and mining in Alaska.

OVERLEAF: *Mount McKinley, known to Alaskans by its Athapaskan name, Denali, is the highest mountain in North America.*

Independence Mine State Historic Park preserves the remnants of a gold-mining camp in the Talkeetna Mountains. At its peak, in the 1940s, the hard-rock mine employed 200 workers and produced over $1.6 million worth of gold.

Wasilla and **Knik** stand at either end of Knik Arm of the Cook Inlet, on the west side. Wasilla, founded in 1917 as a stop on the Alaska Railroad, attained instant importance as a supply point for the gold–mining districts farther up the Susitna River and its tributaries. The **Wasilla Museum** (323 Main Street, 907–376–2005) features Indian baskets, pioneer buggies, and old irons. Behind the museum building is a frontier village with five log buildings, including a smithy and a sauna; the ca. 1934 Herning–Teeland–Mead House; and the town's first school. Down the road toward Knik is the **Knik Museum** (Knik–Goosebay Road, 907–376–7755), home of the Dog Mushers' Hall of Fame, a collection of portraits, memorabilia, and displays dedicated to great dogsled racers.

Just north of Willow, one of the surviving hard–rock mines is now open as **Independence Mine State Historic Park** (Fishhook –Willow Road, off Glenn Highway, 907–745–3975). Renovated buildings include mess halls, bunkhouses, and the mine manager's house, which displays photos, artifacts, and interpretive materials on hard–rock mining. Beyond the mine and on what is now a side road is the town of **Talkeetna**, founded, like Wasilla, as a railroad camp. The town stands at the confluence of three rivers, and its name means "river of plenty" in the language of the Tanaina Indians. The **Talkeetna Historical Society Museum** (one block south of Main Street, 907–733–2487), in an old schoolhouse, has displays on the history of mountain climbing and exhibits the work of local artists.

Talkeetna is a jumping–off point for **Denali National Park and Preserve** (Parks Highway, 907–683–2294). Denali, a Tanaina word meaning "the high one," is the local name for Mount McKinley, at 20,320 feet the tallest mountain in North America. Its summit was first reached by white mountaineers in 1913, but Alaskans like to recall the Sourdough Expedition of 1910, a group of four miners who had never attempted such an ascent. Upon reaching what they had thought to be Denali's summit, they realized that they had only climbed the shorter of the mountain's two peaks.

PRINCE WILLIAM SOUND

Southeast of Anchorage, between the Kenai Peninsula and the mainland, lies Prince William Sound, named by Captain James Cook during his passage in 1778. **Valdez** began as the starting point of a rumored Indian trail to the Yukon. During the spring and summer of 1898 some 4,000 prospectors crossed the Valdez Glacier into the Alaska Interior, but many turned back, unable to withstand the winter chill. They reached the coast but most could not return to the lower forty–eight and were forced to spend the winter camped on the beach, cared for by a small contingent of soldiers left to guard a nearby army post. The town subsisted on small gold rushes, together with more dependable industries like fishing and lumbering, until it became important as the terminus of the Richardson Highway and, today, of the Trans–Alaska Oil Pipeline. Valdez was heavily damaged by an earthquake and tidal wave in 1964 and was totally rebuilt in a different location. Another catastrophe occurred in 1989 when a massive oil spill fouled portions of Prince William Sound, but many of the area's natural attractions, including the nearby Columbia and Shoop glaciers, remain unaffected. Artifacts of the town's history—including photos of the 1964 disaster and a working model of the pipeline terminal—can be seen at the **Valdez Museum** (103 Chenega Avenue, 907–835–2764).

Cordova grew rapidly in the early years of this century as the embarkation point for the copper of the great Kennecott mines, located 195 miles inland. In 1911 Michael J. Heney, the same man who had engineered the White Pass and Yukon Railway, performed another engineering miracle in driving the Copper River and Northwestern Railway to the mines. The **Cordova Museum** (622 First Street, 907–424–6665) contains artifacts of the railroad and copper–mining days, as well as Chugach and Eyak artifacts and a large photo display.

KENAI PENINSULA

The Seward Highway runs south from Anchorage and over a narrow land bridge to the Kenai Peninsula, a wedge of land almost as large as Massachusetts that separates Cook Inlet from the Gulf of Alaska. The climate on the inlet side is mild and, for Alaska, well suited to agriculture. In 1793 Aleksandr Baranov established a Russian shipbuilding operation at the head of Resurrection Bay, near the present-day town of Seward, and Russian settlers built some of the finer Russian Orthodox churches in Alaska in towns along the inlet.

The largest as well as the oldest town on the peninsula, **Kenai** is named for the local Athapaskan tribe. Founded by Russians in 1791, Kenai is today the site of the **Holy Assumption of the Virgin Mary Russian Orthodox Church** (Mission Street and Overland), one of the oldest surviving Russian Orthodox church buildings in Alaska. It was built in 1895, about twenty–five years after the Americans had confirmed their commitment to the area by building **Fort Kenay** (1104 Mission Street, 907–283–4156). A 1967 replica of the log fort is now maintained as a museum and community center with artifacts ranging from mining tools to icons and Indian relics.

South of town on the Sterling Highway is the fishing hamlet of **Ninilchik,** founded by the Russians in the 1830s and not much changed in this century. Several late–nineteenth–century log houses remain, presided over by the 1901 **Holy Transfiguration of Our Lord Russian Orthodox Church** (Coal Street), which overlooks the town.

A former coal-mining town and gold-rush camp, **Homer** is now a recreational center with a lively and varied community of artists. The **Pratt Museum** (3779 Bartlett Street, 907–235–8635) has displays about natural history, Russian settlers, pioneer life in the early 1900s, and Dena'ina and Eskimo artifacts. Accessible only by boat across Kachemak Bay, **Seldovia** is a fishing town—its name is derived from the Russian word for "herring"—whose isolation evokes the remoteness once prevalent in all of Alaska. **Saint Nicholas** (Church Street), another fine old Russian Orthodox church, was built in 1891.

KODIAK ISLAND

Kodiak Island had been inhabited for nearly 6,000 years when Russian settlement first touched Alaska in 1784. Grigori Shelikof and

OPPOSITE: *Saint Nicholas Russian Orthodox Church, Seldovia.*

his men established a post on the southeast tip of the islands at Three Saints Bay, murdered a large number of the Koniag Indians, and took others hostage. Aleksandr Baranov, Shelikof's successor, moved the whole settlement in 1791 to the present-day location of Kodiak, on the northeastern edge of the island, making it more convenient for trade, better protected from Pacific storms, and nearer to important resources like timber. Until Baranov moved to Sitka in 1804, Kodiak was the capital of Russian Alaska. Today the city of **Kodiak** is known for the **Holy Resurrection Russian Orthodox Church** (385 Kashevarof Circle) and the **Baranov Museum** (101 Marine Way, 907–486–5920). Housed in the Erskine House, a Russian American Company fur warehouse constructed around 1808, the museum's collection focuses on the culture of the Koniag and the Aleut as well as Russian and later settlers.

INTERIOR ALASKA

Alaska's Interior starts just above the Alaska Range and runs north to the Brooks Range. The Russians hardly penetrated this region, being more interested in hunting sea otters along the coast. English and American trappers sought furs in the area early in the nineteenth century, but it wasn't until 1865 that the Western Union Telegraph Expedition actually explored the region, surveying the Yukon River and much of the surrounding country to lay a telegraph cable—a project that never came to fruition.

FAIRBANKS

Fairbanks was founded, almost by accident, in 1901. E. T. Barnette and his family were transporting $20,000 worth of trade goods in the hopes of creating "the Chicago of the North" at a strategic point on the Tanana River, but their boat could not navigate the rough, shallow water and they stopped at a point on the Chena. As luck would have it, two prospectors, Felix Pedro and Tom Gilmore, were nearby and in the market for supplies. Barnette was still planning to head upriver when Pedro struck it rich a year later. The ensuing gold rush ensured Barnette a healthy market for his goods right where he was, and Fairbanks—named for Senator Charles Fairbanks—was born.

Through most of the first half of this century, gold was the mainstay of Fairbanks, but since then the city has grown as a hub for

OPPOSITE: *The Alatna River and the Endicott Mountains, part of the Brooks Range.*

commerce, transportation, the military, and education. Its location near the geographical center of Alaska makes it convenient for many destinations: The Alaska Railroad and the Richardson Highway have their northern termini here; the Dalton and Steese highways also end here; and the Trans–Alaska Oil Pipeline passes nearby.

The town has log cabins set next to skyscrapers; among the former is the **George Thomas Library** (Cowles Street and First Avenue), Fairbanks's original public library, built in 1909; among the latter is the **Northward Building,** formerly the Alaska National Bank Building, covering the block between Third and Fourth avenues and Lacey and Noble streets. Not only was this Fairbanks's first skyscraper; it also served as the model for the Ice Palace in Edna Ferber's muckraking novel of that name. The **visitor center** (550 First Avenue, 907–456–5774) provides information on these and other historic buildings, including the 1905 **Falcon Joslin House** (413 Cowles Street); the **IOOF Hall** (First Avenue and Cowles Street), built in 1907 as a miners' bathhouse; and the wood frame **Immaculate Conception Church** (115 North Cushman Street), built in 1904 and moved over the frozen river in 1911.

University of Alaska Museum

The University of Alaska Museum's fine archaeological, paleontological, geographical, and ethnological collections are due in large part to a dedicated amateur named Otto Geist, who made countless collecting trips on the museum's behalf between 1926 and his death in 1963. The museum is organized by region, with all aspects of a region's culture dealt with in a single integrated gallery. Among the remarkable collections are the fortified blockhouse from an 1841 Russian trading settlement; the preserved remains of a 36,000–year–old arctic bison; collections of Athapaskan basketry, Eskimo carving, and Tlingit and Haida potlatch items; and a home-made car constructed in Skagway in 1905, when there was nowhere to drive it. A choice group of paintings with Alaskan themes is also on view.

LOCATION: 907 Yukon Drive on the West Ridge of the University of Alaska campus. HOURS: May and September: 9–5 Daily; June through August: 9–9 Daily; October through April: 12–5 Daily. FEE: Yes. TELEPHONE: 907–474–7505.

Alaskaland Pioneer Park

This forty–four–acre theme park, created in 1967 for the centennial of the purchase of Alaska from Russia, re–creates pioneer life at the turn of the century. The park's attractions include the partially restored, partially reconstructed 1904 Judge James Wickersham House, furnished with period items; the wooden sternwheeler *Nenana*; a gold–rush town with original log cabins moved in from the Fairbanks area; a museum detailing the history of the gold rush; original mining equipment, including a working sluice box; a replica Athapaskan village; a museum of Indian and Eskimo artifacts from around the state; and a narrow–gauge railroad.

> LOCATION: Airport Way and Peger Road. HOURS: *Park:* Always open; *Museums:* June through August: 11–9 Daily. FEE: None. TELEPHONE: 907–452–4244.

North of Fairbanks is the **Dog Musher's Museum,** (Mile 4, Farmers Loop Road, 907–457–6874) tracing the history of dogsledding with interpretive displays and early sleds and equipment.

STEESE HIGHWAY

The Steese Highway, named for the army general who engineered it from Fairbanks to the town of Circle during the 1920s, covers 162 miles and largely follows the trails laid down by turn-of-the-century prospectors. All along the route are spectacular views of the Alaska Range, Mount McKinley, and the Tanana Valley. Just nine miles from the start of the highway lies the restored **Goldstream Dredge Number 8** (Steese Highway, in Fox, 907–457–6058), one of the huge dredges that washed and crushed the gravel from gold-bearing creeks. Guided tours explain how the five-story ship-borne machine worked. Before the road climbs Cleary Peak, at about Mile 16, the **Felix Pedro Monument** marks the creek where prospector Pedro struck gold in 1902, touching off the rush that built Fairbanks. At Mile 127, where the road branches off to Circle Hot Springs, is the still–active mining town of **Central.** The **Circle District Historical Society Museum** (907–520–1893) contains exhibits on small– and large–scale mining as well as on trapping. The terminus of the highway is at **Circle,** so named because the prospectors who founded it thought they were on the Arctic Circle, which is actually fifty miles to the north.

A Serious Case of Gold Fever, *one of thousands of E.A. Hegg's photographs recording the Alaska gold rush. Many such photographs were sent home by the Ninety-eighters.*

EAGLE CITY

Situated on the Yukon River near the Canadian border, Eagle has a population of 200 and an unusually rich history. Founded in 1898 by twenty–eight miners who crossed the border to avoid Canada's restrictive mining laws, the town soon became a trading center for the Interior. In 1899 Fort Egbert was established, and the following year Judge James Wickersham set up the first federal court in the area. Eagle City was incorporated in 1901—the first in Alaska's Interior to do so—and its future looked bright, but by 1904 the miners had shifted westward and the court moved to Fairbanks. The town had another brush with fame in 1905 when Captain Roald Amundsen arrived here, after trekking 900 miles over tundra, to telegraph to the world that he had completed the first crossing of the Northwest Passage.

The **Eagle Historical Society** offers a walking tour of the town and maintains several museums. The restored **Customs Building**

(Front Street) appears as it did when the customs officer lived there in the early 1900s. The courtroom upstairs in the **Wickersham Courthouse** (First Avenue) is restored to its original appearance, and the downstairs rooms feature exhibits on Amundsen, the local Indians, the telegraph, and the pioneers. The remnants of **Fort Egbert** are located on the campground road at the end of the old airstrip. Four of the remaining buildings are open to the public and house exhibits on the history of the fort and the town.

THE WEST AND FAR NORTH

The western and northern coasts of Alaska belong to the Eskimo. The climate is among the coldest on earth: A hot August day in Barrow might reach forty–five degrees Fahrenheit, while in winter the average temperature is around fifteen below zero. Much of the north is covered by tundra, with frozen soil, or permafrost, reaching depths of 1,000 feet or more.

THE ALEUTIAN ISLANDS

Treeless and windswept (but green in summer), dotted with volcanoes, the Aleutian Islands stretch over 1,000 miles from Unimak Island, at the tip of the Alaska Peninsula, to Attu, their westernmost extreme. Vitus Bering estimated the Aleut population to be over 20,000 when he landed on the islands in 1741; he died on the return voyage, but the pelts brought back by his crew quickly brought fur traders to the area. The Russians massacred and enslaved the Aleut, exploiting their superior hunting and trapping skills, and their numbers had dwindled to fewer than 3,000 by the time the United States assumed possession of Alaska in 1867.

The islands' strategic importance became clear during World War II, when Japanese forces bombed Dutch Harbor and occupied the islands of Attu and Kiska. Attu was recaptured by U.S. forces in 1943, after three weeks of fighting, and Kiska was abandoned by the Japanese. Several of the islands are now military bases.

The twin cities of Unalaska and Dutch Harbor form the islands' largest community. **Unalaska,** an ancient Aleut village, was the center of activity during the Russian occupation. The Russian Orthodox **Church of the Holy Ascension,** portions of which date back to 1826, overlooks Iliuliuk Bay; the adjacent **Bishop's House,** now partially destroyed by fire, was built in 1824.

NOME

Nome is located on the south shore of the Seward Peninsula, which at Cape Prince of Wales is only fifty–five miles from Siberia. Although it is 150 miles south of the Arctic Circle, Nome's position between the Bering Sea and the frozen tundra of the peninsula makes it seem thoroughly arctic. If not for gold, Nome would be little more than a village, but a series of rushes beginning in 1898 brought thousands north to the creeks and beaches in this region. At one time, the town may have had over 20,000 inhabitants, but today there are only a sixth that number. Information about Nome's remaining historic buildings is available from the **visitor center** (Front Street, 907–443–5535). The **Carrie McLain Memorial Museum** (Front Street, 907–443–2566) tells of Nome's wild gold days and displays Eskimo artifacts and exhibits about the Bering Strait.

Seward Peninsula juts out to form the Bering Strait between the United States and the Soviet Union. It is here, by way of a land

Fierce-looking teeth distinguish a wooden mask made by the Eskimo of Point Barrow.

bridge, that the ancestors of all native American peoples probably entered the Americas, between 50,000 and 10,000 years ago. Part of the area has been set aside as the **Bering Land Bridge National Preserve** (907–443–2522).

KOTZEBUE

There are thirty–six days in Kotzebue when the sun never sets. Named for Otto von Kotzebue, the first white explorer to sight the region, in 1816, Kotzebue has a largely Inupiat Eskimo population. As the headquarters of NANA (North American Native Association), one of the Eskimo native corporations that administer the Eskimo share of the millions of acres of land and the $1 billion granted to them in the Alaska Native Claims Settlement Act of 1971, Kotzebue is a showcase for Eskimo culture. The **NANA Museum of the Arctic** (corner of Second and Third streets, 907–442–3304) provides a good introduction to Eskimo culture, with excellent dioramas and live demonstrations.

BARROW

Perched on the northernmost point of North America, Barrow is 330 miles north of the Arctic Circle. The sun stays visible here for eighty–two days every summer and disappears for sixty–seven days in winter. Though the city was named for an English explorer, its citizens are mainly Eskimo. North Slope oil revenues have also been flowing into this town, resulting in an almost surreal combination of brand–new, state–of–the–art buildings and traditional Eskimo dwellings. The **National Arctic Research Laboratory** (three miles north of Barrow, on the Chukchi Sea, 907–852–7800), the largest year–round center for arctic research, has a small museum of natural history, with artifacts, photographs, and oddments picked up during its years of research. Among these is part of the wing of the plane in which the humorist Will Rogers and pioneer aviator Wiley Post crashed near Barrow on August 15, 1935. Post had been the first person to fly around the world solo. He and Rogers, an enthusiastic promoter of aviation, were headed for Asia on a good will tour when they crashed after taking off from Barrow. Their deaths stunned the nation: Charles Lindbergh oversaw the return of the bodies; and the funerals were elaborate. The CBS and NBC radio networks went off the air for thirty minutes in tribute.

CHAPTER EIGHT

HAWAII

From Polynesian settlement to American state, Hawaii has had many lives. This hauntingly beautiful archipelago was born some thirty million years ago when magma escaping through vents in the floor of the Pacific Ocean began creating a submerged range of mountains. Slowly the mountains have risen, their tips forming more than a hundred points of land that now stretch nearly 2,000 miles across the sea. The more prominent islands of Oahu, Kauai, Molokai, Maui, Lanai, and Hawaii were first discovered by Polynesian natives of the Marquesas Islands between A.D. 500 and 800. Five centuries later, groups of Tahitians migrated north and made the island of Hawaii, traditionally said to have been named after an ancient homeland, their headquarters. Master seafarers, the Polynesians had navigated their canoes some 2,000 miles using the sun, clouds, currents, waves, and stars—a feat that would not be repeated by Western explorers with nautical instruments until centuries later.

Hawaiian civilization was organized hierarchically, with chiefs, priests, and the upper castes maintaining their power through a complex system of laws known as *kapu* (a variation of the Tahitian word *tapu,* or taboo). Wars of succession and conquest were common. The Hawaiians worshiped numerous gods at outdoor temples, or *heiaus,* where human and animal sacrifices were performed. They were expert fishermen and engineers, constructing large ponds in which they fattened fish for consumption. They tested their courage by diving off high cliffs into the ocean and enjoyed surfing (on boards made of native woods) in the islands' hazardous waters and sledding down steep hills on ti leaves and coconut fronds.

This isolated but highly developed society greeted British captain James Cook at Waimea, Kauai, on January 19, 1778. His landing marked the beginning of Hawaii's westernization, as explorers and traders followed in his wake. Internecine struggles among the islands' chiefs led, by the early nineteenth century, to the unification of Hawaii under Kamehameha I, the first king in a dynasty that would rule the islands for nearly a century.

During the early nineteenth century, the ports of Honolulu on Oahu, Kailua on Hawaii, and Lahaina on Maui flourished as Hawaii's whaling and sandalwood industries attracted international traders. Also drawn to the islands were American missionaries, whose job was made somewhat easier by the abolition of the *kapu* system in 1819. The Hawaiians embraced Christianity; churches were established on all the islands; and the missionaries, by virtue of their close ties with

Hawaiians paddling a double-hulled canoe equipped with a sail. This engraving was based on sketches made by John Webber, an artist who accompanied Captain Cook on his last voyage to Hawaii in the late 1770s.

the Hawaiian royalty, began to play an increasingly important political role. Native Hawaiians referred to the newcomers as *haoles* ("whites"), and later the term "mainlander" came into use.

The mainlanders rapidly established their economic system on the islands. Plantations and ranches owned by missionary families and their descendants sprang up on Hawaii, Maui, and Kauai, with workers imported from Japan and China. Hoping to profit from mainland markets, Hawaiian planters lobbied for a reciprocity treaty with the United States. After two unsuccessful attempts, a treaty was approved by the U.S. Senate in March 1875. In the next five years, the number of sugar plantations more than tripled.

The last quarter of the nineteenth century saw the tremendous increase in political and financial influence of mainlanders in Hawaii. The Big Five sugar agents, Castle & Cooke, Alexander & Baldwin, American Factors, Theo H. Davies & Company, and C. Brewer & Co.—all headquartered in Honolulu and run by families descended from missionaries—dominated the kingdom's economy. In 1893 the last monarch, Queen Liliuokalani, was overthrown and replaced by Sanford Dole, the son of American missionaries, who became president of the islands' short-lived republic and governor after Hawaii was annexed by President McKinley on July 7, 1898. America's frontier on the Pacific Rim, Hawaii joined the union in 1959.

This chapter begins on the island of Oahu, then covers the islands of Kauai, Niihau, Molokai, Lanai, Maui, and Hawaii.

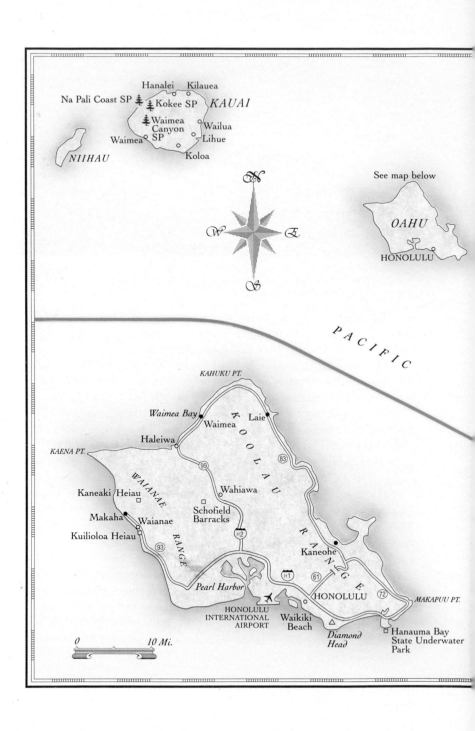

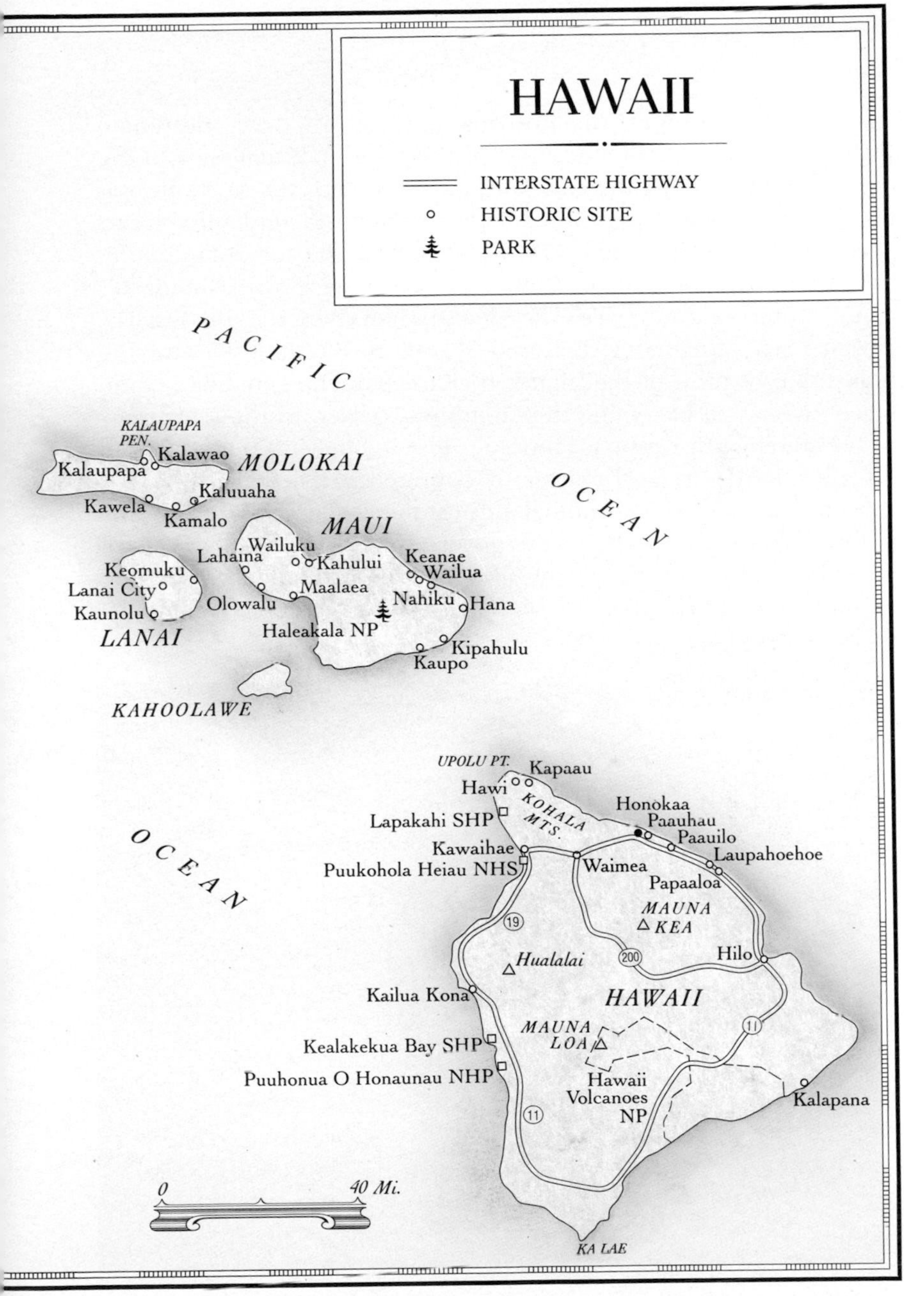

HAWAII

 INTERSTATE HIGHWAY
○ HISTORIC SITE
♣ PARK

PACIFIC

OCEAN

KALAUPAPA PEN.
Kalaupapa ○ ○ Kalawao *MOLOKAI*
Kawela ○ ○ Kaluuaha
Kamalo

MAUI
Lahaina .Wailuku ○○ Kahului Keanae
Keomuku Maalaea ○ ○ Wailua
Lanai City ○ Olowalu ♣ Nahiku ○ Hana
Kaunolu ○ Haleakala NP
LANAI Kipahulu
Kaupo

KAHOOLAWE

UPOLU PT. Kapaau
Hawi ○ ○
Lapakahi SHP □ *KOHALA MTS.* Honokaa
Paauhau
Kawaihae ○ Paauilo
Puukohola Heiau NHS Waimea Laupahoehoe
OCEAN Papaaloa
MAUNA △ KEA
⑲
△ *Hualalai* ⑳⁰ Hilo ○

Kailua Kona ○ *HAWAII*

Kealakekua Bay SHP □ *MAUNA LOA* △
Puuhonua O Honaunau NHP □ Hawaii
Volcanoes Kalapana
⑪ NP ⑪

0   40 Mi.

KA LAE

O A H U

Two mountain ranges, the Koolaus and the Waianaes, dominate Oahu's landscape, hemming most of the state's population into the cities and towns along the coast and in the verdant valleys. Oahu was not always the most populous of the islands. Ancient inhabitants lived on the west side and on the Plain of Kou, the site of Honolulu; but at the time of Captain Cook's arrival in 1778, the kingdom's major centers of power were Hawaii and Maui. With the discovery by Western sea captains of sheltered Honolulu Bay in 1793 and the unification of most of the islands by Kamehameha I in 1796, Oahu was on its way to becoming the kingdom's center. In the early years of the nineteenth century, Honolulu grew, achieving renown as an international port and center of commerce. Though the kings returned to their ancient homelands on the other islands from time to time, Honolulu was the seat of government. In the second half of the nineteenth century, as the influence of mainlanders grew and the monarchy unraveled, Honolulu increasingly became a center of political intrigue.

A group of women selling leis, *garlands of flowers that are the traditional Hawaiian symbol of welcome. The photograph was taken in 1903.*

In addition to missionaries, entrepreneurs, and traders, Oahu also attracted tourists, among them Mark Twain, Robert Louis Stevenson, Jack London, and other literary lights. Once fine surfing grounds for Hawaiian royalty, Waikiki Beach is now overrun with hotels and people, but other stretches of coast on the island remain relatively undeveloped.

This tour starts in Honolulu and its environs, winds east along the coast, then north up to Kaneohe and Kahuku Point, down to Waimea and Haleiwa and through central Oahu down to Pearl Harbor. The section ends with Oahu's west coast.

HONOLULU AND ENVIRONS

Honolulu, Hawaiian for "sheltered bay," became known to the world in the late eighteenth century as a port for Pacific explorers and traders. Among the first Europeans to take advantage of the protected harbor, in 1794, was William Brown, a British fur trader and captain of the *Jackal*, who described it as "small but commodious . . . a few vessels may ride with the greatest safety." However, Brown and others would discover that while the harbor provided protection from the elements, it was far from a peaceful haven. Hawaii's chieftains, with cannons and other weapons acquired from foreigners, were waging war for domination of the islands. In January 1795, Brown and another British captain were killed in a battle for control of Oahu by Chief Kalanikupule. Later that year Kamehameha I conquered Kalanikupule and Oahu. Under Kamehameha I's guidance, Honolulu became Hawaii's premier port and a major Pacific trading center. By the first decade of the nineteenth century, the pilotage and wharfage fees from hundreds of visiting vessels were filling the royal coffers, as were profits from the lucrative sandalwood trade. Hawaiians from the islands' more rural regions began to migrate to Honolulu, among them Kamehameha, who made the city his kingdom's capital from 1804 to 1812. In 1820 Honolulu was a town of grass houses, wood and stone buildings, some 3,000 to 4,000 residents, and increasing numbers of missionaries. A group of Congregationalists from Boston, led by the Reverend Hiram Bingham, landed on the island of Hawaii in the spring of 1820. Bingham built Honolulu's first Christian church in 1821 on the site now occupied by the Kawaiahao Church.

Honolulu prospered in the middle decades of the nineteenth century with the growth of sugar, whaling, and tourism. By 1840 the population had doubled, streets had been laid out, and the town had spread from the waterfront toward the inland swampland and seaside beaches of Waikiki. Commerce was increasingly dominated by *haoles*. The American missionaries, now firmly ensconced, were not only spreading the gospel but also buying and speculating on land and starting to make their fortunes by planting sugarcane. Hawaii's new elite opened offices in Honolulu and built their homes in the heights and valleys of the city. During the 1840s and 1850s, Honolulu and Lahaina became the principal bases for the Pacific whaling industry, welcoming hundreds of whaling ships annually. Although booming Lahaina became the capital for a time, Honolulu reasserted its claim in 1845, when Kamehameha III moved his residence, as well as the legislature, to Oahu's sheltered port. On August 30, 1850, the city was officially declared the capital of Hawaii.

Steamship service was instituted among the islands' ports and between Honolulu and San Francisco in the 1860s–a boon to trade and the nascent tourist industry. Honolulu's natural beauty delighted early travelers, including Samuel Clemens, who spent four months in the islands in 1866, reporting for the Sacramento *Union* under his pen name, Mark Twain. "I moved in the midst of a summer calm as tranquil as dawn in the Garden of Eden," he wrote in one of his letters from Hawaii, after extolling the city's "luxurious banks and thickets of flowers," "wide-spreading forest trees," and "dusky native women."

From the 1870s until the end of the nineteenth century, Honolulu increasingly reflected the division between the native Hawaiians and the powerful American missionary faction. It was, superficially, a grand time for the monarchy. In 1882 King Kalakaua, dubbed "the merry monarch," built Iolani Palace, where he lived and entertained lavishly. He traveled the world while Honolulu's *haoles* and Hawaiians loyal to the monarchy were jockeying for power. In 1887 an armed insurrection led by the Hawaiian League, a secret society of prominent *haole* businessmen, forced the creation of a new constitution, which made the king a puppet and put power in their hands. In 1894, after months of agitation by Honolulu's pro-annexation leaders, Hawaii was declared a republic. On August 12, 1898, Hawaii was annexed to the United States and an American flag was raised over Iolani Palace.

Though steel-and-glass monoliths line the harbor that the British trader William Brown dubbed Fair Haven, the city still offers a landscape of great beauty. To the north and east are the valleys and

*In February 1889 King Kalakaua honored the writer Robert Louis Stevenson with a
luau, an informal dinner. The king is seated at the head of the table, with Princess
Liliuokalani and Stevenson at his right.*

ridges of the Koolau Range; to the west, the Waianae Mountains; and
to the south the ocean, its deep, dark blue giving way, near shore, to
a brilliant transparent turquoise. A prominent waterfront landmark
is the ten-story **Aloha Tower** located at Pier 9. Built in 1925, it was for
decades the city's tallest structure. At Pier 7 the **Hawaii Maritime
Center** (808-536-6373) has exhibits about the achievements of
prehistoric Polynesian navigators and boatbuilders, the discovery of
the islands by Captain Cook, surfing, fishing, shipwrecks, and
maritime medicine. The center maintains two vessels, moored
nearby. One is the *Hokuleia,* a reconstruction of the type of boat used
by the Polynesians to reach Hawaii from Tahiti. The other is the
restored *Falls of Clyde,* a four-masted full-rigged sailing ship built in
Scotland more than a century ago and bought in 1898 by William
Matson, whose Navigation Company used it on the route from San
Francisco to Honolulu.

Just up from the harbor on Bishop Street is the city's financial
district and home of the so-called Big Five companies founded by
prominent missionary families in the 1860s and 1870s as financial
and marketing agents for the kingdom's sugar plantations. The
Alexander & Baldwin Building (822 Bishop Street), built in 1929,

features a Hawaiian-style roof with a high peak and low eaves as well as tile murals, terra-cotta ornamentation, and an inlaid floor of black Belgian marble. Also notable is the **C. Brewer Building** (827 Fort Street), a Mediterranean-style structure with a high double-pitched Hawaiian roof and grillwork in the form of sugarcane.

Iolani Palace

The palace, whose name combines *Io*, the high-flying Hawaiian hawk, with *lani*, which means "heaven and royalty," was the official residence of Hawaii's last king, Kalakaua, and his sister and successor, Liliuokalani. From its completion in 1882 until 1893, the year the monarchy was overthrown and replaced with a provisional government, the palace was the center of the kingdom's political and social life and reflected Kalakaua's infatuation with the royal courts of Europe. In 1895, after an uprising by native Hawaiian monarchists, Queen Liliuokalani was arrested, brought to trial in the palace's Throne Room, and imprisoned in an upstairs bedroom.

With the ascendance of the Americans to power, the palace was converted into legislative halls and executive offices, which remained until the state capitol was built in 1968. Recently restored,

The Hawaiian royal coat of arms appears on the four gates of the Iolani Palace. The motto means "The life of the land is preserved in righteousness."

it is a splendid example of the government residences built in the tropics during the late Victorian period. Glass-paneled portals, elegant woodwork fashioned with native Hawaiian woods of koa, kou, and kamani, and an extensive collection of Davenport furniture are among the palace's treasures. On the grounds are the coral block **Iolani Barracks,** built in 1871 to house the royal guard, the copper-roofed octagonal **Coronation Pavilion,** and the original 1906 territorial archives building, all of which have been restored.

LOCATION: King and Richards streets. HOURS: 9-2:15 Wednesday-Saturday. FEE: Yes. TELEPHONE: 808-522-0832.

Facing the palace on South King Street is the gilded **statue of Kamehameha I,** commissioned by the Hawaiian legislature in 1878 to commemorate the centennial of Captain Cook's arrival. It was unveiled in 1883 during the week of Kalakaua's coronation. The statue, which shows Kamehameha I holding a barbed *pololu* (spear), a symbol of peace, is actually a replica. The first, made in Italy by the American sculptor Thomas Gould, was lost when the ship carrying it sank off the Falkland Islands. The original was later salvaged and now stands in Kohala, Hawaii, Kamehameha's birthplace. Behind

The statue of Kamehameha I in front of the Aliiolani Hale. Often referred to as Kamehameha the Great, he unified the Hawaiian Islands under one ruler.

the statue is **Aliiolani Hale,** the state judiciary building. Designed as a palace for Kamehameha V, one of whose names was Aliiolani, "a chief of heavenly repute," it became, upon its completion in 1874, the house (*hale*) for Hawaii's parliament.

In sharp contrast to the palace is modern Hawaii's center of power, the **State Capitol** (415 South Beretania Street), whose cone-shaped legislative chambers look like volcanoes rising from the sea. Hawaii's governor lives nearby in **Washington Place,** visible from South Beretania Street. This elegant Greek Revival mansion was built in 1846 by a New York sea captain, John Dominis. After his death in 1847, his widow rented rooms to Anthony Ten Eyck, the U.S. commissioner to Hawaii, who established his U.S. legation in the house and named it after George Washington. Dominis's son married Kalakaua's sister, the ill-fated Queen Liliuokalani. When the monarchy was overthrown, the queen returned to the house, where she lived until her death in 1917. More royal history is marked by the early French Gothic-style architecture of **Saint Andrew's Cathedral** (Queen Emma Square), begun in 1867 but not completed until 1958. Made of English sandstone, this Hawaiian headquarters for the Anglican church was commissioned by Kamehameha IV and Queen Emma, who became members of the Church of England in 1862 after the death of their 4-year-old son.

At the top of the Fort Street Mall is the result of the work of some French Roman Catholic missionaries, the **Cathedral of Our Lady of Peace** (1184 Fort Street), dedicated in 1843. It was here, three years later, that Hawaiians were treated to the sounds of the islands' first pipe organ. Here too, in 1864, Father Damien, the Belgian priest who lived and worked among the lepers on Molokai, was ordained.

Kawaiahao Church

Honolulu's most famous testament to the power of the missionary influence, this church was dedicated in 1842, twenty-one years after the Reverend Hiram Bingham and his group of Boston Congregationalists built their first of five churches on this site. It was made from thousands of coral blocks from nearby reefs. Kawaiahao, which means "freshwater pool of Hao" (it was named after a sacred spring), welcomed among its worshipers many members of the royal families, whose weddings, coronations, and funerals were often held here. The church's role as a center for community debate was established as early as 1843, when Kamehameha III, following a brief British takeover, celebrated the restoration of sovereignty with the words that have since become Hawaii's motto: *Ua mau ke ea o ka aina i ka pono*—"The life of the land is preserved in righteousness." The **Tomb of King Lunalilo,** who died in 1874 after a reign of one year, is on the right side of the entrance to the church. Also on the grounds is the **Adobe Schoolhouse,** built in 1835, where several generations of Hawaiian children learned to read and write their own language.

LOCATION: 957 Punchbowl Street. HOURS: 9-3 Daily.

Mission Houses Museum

This complex includes three historic houses that served as the family homes and headquarters for the first Christian mission to Hawaii. Today the houses are restored and furnished with articles from the 1820s to the 1860s. The **Mission Frame House,** built of precut frame shipped from Boston, was erected in 1821 and served as the family home of Reverend Hiram Bingham, Dr. Gerrit Judd, and other prominent missionaries. It is the oldest remaining house in Hawaii. The **Printing Office,** built in 1841, still operates today with demonstrations of typesetting, bookbinding, and printing on a working replica of the mission's original wood-and-iron press. Schoolbooks, hymnals, religious tracts, and government laws were printed here in the Hawaiian language. The **Chamberlain House,** built by Hawaiian workers in 1831 of large coral blocks quarried from the reef flats, was a family home and storehouse. Guided tours, a living history program, and seasonal events are offered.

LOCATION: 553 South King Street. HOURS: 9-4 Daily. FEE: Yes. TELEPHONE: 808-531-0481.

Also on South King Street is the Honolulu Civic Center, which includes **Honolulu Hale** (City Hall). Built in 1929, this California/Spanish-style building boasts a terra-cotta courtyard patterned after the thirteenth-century Bargello Palace in Florence, as well as three colonial-style Mission Memorial buildings erected by the American Protestant mission to Hawaii.

Honolulu Academy of Arts

The Honolulu Academy of Arts, the only museum in the Hawaiian Islands that exhibits a general collection of art, is housed in a building designed in 1927 by Bertram Grosvenor Goodhue Associates to combine the appearance of a traditional Hawaiian structure with the plan of a modern museum. The Academy was founded by Mrs. Charles Montague Cooke, who was born in the islands to missionary parents and who wanted to share the art she had collected with the people of Hawaii. The collection—which now numbers some 22,000 objects displayed in thirty galleries surrounding six garden courts—includes Japanese and Chinese paintings, sculpture, and ceramics, the James A. Michener Collection of Ukiyo-e, European and American paintings from the eighteenth to the twentieth century, the Kress Collection of Italian Renaissance painting, ancient Chinese and Persian bronzes, and the traditional arts of the Pacific and Africa. The Academy also maintains a large research library, and sponsors concert and film programs in their theater.

LOCATION: 900 South Beretania Street. HOURS: 10-4:30 Tuesday-Saturday, 1-5 Sunday. FEE: None. TELEPHONE: 808-538-3693.

Arc-en-Ciel, or The Rainbow, painted by Robert Delaunay in 1913, is part of the diverse collection of the Honolulu Academy of Arts.

Waikiki Beach

This renowned two-mile strip of beach was named Waikiki ("spouting water") for the streams and springs feeding the swampland that once lay behind it. For centuries it was a favorite resort of Hawaii's natives, many of whom surfed on long boards made of planks from the trunks of koa and *wili-wili* trees. Fifteenth-century chants make reference to contests and specific surfing breaks at Waikiki. Captain Cook's men, who sailed past these shores in 1778, were impressed by the "boldness and address" with which they "saw them perform these difficult and dangerous maneuvers." During the early 1800s, Hawaii's kings retreated here from the bustle of Honolulu to their homes along the beach. A dirt road constructed in the 1860s between Waikiki and Honolulu provided a path for buses and tramcars. Numerous hotels and tourists ultimately would transform the area into Hawaii's version of Miami Beach. Some of the hotels built in the early twentieth century—including the **Moana,** the **Royal Hawaiian,** and the **Sans Souci**—still stand, marking Waikiki's social history and its evolution as a resort. The writers Jack London, Robert Louis Stevenson, and Rupert Brooke lived and worked here.

The **U.S. Army Museum** (Fort De Russy, Kalia Road, 808-438-2821) is housed in Battery Randolph, a 1911 bunker. It contains military artifacts and memorabilia that explore the role of the army in Hawaii, Hawaiian military history, and Hawaii's role in national defense. The possessions of Father Damien, who lived and died among the lepers of Molokai, are displayed in the **Damien Museum and Archives** (130 Ohua Avenue, 808-923-2690).

Diamond Head, the volcanic crater at the end of Waikiki Beach, was the site of the Papaenaena Heiau, a temple where Kamehameha I is said to have ordered the islands' last human sacrifices after the battle of the Nuuanu Valley in 1795. The crater was originally known as Laeahi ("brow of the tuna"), a name given, according to Hawaiian legend, by Hiiaka, younger sister of the goddess of fire, who thought the crater's profile resembled that of the yellowfin tuna. In 1825 it was renamed by a group of British sailors who mistook the crater's calcite crystals for diamonds.

Surrounding downtown Honolulu and Waikiki are **Kalihi, Palama, Nuuanu,** and **Manoa,** residential districts that stretch across the valleys and ridges of the Koolau Range.

These two representations of the war god Kukailimoku are in the Bishop Museum. The bust, left, was made in the 1600s from roots of a mountain vine, intertwined with feathers. The dramatic wooden effigy, right, is one of the finest achievements of Hawaiian art. The eight-foot-tall statue was made for a temple in the 1600s.

Bernice Pauahi Bishop Museum

The Bishop Museum was founded in 1889 by the Honolulu banker Charles Reed Bishop as a memorial to his wife, Bernice, the great-granddaughter of Kamehameha I. The collection began with the family heirlooms of Princess Bernice and Queen Emma, wife of Kamehameha IV; today the museum's collection of Hawaiian and Pacific artifacts and natural history specimens is the largest in the world. Its four original buildings were built of coursed lava rock in the Richardsonian Romanesque style; the interiors are of carved koa wood. A fifty-five-foot sperm whale is suspended from the ceiling of the **Hawaiian Hall,** which contains displays on the history of the state and exhibits featuring splendid garments made of thousands of red or yellow feathers from tropical birds and worn by Hawaii's kings. The **Hall of Hawaiian Natural History** focuses on the geology and ecology of the islands; the **Polynesian Hall,** on the Polynesian, Micronesian, and Melanesian cultures. Other galleries feature exhibits on archaeological sites, tropical birds, and Japanese immigration to Hawaii.

LOCATION: 1525 Bernice Street. HOURS: 9-5 Monday-Saturday and first Sunday of the month. FEE: Yes. TELEPHONE: 808-847-3511.

Nuuanu ("cool height") was the site of Kamehameha I's victory over Oahu's Chief Kalanikupule in one of the wars of unification during 1795. Hundreds of Kalanikupule's men were killed, some of them driven over the Nuuanu Pali ("precipice") at the head of the valley, on the windward edge of the Koolaus. A country retreat for royalty in the 1860s and 1870s, Nuuanu became a suburb for Honolulu's wealthy *haole* families at the turn of the century. Their grand Victorian mansions, complete with lush tropical gardens, still stand.

Queen Emma Summer Palace

This relatively modest but elegant house was built in 1847 by a Honolulu businessman and later sold to John Young II, son of one of Kamehameha I's *haole* advisers. In 1857 Young left the house to his niece Emma, who had married Kamehameha IV the year before. Queen Emma, who lost both her son and her husband while still young—Kamehameha IV died in 1862 at age 29—nonetheless held court here until 1875. Restored by the Daughters of Hawaii, *Hanaiakamalama*, as the palace is known, is now a museum containing furniture and artifacts from the period of the queen's residence. Included in the museum's collection are a tiger-claw necklace given to Emma by a visiting maharaja, wedding and baby gifts from Queen Victoria, and an elaborate triple-tiered cabinet made in Germany from Hawaii's native koa wood.

LOCATION: 2913 Pali Highway. HOURS: 9-4 Daily. FEE: Yes. TELEPHONE: 808-595-3167.

Nuuanu is also the site of the **Oahu Cemetery** (2162 Nuuanu Avenue), where many prominent Honolulu citizens are buried. In the center of the cemetery, under a royal palm, is the tomb of Alexander Cartwright, one of the people who drew up the rules of baseball in the 1840s. Cartwright stopped in Hawaii on a trip around the world and liked Honolulu so much that he decided to stay. He founded the city's first volunteer fire department and served as its chief from 1850 to 1856. Across the street and up Nuuanu Avenue is the **Royal Mausoleum,** the burial ground for Kamehameha II, III, IV, and V, King Kalakaua, and Queen Liliuokalani, whose remains were transferred from a tomb on the grounds of the Iolani Palace. Not interred here is Kamehameha I, whose burial place was kept secret. The cemetery's **chapel,** which is in the shape of a cross, was designed in 1865 by Honolulu's first professional architect, Theodore Heuck.

Similar to Nuuanu, the Manoa Valley was a favorite country retreat for Hawaiian royalty. According to missionary accounts, the queen regent Kaahumanu, the widow of Kamehameha I who ruled the islands after the death of Kamehameha II in 1825 (his successor, a younger brother, was not old enough to take the throne), requested she be taken to Manoa when close to death. She died in her small summer cottage in June 1832, allegedly holding a copy of the New Testament in Hawaiian given to her by Reverend Hiram Bingham. The **Punahou School** was founded in 1841 by Reverend Bingham for the children of Congregational missionaries. Located on land bequeathed by Queen Kaahumanu, it still educates many of Hawaii's *haoles*.

THE WINDWARD COAST

Route 72, the Kalanianole Highway, winds east and then north of Honolulu proper along the coast and up the island's windward side. The suburban sprawl along the first few miles gives way to **Hanauma Bay**, which curves around an eroded volcanic crater. In **Kailua** a large temple platform is preserved as **Ulu Po State Monument** (Off

Hawaiian women, above, surfing off Waikiki in the 1870s. OPPOSITE: *Queen Liliuokalani, the last Hawaiian monarch, who was deposed in 1893.*

Route 61). The temple cannot be accurately dated. The Koolau Mountains dominate the landscape between Makapuu and Kahuku points with their falls, valleys, and cliffs. North of Kaneohe are the fish ponds of **Heeia, Kahaluu, Molii,** and **Huilua.** The island once boasted nearly a hundred of these structures, which the early Hawaiians used to fatten stocked fish. Some ponds are still used today. Covering eighty-eight acres, Heeia is the island's largest pond, with a wall 5,000 feet long and 12 feet wide.

NORTH SHORE

Oahu's northwestern flank, from Kahuku to Kaena points, is dangerously rugged, with waves that challenge surfers and have been known to wreak havoc upon the communities lining the coast. Above Waimea Bay, off Pupukea Road, is the *heiau* (open-air temple) called **Puu o Mahuka,** built in the middle or late 1700s. One of the largest temples on the island, it was used in ancient times for human sacrifice. According to some accounts, the crew members of the British ship *Dedalus* were sacrificed here in 1794 after their capture at the mouth of the Waimea River. **Haleiwa,** which flourished as a fashionable resort at the turn of the century, is the locale of the **Liliuokalani Church** (66-090 Kamehameha Highway), built in 1861. In 1890 Queen Liliuokalani presented the church with a clock whose hours are marked by the letters of her name.

CENTRAL OAHU

Wedged between the Koolau and the Waianae ranges is the Leilehua Plateau, the site of military installations and pineapple plantations. The center of Hawaii's fruit business is Wahiawa, where in 1899 the Oahu entrepreneur James Dole planted sixty acres and two years later founded the Hawaiian Pineapple Company. The history of the industry is told at the **Dole Pineapple Pavilion** (64–1550 Kamehameha Highway, 808–621–8408).

    Schofield Barracks, west of Wahiawa, is headquarters for the Twenty-fifth Infantry Division. It was attacked by Japanese bombers flying through Kolekole Pass on December 7, 1941. The town is also known for its **Birthing Stones** and **Healing Stones.** The Healing Stones, thought to have the power to relieve physical ailments, were visited regularly by pilgrims in the 1920s and still draw some believers today. The wives of ancient Hawaiian chiefs delivered their children on the Birthing Stones in a spot surrounded by eucalyptus trees.

PEARL HARBOR

The United States was granted the exclusive right to use Pearl Harbor in 1887, but it was not until 1899 that Congress approved the site as a naval base. Channel-dredging of the harbor, called Wai Momi (Pearl River) because of its oyster beds, was completed in 1902, and the base was dedicated in December of that year.

The United States entered World War II after the surprise Japanese attack here on December 7, 1941. When Japan was laying plans for war with the United States, Admiral Isoroku Yamamoto urged that the first blow fall upon Pearl Harbor: "We will have no hope of winning," he said, "unless the U.S. fleet in Hawaiian waters can be destroyed." At about 8:00 AM on December 7 the first wave of 343 Japanese bombers, torpedo planes, and fighters, launched from six aircraft carriers, swept over Oahu's airfields and the 94 U.S. ships in the harbor. An armor-piercing bomb penetrated the deck of the battleship *Arizona* and caused a magazine to explode—the ship erupted in flames, split in two, and sank with 1,100 officers and men. The battleships *West Virginia* and *California* also sank; *Oklahoma* capsized. In all, 2,403 Americans died in the two-hour attack, and nineteen ships were wrecked. However, the American aircraft

Its magazine penetrated by a bomb, the destroyer Shaw *explodes during the Japanese attack on Pearl Harbor, December 7, 1941.*

The battleship Arizona, *which was sunk during the Japanese attack, lies on the bottom of Pearl Harbor, still holding the remains of its crew. A memorial with exhibits about the attack is moored above the hulk.*

carriers were at sea that day, and thus survived to form the bulwark of U.S. defenses in the Pacific; the Japanese pilots also neglected to strike critical fuel dumps and repair facilities. The next day, President Franklin D. Roosevelt asked Congress for a declaration of war against Japan, saying that December 7 would be "a date which will live in infamy." Pearl Harbor, its facilities repaired, became the major U.S. base in the Pacific during World War II.

The wreck of the *Arizona* lies undisturbed where it sank, still holding the remains of its crew. Its mast, protruding from the water, is surrounded by a floating platform, the **Arizona Memorial.** Another monument has been built next to the hulk of the *Utah* (not accessible) on Ford Island. The navy runs boats to the *Arizona* Memorial from the Halawa Landing.

LOCATION: Pearl Harbor. HOURS: 8-3 Daily. FEE: None. TELEPHONE: 808-471-0281.

WEST SIDE

Also known as the Waianae Coast, Oahu's west side is drier, hotter, and less populated than the island's other regions. However, the area's good fishing grounds made it one of the hubs of the islands' ancient civilization. At the end of Kaneilio Point, on the south side of Pokai Bay, is the **Kuilioloa Heiau.** Made of coral and lava rock, the temple was built in the fifteenth or sixteenth century in honor of Ilioloa (Long Dog), patron of travelers along the coast. Another temple, **Kaneaki,** is in the Makaha Valley and was built by a Hawaiian chief in the seventeenth century. Finely restored by the National Park Service, the Bishop Museum, and the Makaha Historical Society, Kaneaki was originally an agricultural temple. There is speculation that it may have been reconditioned in 1796 for use as a temple of human sacrifice by Kamehameha I, who was preparing to launch an invasion of Kauai. His fleet of war canoes was wrecked by bad weather and another attack in 1804 was forestalled by an outbreak of disease.

K A U A I

The oldest of Hawaii's inhabited islands, Kauai was created some 5 million years ago by the upward thrust of Mount Waialeale. Later volcanic activity left a massive caldera, filled today by the Alakai Swamp, a dense jungle of rare birds and plants that covers the center of the island. In this area and in the drier areas to the north and west has been found evidence of Kauai's first settlers, who arrived some time around A.D. 800. In 1778 Captain James Cook landed at Waimea. The island managed to stay out of the fray during the wars of unification, and in 1810, to preserve peace, King Kaumualii decided to yield the island to Kamehameha I. Missionaries and sugar planters settled on this island in the mid-nineteenth century, establishing churches and plantations in Koloa, Hanalei, and Lihue. Today most of Kauai's residents live on the island's rim in small towns surrounded by fish ponds, splendid beaches, a wealth of streams, and rugged cliffs.

This section begins in Lihue and traces two routes: one heads south on Route 50 to Koloa and Waimea (with a detour on Route 550 into the Waimea Canyon); the other covers the island's northern flank, including Hanalei, and ending at the Na Pali Coast.

The spectacular Na Pali Coast.

LIHUE

Like many of Kauai's towns, Lihue was born of Hawaii's flourishing sugar industry, which began in the mid-nineteenth century. William H. Rice, patriarch of one of the island's powerful missionary families, dug one of the state's first irrigation ditches here in 1856. George Wilcox, a member of Kauai's other influential missionary clan, established his own plantation in 1864. Now a museum, the restored **Grove Farm Homestead** (808-245-3202, reservations required) includes the main plantation house, the guest cottages, and the camp houses of the workers. Also in Lihue is the **Kauai Museum** (4428 Rice Street, 808-245-6931), which includes exhibits of artifacts and photographs depicting the island's history.

South of Lihue is the **Alekoko Fish Pond,** built, as the story goes, by the *menehunes*. According to legend, these two-foot-tall people from the Marquesas Islands were the first inhabitants of Hawaii. Working only at night, it is said they were able to perform such prodigious feats as the construction of this fish pond's 900-foot wall.

KOLOA

The American firm of Ladd and Company established Hawaii's first major sugar plantation at Koloa in 1835. Natives were given twelve and a half cents a day, fish, and poi (a paste made from taro root) to work under miserable conditions against the wishes of the local chiefs. (It has been recorded that forty natives were hitched to a plow when no draft animals were available.) In 1836 the manager complained about the reluctance of his work force: "I have had more annoyance from the chiefs and difficulties with the natives than I had thought it possible for a white man to bear." The ruins of the original mill are still here, and the McBryde Sugar Company operates another mill just north of town. Among the town's weathered wooden buildings are some Japanese temples (plantation owners imported Chinese and Japanese labor) and a cluster of mission buildings. Most of the buildings are still in use; one temple (Jodo Mission) has been restored.

WAIMEA

Waimea and its bay played a prominent role in the opening of Hawaii to the outside world. Captain James Cook dropped anchor here on January 19, 1778, the first white man to land on the islands. His coming was marked by tremendous excitement among the natives, who thought he was a god. "That can be nothing else than the *heiau* of Lono," said one priest of Cook's ship, ". . . and the place of sacrifice at the altar." Cook spent five days in Waimea, visiting with the island's chiefs, trading iron for pork, potatoes, and taro, and sailing to the offshore island of Niihau before departing for the Pacific Northwest on February 2. In the spring of 1792, Captain George Vancouver's crew was greeted far less civilly: Four of his men were killed during an excursion ashore for water.

The nineteenth century brought more *haole* involvement. The island's ruler, Kaumualii, desired to be free of the overlordship of Kamehameha and attempted to use his recent affiliation with the Russians to equip an army to invade Oahu. In 1817 Georg Anton Schaeffer, a representative of the Russian American Fur Company, secured permission from Kaumualii to build two forts on the island. The ruins of **Fort Elizabeth,** also known as the **Russian Fort,** can still be seen at the mouth of the Waimea River. Alarmed at the budding alliance between Kaumualii and Schaeffer, Kamehameha ordered

Known as "the Little Grand Canyon," Waimea Canyon is one of the most rugged landscapes in the Hawaiian Islands.

the Russians expelled, and Schaeffer was ultimately repudiated by the czar. The Hawaiian government completed the fort, which was used for a variety of purposes until 1864, when it was ordered dismantled.

Route 50, which runs parallel to the island's southern coast, ends at Mana. Inland, accessible via Route 550, are the **Waimea Canyon** and **Kokee state parks.** The **Kokee Museum** (808-335-9975) features exhibits on the geology and natural history of the parks, the neighboring Alakai Swamp, and the rest of the island.

THE NORTH SHORE

Route 56, which begins in Lihue, winds around the eastern and northern flanks of Kauai past lovely beaches—including Lumahai, where the movie *South Pacific* was filmed—falls, and caverns. The region around **Wailua** was also important to ancient Hawaiians, who built some of their most sacred temples here. At the mouth of the Wailua River several temple sites are preserved in **Wailua River State**

Farmlands in the lush Hanalei Valley, where taro is grown. The valley is also the site of a national wildlife refuge.

Park (Route 56), including a birthing place and the restored **Holo-Holo-Ku Heiau.** Farther up the coast is **Kilauea,** whose lighthouse, now automated, was built in 1913.

Hanalei

New England missionaries built the **Waioli Mission House** (808-245-3202) in 1836. Restored by their descendants, it is now a museum with period furniture and artifacts. In the same year that the mission house was built, silk production was started. The silkworm eggs were imported from China and America, mulberry trees were planted, and some good cocoons were produced, but insects and bad weather brought the enterprise to an end in 1845.

Route 56 ends at the beginning of the **Na Pali Coast** (*na pali* means "the cliffs"), most of which is under state jurisdiction. This lush, rugged region, accessible only to helicopters, boats, and intrepid hikers on narrow, precipitous trails, was inhabited until the early years of this century. Two of the old coastal communities, **Nualolo Kai** and **Milolii,** are both part of the **Na Pali Coast State Park.** Some of the stones used to build the taro paddies and lodgings of Nualolo still remain.

Seventeen miles to the west, across the Kaulakahi Channel, is the tiny island of **Niihau.** It is owned by the Robinson family, whose relatives James and Francis Sinclair bought Niihau from Kamehameha V for $10,000 in 1864. Most of the inhabitants—who are all employed on the Robinson ranch—are native Hawaiians, now a minority in the state, and Hawaiian is the island's prime language. Niihau was the only precinct to vote against statehood in the 1959 plebiscite.

M O L O K A I

Just thirty-eight miles long and seven miles wide, Molokai is small but topographically diverse. Two sets of volcanic mountains form the eastern and western parts of the island, which are divided by the plain of Hoolehua. Western Molokai, dominated by the 67,000-acre Molokai Ranch and fields of pineapple, is drier, with brown hills rolling down to beaches. The east side is marked by a lush forest. At its tip lies the Halawa Valley, now a county park, which was inhabited until a tidal wave in 1946 forced its residents to evacuate. Historically Molokai has been a place of refuge. Ancient Hawaiians fled to the city of Kawela, whose powerful priests were respected throughout the islands. Later, in the 1860s, the kingdom's victims of leprosy were isolated on the Makanalua, or Kalaupapa, Peninsula on the orders of Kamehameha V. They lived impoverished and in exile until 1873, when the Belgian priest Joseph De Veuster, known as Father Damien, joined their community.

This section begins at Kaunakakai, Molokai's major town, heads east on Route 450 past the fish ponds of the island's south coast, then swings up and around the eastern tip to the Kalaupapa Peninsula.

KAUNAKAKAI AND THE SOUTH SHORE

This small, quiet town of false-front wooden buildings is the island's major urban center. In the 1930s its wharf bustled with barges of pineapples ready for shipment to canneries on Oahu. Near the harbor are the remains of the home of Kamehameha V, who spent summers here from 1863 until his death in 1872. Farther west are the thousand coconut trees of **Kapuaiwa Grove**—planted, it is said, by the king in the 1860s. Along Route 450 (also known as Kamehameha V Highway) lie numerous **fish ponds,** which were built of coral and basalt and used to fatten fish for consumption by Hawaii's royal chiefs. **Kawela,** a city of refuge for ancient Hawaiians, was also the site of one of Kamehameha I's battles in his campaign to unify the islands.

Father Damien built two churches on Molokai's southern coast: the white, wood-frame **Saint Joseph** in Kamalo, which dates to 1876, and **Our Lady of Sorrows** in Kaluuaha, completed in 1874. Both churches have been restored. Also in Kaluuaha is **Kaluuaha Church,** Molokai's first Christian church, built in 1844 by one of the island's early missionaries, the Reverend H. R. Hitchcock. Up from the coast in the Mapulehu Valley is **Iliiliopae Heiau,** one of Hawaii's largest temples. It was built in the thirteenth century of stones transported, one by one, from the Wailau Valley and was a site of human sacrifice.

KALAUPAPA

Molokai's north coast peninsula, **Makanalua,** is a small plateau separated from the rest of the island by a 2,000-foot cliff. It has been home since the mid-nineteenth century to Hawaiian victims of leprosy, now called Hansen's Disease. Although the disease was identified on the islands as early as 1830—it was called *mai pake* (the Chinese disease) for its presumed country of origin—it was not widespread until the 1860s. "The increase of leprosy has caused me much anxiety," Kamehameha V told the legislature in 1864, "and is such as to make decisive steps imperative upon us." Two years later, the first group of lepers was tossed from boats and forced to swim to the peninsula, where they founded a settlement at **Kalawao.** Their isolation was broken in 1873 by Father Damien, who ministered to their physical and spiritual needs until 1889, when he succumbed to the disease. **Saint Philomena's,** the church he built in 1873, still stands. The colony moved from Kalawao to the drier and less windy Kalaupapa, where Father Damien helped create a community that included houses, a hospital, and farms, work for which the "Martyr of Molokai" was honored by the Hawaiian government.

OVERLEAF: *The Kapuaiwa Coconut Grove on Molokai, with a thousand trees said to have been planted by royal hands a century ago.*

Fewer than a hundred people live on the peninsula today—sulfone drugs, introduced in the 1940s, have brought leprosy under control—and patients may now leave the colony. The area has been designated the **Kalaupapa National Historical Park** (808-567-9093). Visitors must obtain permission to tour the peninsula, which is accessible by air, car, or by mule over a trail with spectacular views. Jack London, who wrote of the Kalaupapa residents in *The Cruise of the Snark* (1911) and in later short stories, followed the three-mile-long mule trail to the village in 1907.

L　A　N　A　I

Named for its shape—Lanai means "hump" or "swell" in old Hawaiian—this small island was once, according to legend, overrun by evil spirits. Hawaiians began to settle here after the banished nephew of one of Maui's chiefs drove out the demons. European explorers and traders made note of the rich fishing grounds and taro farms of Lanai's south shore. Early attempts to grow sugar on the island, starting in 1802, were unsuccessful, as was an effort to establish a Mormon colony in 1855. Lanai was primarily used for grazing until 1922, when Jim Dole purchased the island from the Baldwin missionary family to grow pineapples. Today most of Lanai's 2,100 residents still work for Dole's company, which is now owned by Castle & Cooke, one of Honolulu's Big Five companies. The entries here include Lanai City, Kaunolu Bay, the Munro Trail, and some sites on the island's windward side.

LANAI CITY

Set amid Norfolk pines on a high central plateau, Lanai City is the island's major urban center. It was founded by Jim Dole in 1924, two years after his Hawaiian Pineapple Company purchased the island for $1.1 million. Like Kaunakakai on Molokai, which has also remained relatively untouched by tourism, Lanai City retains the flavor of 1930s Hawaii. One of the forks of Route 440, which originates in Lanai City, winds in a southwesterly direction toward Kaumalapau Harbor, where more than a million pineapples are loaded daily onto barges destined for canneries on Oahu.

OPPOSITE: *The rusting hulk of a freighter off Shipwreck Beach on Lanai. Molokai is across the channel.*

A four-wheel-drive vehicle is needed for the road to Kaunolu Bay, a few miles south of the island's airport. **Kaunolu Village,** where Kamehameha I summered and fished, is a rich archaeological site. Dr. Kenneth Emory of Honolulu's Bishop Museum uncovered the remains of stone platforms, shelters, gravestones, and garden plots during excavations here in 1921. Nearby are **Halulu Heiau** and **Kahekili's Leap,** where warriors, in a test of bravery, jumped sixty feet from a ledge into the water, clearing a fifteen-foot outcropping of rock.

Munro Trail, which extends from Koele, above Lanai City, to the summit of Mount Lanaihale, was named for George C. Munro, a New Zealander who came to the island to manage the Lanai Ranch in 1910. An amateur naturalist, he liked to ride through the mountains sowing seeds. From his wanderings sprouted Norfolk pines, moisture-gathering trees that are now a common sight on the island. Along the trail is **Hookio Ridge** above Maunalei Gulch, the site of a Hawaiian invasion in 1778.

WINDWARD LANAI

North of Lanai City along the island's arid coast is **Shipwreck Beach,** where for centuries strong trade winds between Maui and Molokai have driven boats up the reef. It is still possible to see the remains of a rusty World War II ship. Several miles east are the remnants of **Keomuku,** a village abandoned after the failure of a sugar company in 1901. Nearby are the **Luahiwa petroglyphs,** carved into a hillside.

M A U I

Geologists believe that Maui began as two distinct volcanic peaks that fused together thousands of centuries ago. Polynesian mythology offers a different theory of its genesis. According to one legend, the demigod Maui, in an effort to prove his worth to his scornful brothers, snared on his line not a fish but this entire island, the first of the Hawaiian chain.

Kamehameha I also snared Maui, after a fierce battle in the Iao Valley in 1790. Within a few years, he had unified his kingdom and established a residence at Lahaina, where European explorers and traders, among them Captain George Vancouver, began to seek him out. Upon Kamehameha's death in 1819, his son and successor made Lahaina Hawaii's capital, which it remained until 1845. During those decades, Maui was a magnet for whalers and missionaries, whose different views of life and morality caused a good deal of friction. The whaling industry declined in the second half of the nineteenth century as sugar became the mainstay of Hawaii's economy. In the late 1870s the Hamakua Ditch, Maui's first irrigation effort, was built to bring water from Haleakala's wet northern slopes to the island's arid central plain, transforming it into fertile land for raising sugarcane. Sugar is still a major industry, along with agriculture and tourism. While Maui's sunny and dry western coast continues to draw resort developers, the more rugged and wetter eastern half remains fairly pristine.

This section starts in Kahului and Wailuku, Maui's twin cities, then goes on to Lahaina, crosses over to the east and the Hana Coast, and ends with Haleakala National Park.

WAILUKU AND KAHULUI

Known as Maui's twin cities, Wailuku and Kahului lie at the northern end of the isthmus that joins the island's two volcanic craters. Kahului, Maui's port, is a modern commercial center. However, just off Route 36 between the city and the airport is the ancient **Kanaha Pond,** today the state's major sanctuary for waterfowl. In **Puunene,** south of Kahului on Puunene Avenue, is the **Alexander & Baldwin Sugar Museum** (808-871-8058), housed in an old plantation overseers' house across from the C & H Sugar Mill. The museum contains working models of sugar-processing machinery, photographs, and artifacts. Outside the museum is a restored 1882 steam locomotive from the Kahului Railroad. In Wailuku's historic district, on the west side of High Street, is **Kaahumanu Congregational Church.** Built in 1837 of wood and plastered stone, it was named for one of Kamehameha I's wives, who was born in Hana and promoted the work of the missionaries during her reign as queen regent from 1825 until her death in 1832. Nearby on Main Street is the **Bailey House Museum** (808-244-3326), operated by the Maui Historical Society. It is housed in the former home of Edward Bailey, headmaster of the Central Female Boarding Seminary, which opened at Wailuku in 1837. Ancient Hawaiian artifacts, paintings, and furnishings from the missionary era are featured.

Three miles from Wailuku is the **Iao Valley,** once the burial place of Maui's royalty. It was also the site in 1790 of Kamehameha's victory against rival chieftain Kalanikupule in a battle known as Kepaniwai, which means "the damming of the waters," a name said to refer to the carnage that choked the Iao Stream after the bloody battle. Kalanikupule escaped to Lahaina and then to Oahu, but he was captured during the Battle of the Nuuanu Valley in 1795.

South on Route 30, the Honoapilani Highway, is **Maalaea,** a small coastal town whose bay is a calving ground for humpback whales. Farther up the coast, **Olowalu** was the scene of the brutal massacre of more than a hundred Hawaiians in February 1790 by Captain Simon Metcalfe, one of the first Americans to visit the islands. Anchored at Maui after a fur-trading journey to America's Pacific Northwest, his ship, the *Eleanora,* was attacked by Hawaiians. In retaliation for the killing of a crew member, Metcalfe fired on the natives, burned their village, and later, after falsely declaring a peace, slaughtered the Hawaiians who had paddled out in canoes to barter.

LAHAINA

Captain Cook's voyage in 1778 opened Hawaii to the world, and within less than two decades Lahaina had become a favorite port of call for explorers and traders. After the Battle of Kepaniwai in 1790, Kamehameha I had established a residence in the port. Three of his children were born here, including Liholiho, who assumed the throne as Kamehameha II in 1819 and made Lahaina the kingdom's capital, which it remained until 1845.

From the 1820s to the 1860s the port was busy with missionaries and whalers, a combination that was sometimes explosive. Hawaii's chiefs, increasingly under the influence of the Christian *haoles,* banned gambling, drunkenness, and other vices in 1825. Two years later, a group of angry sailors in Lahaina fired some cannon shots into the house of the American missionary William Richards. Henry Cheever, a minister who visited Hawaii in the early 1840s, described the town as "one of the breathing holes of hell." Herman Melville, who sailed into Lahaina in 1843 and spent six months in the islands, would describe the missionaries later in his appendix to *Typee* as ". . . a junta of ignorant and designing Methodist elders in the councils of a half-civilized king, ruling with absolute sway over a nation just poised between barbarism and civilization." Nevertheless, both whaling and Christianity flourished. Hundreds of ships stopped at

OPPOSITE: *Poolenalena Beach on Maui.*

A statue of Buddha at the Jodo Mission, a nineteenth-century Buddhist temple built to serve Japanese laborers in the town of Koloa.

Lahaina and Honolulu until the Pacific whaling industry declined in the 1860s. The missionaries, led by Reverend Richards, consolidated their power by founding a seminary and currying favor with Hawaii's kings. Richards, who became a close adviser to Kamehameha III in 1836, encouraged the king to establish a constitutional monarchy. In 1839 Kamehameha III issued a declaration of rights and laws protecting religious freedom, followed a year later by the kingdom's first constitution.

By the late nineteenth century, sugar had replaced government and whaling as Lahaina's major industry. Today a small and lively town, Lahaina contains landmarks that reflect its rich—and sometimes wild—heritage. A legacy of the town's earliest missionaries, the **Lahainaluna School** sits at the foot of the West Maui Mountains. The school's first building was built of poles and grass in 1831 by its students. Originally a seminary, it is now a high school. On the campus is the restored **Hale Pai** (house of printing), where, in 1834, Hawaii's first newspaper, *Ka Lama Hawaii* (Hawaiian Luminary), was printed on a Ramage press.

At the junction of Lahainaluna Road and Route 30 is the **Pioneer Sugar Mill,** whose smokestack is a familiar local landmark. The mill was built in 1860 by James Campbell, whose Pioneer Mill Company went on to become one of Maui's major sugar producers.

The **Baldwin House,** on Front Street (808-661-3262), is a memorial to Reverend Dwight Baldwin, an American missionary from Connecticut who was transferred to Lahaina in 1835 for his health and became the community's doctor. His two-story white stucco house, restored by the Lahaina Restoration Foundation, is now a museum and the foundation's headquarters. On Front Street is the restored **Wo Hing Temple** (808-661-5553), a museum devoted to Hawaii's Chinese heritage. Chinese immigrants came to Maui to work on the plantations and sugar mills, and also to build tunnels and an irrigation system throughout the west Maui mountains. The Chinese residents of Lahaina formed the Wo Hing Society in 1909 and built their temple in that year. A Buddhist shrine is maintained on the second floor, and a film about Chinese Hawaiian history is shown in a small theater.

Overlooking the harbor, on Wharf Street, is the **Pioneer Hotel,** one of Hawaii's two oldest hotels (the Moana on Waikiki Beach opened the same year). Built in 1901 by a Canadian, George Freeland, its original house rules, which are still posted, reflect the missionaries' moral influence: "Women is not allow in you room; If you wet or burn you bed you going out; You are not allow to gambel in you room; Only on Sunday you can sleep all day." Also on Wharf Street is the **Lahaina Courthouse,** built in 1859 of stones originally used for King Kamehameha III's now-demolished palace. Open for inspection is the town's old prison, **Hale Paahao** (Stuck-in-irons House), built in the 1850s to hold drunken sailors and others convicted of such sins as working on Sunday. Its walls are coral. In the Whaler's Village shopping complex is the **Whaler's Village Museum** (808-661-5992), which maintains a collection of more than one hundred artifacts from Hawaii's whaling days, including nineteenth-century surgeons' tools and a six-foot model of a whaling vessel.

The diversity of Lahaina's nineteenth-century citizenry is apparent in the **Waiola Churchyard** (Wainee Street), the burial place of Queen Keopuolani (one of the wives of Kamehameha I and the mother of Kamehamehas II and III); missionary families; sailors; and other townspeople.

THE HANA COAST

This stretch of coast from Kahului to Hana, along Maui's northeastern flank, is celebrated for its beauty. Ravines, cliffs, waterfalls, stunning flora, and dense foliage define the region, which is accessible via the winding Hana Highway. At the turn of the century, the fertile coast attracted entrepreneurial pioneers, who planted sugar, pineapple, cotton, eucalyptus, and rubber. **Nahiku** was the site of America's first rubber plantation, built in 1905. Many of the entrepreneurial ventures failed because of the coast's relative inaccessibility. However, a trans-island irrigation system of ditches, pipelines, and flumes, started in the late 1870s by two entrepreneurs, Samuel T. Alexander and Henry P. Baldwin, and by Claus Spreckels, a sugar baron, is responsible for the transformation of Maui's arid central plain into a rich agricultural region.

The missionaries also made inroads here. In 1856 the Congregationalists built a church in **Keanae,** which, along with a small cemetery, still stands. **Wailua** is home to **Saint Gabriel's,** one of the area's first Catholic churches, which was built in 1860. At the end of the road is **Hana.** Today a peaceful town, Hana was for centuries a stronghold against invading armies from the island of Hawaii. **Kauiki Hill,** a large cinder cone adjacent to Hana Bay, was once the site of a large fortress guarded, according to legend, by a fierce idol who kept the Hawaiian invaders from conquering Maui.

South of Hana is **Kipahulu,** a tiny town so loved by the aviator Charles Lindbergh, who had a home on Maui, that he chose to be buried there. His grave is in the small cemetery of the **Kipahulu Hawaiian Church** (Hana Highway), which was built in 1850. Farther down a road that is recommended for four-wheel-drive vehicles only is **Kaupo,** site of the **Kaupo Ranch,** which was founded in the late nineteenth century, and the restored **Huialoha Church,** built in 1859, when Kaupo could be reached only by sea and a primitive trail.

HALEAKALA NATIONAL PARK

This 28,000-acre park is dominated by the enormous dormant volcano Haleakala (House of the Sun). In the beginning, say Polynesian legends, the island had few hours of daylight; the sun preferred to sleep and race across the sky. One day, however, the demigod Maui, upset by his mother's difficulty with drying cloth, decided to bring the sun to task. Perching on the edge of Haleakala one evening, he waited until dawn and then lassoed the sun. When Maui's captive agreed to move more slowly across the sky, the god released him. Samuel Clemens, who spent six months in Hawaii in 1866, wrote of how he "froze and roasted by turns all night" on Haleakala's summit, only to awaken to a sunrise that was the "sublimest spectacle" he had ever seen. Many before him had climbed the crater—including New England missionaries in 1828 and members of the U.S. Exploring Expedition in 1841—and many have climbed it since. There are more than thirty miles of hiking trails in the park. The area's geology and ecology are described in exhibits at the park's visitor center.

LOCATION: Entrances off routes 378 and 360. HOURS: Always open. FEE: Yes. TELEPHONE: 808-572-9306.

H   A   W   A   I   I

Hawaii is thought to have been the first island in the Hawaiian chain to be settled by the Polynesians from the Marquesas Islands, who migrated here between A.D. 500 and 800. Some 500 to 600 years later, the Tahitians established their headquarters here, according to tradition naming it for an ancient homeland. It was on the island's northern peninsula of Kohala that Kamehameha I was born about 1758. From the isolated Waipio Valley he launched attacks against rival chiefs in the wars of unification. Kailua also saw the abolishment of Hawaii's ancient *kapu* system by Kamehameha II in 1819 and the kingdom's introduction to Christianity by Boston Congregationalists in 1820.

Ranchers, coffee growers, and sugar planters followed on the heels of the missionaries, ultimately attracting an international labor force. Cowboys from Central and South America came to work on the mammoth Parker Ranch. Filipinos, Japanese, Chinese, and Portuguese filled the sugar plantation towns on the Hamakua Coast, above Hilo. This rich mix of cultures is reflected in Hawaii's urban and rural areas. The history of these immigrants and that of the kings and ancient Hawaiians is well preserved through the island's monuments and sites.

This section begins with Hilo and circles the island counterclockwise, winding along the Hamakua Coast northwest to the Waipio Valley and Kohala; then traveling down the west coast to

A thirty-acre Japanese garden, named for Queen Liliuokalani, now covers a portion of Hilo that was flattened by a tidal wave in 1960.

Kailua-Kona and back along the southern flanks to Hawaii Volcanoes National Park.

HILO

Situated on a sheltered bay at the mouth of the Wailuku River, Hilo has always been a small center of trade. Early Hawaiians came to the river to barter, and in the eighteenth and nineteenth centuries sailing ships and then steamers docked here, carrying merchants, missionaries, whale oil, sandalwood, coffee, bananas, sugar, and livestock. Hilo's oldest building is part of the **Lyman House Memorial Museum** complex (276 Haili Street, 808-935-5021). The house was built in 1839 by the Reverend David Belden Lyman, who arrived with his wife and a group of missionaries in 1832. Restored and furnished with original and donated period pieces, it depicts family life from 1840 to 1880. Next door is a museum with exhibits about the region's natural history and the island's ethnic groups and missionaries.

HAMAKUA COAST

This peaceful and scenic stretch of coast just north of Hilo was, in the 1780s, a battleground for the forces of Kamehameha I and rival chiefs Keawemauhili and Keoua, who were competing for domination of the island. A century later, with the flowering of the sugar industry, the region attracted large numbers of imported laborers. Chinese, Japanese, Filipino, and to a lesser extent, European workers filled the towns that had sprung up around the plantations. The villages of **Papaaloa, Laupahoehoe, Paauilo,** and **Paauhau,** which lie off Route 19 and the old Mamalahoa Highway, have changed little. Their wooden churches, iron-roofed cottages, and small shops give a sense of plantation life in the late nineteenth and early twentieth centuries.

Nine miles beyond Honokaa, on Hawaii's northeast coast, is the **Waipio Valley,** a canyon bounded by 2,000-foot cliffs and a mile-long beach. The valley was home to Hawaii's chiefs in the century before the arrival of European explorers. Kamehameha I spent time here as a child, and later, in 1791, he fought Maui's chief offshore with cannons acquired from Western traders.

WAIMEA

This town in the foothills of the Kohala Mountains is headquarters for the **Parker Ranch.** Its founder, John Parker, came to Hawaii from Massachusetts in 1809, at which time goats, sheep, and cows—presents to Kamehameha I from visiting Europeans—were destroying the island's farmlands and trees. In exchange for a homestead, Parker offered to bring the situation under control. To help him rope and brand the wild cattle, Parker imported Spanish-American cowboys, whom the Hawaiians called *paniolo*, from *españole* (today all Hawaiian cowboys, regardless of nationality, are so named). In 1847 Kamehameha III gave Parker two acres on the island, and by the turn of the century, his homestead was on its way to becoming America's largest ranch under individual ownership. Armine von Tempski, whose father was a ranch manager in Maui in the early 1900s, marveled at its size in her memoir, *Born in Paradise:* "The scope of the place was almost beyond comprehension as we moved across the plains to meet the herd. . . .five thousand head of cattle, gathered from the hundred-thousand-acre pasture they grazed in."

Today the ranch covers some 225,000 acres and runs 50,000 head of cattle. The **Parker Ranch Visitor Center and Museum** (Parker Ranch Shopping Center, Kamuela, 808-885-7655) contains exhibits on the history of the Parker family and the ranch. Tours depart from here to visit the original Mana Hale Homestead, the Parker family cemetery, working field areas, and the historic homes at Puuopelu. The residence of the ranch's present owner, **Puuopelu** is open as an art gallery exhibiting the works of Renoir, Chagall, Hassam, and others. Nearby is the reconstructed Mana home, originally built in the 1840s in the New England saltbox style. Its interior is made entirely of koa wood. In **Kamuela** at the junction of Routes 19 and 250 is the **Kamuela Museum** (808-885-4724), founded by J. P. Parker's great-great-granddaughter. It contains a small but eclectic collection, including artifacts from Hawaii's royalty and memorabilia of space flights. The clapboard **Imiola Congregational Church** (Church Row, Kamuela), built in 1857, is a fine example of *koa* woodworking. All the interior woodwork is made from native timber.

KOHALA

Hawaii's northernmost peninsula is dominated by the Kohala Mountains, which divide it into two different geographical regions: North Kohala is densely forested; South Kohala, hot and dry. On **Upolu Point** there is a marker commemorating the birth (about 1758) of Kamehameha I. He was also buried in this area, at an unknown site. **Kapaau** possesses the first **statue of Kamehameha,** made by the American sculptor Thomas Gould in 1880 and salvaged from a wreck off Port Stanley in the Falkland Islands.

Near **Hawi,** a plantation town on the tip of the peninsula, is **Mookini Heiau.** Probably built in the 1300s and 1400s and rebuilt at different times by later rulers, it was an important sacrificial temple for the rulers of Hawaii. The ruins of a fishing village built between 1200 and 1800, including houses, shrines, and a games area, were discovered by archaeologists and restored at **Lapakahi State Park** (808-889-5566), just a few miles south on Route 270. The visitor center offers maps and tour information.

KAWAIHAE

Kawaihae was a bustling harbor in the early days of the Hawaiian kingdom when Kamehameha I used it as a base during the wars of unification. In 1820 a member of Hawaii's first group of New England missionaries came to teach the gospel to the chiefs. The late nineteenth century saw the strange sight of Samuel Parker's cattle being herded to the ocean at Kawaihae and forced to swim to steamers, where they were hauled aboard for the trip to Oahu.

Just south of this now sleepy town is the **Puukohola Heiau National Historic Site** (808-882-7218). This huge stabilized temple, 224 by 100 feet, was built by Kamehameha I in 1791 at the suggestion of a renowned Kauai *kahuna,* an expert in certain fields such as prophesy, canoe building, and religion. The *kahuna* predicted that if Kamehameha built the temple and dedicated it to the war god, Kukailimoku (of whom Kamehameha was guardian), he would then gain his *mana* (spiritual power) and be able to conquer the islands of Hawaii, which thus far had eluded his grasp. When the temple was completed in 1791, Kamehameha invited his rival to the dedication, had him killed, and sacrificed him to the war god. By 1795, Hawaii, Maui, Lanai, Molokai, and Oahu were united under Kamehameha's rule. Kauai and Niihau joined the kingdom in 1810. The *heiau,* still considered sacred by some Hawaiians, cannot be entered. The visitor center provides a map of the park, which also includes the site of Kamehameha II's residence before he became king and the ruins of the house of John Young, one of his *haole* advisers.

KAILUA AND THE KONA COAST

Called Kailua-Kona to distinguish it from Oahu's Kailua, this area is marked by lava flows from Hualalai. Kailua was a royal retreat during the early days of the Hawaiian kingdom. Kamehameha I left Honolulu in 1812 and lived here until his death in 1819. His residence, **Kamakahonu,** a complex of thatched huts, fish ponds, and **Ahuena Heiau,** the temple where he conducted government meetings, has been restored by the management of the Hotel King Kamehameha (on whose grounds it is located), under the direction of the Bishop Museum. After Kamehameha I's death, Kamehameha II abolished the ancient *kapu* (taboo) system in November 1819 during a symbolic feast at Kamakahonu in the company of his father's wives Kaahumanu and Keopuolani. Previously it had been taboo for women and men to eat together. Hawaii's first Christian missionaries arrived in Kailua in the spring of 1820. Their leader, Hiram Bingham, went on to Honolulu, but Asa Thurston remained to build the island's first church in 1823. This thatched structure was replaced in 1837 by **Mokuaikaua Church,** which still stands on Alii Drive.

Mokuaikaua Church, built in 1837.

Hulihee Palace

This elegant two-story stone house, built in 1838 by John Adams Kuakini, a cousin of Kamehameha I, was a favorite retreat for members of the royal family. Kamehameha IV and Queen Emma moved the royal court to Hulihee for four months in 1858, a time they both enjoyed, but one of their servants did not. As the king's secretary wrote: "What can be done in a place where nothing is to be seen but blank masses of lava . . . not grass enough to feed a horse . . . and scarcely a tree within miles of us." Queen Emma wrote that her British butler, who got lost looking for alligator pears in the uplands one day, felt "like a fish out of water." Kalakaua, who traveled widely after becoming king in 1874, remodeled the house and furnished it with rugs, paintings, photographs, and Victoriana.

Restored by the Daughters of Hawaii, Hulihee has been a museum since 1928. It is furnished with period pieces of native woods and contains such royal artifacts as Kamehameha I's stone exercise ball and King Kalakaua's medals and guitar.

LOCATION: 75-5718 Alii Drive. HOURS: 9-4 Daily. FEE: Yes. TELEPHONE: 808-329-1877.

KEALAKEKUA BAY

On a wooded spit that forms the north head of this bay is the twenty-seven-foot **Captain Cook Monument,** erected in 1874 in honor of the celebrated explorer, who died on a nearby beach in 1779. Cook's arrival on Kauai in 1778 had provoked much excitement, and some talked as if they thought him a god. When he dropped anchor in Kealakekua Bay in January 1779 the reception was equally enthusiastic. After two weeks of provisioning and refitting the *Discovery* and the *Resolution*—a stopover that included visits with the local chief—Cook headed north. A severe storm off the coast of Kohala, however, sent him back to the bay. Relations with the natives were less amicable this time, and when a cutter was stolen Cook attempted to take the Hawaiian chief hostage. In the scuffle that followed, a native clubbed Cook and was taken aback by his groan. According to one native account, "The people immediately exclaimed, 'He groans–he is not a god,' and instantly slew him."

Just south of the Cook memorial, at 160 Napoopoo Road, is the **Royal Kona Coffee Mill and Museum** (808-328-2511). It displays processing equipment and photographs of harvests on the Kona Coast, which still is a major coffee-producing region.

The colorful interior of Saint Benedict's Church, called the "Painted Church," on the Kona Coast.

PUUHONUA O HONAUNAU NATIONAL HISTORICAL PARK

In ancient Hawaii defeated warriors or those who broke sacred laws sought refuge in sanctuaries, where they would be absolved by a priest. This *puuhonua* ("place of refuge") has been beautifully restored. It contains a great lava wall, which was constructed in 1550, thatched huts, petroglyphs, and several temples. A self-guided tour map is available at the park's visitor center.

> LOCATION: Honaunau, off Route 160. HOURS: 7:30-5:30 Daily. FEE: Yes. TELEPHONE: 808-328-2336.

Ka Lae (South Cape) is the southernmost point of the United States. This dry, windswept cape is believed to be the place where Hawaii's earliest Polynesian inhabitants first settled. Remnants of the temples discovered here date to A.D. 700.

HAWAII VOLCANOES NATIONAL PARK

Established in 1916, this park encompasses two young active volcanoes, Mauna Loa and Kilauea. Their colorful, but thus far nonexplosive, eruptions allow spectators to observe at remarkably close range the geological forces that created the Hawaiian Islands. According to Polynesian mythology, the park's centerpiece, the Kilauea caldera, is home to Pele, goddess of fire. In flight from her sister, the goddess of the sea, Pele searched the island for a place to rest, finally settling in the Halemaumau crater, from which she sends lava down the cliffs into her sister's domain. The park contains many hiking trails and roads. One paved path crosses the Kau Desert where in 1790 soldiers fighting Kamehameha I were caught in a fatal lava flow during an eruption of Kilauea. The Kilauea Visitor Center runs a short film on the volcanoes and also provides maps of the park.

> LOCATION: Route 11 to Chain of Craters Road. HOURS: *Visitor Center:* 7:45 AM-5 PM Daily. *Park:* Always open. FEE: Yes. TELEPHONE: 808-967-7311.

In **Kalapana,** a small town on the lava-lined Puna Coast south of Hilo, is the **Star of the Sea Church.** The interior contains vividly colored murals painted by Belgian priest Evarist Gielen in the 1920s.

OPPOSITE: *A modern reconstruction of the Ahuena Heiau in Kailua-Kona.*

NOTES ON ARCHITECTURE

HISPANIC

MISSION SAN DIEGO DE ALCALÁ, CA.

Franciscan missionaries built a series of missions along the California coast that were provincial adaptations of Mexican baroque, which in turn was an adaptation of seventeenth- and eighteenth-century Spanish architectural styles. California missions are characterized by massive masonry walls, bell towers, tile roofs, and dependent buildings placed around arcaded courtyards. Hispanic domestic buildings were simple one-room-wide adobe structures with few decorative flourishes.

GREEK REVIVAL

The Greek Revival manifested itself in severe, stripped, rectilinear proportions and, occasionally, a set of columns or pilasters. It combined Greek and Roman forms—low pitched pediments, simple moldings, rounded arches, and shallow domes—and was used in public buildings and many private houses. The style was brought to California by Yankee traders in the 1820s; when it was adapted to construction in adobe the result was the Monterey Style—

adobe walls, a pitched roof, and two stories with a cantilevered second-story balcony. In the other Pacific states, the Greek Revival followed the model of the rest of the United States.

GOTHIC REVIVAL

SAINT JAMES EPISCOPAL CHURCH, CA.

After about 1830 darker colors, asymmetry, broken skylines, verticality, and the pointed arch began to appear. New machinery produced carved and pierced trim along the eaves. Roofs became steep and gabled; porches became more spacious. Oriel and bay windows were common and there was greater use of stained glass.

ITALIANATE

BIDWELL MANSION, CA.

The Italianate style began to appear in the 1840s, both in a formal, balanced "palazzo" style and in a picturesque "villa" style. Both had round-headed windows and arcaded porches. Commercial structures were often made of cast iron, with a ground floor of

large arcaded windows and smaller windows on each successive rising story.

QUEEN ANNE

SHELTON-MCMURPHEY HOUSE, WA.

The Queen Anne style emphasized contrasts of form, texture, and color. Large encircling verandahs, tall chimneys, turrets, towers, and a multitude of textures are typical of the style. The ground floor might be of stone or brick, the upper floors of stucco, shingle, or clapboard. Specially shaped bricks and plaques were used for decoration. Panels of stained glass outlined or filled the windows. The steep roofs were gabled or hipped, and other elements, such as pediments, Venetian windows, and front and corner bay windows, were typical.

SHINGLE STYLE

The Shingle Style bore the stamp of a new generation of professional architects led by Henry Hobson Richardson (1838–1886). Sheathed in wooden shingles, its forms were smoothed and unified. Verandahs, turrets, and complex roofs were sometimes used, but they were thoroughly integrated into a whole that emphasized uniformity of surface rather than a jumble of forms. The style was a domestic and informal expression of what became known as Richardsonian Romanesque.

RENAISSANCE REVIVAL OR BEAUX ARTS

SPRECKELS MANSION, CA.

In the 1880s and 1890s, American architects who had studied at the Ecole des Beaux Arts in Paris brought a new Renaissance Revival to the United States. Sometimes used in urban mansions, but generally reserved for public and academic buildings, it borrowed from three centuries of Renaissance detail— much of it French—and put together picturesque combinations from widely differing periods. The Beaux Arts style gave rise to the "City Beautiful" movement, whose most complete expression was found in the late nineteenth- and early twentieth-century world's fairs in Chicago and San Francisco.

CRAFTSMAN OR ARTS AND CRAFTS

GAMBLE HOUSE, CA.

Almost always used for domestic structures, the Craftsman style had its origins in the English Arts and Crafts movement, but it developed quite differently from its progenitor. The Craftsman style employed simple boxlike forms, low-pitched roofs, an intimate scale, and exposure of some structural components, especially roof rafters. The acknowledged masters of the style were the California architects Greene and Greene. Its influence can be seen in many modest California bungalows.

MISSION AND SPANISH COLONIAL REVIVAL

CASA DEL PRADO, CA.

Beginning in the 1890s in California, and spreading across the country by the first decade of the twentieth cen-

tury, the Mission Revival appealed to those inspired by the romantic view of California presented in Helen Hunt Jackson's 1881 novel Ramona. The Mission Revival style employed massive masonry walls, tiled roofs, arches, and thin wooden details. Two decades later, the Spanish Colonial Revival, inspired by Bertram Grosvenor Goodhue's buildings for the 1915 San Diego exposition, relied on more sophisticated forms closer to the Spanish sources, including decorative iron grillwork, French doors leading to terraces and pergolas, and cast concrete or terra-cotta ornament. Its popularity peaked between 1920 and 1930.

ECLECTIC PERIOD REVIVALS

SAN SIMEON, CA.

During the first decades of the twentieth century, revivals of diverse architectural styles became popular in the United States, particularly for residential buildings. Architects designed Swiss chalets, half-timbered Tudor houses, and Norman chateaux with equal enthusiasm. In Europe such architecture is found in the countryside; in America the styles were transplanted to the suburbs.

I N D E X

The editors gratefully acknowledge the assistance of Ann J. Campbell, Kathy Casey, Thomas Dickey, Fonda Duvanel, Julia Ehrhardt, Ann ffolliott, Steven Gray, Ruth Horie, Amy Hughes, Carol Kewhok, Kevin Lewis, Carol A. McKeown, Paul Murphy, Linda Venator, and Patricia Woodruff.

Composed in Basilia Haas and ITC New Baskerville by Graphic Arts Composition, Inc., Philadelphia, Pennsylvania. Printed and bound by Toppan Printing Company, Ltd., Tokyo, Japan.